Britain and the
Widening War
1915–1916

Britain and the Widening War 1915–1916

From Gallipoli to the Somme

Edited by

Peter Liddle

Pen & Sword
MILITARY

First published in Great Britain in 2016 by
PEN & SWORD MILITARY
An imprint of
Pen & Sword Books Ltd
47 Church Street
Barnsley
South Yorkshire
S70 2AS

ISBN 978-1-47386-717-8

A CIP catalogue record for this book is available from the British Library.

Typeset by Concept, Huddersfield, West Yorkshire, HD4 5JL.
Printed and bound in England by CPI Group (UK) Ltd, Croydon CR0 4YY.

Pen & Sword Books Ltd incorporates the imprints of Pen & Sword Archaeology, Atlas, Aviation, Battleground, Discovery, Family History, History, Maritime, Military, Naval, Politics, Railways, Select, Social History, Transport, True Crime, and Claymore Press, Frontline Books, Leo Cooper, Praetorian Press, Remember When, Seaforth Publishing and Wharncliffe.

For a complete list of Pen & Sword titles please contact
PEN & SWORD BOOKS LIMITED
47 Church Street, Barnsley, South Yorkshire, S70 2AS, England
E-mail: enquiries@pen-and-sword.co.uk
Website: www.pen-and-sword.co.uk

Contents

List of Plates

Acknowledgements

I thank all my colleagues who have generously contributed to this volume. As with all such books, chapter authors, for scant reward, are challenged with a time-taking commitment under deadline terms. By definition the challenge is within the area of their research expertise but it is to be managed in addition to over-filled writing, teaching, academic and family obligations. I am truly grateful for all the time, research, hard work, thinking and scholarship freely given. I have thoroughly enjoyed working with new and old friends on this project. It is all to their credit and is a tribute to more than just the professional factor. In relation to the work of my colleagues, formally I thank on their behalf the trustees of institutions and officers of agencies for permissions granted to reproduce illustrations and quotations.

It is my pleasure to thank Rupert Harding of Pen & Sword Books, who had the vision to commission the book, and Sarah Cook, the volume's copy editor, who has brought sharp-eyed, well-informed judgement to bear, cover to cover.

In conclusion I thank my best friend and beloved wife Louise, who has helped from the earliest stages of drawing the book together. If formatting and the finding of additional maps and appropriate illustrations were to be a particular area of indebtedness, figuratively they should be but two pennants in an endless line of appreciative bunting.

Peter Liddle
Mickley, North Yorkshire, 2016

Preface

For the Editor of *The Widening War* there was first the challenge of drawing up a list of topics which incontestably had to be covered in a book under this title. Then there was the burgeoning excitement of going beyond that list to consider topics less to be anticipated by the general reader but with a claim through current research to being fundamental in understanding how a clash of arms between Great Powers in August 1914 transformed their societies and engulfed a wider world with related impact by the end of 1916.

The failure to achieve an early victory, two further years of intensifying struggle, hitherto undreamt of manpower and industrial needs, the world-wide colonial factor – in Britain's case the Dominion factor too – new opponents, new allies, all this together provides a framework within which the phenomenon of a widening war might be examined. However, there are aspects of the transformation of societies at war which, in all likelihood, would still have received but slight reference in a volume of this nature if the editor were not to have been determined to recruit authors who could quite specifically address such issues. Choices had to be made and with every topic selected, by implication, another was threatened. Getting a justifiable balance has been a challenging task.

The years 1915 and 1916 simply demand examination of the Dardanelles/Gallipoli concept and campaign, of Verdun and the Somme of course, of Jutland too and of the first stage of the campaign in Mesopotamia. They require a consideration of British, French and German High Command, with regard to Britain in particular, the inter-relationship between civil and military High Command. To this list of essential topics might reasonably be added the strategic purpose, the tactical methods and the means of warfare, weaponry, warships and machines by which it was waged on land, at sea and in the air in these 'middle years' of the war.

Then, if one were to look for topics more usually dealt with in specialist journals or in scholarly monographs, hence much less likely to gain the attention of the general reader, a serious claim can be made that addressing such subjects in their wider context would certainly contribute to a better understanding of the Great War. Some such topics readily spring to mind, such as what kept the United States out of the war for so long; or looking at the nature, composition and service record of the Indian Army on a specific front; certainly at what impact on Faith was exerted by the war years, or how isolated and harsh was the lot of the young men who chose the exceptional stance of conscientious objection.

Familiar to the specialist, but much less so to others, is the subject of the experimental work of facial reconstructive surgery after wounds or burns, and then another more basic and much wider issue – one I would guess far too little visited by any of us – the various 'modern' developing means of army communication in the Great War, telecommunications. Then there is the supportive role of women in the war beyond that of substitute labour, nursing and in uniformed service, and the striking impact of the war, not entirely negative, on boys caught by the outbreak in their mid-teen years.

There were further topics the Editor was keen to add: a study of the nature of the gallantry of a man who did not fit into the 'received wisdom' image of the 'hero'; the war effort and response in its full range of a single town during the war years, in the chosen instance, Halifax in West Yorkshire; and the manner by which both professionally and in an amateur way pictorial images of the war on the Western Front were drawn, the production of artwork flourishing like poppies in the torn landscapes of Belgium and France.

A topic the Editor considered fundamental, yet in general works seldom addressed, was bereavement, grief and coping with loss. Why had this not automatically claimed its due place in every book which sought to grasp the essence of the war as a human experience? Here, while recognising that the war offered new opportunities, new purpose and new experiences for women, the loss to be endured was on a monumental scale for mothers, sisters, wives, fiancées, friends, and loss for men too, as comrades, fathers, brothers and friends. In this volume one aspect of an emotionally charged issue, the practical problems faced by the newly bereaved, is searchingly explored.

It was the centenary anniversary years of the Great War which made the final chapter selection for the book so appropriately symbolic, illustrative of the lasting impact of the war even today, its various surviving physical vestiges in Britain fascinatingly available to an informed eye a century after their locational significance.

Of course there had to be choices but what about the omissions, all regrettable and some arguably inexcusable – nothing about the essential increase in home-produced food, nor about coal, shipbuilding and steel output, and the vital part played by the railways. There could well have been chapters on the German, Austro-Hungarian and Ottoman home fronts, France, Russia and Italy too. In notable cases their military campaigning has been wholly neglected, as with Russia, Austria-Hungary and Italy, but this might also be remarked of Serbia, Bulgaria and Romania.

Africa, in the North East with the Senussi, and certainly in the West – Togoland and the Cameroons; in the South – rebellion and also the campaign in German South West Africa; and then perhaps above all, in the East, could have justifiable claim for inclusion. Patently in a book which seeks to tackle in some depth subjects of either major significance or compelling and relevant interest, difficult choices had to be made and if there were to be a follow-up volume to this, a book dealing with the concluding years of the war, then some of the omissions here could perhaps be addressed in that volume.

As might be expected, concerning many of the chosen subjects, there were well known historians distinguished in those fields to approach. The approach was made and the invitations in almost every case accepted. I was aware of the work of some younger scholars writing in areas which I was keen to have covered and was given helpful advice on where I might go for others. In short, I had little difficulty in getting, I believe, just the right people for the topics selected. Without exception I have learned from the work of my colleagues, most notably with regard to army communications. Almost everyone reading this chapter will surely feel that he or she should have been more familiar with so fundamentally important a subject. Something similar might be said of the chapter specifically focusing on the contribution of British youngsters to the war effort. However, there are chapters the attraction of which lies in their challenge to 'received wisdom', or rather ignorance. A striking example is the one linking Verdun and the Somme in terms of their 1916/1918 significance and their mistaken memorialisation, however explicable and understandable that mistaken perspective. Not unrelatedly the real significance of the Battle of Jutland is made abundantly clear, a more 'material' explanation than usual is given for 1915 BEF offensive failures, and we are encouraged to look differently at the war in the air in 1915 properly to understand what was really being contested.

The list of contributors and the list of chapters are, in a 'filmic sense', rather like a 'trailer' for those with a committed interest in the Great War, along the lines of 'authors you *must* read and topics you *must* consider'. I believe it could well be added: 'Insights which will stay with you.'

A final point of some interest: the chapters seem to the Editor to reflect an intriguing development with regard to writing about the First World War – a less judgemental tone than that to which one has become accustomed. If the reader were to detect this too, then perhaps the volume is indeed making a contribution to understanding from a twenty-first-century perspective a war now distant by a hundred years yet still so near in our thinking about the past.

PART ONE

Chapter 1

The Dardanelles/Gallipoli Campaign: Concept, Delivery and Experience

By Peter Liddle

The Dardanelles is the narrow, natural, strategic waterway that leads from the Aegean Sea into the Sea of Marmara and so to Istanbul, in 1914 Constantinople, and another narrow passage, the Bosphorus, into the Black Sea and so to Russia. The Gallipoli Peninsula is a finger of land, part of the then Ottoman Empire's territory in Europe, projecting into the Aegean and forming the northern shoreline of the Dardanelles across which was the Ottoman Empire's Asian territory.

At the opening of the Great War, the Ottoman Empire, modern Turkey, was neutral. Circumstances, in the escape from British pursuit of the modern German warships *Goeben* and *Breslau* into the Dardanelles, gave advantage to Germany in diplomatic, military and naval persuasion to influence the neutral power to throw in her lot with the Central Powers rather than with Britain, France and Tsarist Russia. The British government's decision to hold on to two newly-built dreadnought battleships commissioned by the Ottomans further weighted the alignment question scales towards Berlin and indeed, at the end of October, by naval shelling of Russian Black Sea ports, the Ottoman Empire became an ally of Germany and Austria, adding at one blow hugely to the range of British defence responsibilities: the Suez Canal and shorter sea route to India and East Africa could no longer be considered secure, nor British and French interests in North Africa and the Middle East, most notably the oil resource outlet of the then Persian Gulf. The possibility of *Jihad* being proclaimed against the Entente raised serious anxieties for Britain concerning the security of the Indian subcontinent and allegiance of Moslem soldiers in the Indian Army.

Towards the end of 1914, such was the stalemate in the struggle to throw the Germans out of Belgium and northwestern France, it was worryingly clear to the British War Council that there was no prospect of an early victory in the war. For how long could the all-consuming needs for more men in uniform, for munitions of war and food production on an unprecedented scale, for financial reserves previously unenvisaged, and for national willpower to accept the strain, be fulfilled?

Among a range of ideas to break the deadlock, and in the belief that to knock the Ottoman Empire out of the war would bring significant benefits additional to those listed above, – aid to imperilled Serbia, munitions to Russia, wheat in return, potential support of Italy, Greece, Bulgaria and Rumania, even a Danube conduit threat to the heart of the Austro-Hungarian Empire – the idea of a major allied landing on the Gallipoli Peninsula was put forward for discussion in late

November by the First Lord of the Admiralty, Winston Churchill. There were sufficient reasons against such a venture to account for its failure to gain approval. To give but one example, it had hypothetically involved a military contribution from neutral Greece, something considered within the War Council difficult to engineer, and, if achieved, a development scarcely to be welcomed by Russia with both those nations ambitious for control of the Dardanelles.

The next four weeks brought no news from France to encourage the prospect of victory for the Entente. On 26 December, reviewing the strategic options available, the secretary to the War Council, Lieutenant-Colonel Maurice Hankey, revived the Gallipoli Peninsula project in a memorandum which can be seen in itself as both an indication of the degree of anxiety over the stalemate, and as his measured judgement of the best way forward among the strategic choices open. Hankey listed the prospective consequences from securing the Dardanelles, allowing the Royal Navy secure passage into the Sea of Marmara and thus to be able to threaten bombardment of Constantinople. The list, as originally 'floated' by Churchill, was collectively impressive, perhaps, in the dilemma facing the War Council, so impressive as to undermine the need for serious scrutiny of each element separately and then the paramount consideration of whether there were the necessary military strength spare, that is over and above what was essential for France and for the defence of overseas possessions.

However, any careful weighing of such factors was further discouraged by a new circumstance. On 2 January 1915, in what appeared a military emergency on the Russo/Turkish battlefront in Armenia, Russian Grand Duke Nicholas appealed to Russia's British and French allies for a diversionary attack on the Turks. With Churchill increasingly convinced that an alternative strategy from the Western Front must be found, here was a golden opportunity to re-focus upon the Dardanelles. It might also be remarked in retrospect that it was the moment when, delusively, the Ottoman Empire for Britain changed from being a problem area to one offering an opportunity swiftly to be grasped.

Churchill signalled Sir Stuart Carden, the admiral in command of the Royal Naval squadron in the Eastern Mediterranean, asking him about the feasibility of his warships bombarding the forts defending the minefields barring access and passage through the Dardanelles to the Sea of Marmara and so to Constantinople. To so challenging a question Carden replied cautiously to the effect that it might be done by progressive bombardment.

Churchill had secured what he needed – professional endorsement of what could be argued as an attractively 'economic' way forward. He put to the War Council the idea of using older battleships, that is Carden's squadron, to do the work hitherto considered only possible in a combined operation with an allied military force. At a stroke he had taken the wind out of potential objections from his two most powerful colleagues, the Secretary of State for War, Lord Kitchener, from whom he was asking for no troops, and the First Sea Lord, Admiral of the Fleet, Lord Fisher, from whom he was asking for no modern warships.

Correspondence and informal meetings between the principals prepared the groundwork for general approval and then, at a meeting of the War Council on

13 January, Churchill's persuasive eloquence secured assent. It must be stressed: there were no dissentients. The decision was one of collective responsibility.

No serious question has ever been raised about the political or professional qualification of the members of the War Council concerning entitlement to their particular office-holding responsibility. Were they then all bereft of common sense as is implied by the judgement of an historian who recently has indicted the whole Dardanelles/Gallipoli concept as a 'lunacy'?[1] Surely there has to be some danger of this armchair critic, blatantly shelling from his arsenal of hindsight, inviting such scorn to his own account. Estimating the degree of perplexed anxiety, even desperation, in the War Council in February 1915 as to how the war might be won, is difficult and would then be debatable. However, an indicator is provided by the fact that only one member, Kitchener, had from the start been convinced that waging the war would be a long, long haul, and it had not lain in his vision that in addition to the years ahead, the political commitment of the United States, with her industrial might and transformed military potential, would be needed for victory over Germany in France.

The historian holds in his hand a blade without a handle, 'hindsight'. In wielding it he is likely to wound himself but perhaps it *is* reasonable to put forward that the men who sanctioned the Dardanelles endeavour were searching for a means to avoid the fearsome prospect of a war without end – and, in the event, there were three and a half years still to go, something conceivable to just one member in February 1915.

It so happens that as this chapter is being written, ways forward for a British Cabinet facing exceptional challenges may lead to decisions taken which will be derided in the future. The historian will then have the benefit of knowing how things panned out but will he or she have soundly measured the anxieties being evaluated today over choices concerning Defence needs, political/military initiatives to be essayed in the Middle East and North Africa, measures taken over migration/immigration and concerning the European Union? There is a century dividing these points of comparison but no such gulf in complexity. Whether in a democracy or an autocracy the foresight of decision-making will always be weighed and re-weighed on the scales of 'whatever ensued', but so will those who make judgemental assessment upon them from the privileged position of knowing what happened.

Despite the case as argued above, it cannot be denied that the wording in the minuted conclusions to the 13 January 1915 War Council left a serious hostage to fortune in that the Admiralty was to 'prepare a naval expedition to invade and take the Gallipoli Peninsula'.[2] The invading and taking of land by warships and their crews, presumably the Royal Marines, does seem to imply that Ottoman defence will collapse at first sight of the foe. Indeed it seems to distort history's indifferent record of ships shelling forts and minimize the difficulty of mine-sweeping with the presumption of conclusive demolition of the forts protecting the minefields.

The French government endorsed the British War Council's decision, approving French naval participation. The attempt went forward, bombardment commencing on 19 February. In the War Council, and directly to Lord Kitchener, Churchill pressed for troops to be available in the region in the event of their being necessary. The story of Kitchener's enthusiasm for the venture and then, in the event, reluctance to provide the troops because of his underlying conviction that the decisive theatre would be in France, is as interesting as that of Lord Fisher's support and then implacable opposition to the Dardanelles with a related awareness on his part that the North Sea was where the war would be decided.

The War Council came to appreciate that troops needed to be on hand and they were assembled in Egypt. A force commander, Lieutenant-General Sir Ian Hamilton, was rushed out to the Eastern Mediterranean, arriving in fact just in time to view the outcome of the naval attempt at close-range bombardment of the forts defending the minefields. Shore-landing parties to complete by demolition the work of the naval shelling had met with increasing resistance and so the hazard from un-swept mines and still active fixed and mobile shore batteries was to be accepted by the huge, if old, battleships. They were to enter the Narrows completely to destroy all resistance at what was for such warships point-blank range.

The bombardment of 18 March, witnessed by Hamilton, met with severe losses in warships – three British battleships and a French battleship – and with serious damage to others from striking un-swept mines and from shelling from the shore. There was considerable loss of life too, in particular from the French battleship *Bouvet*. The naval attack could not have been continued the following day even if this were to have been deemed necessary to maintain pressure upon defence of the Narrows regardless of allied losses – the weather became unfavourable – but should the enterprise now have been called off? The concept as authorised had patently failed. The Turks were alerted; opposition to any landings was now certain; what little surprise there may have been in relation to the commencement of the bombardments on 19 February had of course gone.

On the other hand, should the naval assault have been resumed when weather conditions allowed – a conviction held at the time and lastingly by Roger Keyes, Chief of Staff to the admiral who had succeeded the sick Carden in command, Vice-Admiral John de Robeck? The Ottoman government, having drawn such an onslaught from the two Great Powers of Britain and France, must surely have been reeling and in all likelihood the forts would be running low in ammunition? Such questions, with a ready answer implied, are much easier for opposing pro-tagonists to answer today than they were in late March 1915.

General Sir Ian Hamilton conferred with the British and French admirals and a decision was taken, endorsed by the War Council, to mount a combined opera-tion, the Navy to land troops on the Peninsula to secure it, neutralizing Ottoman defence of the northern shore of the Narrows thus facilitating mine-sweeping and safe naval passage through to the Sea of Marmara.

Had there been any serious study of the availability of the troops and artillery needed for such a large-scale enterprise, and one the needs of which might well expand? No, there had not, and if this were to seem inexcusable there is both a personal and a material explanation, explanations insufficient to satisfy many without expressions of disdain, reasonable or otherwise, but that was 'how things transpired'.

Churchill, unauthorised, had issued a Press release at an early stage in the bombardment that all was proceeding well. It was a calculated indiscretion undermining what had been discussed in the War Council that in the event of a naval failure the force could be withdrawn without serious loss of face. After international consumption of such a claim, how could the affair have been called off without damaging loss of reputation to the allied cause? Then, directly consequent upon what supportive preparations had been undertaken with regard to the assembling of troops and appointing of a Commander in Chief, and to take military and psychological advantage of the blows inflicted on the Ottomans, the 'motor of war' – seldom easy to arrest – almost decreed the next step, the landing of troops. The British and French governments, having invested materially in success, were in spiritual accord, desperate to achieve it. Yes, the concept had changed but such niceties and the military resource calculations bound up with them were swept aside by that by no means rare inducement to 'seize the moment'.

The plan worked out to capture the Peninsula – more specifically to secure the Dardanelles Narrows – was imaginative but complex. At the tip of the Peninsula, Cape Helles, there were to be five separate beach landings by British troops, there being no single beach large enough, and, to the defenders, vulnerable enough, to land the division, the 29th Regular Army Division, charged with the task. The Division was to advance to capture the village of Krithia beneath the dominant rise, Achi Baba, which overlooked all approaches from Cape Helles. With the immediate landing objectives seized, the advance would enable the secured beaches to be linked, the village taken, Achi Baba to be outflanked and Ottoman defence of the entrance to the Dardanelles wiped clear.

Approximately 9 miles further north on the Aegean coast of the Peninsula, Australian and New Zealand troops were to be landed. They were to hasten to secure the higher ground overlooking their intended point of landing just north of a prominent headland, Gaba Tepe. The higher ground was not just an 'obstacle' to the invaders, it commanded the southern coastline of the Peninsula thus affording the Australians and New Zealanders the potentially decisive challenge of cutting off the Helles defenders from withdrawal and, with their elimination, the Narrows, on the European shore, would be in allied hands.

As a temporary diversion, French troops were to be put ashore on the Asiatic side of the entrance to the Dardanelles and two decoy diversions were arranged further to confuse Ottoman defence under its German direction.

The plan had indeed broken away from the established principle of concentrating rather than dispersing one's force but the local circumstance determined that, and if, as was the case, Hamilton's command philosophy were to devolve his authority upon his commanding officers at Cape Helles and where the Australasians were to land, this can be approved before the event as a commonsense freedom from constraint being exercised from a distance, just as much as risking a high dependency on untested ability.

In a remarkable example of the completion of highly detailed staff work, of naval/military cooperation in getting the troops and their not necessarily well stowed needs from Egypt into the immediate area for their operation and then

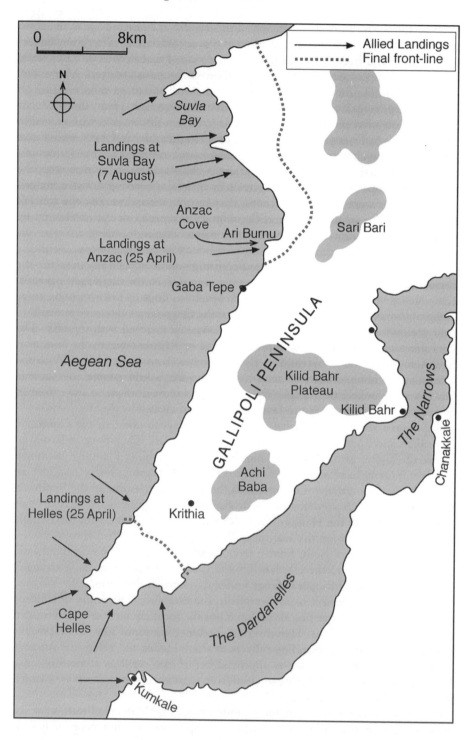

training them for shore landings with little time to do any of these essentials effectively, in but five weeks, on 25 April, the campaign was launched. At Helles, two inadequacies were tragically demonstrated: the limited effect of naval bombardment on defensive emplacements and, related in grim significance, the lack of armoured protection of the open cutters being towed and then rowed into shore, troops packed within them.

From the most northerly beach, designated 'Y', an opportunity of taking advantage of an initial lack of opposition may have been missed. Immediate local command, the exercise of Divisional authority, and that of High Command have a case to answer here but whether the opportunity were potentially decisive is doubtful. Two of the beaches, 'V', with designed protection for large numbers of men in a converted collier, *River Clyde*, run ashore, and 'W', with Lancashire Fusiliers landed into devastating fire, witnessed tragic drama on an epic scale, but for all the heroic endeavour, no conclusive result was obtained.

Those miles further up the Aegean coast, the men were landed by navigational error a mile further north than had been intended, the indifferent early-dawn light, a mistaken headland, and the current, contributing to the unintended location. The immediate strength in numbers of the defenders may, by the error, have been less but the precipitous contorted heights to assail made the challenge exceptionally difficult. It proved beyond the grasp of the Australians and New Zealanders; indeed for some time it looked as if the troops were to be withdrawn but Hamilton's adamant refusal to sanction such procedure averted so serious a repulse.

Ironically, in view of such high political expectation, but with hindsight predictably to a considerable extent given the defender's advantage at that time over the attacker, a new Western Front stalemate was born. Of course it was under very different climatic conditions. In the case of the Australasians above their beach which became known as Anzac Cove, the geographical conditions were extraordinarily different too.

Furthermore, in contrast to France, it was at the end of an over-extended supply line, one making heavier and heavier demand on resources under constant requirement for the Western Front. On the Gallipoli Peninsula, High Command, command at all levels, and the men themselves, had drawn the short straw.

Warfare in 1915, without over-powering force in heavy artillery with a limitless supply of ammunition, – a circumstance beyond British and French capacity in France and out of the question beyond, – so advantaged the well dug-in, armed, ammunitioned, adequately fed, led and motivated defender, that nigh ruinous loss without gain would attend the attacker's every effort to cross the approach to concealed positions. And so it proved on the Peninsula.

Does this free the commander from blame when plans and orders bring but costly failure? By no means, but the political, strategic and tactical imperative of his having to attack against all advantage must be the framework from which legitimate criticism is made. Of course what informs or overshadows all such considerations is the human cost without evident advantage – in the case of Gallipoli almost 55,000 British, British Commonwealth and French dead. Defeat, colossal commitment of material resources, considerable humiliation and the war un-shortened must be added to that utterly tragic debit. How could one be dis-passionate about this? – but if that were possible, would the grim answer to such an issue be that if, politically, you were to have gone to war at that time, that is 'what you got'. This may seem miserably inadequate, and to some who believe that the war came about through diplomatic failure or shared capitalistic greed, it is grossly evasive of more fundamental issues. A far greater majority, this author suggests, would conclude: 'that was the past, and we can understand with sadness why it happened as it did'.

After April 1915 on the Peninsula, reinforcements came in stages, then in the summer they were sent in greater number to be deployed in a new strategic plan to take the heights above Anzac Cove and with a new landing, just north of that position, at Suvla Bay, decisively beat the Turks. The plan called for major diver-sionary attacks at Helles and on the right flank at Anzac in front of positions named Lone Pine and the Nek.

Previously there had been costly assaults at both Cape Helles in unavailing attempts to take the village of Krithia, notably an attack across the 'Daisy Patch', and from the Anzac beach-head, but now, in August, the diversionary assaults on both sectors were in indisputable fact disastrous and arguably of the most slender benefit to the operations they were designed to assist. Concerning the vital Anzac assault of the heights, a great deal physically was demanded of the men involved. The reinforcement troops here were in good condition but inexperienced, never having encountered in training, ground of the nature of their task; the Australians and New Zealanders had the experience but had been drained by that experience, were weary and further weakened by dysentery. Additionally, all had to make their way by night, as quietly as possible climbing up one of three steep, un-reconnoitred gullies, thickly tangled with undergrowth, and with the men burdened by apprehension, but no fore knowledge, of from where and when devastating defensive fire might be encountered.

Location identification, inter-communication, coordinated Field and Naval artillery support, by definition unregistered, command control, were all fiend-ishly difficult to manage. What was required of senior and regimental officers and their men here proved beyond their capacity in very challenging circumstances. It might even be said fairly that the circumstances made the task beyond achievement.

The new landing in Suvla Bay was not pressed forward as was necessary to provide a dangerous threat to Ottoman defence of the higher ground overlooking the bay and here in particular blame can fairly be apportioned to the 9th Corps officer in command, Lieutenant-General Sir Frederick Stopford, two divisional and one brigade commander, and to Hamilton himself whose delayed inter-vention to inject urgency only added to the confusion. A base and a new front were established, not a thrust perilous to the Turks. From the end of August no serious threat to defence of the Peninsula remained. A senior Turkish regimental officer wrote to his father on 2 September: 'The hopes of the British have col-lapsed. Will they bring up fresh troops, perhaps Italian, and land them on the beaches – or elsewhere? We are used to it and let them come if they like. In one respect it helps our soldiers, who strip the British dead of their boots, and now have fine British boots on their own feet.'[3] Presciently the officer, Lieutenant-Colonel Fahrettin Altay, added that when the rains came, the British in their positions on the lower ground would find themselves in serious difficulty.

With the Turks holding the higher ground now on all three fronts and that ground having proved impossible to capture, weather conditions ensured that the troops, particularly at the exposed Suvla Bay, first baked in the sun and then, in late November, were deluged with rain and flooding, before enduring snow and freezing temperatures.

With Hamilton removed from his command in mid-October and replaced by General Charles Monro, the new Commander in Chief visited each Peninsula front on arrival, judging evacuation necessary. This potentially disastrous procedure was not sanctioned from London until Lord Kitchener himself had carried out a lightning personal inspection, but there was no alternative. Planning for evacuation had begun on 22 November, appreciably before it was finally authorized from London on 7 December.

In London most particularly, dire consequences were anticipated in any attempt at withdrawal with the Turks exercising close and overlooking observation on all three sectors. However, by brilliant planning, clever, imaginative deception and meticulous execution, it was achieved on each front without loss, an almost astounding accomplishment. There was a progressive reduction of the establishment from each front with cunning disguise that this was taking place and then, from Anzac and Suvla first, on the night of 19/20 December, and from Cape Helles on the night of 9 January 1916, the withdrawal was successfully completed though with great loss of equipment and stores, all destroyed as far as possible by concealed methods or by fire and explosion as the last men left.

During the subsequent months, then years of the war, the campaign was a scandal for its failure, bringing down temporarily, and damaging lastingly, Churchill, its chief progenitor, for his over-optimism about what might be achieved, and his under-estimation of the Turk. Even though political and public focus upon responsibility for the 'shame' of Gallipoli were to have its twin in just a few more months of war with the British surrender at besieged Kut in Mesopotamia, post-war, and even at the recent centenary of the campaign, Gallipoli has for many been legendary for political and military incompetence, set against soldier heroism, sacrifice and suffering. In this chapter the author has argued for a more reasoned assessment of the 'incompetence' but thoroughly endorses the soldier record.

Before looking at evidence of that record, something must be said additionally about the longer-term significance of the campaign and in a positive not exculpatory sense. In four and half years of war it was, after all, the only innovative attempt by the Entente offering any prospect of success in outflanking the Central Powers and achieving strategic advantage which might bring about their defeat. By no serious argument can the landing and subsequent campaign from Salonika be considered of the same order.

The Gallipoli Campaign should be acknowledged as an amphibious, combined, allied operation, of a nature and on a scale wholly unique in the waging of the First World War. It saw pioneer development in the utilisation of military action from the air, initiated from both land and sea, had elements of special experimental development with regard to reconnaissance, naval and military artillery cooperation, bombing, propaganda leafleting and air-launched torpedoing, so evidently that early stages in the development of air power can be traced directly to the Dardanelles in 1915.

If no such exceptional claim can be made for the development of undersea warfare, the use of the submarine, it can nevertheless legitimately be claimed for the German U-boat on the one hand, and the British submarines on the other, that their successes were far more materially of influence upon the conduct of the campaign. For the Germans, their sinking of three British battleships in May, within weeks of the landing of the troops, forced the withdrawal from the Narrows of the modern dreadnought HMS *Queen Elizabeth*, and the much older battleships too, leaving the invaders shorn of the actual and spiritual comfort hitherto provided by the great grey warships with their powerful guns.

For the submarines of the Royal Navy, such were their successful exploits in the Sea of Marmara, and quite extraordinarily off the Golden Horn at Constantinople, – the sinking of troopships and supply vessels, shelling of shore targets and rail transportation demolitions, – that Ottoman reinforcements and supplies of munitions and food had increasingly to reach the Turkish positions on the Peninsula by the slow land route, a factor compensating to some extent for the much longer allied supply line.

The diversity in ethnic as well as national make-up of the attacking force is particularly striking and deserves recognition: Senegalese, Moroccan, Metropolitan French, Gurkhas, Sikhs, Punjabis, Russian Palestinians, Newfoundlanders, Australians, New Zealanders, English, Welsh, Scots and Irish. The range of service experience was extensive too, from Regular Army, Territorial, to New Army, and their French equivalents.

Any listing of the lastingly important aspects of the campaign would have near its premier place the part it played in the forging of Australian and New Zealand nationhood and similarly, though less a matter of public awareness, was the inter-war, international, detailed study of the campaign for the lessons it taught concerning for example, surprise, deception, force sufficiency, command, communications and supply lines, lessons not always taken on board, as for example the British in Norway in 1940, but emphatically followed in preparations for Normandy in 1944.

To our full, if uncomfortable, enlightenment, personal experience on every First World War fighting front is well documented. In addition to assaulting across no-man's-land almost impregnably defended positions, as in France and elsewhere, Gallipoli had special, testing features: the opposed shore landings of 25 April at Cape Helles and at what became Anzac Cove, and then the conditions of stalemate in high temperatures with unburied dead between close front lines, circumstances exacerbated by the stress of underground mining. Even in East Africa and in Macedonia where disease was a very serious problem, the weakening of troops on the Gallipoli Peninsula by forms of dysentery has no parallel. There is too the awful trial of the flooding and freezing temperatures of late November where the troops at Suvla were worst affected and finally the experience of the evacuation from all three fronts, again to which there is no First World War parallel. All should be exemplified for the reader to offer at least some approach to the actual experience. For those in the Eastern Mediterranean Squadron too there were experiences of action distinctively different, however kindred, to the major battles at sea and to the storming of the Mole at Zeebrugge. Such experiences would include at least the February landings in an attempt to demolish the forts, the drama of the losses on 18 March, landing the troops on 25 April, submariner service in the Sea of Marmara and evacuation of the troops in December 1915 and January 1916.

A midshipman from HMS *Vengeance* got a close view of what happened when a demolition party from his ship reached the shore at Kum Kale on the Asiatic side of the entrance to the Dardanelles on 26 February. The party separated into two and the men going towards one fort:

> were fired on by Turks in the windmills at Yeni Shehr which were soon brought down by us and Dublin. When the party got to number 4 fort they smashed up a searchlight and several wires connecting mines but did not blow up the guns. On the way back they were cut off by some Turks in a cemetery. We had some difficulty in finding the point of aim owing to the wrong bearing having been passed up. The captain got furious and came and trained the gun himself. He cursed me ... The Turks were driven off and our Marines got back to their boats. I did not expect half of them to get back. Only one was killed and three wounded.[4]

Of 18 March, a seaman of *Lord Nelson* kept a diary account of seeing the French battleship *Bouvet* 'turn turtle in less than two minutes', six hundred men lost in that tragedy. Of *Lord Nelson* under fire, he wrote: 'I was not very cheerful in the maintop with too many splinters flying around.' He was witness to the serious damage suffered by HMS *Inflexible*: 'Her foretop was smashed in and soon she was hit on the forebridge setting it on fire. It was a sight to see her blazing away and firing her 12 inch guns at the same time.'[5]

The role of many midshipmen on 25 April was in the picket boats towing strings of cutters towards the shore, then releasing them for sailors aboard to row them in. The midshipmen were all by definition young but one was not yet sixteen. A letter home on naval message paper graphically illustrates the daunting duty faced by a midshipman at 'W' beach:

> We slipped [the towed boats] about 30 yards from the beach but my boat was closer as we had come round the corner. We were nearly on the rocks and only just slipped in time. All the tows slipped alright and pulled in without fouling each other. There were two rows of barbed wire the whole length of the beach. The Turks opened fire with maxims, pompoms, rifles, just as we slipped. You could see them standing up in the trenches which obviously had not been properly shelled. They were pouring a terrific fire down on us and it is a most

extraordinary thing how any men survived it. The soldiers had to jump out into three feet of water and it was a most awful sight seeing them being shot down as soon as they got into the water and the wounded men must have drowned.[6]

The diary of a submariner in the Sea of Marmara illustrates perfectly a range of operations totally outside the service experience of a submariner in the Mediterranean never mind seas and oceans further west. On 13 August submarine *E2* had entered the Straits, got caught in the anti-submarine net, but freed herself though in so doing exploded a mine above her. She was pursued by a destroyer but eluded her, sank a gunboat by torpedo, picked up a dhow and burned her, dived to escape the attentions of an enemy aircraft, made rendezvous with *E11*, replenished her with ammunition and received a bag of apples in exchange. More dhows were burned, their cargoes thrown overboard. A gunboat and a troop transport were torpedoed, forts, a railway line and a munitions works were shelled. The sea bottom was hit but the submarine seemed undamaged. Of course at night the boat had to surface for ventilation and recharging of the batteries.

On 6 September, among islands in the Marmara, sixteen dhows were sunk during the day but on the 7th, following the landing of an officer with a gun-cotton charge prepared by the diarist, the officer failed to make the return rendezvous after his railway damage attempt. 'Should very much like to see him back for he was too good to lose.' Though shelled from Kum Kale on her return, *E2* reached her base on the Isle of Imbros on 14 September. Petty Officer Stephens recorded in his diary: 'Think we must have scared pretty well everything out of the sea of Marmara as there is nothing to get hold of anywhere.'[7]

The distinctive challenges of soldiering experience on the Peninsula should begin with the landings. 'W' beach, the 1st Battalion Lancashire Fusiliers, and the interviewed recollections of James Grimshaw, earning here the Victoria Cross by battalion ballot, have to be soundly representative of circumstances at Cape Helles though of course there were marked differences on other beaches. Grimshaw wasted few words in describing the approach to the beach in unprotected cutters being rowed in by sailors. It is not known if he were in the line of tows whose approach was described above by Midshipman Wilson.

It was impossible to tell who had been hit as they were prevented from falling inboard or overboard by the crush. The firing broke out all at once and the water seemed to be boiling all around us. I managed to get over the barbed wire which was in the water and then through the stuff on the beach but later when some of us got to the base of the cliff I found that my cap badge had been hit by a bullet, and my pack and water bottle riddled. One thing paramount was the effect of water and sand on your rifle mechanism and the only way to deal with this was to try and urinate on your rifle bolt. By the time we got to the top of the cliff just the remnants of the defenders had retired a couple of hundred yards. They wore a sort of balaclava helmet and a grey uniform and we saw them in the act of trying to prepare trenches. We rushed those trenches and cleared the people out. I didn't use my bayonet: just pressed the trigger. You are carrying your rifle at the trail or held in front of you.[8]

Serving in the broken-ridged, precipiced terrain above the Anzac beach-head was New Zealander J.W. Gascoigne, whose diary is of assistance in making the point of how astoundingly close the opposing positions could be in this sector and additionally the stress of both sides digging tunnels to explode charges to blow the opposition to smithereens:

> We are continually sapping towards the trenches in our front and have now only a few feet to go. The Australians are sapping towards the Turks' trenches and are now only ten yards away. The Turks have only to put their rifles over their trenches and shoot straight down onto our trenches. Hand bombs are being hurled every few minutes.

The diarist was killed two days after this entry.[9]

Another New Zealander, J.G. Gasparich, described the circumstances under which dysentery became endemic:

> The flies flew in their thousands from swollen, rotten bodies lying in the scrub. From this oozing matter where they bred so promiscuously they would move to the open latrines and so to the men themselves. They sought moisture from our ears, our noses, our eyes, our mouths. Men wrapped their heads in hessian in an endeavour to escape them until they were nearly suffocated in the heat but still the flies managed to get in. Liquid spilled on the floor was soon covered by layers of furiously struggling flies fighting to reach the dampness. You had to keep a moving hand over any morsel of food and drink in a forlorn attempt to keep the flies from entering your mouth.[10]

A series of entries in another diary contributes to our understanding of how men in their weakened state coped, as soldiers do, and did what was required of them. For this man, death, encountered regularly, is met with resilience, and dysentery, almost a constant, is recorded with ironic humour:

> June 24. Sorting out Nunn's kit (killed yesterday). Busy till late with various correspondence. Treacle for tea.
>
> July 12. Webster killed by shrapnel in communication trench. Bombardment continued all day. Huge mail in evening. Got my parcels at last. Supper party with Murphy, Dixon, Thomas and Harris – rice, pineapple and coffee. Webster's funeral after dark – (buried) next to Nunn.
>
> July 18. Feeling rotten. Stayed in dugout and slept all day. Kept off grub. WC with seat to it near incinerator! Great luxury. Patronised it all day.[11]

Then there is documentation of the November storm. The entrenched troops on the flat Suvla plain where the new landing had been made in August were to have a grim late November experience, first with deluging rain which led to a torrent of flood water, bearing debris and corpses of men and mules, racing through the trench system from the hills above, forcing the men out of the trenches until the flood eased, and then with freezing temperatures came a blizzard of snow. An officer in the Warwickshire Regiment recalled having supervised the return of his men into their trenches, and responding to a cry for help from someone still outside the cover offered by their sheltered quagmire:

> I got out of the trench feeling as if the guns of the entire Turkish Army were turned on me and slithered over to where the head and shoulders of a man were showing over the mud in the communication trench. Every effort I made to drag him out proved futile until I managed to haul soaked heavy sandbags to place either side of him, stand on them and pull him up vertically. Utterly exhausted, we returned to the trench. The temperature dropped dramatically to below freezing during the night. I shared a dugout with a fellow officer who rocked and moaned in the cold. In the morning a howling blizzard blocked out every other sound, forcing snow down the throat if one's mouth opened. A man tried to sing to keep warm or to raise morale but his efforts failed on both counts – he died. I had taken my boots off to wrap my puttees around my swollen feet, but found I could not walk so had to crawl on hands and knees towards a fire.

From here he was carried down to the beach where wounded and frost-bitten men awaited evacuation by hospital ship, leaving him with memories of a further painful misery, having to crawl to the ship's latrine, his blackened, blistered feet too painful to be allowed to touch the deck.[12]

And finally to something more cheerful, though an acknowledgement of complete defeat: a brilliant and wholly unexpected success, the two-stage evacuation of all the men, first from Anzac and Suvla in December, and then from Cape Helles on 9 January, almost unbelievably without a man lost – superb planning, imaginative means of deception, procedures meticulously carried out, pathways through the communication trenches for night-time evacuation to the beach marked by flour, straw at the bottom of the trenches, boots wrapped in sacking, rifles left in place to be fired by water weight from tins being slowly filled, mines exploding by delayed action fuses – all to give the impression that normal defence of their positions was in place. There was even what was called a 'silent stunt' during which troops at Anzac showed no hostility at all, but by their still being in position accustomed their foe to inactivity. The diary of New Zealander C.J. Walsh documents the rumours, uncertainties, preparations, personal advantage sometimes being taken from them, and his emotional reaction to the evacuation:

> 13 December: It certainly looks as though we are going to evacuate. No more reinforcements or returned sick are to join up here. I'd like to know something. Lot of artillery, Gurkhas, Sikhs and Australians got away late.
>
> 14 December: Heard that good things were to be had on the beach, got loaded up with jam and cheese and also a bag of cabbage and onions. Everything points to a complete evacuation. Railway being torn up. From our bivvy we can see about ten transports near Williams' Pier at 8.30pm. All lists for embarkation been made out.
>
> 15 December: Got orders through that no bivvies are to be disturbed and all roofs are to be intact. On the beach the authorities are tipping out rum and

whisky in Mule Gulley and a terrible lot of rum etc was tipped out and formed a pool. All hands were there with jam tins, dixies etc lapping it up. Have just received final orders for HQ Signals. For last twenty-four hours seven men to remain to man phones and for the last few hours I think it is going to be rather nervy. Password for tonight is Corkscrew.

16 December: Our HQ Signals orders cancelled. Only two men are to stay and man the phones, Sgt Calame and myself. All barges busy getting men off. The last ones to go are Walker's Ridge, Quinn's and Courtney's and all are to be heavily mined.

17 December: Just got orders through that all arrangements are to be postponed twenty-four hours. Password Havelock. Very bright moonlight. Can see shipping as clear as day.

18 December: On 3am to 6am Watch this morning. Went out about 5am to waken officers and saw a great glare in the direction of Anzac. Evidently the heads burning all stores etc. Seems fairly cheeky though. At 9pm most of the boys got away. Everything going satisfactorily – only occasional burst of fire disturbing the night . . . We are leaving everything as they stand. Our funk holes, or at least our HE shelters, once our pride and joy, are now filled with all sorts of rubbish, empty bully tins, old socks, burnt paper, broken helios etc. Burnt all our intelligence department stuff such as old messages etc.

19 December: Last night all went without a hitch. About twelve o'clock the nasty-tempered brutes of Turks started lobbing shells all over the place. Got orders to get into our funk holes. No damage done. Had a wash and clean-up to celebrate what we fondly hope will be our last day on Gallipoli. I'll feel quite at ease when I see the shores of Anzac fade away over the horizon.[13]

The New Zealander did get safely away the following night but the chance of similar good fortune attending those remaining at Cape Helles in their endeavour to escape without heavy loss must have seemed remote.

The preparations were again progressive and again thorough but predictably there was more Ottoman aggression hampering procedure.

The diary of Eric Wettern, a sapper in the Royal Naval Division Engineers, makes abundantly clear that every effort to prevent precipitate enemy pursuit to the shore was undertaken:

5 January, Carrying stuff for barricades. Turks apparently spotted something and plonked a few big 'uns round about making a mess of trenches in two or three places. Had to get night working party from Howes (RND) to shift the muck. With Stout fixing up the barricades got most of the work done.

6 January, Completing barricade arrangements. Fixed up everything to drop in instantly. Rehearsal with Rugg.

7 January, General rehearsal at 2. Attack by Turks on Fusilier Bluff preceded by bombardment of whole line . . . I went up to tie white tape on crinolines [barbed wire obstructions as barricades] . . . Rest of company left leaving only ten of us. Part of firing line went off.

8 January, Hoods (RND) on our left moved out very quickly ... Straw down and muffled feet. 23.45 All moved out. We put down crinolines and umbrellas [further obstructions] at Supports ... Waited for Dumezil and bomb people at Ligne de Repli barricade. Further wait at Post 11 for Thompson ... longish wait for Blake. Barricaded road. Put gear on, proceeded down. Very quiet.[14]

There were further delays for Wettern as he played his part in putting obstacles in place after the passage through of the last men on his route to the shore, where in due course, via a beached French warship, he reached the destroyer *Grasshopper* for evacuation.[15]

Who knows who was the last to leave the Peninsula, but Midshipman Tom Traill may have some claim. He had been ordered to go ashore and search for stragglers:

Not relishing a cold dark swim ashore, I had truly astonishing good fortune when a ten-foot-long, flat-bottomed, carpeted Turkish pleasure punt bumped against my cutter and allowed an easy transfer for a dry examination of the coast. The punt, held on a line by the crew of the cutter, drifted against a breakwater in Morto Bay and with my revolver in hand, I wandered along the beach calling, 'Anybody about?' and hoping the reply would not be in Turkish. After some time, the explosion of the ammunition dump at the very point of the Peninsula convinced me that my search for lost and bewildered troops was no longer necessary and I made my way back to the breakwater. It was a sobering thought that I was probably alone in presenting the allied threat to Constantinople.[16]

The whimsical manner in which Sapper Eric Wettern expressed his opinions in letters from the Peninsula retains its attraction today. On 15 January, now away from the Dardanelles, he wrote to his brother: 'I expect you are feeling fairly disgusted at our magnificent bunk from Gallipoli ... As a matter of fact we aren't exactly sorry to leave dear old Gallipoli. I think we could have stuck it all right, though it was getting a bit warm, but I suppose they thought we should never do any good by staying there.'[17]

In the judgement of most historians, and in public perception, the men should not have been sent there in the first place and, on being sent, were poorly led when they got there. The author senses that these may be harsh assessments, 'benefitting' too much from hindsight in the case of historians, and from 'received wisdom' in the case of popular opinion. If the case as tentatively advanced by the author were to go to Appeal, then Counsels for both Prosecution and Defence would have more work to do, and there is too the knotty consideration that in general terms the men who were there and survived left scanty evidence of bitter recrimination in recall.[18] Is this distance lending enchantment? Yes, perhaps it is, but also I think it is because they felt pride in having taken part in an epic struggle, a sort of satisfaction in having been 'tested and proved'.

Gallipoli a hundred years on can still inspire a range of emotions, sometimes seemingly in contradiction: anger, astonishment verging on awe, admiration, pity, sympathy, sorrow, disgust, disbelief, incomprehension. There is evidential validity for them all, but comprehension today offers a challenge intellectually within our reach.

Notes

1. P. Hart, *Gallipoli* (London: Profile Books, 2011), p. vii.
2. National Archives, Cab 22/1 3623.
3. Lieutenant-Colonel Fahrettin Altay, letter to father, 2.9.15 (Liddle Collection, University of Leeds).
4. Midshipman P.B.R.W. William-Powlett, HMS *Vengeance*, diary (Liddle Collection).
5. Seaman G.E. Keeler, HMS *Lord Nelson*, diary (Liddle Collection).
6. Midshipman H. Wilson, HMS *Euryalus*, letter to mother, 4.5.15 (Liddle Collection).
7. Petty Officer Stephens, HM Submarine *E2*, diary (Liddle Collection).
8. Private J.E. Grimshaw VC, 1st Battalion Lancashire Fusiliers, tape-recorded recollections (Liddle Collection).
9. J.W. Gascoigne, diary, 18.5.15 (Alexander Turnbull Library, Wellington, New Zealand).
10. J.G. Gasparich (Sergeant, Canterbury Regiment), manuscript recollections (Liddle Collection).
11. Sapper E.F. Wettern, 2nd Field Company, RND Engineers, diary (Liddle Collection).
12. Charles Mackintosh (2nd Lieutenant, 9th Battalion Royal Warwickshire Regiment), tape-recorded recollections (Liddle Collection).
13. C.J. Walsh (Private, 1st Auckland Battalion), diary (Liddle Collection).
14. Sapper E.F. Wettern, No. 2 Field Company, RND Engineers, diary (Liddle Collection).
15. Ibid.
16. Midshipman Tom Traill (Midshipman, HMS *Lord Nelson*), tape-recorded recollections (Liddle Collection).
17. Sapper E.F. Wettern, No. 2 Field Company, RND Engineers, letter (Liddle Collection).
18. See Liddle Collection in the Brotherton Library, University of Leeds, for original and recollected testimony of approximately 650 Dardanelles/Gallipoli men.

Suggested Further Reading

Best, Geoffrey, *Churchill: A Study in Greatness* (London: The Hambledon Press, 2002)
Burness, Peter, *The Nek: A Gallipoli Tragedy* (Barnsley: Pen & Sword, 2013)
Cassar, George H., *Kitchener's War, British Strategy from 1914 to 1916* (Washington DC: Brassey's Inc., 2004)
Chambers, Stephen, *Suvla: August Offensive* (Barnsley: Pen & Sword, 2011)
Hart, Peter, *Gallipoli* (London: Profile Books, 2011)
Hickey, Michael, *Gallipoli* (London: John Murray, 1995)
Jones, John Philip, *Johnny: the Legend and Tragedy of General Sir Ian Hamilton* (Barnsley: Pen & Sword, 2012)
Liddle, Peter, *The Gallipoli Experience Reconsidered* (Barnsley: Pen & Sword, 2015)
Macleod, Jenny, *Reconsidering Gallipoli* (Manchester University Press, 2004)

Chapter 2

'Toothless Lions': Firepower and Equipment in the British Army on the Western Front, 1915

By Spencer Jones

The year 1915 surely ranks as one of the worst in the long history of the British Army. By the end of the year the Army had been defeated on all fronts. Operations in East Africa had stagnated, the expedition to Gallipoli had failed utterly, the advance in Mesopotamia had been reversed and the Turks were laying siege to Kut, and the Western Front had proved impregnable. Between March and October the Army fought five major battles on the Western Front: Neuve Chapelle (10–13 March), Aubers Ridge (9 May), Second Ypres (22 April–25 May), Festubert (15–27 May) and Loos (25 September–14 October). With the exception of the defensive battle of Second Ypres, in each of these engagements the British Expeditionary Force (BEF) failed to achieve its intended objectives and suffered heavy casualties for negligible gain. Indeed, the BEF's offensives were so ineffective that by the end of the year senior German officers had come to the conclusion that they had nothing to fear from British attacks.

The verdict of history has been damning. Sir James Edmonds pulled no punches in the *Official History*, lamenting the 'awful slaughter and pitiably small results of the battles of 1915' and noting that the year was 'not one on which the Nation or the Army can look back with satisfaction'.[1] Douglas Haig recalled the 'terrible conditions' faced by the Army and commented to Edmonds, 'I hope the British people will realize what "unpreparedness for war" cost the Empire in flesh and blood.'[2] In his controversial memoirs, David Lloyd George raged against what he regarded as 'futile' and 'criminal attacks' that had seen British forces dashed to pieces against seemingly impregnable German defences.[3] A generation later Alan Clark, taking his cue from Lloyd George, penned his dubious polemic *The Donkeys*, which laid the blame for the defeats of 1915 at the feet of the British generals and popularised the term 'lions led by donkeys'. Subsequent historians have exposed the flaws and untruths present in the work of Lloyd George and Clark, but the terrible cost of 1915 remains undeniable. As Gary Sheffield commented in his celebrated revisionist study, *Forgotten Victory*: 'If any year in the Great War comes close to fulfilling the stereotype promoted by *Oh! What a Lovely War*, it is 1915.'[4]

The litany of disasters that attended British attacks can give the impression that the BEF was utterly static in its methods. Lloyd George was certainly of this opinion[5] and it was wryly summed up by C.S. Forester in his novel *The General*:

[Discussion amongst British generals] was like the debate of a group of savages as to how to extract a screw from a piece of wood. Accustomed only to nails, they had made one effort to pull out the screw by main force, and now that it had failed they were devising methods of applying more force still, of obtaining more efficient pincers, of using levers and fulcrums so that more men could bring their strength to bear. They could hardly be blamed for not guessing that by rotating the screw it would come out after the exertion of far less effort; it would be a notion so different from anything they had ever encountered that they would laugh at the man who suggested it.[6]

The judgement has been deemed harsh by modern historians, who have identified the steady evolution of British command throughout the war, although the debate regarding the effectiveness of British generalship continues to excite interest and controversy.[7] However, in concentrating upon the personalities, opinions and rivalries of High Command, the experiences of the officers and men in the front line can become obscured. Any discussion of the effectiveness of command must also take account of the fighting capabilities of the Army as a whole. Indeed, it was in this latter field that the fundamental problems of 1915 can be found. The question of equipment and tactics is essential to understanding the nature of combat in the early months of trench warfare. This chapter explores the 'sharp end' of battle and will show how the British Army was severely disadvantaged owing to limited firepower and inadequate kit. As a result, the BEF was only able to achieve limited, local success and often met with outright disaster.

There is a common misconception that trench warfare was an entirely new phenomenon to the British Army of the First World War. In fact, the British had more recent practical experience of assaulting enemy trenches than any other power engaged on the Western Front.[8] The Boer War (1899–1902) had introduced the Army to the unpalatable problems associated with attacking dug-in opposition armed with modern weapons.[9] Bitter experience prompted the emergence of two solutions. In the wide grasslands of Orange Free State, the Army had used cavalry and mounted infantry to outflank the Boer trenches and force their defenders to evacuate the position. Amongst the rugged *kopjes* of Natal, British forces adopted artillery-centric methods, firing a hail of shrapnel and lyditte[10] shells to suppress the Boer riflemen whilst infantry stormed forward. The value of these solutions seemed to be confirmed by observations of the Russo-Japanese War (1904–1905).

However, it was not trench warfare *per se* that puzzled the British in 1915 but rather its uniquely immense scale and growing complexity. The Western Front stretched unbroken from the English Channel to the Swiss border. There were no flanks to turn and therefore every assault was, by definition, a frontal one. Furthermore, the trenches of 1915 were noticeably different from those of earlier conflicts. The Germans built their defences in depth and along much of the Anglo-German front the enemy position consisted of three distinct trench lines arrayed one behind another. Each line was linked by a network of communication trenches and the position as a whole was studded with hidden machine-gun nests and other concealed strongpoints. Meanwhile, German artillery batteries lurked out of sight in the rear, ready to bring fire down on any attacker who threatened to penetrate their defences. Even reaching the trenches was a challenge, as these formidable positions were screened by a maze of barbed wire that prevented movement unless it were breached.

It was the combination of fearsome German firepower and movement-inhibiting barbed wire that posed the immediate problem for the British Army. Pre-war tactics had stressed the value of 'fire and movement', urging infantry to advance by bounds, the fire of one group covering the movement of the next. Such methods had proved highly effective in the mobile battles of 1914 but the ubiquitous presence of barbed wire in 1915 greatly hampered their implementation. It is a military truism that an obstacle that is not protected by firepower is merely an engineering problem; unfortunately, German barbed wire belts were covered by rifle, machine-gun, mortar and artillery fire. This produced lethal synergy. Advancing infantry encountering unbroken wire would be forced to halt in no-man's-land where they would be left cruelly exposed to the withering fire of German defenders. Although it was possible for infantry to breach German wire using 'nippers' and similar devices, this was a slow process that was all but impossible under heavy fire. Becoming 'stuck on the wire' was a fate feared by all infantrymen. The Royal Artillery therefore had two crucial duties: to breach the German wire and to beat down the fire of the defenders.

In a rebuttal to the opinion of those who regard the British Army of the First World War as an unthinking, ignorant institution, the Royal Artillery immediately identified the crux of the problem and set about devising solutions. In early 1915 the gunners constructed a series of mock German trenches and carried out live fire exercises against them to gauge their ability to resist damage.[11] At this stage of the war German trenches were relatively shallow. This was especially true of the trenches facing the British in the Aubers Ridge sector, where the high water table prevented deep digging. To increase the strength of the position the Germans reinforced their trenches with loop-holed parapets, often several feet high, constructed from an irregular jumble of sandbags, corrugated iron and wood. The Royal Artillery's experiments were broadly encouraging. High explosive (HE) rounds proved effective at blowing apart German parapets, thereby removing much of the defenders' protection against shrapnel and bullets. Similarly, the barbed wire belts seemed to be vulnerable to accurate fire. At this stage of the war, the great spiral belts of wire that defined the latter years of the conflict were not in evidence, and most German wire was placed on simple wooden stakes. If these stands were destroyed the wire typically fell flat to the ground where it could be crossed with relative ease by the infantry.

However, the Royal Artillery's experiments, combined with ever-growing combat experience, revealed three problems that would not be definitively solved until much later in the war. The first was how best to distribute fire onto the German position. Four key targets required attention: the barbed wire belt, the front line trenches, concealed machine-gun nests and, finally, the enemy artillery. Battle experience would also demonstrate the value of targeting enemy communication trenches and bringing fire onto reserve assembly areas. Engaging such a multitude of targets inevitably diluted the weight of fire, but leaving any one of them untouched was considered an intolerable risk. The second problem, related to the first, was the length of time required for an effective bombardment. Sudden hurricane bombardments lasting less than an hour were favoured in the early part of 1915 and achieved success at the Battle of Neuve Chapelle (10–13 March 1915) but the catastrophic failure of a similar barrage at the Battle of Aubers Ridge (9 May 1915) prejudiced commanders against the method. A day after the battle, Field Marshal Sir John French informed General Sir Douglas Haig:

> It is of great importance that the infantry should not attack until the artillery preparation has been effective. The results of your attacks on the 9th show that the artillery preparation was not effective, and the Commander in Chief does not feel sure that sufficient time is being allowed on this occasion.[12]

Haig had already arrived at a similar opinion and would emphasise the importance of 'thorough preparation' for future action.[13] From the Battle of Festubert (15–27 May) onwards, slow, deliberate bombardments lasting several days were fired with the intention of methodically destroying the German position. In doing so, it was hoped that no targets would be missed and enemy resistance would be thoroughly weakened before the infantry advanced. This latter point was important as it offered a solution of sorts to the third and final problem: how to continue to provide fire support once the infantry assault had gone beyond the enemy front line. An accurate and devastating preliminary bombardment would reduce – although not entirely remove – the need for additional fire support once the attack was under way. Bitter combat experience proved that once the attackers had moved beyond visual range of Forward Observation Officers, it was all but impossible to provide accurate, responsive fire support. Observers who went forward with the infantry found that their telephone lines were soon cut, and hand-carried messages were uncertain to arrive and desperately late even when they did. Various earnest attempts were made to overcome the problem. Aerial observation and air-to-ground communication held promise but remained a novel concept in 1915.[14] Other methods included efforts to bring guns forward to engage over open sights. Mountain artillery was tried in this role, as were armoured cars with turret-mounted 3-pounder guns, but both methods proved disappointing. At times, notably at the Battle of Loos (25 September–14 October), 18-pounder batteries were brought into no-man's-land to provide direct support. Yet ultimately all the methods were found wanting. This meant that there was greater pressure on being able to deliver a highly effective pre-battle bombardment.

The move towards prolonged bombardment has been viewed as an error of judgement.[15] Critics argue that the Royal Artillery had failed to realise that it was not the weight but rather the *density* of fire that mattered: intense bombardments with a high density of shells per yard of trench – as had been fired at Neuve Chapelle – were more effective at crushing positions and suppressing defenders than the slower pace of shelling that was used at Festubert and Loos. It is true that this concept seems to have been poorly understood in 1915 but one must be wary of making judgements with the benefit of hindsight. The decision to adopt prolonged bombardment was made as a result of the Battle of Aubers Ridge, an unmitigated disaster that was proportionally one of the bloodiest days in British Army history. The BEF could not risk another debacle and therefore adopted the methods of her ally, for the French had achieved striking success using a heavy and methodical bombardment during their assault on Vimy Ridge in May.

However, no matter what type of bombardment was employed, two exterior factors complicated the artillery's problems considerably. First, the Germans proved a resourceful and adaptive foe. Startled by the effectiveness of the British hurricane bombardment at the Battle of Neuve Chapelle, the Germans responded by greatly strengthening their defences. Trenches were deepened, parapets were reinforced and machine-gun nests multiplied. To break down these defences the Royal Artillery required ever greater weight of firepower. It was here that the second exterior factor came into play. For the entirety of 1915 the British Army was in the grip of a procurement crisis that left it short of crucial equipment. Nowhere was this shortage more pronounced than amidst the artillery. The problem of pre-battle bombardment was thus compounded; by mid-1915 the German ability to improve their defences threatened to outstrip the Royal Artillery's ability to destroy or suppress them.

The difficulties of the Royal Artillery in this period cannot be overstated. The arm was in the midst of the greatest expansion in its history and this process swiftly exhausted stocks of modern weapons. As early as October 1914 the newly formed 7th Division found itself marching to war with a heavy battery composed of vintage 4.7-inch guns rather than modern 60-pounders. The situation worsened as more divisions were deployed. The reliable 18-pounder field gun was soon in short supply. By July 1915, of 2,148 18-pounders ordered, only 803 had been delivered.[16] The supply of heavy calibre weapons was even worse. In June 1915 there were just sixty-five modern heavy pieces, in an assortment of types and calibres, available to the BEF in France.[17] By comparison, the German Army on the Western Front deployed almost ten times the number of heavy guns available to the British.

Short of modern equipment, the Royal Artillery was forced to make do with whatever was available. In reality, this meant that guns of Boer War vintage, many of which had lain mothballed for years, were suddenly sent to the Western Front. In the absence of 18-pounders the Army deployed obsolete 15-pounders, an aged weapon that had been phased out after a disappointing performance in South Africa. Similarly, the 4.7-inch gun had been a Boer War improvisation designed to deal with the Boer 155mm 'Long Tom' guns. It had emerged from this earlier war with a decidedly mixed reputation and was derided by many as the 'cow gun'.[18] However, the desperate necessity for weapons in 1915 saw it return to action. Lacking range or weight of shell, and further limited by worn and degraded barrels, the 4.7-inch gun gained a notorious reputation for inaccuracy. Soldiers dubbed it 'strict neutrality', for it shelled friend and foe alike.[19] Artillerymen themselves were not immune from the 4.7-inch gun's baleful effects, as it suffered from a disturbingly high proportion of 'prematures', which often killed or injured the crew. The fact that such unsuitable weapons were deployed in large numbers is indicative of the shortages facing the gunners.

Even when guns were available, their employment was constrained by a chronic shortage of ammunition. In February 1915 the field guns of the Royal Artillery were officially limited to ten rounds per gun per day. The Battle of Neuve Chapelle in March all but exhausted the BEF's artillery stocks with the result that in April guns in quiet sectors were limited to a mere three rounds per gun per day.[20] Similar shortages occurred in the quiet months of June and July. In June Sir William Robertson, then serving as the BEF's Chief of Staff, commented bitterly: 'For the past three days we have received a total of three rounds for our three 15-inch howitzers. The Germans yesterday fired forty-seven rounds of this calibre at certain places merely as a joke.'[21]

Ultimately, the Army's frustration with the lack of ammunition boiled over into the notorious 'Shell Scandal' of May 1915 but no amount of press agitation could make up for the fundamental weakness of the British arms industry. At this stage of the war British industry could not meet the insatiable demand for ammunition. Barely half of the orders placed in 1914 had been fulfilled by mid-1915. Furthermore, hasty expansion of factories and dilution of skilled labour sometimes resulted in shoddy work. At the Battle of Loos it has been estimated that around 25 per cent of British shells failed to detonate. There are no comparable statistics for earlier engagements, but it is reasonable to assume that the Royal Artillery suffered from a similar proportion of 'duds' throughout the year.[22]

Chronic shortage of guns and ammunition, combined with ever-strengthening German defences, did not augur well for offensive action. As early as March 1915 Sir Henry Rawlinson, then commanding IV Corps, had identified that:

> ... an undertaking such as that which is under consideration [the Battle of Neuve Chapelle] depends for its success almost entirely upon the correct and efficient employment of the artillery. It is primarily an artillery operation and if the artillery cannot crush and demoralise the enemy's infantry by their fire effect, the enterprise will not succeed.[23]

Robertson expressed his feelings on the matter in May 1915:

> I do not think that people without the experience we have had sufficiently realise what modern warfare is like in a situation such as ours in which there are no flanks and therefore can be no manoeuvre until a hole right through the defence is made. There is no doubt in our minds that it could be made if the means were forthcoming.

Yet unless those 'means' – guns and ammunition – were available, 'we had better get into our holes and stay there and see what the French can do'.[24]

Unfortunately, the harsh reality of 1915 was that the BEF was compelled to fight in support of its French allies but rarely had sufficient artillery 'means' to achieve its objectives. Inadequate equipment, inexperience amongst the officers and men of the expanding Royal Artillery and the ever-strengthening German defences posed a tremendous set of challenges for the British gunners. As a result, the effectiveness of pre-battle bombardments in 1915 was inconsistent and frequently left the infantry facing the unenviable task of attacking relatively intact German positions.

Once the barrage lifted, it was up to the infantry to carry the assault forward. Devising a successful 'art of attack' was a problem that bedevilled all armies in the First World War. The ideal situation was for the infantry to advance on a thoroughly devastated front line, sweep through the handful of concussed defenders, and move forward deep into the enemy position. In reality, this ideal was rarely achieved. Assuming that the bombardment had been at least reasonably successful, and leaving aside the immense logistical and administrative work required to assemble, organise and provision assault troops, the tactical problems of the attackers were threefold. First, the infantry had to cross no-man's-land at sufficient speed to minimise exposure to fire without losing cohesion. Once the attackers had reached the enemy trenches, assuming that the barbed wire had been cut to allow access, they encountered the second problem. The Germans were not willing to surrender their trenches without a fight. To secure the position, the attackers had to engage in brutal, close-range combat with bayonets, rifle butts and, above all else, grenades. Pockets of enemy resistance had to be eliminated and counterattacks beaten back before the German position was consolidated. Once this had been achieved, the third and final problem emerged: how to sustain the attack. After advancing across no-man's-land and engaging in trench combat, the attackers would be bloodied, tired and disorganised and it would be difficult for them to renew the advance. Reinforcements were required, but knowing where and when to commit reserves without real-time communications proved an intractable problem of the First World War.

In 1915, with some notable exceptions such as the disaster at Aubers Ridge, British assault troops were generally able to cross no-man's-land and enter the German lines.[25] However, once locked in combat within the trenches, the infantry found themselves hamstrung by the same shortage of equipment that bedevilled the artillery. British infantry lacked intrinsic firepower beyond its rifles and supporting machine guns. The latter were too heavy and unwieldy to carry forward in the assault. The former, although a vital weapon, was of limited value in close-range actions fought amidst ruined trenches and shell craters. In trench fighting it was soon discovered that the grenade was king.

Before the war the British Army had regarded grenades as a specialised item of siege warfare equipment. In 1914 the Army possessed one pattern of grenade, the 'Hand Grenade No. 1', a percussion device designed to explode on impact. The grenade consisted of an explosive 'head' on the end of a 16-inch cane handle. Although possessing a powerful blast effect, it was expensive to manufacture and the combination of an awkwardly long handle and a sensitive percussion detonator meant that it required a great deal of skill to use, especially in the close confines of a trench, or else it became 'a weapon probably more dangerous to the thrower and his comrades than to the enemy'.[26] Whatever the merits of the weapon, it was in perennially short supply. As early as September 1914 the BEF was requesting a far greater supply of grenades and this pressing need was reinforced by the experience of the Battle of Neuve Chapelle, where post-action reports noted, 'The outstanding feature of these operation was the success of the hand grenade in trench fighting.'[27] William Robertson put it with characteristic bluntness: '[the grenade] seems to be the chief form of attack and defence, and without them it is considered to be practically impossible to hold trenches. The Germans have a large number of them and are constantly using them.'[28]

Supplies from Britain arrived at a snail's pace, prompting the British Army to develop a cottage-industry of grenade manufacture to meet the demand. The Indian Corps took the lead in improvised manufacturing with its 'jam-tin bomb' design. James Edmonds remembered:

> The recipe for making the 'jam pot' hand-grenade of the period was: take a tin jam pot, fill it with shredded guncotton and tenpenny nails, mixed according to taste. Insert a No. 8 detonator and short length of Bickford's fuze. Clay up the lid. Light with a match, pipe, cigar or cigarette, and throw for all you are worth. . . . As may well be imagined . . . these extemporised missiles proved far from reliable.[29]

The cottage-industry was considerably developed in 1915 under the aegis of the Trench Warfare Department, which pioneered at least ten different grenade designs in the first six months of the year.[30] In addition, British arms companies sent out their own weapons for field evaluations. These extemporised grenades inevitably suffered from drawbacks. The Pitcher grenade, issued in large numbers in mid-1915, was so prone to premature detonation that bombers trained in its use were referred to as 'the Suicide Club'.[31] Other grenades were equally dangerous to the user or those nearby. In April 1915 the commanding officer of 7th Division, Major-General Sir Thompson Capper, was hospitalised after being wounded at a grenade demonstration, and one can well imagine how much greater the dangers of throwing grenades in battle must have been. Even designs that did not kill or maim their users suffered from problems. At the Battle of Festubert the Battye bomb was in common usage and it possessed a complex system of igniting the fuse:

> The bomber had to unwind a sticky tape, pull out a safety nail, and then (with the finger of his left hand, always clumsy and often cold and wet, and frequently nervous in addition) take the cardboard lighter, wobbling on the top of two inches of pliable fuse and secured to the bomb with a bit of wire, to twist the upper thimble on the lower one.[32]

Later in the year the Ball grenade emerged as a superior replacement and was employed in considerable quantity at the Battle of Loos. It was described by Edmonds as 'a heavy iron sphere as large as a cricket ball'.[33] To use the weapon it was necessary to light an exposed fuse poking from the top of the grenade. But, as Sir Hubert Gough recalled: 'The fuse of this could only be lit by striking it on a piece of emery paper and this was sewn on the man's left sleeve, but by 8.30 on the morning of the 25th [September] the rain was coming down heavily, the emery paper was soaked and the bomb useless.'[34] The 7th Division estimated that 80 per cent of its grenades were disabled by the wet conditions at Loos.[35]

By the end of the year the BEF had adopted the effective Mills bomb design but supply problems meant that a multitude of peculiar grenade types remained in service well into 1916. Crucially, all but the Mills design were deemed inferior to the German 'Potato Masher' stick grenade. The need to rely upon limited quantities of inadequate grenades placed the British infantry at a severe disadvantage in trench fighting.

In addition to the problems with grenade provision, there were other equipment shortages which hampered the assaulting infantry. The most serious of these was the lack of lightweight mortars suitable for close-range action. The British Army had given little consideration to mortars prior to the war, regarding them as specialised and rather old-fashioned, and it went to war without any in its arsenal. By contrast, the German Army, anticipating siege operations against the fortresses of Belgium and France, equipped its forces with powerful *minenwerfer* – 'mine throwers' – in a variety of calibres. These weapons were especially valuable during trench fighting. There was little protection from the high angle fire of the *minenwerfer*, which could drop shells directly into trenches, dugouts or shell craters. The dull 'thump' as a *minenwerfer* fired, followed by the distinctive high-pitched whistle as its shells plummeted to earth, was a sound that was dreaded by British infantry. A soldier of the 1st Somerset Light Infantry recalled: 'Trench mortar bombs, which we call "flying pigs", hurtle through the air to burst with terrific force, blowing up parapets, traverses and dugouts. Men are just battered about, mere cannon-fodder for the open mouthed guns.'[36]

The British Army reacted quickly to the need for mortars. In October 1914 Sir John French wrote to the War Office, enclosing a pamphlet detailing the design of a German *minenwerfer* and requesting a version suitable for employment with the BEF. But such was the pressure on British industry that there was simply no spare capacity to begin manufacture of the weapon. Instead, the Indian Corps took the lead in improvised designs, deploying their first home-made 'bomb gun' in November 1914 and developing the concept throughout the coming months.[37] The first version of this weapon was little more than a length of pipe with an exposed fuse firing a large 'jam-tin bomb', but the Indians worked on refining the design throughout the coming months. These extemporised mortars were gradually joined by War Office patterns in a variety of calibres but, as with grenades, early designs were often inadequate and the supply was uncertain.

The absence was unfortunate, for mortars were in constant demand, especially those light enough to operate from the British front line or capable of being manhandled forward to support troops in captured positions. In particular, they were useful for destroying enemy machine-gun nests and strongpoints which the pre-battle bombardment had missed. Unless eliminated, these emplacements could inflict withering casualties on attackers and hold up an advance for hours. Yet there were never enough mortars to meet the demand and the infantry often suffered as a consequence. Furthermore, British mortar teams laboured under a variety of disadvantages. Their extemporised weapons were outranged and outgunned by German *minenwerfer*, proved alarmingly prone to malfunction, and were perennially short of ammunition. The BEF would remain chronically short of effective mortars throughout 1915 and it was not until the following year, when the Stokes mortar became available in large numbers, that the problem was solved.

It was not merely grenades and mortars that were in short supply. Before 1914 the BEF had been equipped for mobile field warfare on a relatively small scale.

Faced with a far larger war in 1915, it found itself lacking a variety of items useful in trench fighting, ranging from sandbags and field telephones to trench periscopes and telescopic sights for snipers. Heavy machine guns were always in short supply and the light Lewis machine gun was a rare novelty. Even rifles were lacking. Some indication of the parlous state of British military stores is given by the fact that the BEF lacked a standard pattern of rifle in 1915. Regular and Indian troops used the modern Short Magazine Lee-Enfield, but most Territorials used the Boer War vintage Long Lee-Enfield and Canadian soldiers were equipped with the notoriously unreliable Ross rifle.

The cumulative effect of these equipment shortages greatly diminished the fighting power of the British Army. This was further compounded by the near universal inexperience amongst officers and soldiers in the rapidly growing force. The hardened cadre of Regular soldiers was soon subsumed by a flood of wartime volunteers. These men did not want for courage, but bravery alone was not enough. The assertion that British soldiers were 'lions' has not been seriously questioned, but lack of firepower meant that they were often toothless. James Edmonds lamented after the war that 'Too many of our bravest and best perished, seeking to compensate by valour for lack of experience and shortage of munitions.'[38] But the result was a tragic cycle, for high casualties in one battle ensured inexperience in the next.

Tactically, the BEF became locked into a recurring nightmare. Unless the artillery had thoroughly prepared the way, the infantry lacked the weaponry and fighting power reliably to fight through enemy positions. This unpalatable fact put ever-greater pressure on the artillery to perform, but the gunners had neither weaponry nor ammunition to be certain of breaching the increasingly sophisticated German defences. Attempts to reduce the dependence on the pre-battle bombardment, such as the deployment of poison gas at the Battle of Loos, did nothing to address this core problem. In 1915 the British Army was simply not equipped for trench warfare against a first-rate opponent. This in turn was compounded by inexperience at every level of the BEF, which could be manifest in careless, costly mistakes at the front and grotesque errors of judgement amongst the senior ranks.[39] A consistent problem was the failure of British planning to take account of the lack of firepower available to its troops. Soldiers were frequently asked to do too much with too little, and paid a terrible cost in lives as a result.

Throughout 1915 superior German training and equipment gave them a battlefield edge which the novice BEF could not match. Edmonds admitted without shame 'the enemy undoubtedly had the best of the fighting' but also placed the bloody year in its context: 'In the remembrance of the final victory, we are apt to forget the painful and weary stages by which it was reached, and the heavy cost in our best lives during these stages.'[40]

Notes

1. James Edmonds and G.C. Wynne, *Official History of the Great War: Military Operations France and Belgium 1915*, Vol. 1 (London: MacMillan, 1927), p. vi; Vol. 2, p. xi. (Hereafter Edmonds, *Official History*. Unless otherwise specified, all references are to the 1915 volumes.)

2. Quoted in Edmonds, *Official History*, Vol. 2, p. x.
3. David Lloyd George, *War Memoirs of David Lloyd-George*, Vol. 1 (London: Odhams Press, 1938), p. 292.
4. Gary Sheffield, *Forgotten Victory: The First World War, Myths and Realities* (London: Headline, 2001), p. 133.
5. Lloyd George, *Memoirs*, Vol. 1, pp. 289, 291.
6. C.S. Forester, *The General* (William Collins, 2014; Original, 1936), p. 212.
7. For a useful summary of changing attitudes, see Brian Bond, *The First World War and British Military History* (Oxford: Oxford University Press, 1991) and Brian Bond, *The Unquiet Western Front: Britain's Role in Literature and History* (Cambridge: Cambridge University Press, 2002).
8. It must also be remembered that Russia and Japan had engaged in trench warfare in the Russo-Japanese War (1904–05). This war served as the primary guide for both France and Germany, neither of whom had any recent experience of trench combat.
9. See Spencer Jones, *From Boer War to World War: Tactical Reform of the British Army 1902–1914* (Norman: University of Oklahoma Press, 2012).
10. Lyditte was a form of high explosive favoured by the British Army and Royal Navy.
11. Edmonds, *Official History*, Vol. 1, p. 78, fn 2.
12. Sanders Marble, 'The Infantry Cannot Do With a Gun Less: The Place of the Artillery in the BEF, 1914–1918', available at: http://www.gutenberg-e.org/mas01, Chapter 3: Preparing the Attack.
13. Ibid.
14. For more on this topic, see Peter Hart, 'The BEF Takes Off: The Royal Flying Corps in 1915', in Spencer Jones (ed.), *Courage without Glory: The British Army on the Western Front 1915* (Solihull: Helion & Co., 2015), p. 141.
15. Robin Prior and Trevor Wilson, *Command on the Western Front: The Military Career of General Sir Henry Rawlinson 1914–1918* (Barnsley: Pen & Sword Military Classics, 2004), pp. 83, 85.
16. Edmonds, *Official History*, Vol. 1, p. 55.
17. Ibid.
18. Jones, *Boer War to World War*, pp. 121–3, 127. The weapons were known as 'cow guns' due to the habit of using oxen to tow them in South Africa; it was also a cynical comment on their slow movement speed compared to the dashing batteries of the field and horse artillery.
19. Edmonds, *Official History 1914*, Vol. 2, p. 164.
20. Edmonds, *Official History*, Vol. 1, p. 56. This restriction did not apply to guns engaged at the Second Battle of Ypres.
21. Quoted in John Spencer, 'Friends Disunited: Johnnie French, Wully Robertson and "K of K" in 1915', in Jones (ed.), *Courage without Glory*, p. 89.
22. John Mason Sneddon, 'The Supply of Munitions to the Army, 1915', in Jones (ed.), *Courage without Glory*, p. 66.
23. Quoted in Patrick Watt, 'Douglas Haig and the Planning of the Battle of Neuve Chapelle', in Jones (ed.), *Courage without Glory*, p. 191.
24. Quoted in Spencer, 'Friends Disunited', p. 88.
25. It must be noted that there would often be local repulses against portions of the German line where the wire was not breached or enemy resistance was especially strong. Such incidents had first been noted at the Battle of Neuve Chapelle; whilst the assault was successful along most of the line, the 2nd Middlesex and 2nd Scottish Rifles advanced into unbroken German wire and suffered terribly as a result. Similar localised disasters occurred during all the major British offensives of 1915.
26. John Ewing, *The History of the 9th (Scottish) Division 1914–1919* (London: J. Murray, 1921), pp. 13–14.
27. National Archive, WO 95/1628, 7th Division War Diary, Narrative of Operations, Neuve Chapelle, March 10th to 14th 1915.
28. Michael Woods, 'Gas, Grenades and Grievances: The Attack on the Hohenzollern Redoubt by 46th (North Midland) Division, 13 October 1915', in Jones (ed.), *Courage without Glory*, pp. 425–6.
29. Edmonds, *Official History*, Vol. 1, p. 7.

30. For a full account of the Trench Warfare Department, see Sneddon, 'Supply of Munitions'.
31. Ibid., p. 74.
32. Quoted in Robert Williams, 'The Battle of Festubert', in Jones (ed.), *Courage without Glory*, p. 279.
33. Edmonds, *Official History*, Vol. 2, p. 248.
34. Hubert Gough, *The Fifth Army* (London: Hodder & Stoughton, 1931), pp. 121–2.
35. Brian Curragh, '"A Great Victory All But Gained": The Battle of Loos, 1915', in Jones (ed.), *Courage without Glory*, p. 387.
36. Quoted in Mike LoCicero, '"A Coda to the Second Battle of Ypres": International Trench, 6–10 July 1915', in Jones (ed.), *Courage without Glory*, p. 319.
37. Sneddon, 'Supply of Munitions', pp. 76–8.
38. Edmonds, *Official History*, Vol. 1, p. vii.
39. For an example of the latter, see Woods, 'Gas, Grenades and Grievances', pp. 413–16.
40. Edmonds, *Official History*, Vol. 1, p. vi.

Suggested Further Reading

Edmonds, James and Wynne, G.C., *Official History of the Great War: Military Operations France and Belgium 1915*, Vol. 1 (London: MacMillan, 1927) and Vol. 2 (London: MacMillan, 1928).

Jones, Spencer (ed.), *Courage without Glory: The British Army on the Western Front 1915* (Solihull: Helion & Co., 2015)

Lloyd, Nick, *Loos 1915* (Stroud: Tempus, 2006)

Mitchinson, K.W., *The Territorial Force at War 1914–1916* (Basingstoke: Palgrave Macmillan, 2014)

Morton-Jack, George, *The Indian Army on the Western Front: India's Expeditionary Force to France and Belgium in the First World War* (Cambridge: Cambridge University Press, 2014)

Prior, Robin and Wilson, Trevor, *Command on the Western Front: The Military Career of General Sir Henry Rawlinson 1914–1918* (Barnsley: Pen & Sword Military Classics, 2004)

Simkins, Peter, *Kitchener's Army: The Raising of the New Armies, 1914–1916* (Barnsley: Pen & Sword, 2014)

Chapter 3

'A Second Trafalgar?' Jutland and its Impact, 1916–18

By Duncan Redford

Around 2.15pm on 31 May 1916 a signal flashed out that the Battlecruiser Fleet had been waiting to hear for over a year (and longer for the Grand Fleet): 'Enemy in sight.' HMS *Galatea*, one of the Battlecruiser Fleet's reconnaissance screen, had spotted a small steamer to the east which was blowing off steam – a sign it was stopped. Within seconds, the lookouts and officers on *Galatea*'s bridge had seen that a two-funnelled ship was close by the stopped steamer. As *Galatea* and her fellow light cruisers of the 1st Light Cruiser Squadron approached these strange ships to investigate, it became clear that they were cruisers and not friendly ones either.

This was the start of a battle – the Battle of Jutland – that was perhaps the most significant engagement of the First World War, one that would shape the war on sea and on land. The result of the battle was also felt far inland by civilians of both sides as the directors of their national war endeavours reinvigorated their economic blockades. Quite simply, Jutland directly and indirectly won the war for the allies. This may sound an ambitious claim for a sea battle. After all, man lives on the land and not at sea. Moreover, it was a battle that the Germans claimed to have won, and one that sowed discord for years after the war throughout the Royal Navy as rival factions tried to justify their actions whilst mourning the fact that the battle had not been a second Trafalgar destroying the Kaiser's naval power. Yet the battle also indicates the ways by which seapower can influence operations on land and sea, even when fleets are not in combat. To paraphrase Sir Julian Corbett, the most important observer of national strategy, what matters about seapower is not what it allows you to do at sea, but what influence it allows you to exert over the land and Jutland was in many ways a catalyst for how seapower could exert influence on land.

The battle was, despite German propaganda claims, a victory for the Royal Navy – a pyrrhic victory at the tactical level perhaps, but one that at the operational and strategic level was a clear success for the British and one that had a profound impact on the rest of the war. First, it safeguarded the British economic blockade of Germany. Second, it demonstrated to the Germans that they could not wrest command of the North Sea away from the British and that they would have to find a different way of trying to break Britain's stranglehold. These two issues had huge consequences – intended and unintended – and would dictate who would win the war on land as well as at sea. This chapter will explore the impact of the Battle of Jutland, but first, for the benefit of those whose view of the sea has been obscured by life in the trenches, it will outline the battle that won the war for the allies.

The Battle

As soon as Beatty, commanding the Battlecruiser Fleet (BCF), received the 'Enemy in sight' signal, he immediately turned his ships off their northerly course which had been taking them towards a rendezvous with the rest of the Grand Fleet under Admiral Sir John Jellicoe some miles to the north, and headed south-east to cut off the escape of the enemy ships. Beatty's force was also accompanied by the seaplane carrier HMS *Engadine* and there were frantic but successful efforts to get a seaplane launched and in the air. Unfortunately for the British, things now started to go wrong.

The signal to turn to the southeast was missed by the 5th Battle Squadron (5BS) which Beatty had stationed about 5 miles to his northwest. This squadron was the most powerful unit in the Grand Fleet, consisting of four of the five super-dreadnoughts of the *Queen Elizabeth* class – HMS *Barham*, HMS *Warspite*, HMS *Valiant* and HMS *Malaya*, all armed with eight 15-inch guns and with oil-fired steam turbines making them almost as fast as Beatty's coal-powered battlecruisers. After much nagging, 5BS had been lent to Beatty while one of his battlecruiser squadrons was away at Scapa Flow for some badly needed gunnery practice. But, thanks to the missed signal, 5BS was now heading in almost the opposite direction to Beatty's battlecruisers. By the time the mistake was recti-fied, 5BS was about 10 miles behind the BCF.

As *Barham* and the super-dreadnoughts of 5BS belatedly altered course to follow the BCF, another signal was arcing across the wireless system: *Galatea* had sighted a large amount of smoke to the north-east – in fact so much smoke that it could only be from an enemy fleet. The German High Seas Fleet had sailed. Of course the Admiralty, thanks to its code-breakers in Room 40, knew the whole High Seas Fleet was going to mount an operation – this was why the Grand Fleet and BCF had been ordered to sea and to patrol the area of Jutland Bank. But for the Grand Fleet and the BCF as they sailed across a dull flat sea on the morning of 31 May, it seemed that this sortie was shaping up to be like so many sweeps of the North Sea before it – no sign of the enemy, no action and then back to base.

The indistinct shapes on the horizon soon solidified into the battlecruisers of Hipper's 1st Scouting Group, and it was the Germans who opened fire first at 3.45pm as both sides charged south. The reason for the German course was simple – they were trying to draw the six battlecruisers of the BCF onto the guns of the rest of the High Seas Fleet, while Beatty had the dual task of trying to destroy Hipper's force and tell Jellicoe the position of the German main fleet. Unfortunately for the British, the German shooting was far more accurate than that of the BCF. In the first twelve minutes of the battle the BCF was hit by perhaps fifteen heavy shells; the Germans were hit by just four. Then, at 4pm, Beatty's flagship, HMS *Lion*, was hit on Q turret. The shell penetrated the armoured roof of the turret and exploded, destroying the turret and sending flames lancing down towards the magazines, feeding on cordite charges waiting in the turret trunking to be fired and sending a plume of flames high into the air. Only the order to flood the magazines, apparently given by Major Francis Harvey, Royal Marines, as he was dying, prevented a catastrophic explosion that would have destroyed the ship. (The act was to see him awarded a posthumous Victoria Cross.) Minutes later, several heavy shells hit HMS *Indefatigable* and after a delay of perhaps thirty seconds, she blew up; there were just two survivors. However, 5BS had been slowly closing the gap and at 4.08pm the 5BS battleships were able to open fire on the rearmost German battlecruiser, *Von Der Tann*. Soon two of Hipper's ships, *Von Der Tann* and *Moltke*, were being hit – and hit hard – by 15-inch salvos from the *Queen Elizabeth*s. Twenty-four minutes after the destruction of HMS *Indefatigable*, HMS *Queen Mary*, which had been targeted by *Derfflinger* and *Seydlitz*, seemed to be hit almost simultaneously by a large number of shells and she disintegrated. All Beatty could say was: 'There seems to be something wrong with our bloody ships today.'

At almost the moment that *Queen Mary* exploded, Commodore Goodenough's 2nd Light Cruiser Squadron, which had been working hard to get back ahead of the BCF during the opening stages of the battle, sighted numerous masts ahead, together with a great deal of funnel smoke. Minutes later, at 4.47pm, the squadron was wirelessing that it had sighted the main enemy battlefleet. Beatty had been drawn onto the guns of the High Seas Fleet by Hipper, as the Germans had intended.

Beatty's reaction was to try to turn the tables on the Germans by turning round and trying to lead them into the arms of the Grand Fleet coming down from the north. But now, a combination of poor tactical decision-making by Beatty and ineffective signalling meant that as Beatty headed north, he passed 5BS heading south, and he allowed them to continue south for some time before ordering them to reverse course and escape the trap. This made 5BS the centre of attention for the Germans and it was deluged with shells, with several of the super-dreadnoughts being hit as they turned. During the run north the BCF pulled out of range, but 5BS, further behind, fought on alone against the combined German forces for at least thirty minutes.

Jellicoe, away to the north and moving south to support Beatty, had been wondering where exactly the enemy was since the sighting reports at around 4.45pm. The position, course and speed of the enemy were vital information if the Grand Fleet were to deploy from its cruising formation to line-of-battle in the right direction and at the right time. Quite simply, Beatty failed to ensure that his Commander-in-Chief had good information about what was happening over the horizon and where the High Seas Fleet was going. The first indication as to the direction for the enemy came as Beatty's ships raced into sight at about 6pm. After some pointed signals, Beatty finally seems to have remembered what he was there for and sent a barely adequate indication of the enemy's course and direction. However, Jellicoe had already worked it out and ordered the deployment of his fleet at 6.16pm in a direction that would ensure Admiral Scheer's High Seas Fleet had a very unpleasant shock.

As Beatty's and Jellicoe's forces met, the battlecruisers headed for the front of the British line, while 5BS, still some distance behind Beatty's ships, headed for the rear. The mass of cruisers and destroyers manoeuvring to try to take their correct station as the Grand Fleet dreadnoughts turned to form a single line of twenty-four ships, 6 miles long, across the path of the German fleet, caused a great number of rapid course changes – with enemy shell-fire adding to the tension of the developing situation. For reasons best known to himself, Rear-Admiral Arbuthnot, commanding four obsolescent large armoured cruisers, moved with HMS *Defence* and HMS *Warrior* (his other two ships were unable to follow him due to the onrushing British fleet) into the gap between the opposing fleets to reach his allocated position, rather than going behind the British fleet. His ships set upon a disabled German cruiser, *Wiesbaden*, just as Scheer's dread-noughts and Hipper's battlecruisers loomed out of the murk. *Defence* exploded under the weight of heavy shell hits, and *Warrior* was comprehensively wrecked by shell-fire, but managed to limp out of the way. *Warrior* was saved by the 'antics' of *Warspite* (5BS) whose steering gear chose this moment to jam and she steered two complete circles between the British fleet and the enemy, becoming the centre of attention for the entire High Seas Fleet, and suffering for it. By the time *Warspite's* recalcitrant steering gear was put in some order, she had been hit many times and, despite trying to remain in the battle line, was too badly damaged, forcing her to retire from the battle.

At the head of the British line, the 3rd Battlecruiser Squadron (the one that had been swapped for 5BS to allow gunnery practice), which had positioned itself in front of Beatty's battlecruisers, was treated to the sight of Hipper's battlecruisers at a range of 9,000 yards and opened a heavy fire on them at about 6.21pm. *Lutzow* and *Derfflinger* in particular were hard hit by shell-fire from HMS *Invincible*, HMS *Inflexible* and HMS *Indomitable*. But then the mists blocking the German view cleared and *Invincible* felt the full weight of fire from Hipper's ships. Hit on her centre turret, the middle of the ship disintegrated, leaving the bow and stern jutting up from the seabed and six survivors – out of a ship's company of 1,032 – clinging to the wreckage.

As the Grand Fleet's dreadnoughts turned into line at one minute intervals after Jellicoe's 6.16pm order to deploy, they opened fire on the head of the approaching German line. The crescent of gun flashes across the horizon showed Scheer exactly what he had blundered into: the Grand Fleet, the very thing he had to avoid. Scheer then ordered a 'battle emergency turn away', which involved the rear ship turning first, then each successive ship turning once it saw the ships astern starting to turn. The result was that just as the Grand Fleet's gunners were getting into their stride, the German fleet seemed to disappear in the mist. By 6.45pm the British guns were falling silent.

Once Scheer had moved some distance to the south, he made the mistake of turning back in order to try to cut across the rear of the British. Unfortunately for the High Seas Fleet, all he succeeded in doing was blundering into the middle of the Grand Fleet, which again poured fire onto his ships. A second, far more disorganised, emergency turn away occurred in the worsening visibility as the Germans desperately tried to escape. Hipper's battlecruisers were ordered at 7.14pm to attack the head of the British line, while the German destroyers launched a mass torpedo attack to cover the flight of the High Seas Fleet. This attack led to the Grand Fleet turning away to avoid the torpedoes running towards it, with the result that contact was lost with the German heavy units.

The Grand Fleet, after the torpedo attack, slowly edged south. The High Seas Fleet tried to avoid being pushed further west and came round towards the southeast. Visibility was very poor and the sun was setting so that there were but sporadic outbreaks of gunfire as the opposition was glimpsed, but Jellicoe had no firm idea where the enemy fleet was, or the course it was taking. In the darkness that followed, both fleets bumped against each other as the Germans tried to pass round the Grand Fleet and head back to base. Intense action occurred between each side's flotilla forces; in the darkness the armoured cruiser HMS *Black Prince* blundered into the path of German battleships and was destroyed, leaving no survivors. The British, however, were not trained in night fighting, so the dreadnoughts did not force an action. By dawn, the High Seas Fleet had escaped and was safe behind its defensive minefields.[1]

The Germans, having reached port first, claimed a victory and their propaganda machine went into overdrive with the neutral Press. The British ships, getting back to base twenty-four hours or more after the Germans, were greeted with a degree of dismay that the Germans had not been utterly destroyed. Propaganda aside, and despite their losses in ships (which the British could afford), the failings experienced with their shells, their command and control – especially the desire of senior officers to get to grips with the enemy without waiting for orders to do so – and their lack of training for night fighting, the British had managed to achieve a strategic victory as well as a tactical win, even if it was somewhat closer to being a pyrrhic victory than was comfortable. That the British were dissatisfied with the result of the battle does not mean that they had lost it.

The Germans had attempted to destroy a significant part of the Grand Fleet in isolation and had failed in their aim. They had not destroyed enough of the Grand Fleet to make British command of the sea untenable. The British economic blockade was still in place, as were the British Army's supply lines across the Channel to the Western Front. Also, the German fleet suffered proportionally more damage than the British. Indeed, apart from their propaganda, the Germans had very little to show for the battle and their fleet's morale had received a severe shock. Tactically, the Germans were in much worse shape than the British during and after the battle. Their commander, Scheer, had made a number of potentially fatal errors, from the full consequences of which only British cack-handedness had allowed him to escape.

The chief failing on the British side – command and control – was caused by a corporate culture stretching back decades that stifled initiative and where obedience to orders was paramount.[2] With regard to the loss of three battlecruisers, again much of the blame must be laid at the Navy's own confusion as to what fast armoured cruisers were actually for: either trade defence or as a high speed section of the battle line. However, the poor magazine safety standards that were endemic within the BCF cannot escape some of the blame, and for that Beatty, who had tried to compensate for his force's reputation for poor gunnery by rapid firing and less attention to safety, must shoulder much of the responsibility.

What a state, or a navy, does with its seapower is the important issue. The German High Seas Fleet was effectively impotent and remained impotent after Jutland. As Scheer reported to the Kaiser on 4 July 1916, 'there can be no doubt that even the most successful result from a high seas battle will not compel England to make peace'.[3] However, the British had been unable to wean themselves off the image of the battleship and then the dreadnought as the arbiter of seapower, with the result that they wanted a second Trafalgar, even if strategically one was perhaps not necessary to neutralise German naval power in the North Sea. For both sides, Jutland signalled a change in the war at sea.

The Economic Blockade – Starving Germany

The most significant impact of the Battle of Jutland was that the British economic blockade of Germany could continue unchallenged, enforced by patrolling armed merchant cruisers north of Scotland and backed by the unbeaten might of the Grand Fleet. While the blockade in the early years of the war had not been enforced as rigorously as the Admiralty wanted, by the end of 1916 it had become much tighter. However, the Germans could and did receive goods and foodstuffs via neighbouring neutral states, but thanks to the efforts of the Ministry of Blockade, diplomatic pressure had ramped up against neutral trading with Germany.

The increasing effectiveness of the blockade through diplomatic measures, the continuing patrols by the Navy to catch blockade runners, and the day to day interception of neutral vessels to ensure they were not carrying contraband meant that in the winter of 1916/17 Germany experienced real food shortages.

German imports of foodstuffs (in thousands of tonnes)				
		Average net imports 1912–13	*Imported 1917*	*% decrease*
Breads/cereals		5,538	17.6	99.7
Animal fats		161.6	5.2	96.7
Fish		361.3	161	55.4
Eggs		169	40	76.3
Leguminous vegetables		310.8	1.7	99.5
Fruits		850	220	74.1
Vegetable fats & oils		155.3	Not given	
Oilseeds		1,595.4	17.1	98.9
Cattle foods	– oilseeds	1,571.9	14.8	99.1
(not including pig	– bran	1,744.9	10.2	99.4
fodders like maize)	– oilcake	532.5	2	99.6
	– other	359.2	18.6	94.8

Source: National Archive, ADM 186/603, CB 1554, The Economic Blockade, p. 21.

Before the war the average calorie intake per person per day in Germany was 3,215; by the autumn of 1916 it had fallen to 1,344 before rising very slightly in November to 1,431 calories. (An average working man needs about 2,500 calories to remain healthy, and if involved in heavy manual labour might need up to 4,000.) Around 763,000 people died prematurely in Germany as a result of the economic blockade.

The shortage of fertilisers and fodders, which had previously been imported and were now covered by the blockade, only made the German situation worse. Fortunately for the Allies, the Germans had experienced poor weather and a poor harvest during 1916, which was exacerbated by a lack of agricultural labour. Indeed, the restrictions on fertilisers would continue to compound German woes, and the corps of wheat, oats and potatoes in 1918–19 was only half what they had been in 1912–13. Germany, thanks to British command of the sea, unbroken by the High Seas Fleet at the Battle of Jutland, was being starved out of the war, a process that was aided by the prestige seapower was giving to allied diplomatic efforts to reduce contraband reaching Germany via neutral neighbours. The result in 1918 was political revolution and the Armistice.

However, the tightening British blockade encouraged Germany to revisit a mode of warfare that neutral pressure earlier in the war had forced them to abandon – unrestricted submarine warfare.

The Economic Blockade – Starving Britain

Jutland may have ended German enthusiasm for ambushes on parts of the Grand Fleet, but it did not end their attempts to impose an economic blockade on Britain. Surface raiders were, however, a trifling issue and mines could be contained by laborious and constant efforts. The main threat after Jutland was the submarine and unrestricted submarine warfare. Neutral pressure in 1915 and the fear that America would enter the war on the allied side in that year saw Germany call off its first unrestricted submarine warfare campaign. However, despite the German move back to restricted submarine warfare, allied losses rapidly increased after June 1916. In October, the worst month of 1916, 314,239 tons of shipping was lost to U-boats; from September to the end of the year more than 200,000 tons of shipping was sunk by enemy submarines per month. Worse still was the lack of success of anti-submarine measures. From 1 June to the end of 1916 only fifteen U-boats (in all theatres) were sunk by allied countermeasures. Of these measures, mines were the most effective, while British submarines were almost as effective as surface ships, sinking two U-boats. Surface ships sank two with depth-charges and one was sunk by a Q-ship.

It was obvious that the British and the Royal Navy had not managed to find a solution to the submarine problem and the established countermeasures – patrolling shipping routes and focal points, diverting shipping, laying minefields, giving merchant ships defensive guns, deploying Q-ships and the Dover barrage with its nets, mines and surface patrols – were not coping with German submarines. In October 1916 Jellicoe, as Commander-in-Chief of the Grand Fleet, told the First Lord (Balfour) and First Sea Lord (Henry Jackson) that 'the very serious and ever-increasing menace of the enemy's submarine attack on trade is by far the

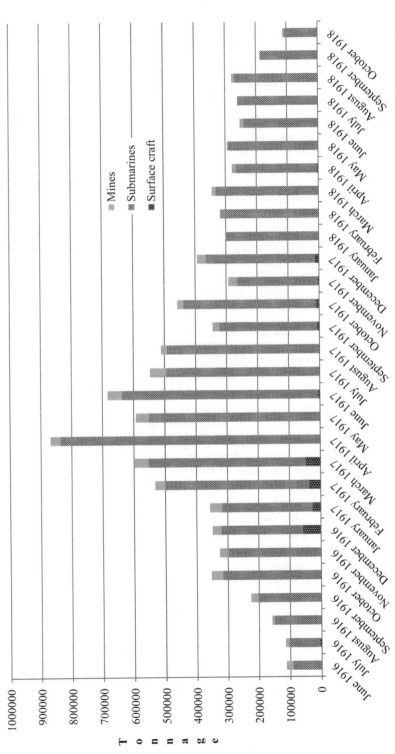

British, allied and neutral merchant vessels destroyed by enemy action, 1 June 1916–31 October 1918. In May and June 1917 and in April 1918 a small percentage of losses were also attributed to aircraft.

Source: NHB, *Statistical Review of the War Against Merchant Shipping* (London: HMSO, 1918), p. 22.

most pressing question at the present time'. A few days later Jellicoe was mooting the possibility that 'we are risking all the advantages we may gain by successes on shore if we are forced to conclude peace because we cannot feed the country'.[4]

The inability of the Jackson/Balfour administration to get on top of the submarine menace was one of the chief reasons for their removal: Jackson, worn out by overwork and unable to delegate effectively, was dismissed in November; Balfour went in December. It was hoped that their replacements, Jellicoe as First Sea Lord (Beatty got the command he had lusted after – the Grand Fleet) and Sir Edward Carson as First Lord, would be able to get a grip on the problem. And there was hope for betterment; hydrophones were improving, giving a means of locating (eventually) a submerged U-boat, and the entry into service of depth-charges gave warships a more effective weapon against a dived submarine than bludgeoning it with their bows.

However, after Jutland, the Germans had been discussing how to prosecute the war against Britain and had come to the conclusion that their only hope lay in resuming unrestricted submarine warfare. This they did on 1 February 1917 and the results were dreadful for Britain. In February 1917 U-boats sank 464,599 tons of allied shipping and by the end of April the monthly tonnage lost had risen to a horrifying 834,549 tons; for the rest of the year the monthly tonnage lost never fell below 300,000 tons. As allied shipping was massacred between February and April, it seemed to Jellicoe and others that Britain would be starved out of the war. Certainly Jellicoe, exhausted after years of shouldering the burden of command of the Grand Fleet, was extremely pessimistic about Britain's ability to continue the war into 1918 unless a solution were found. On the other hand, American outrage over the German resumption of unrestricted submarine warfare positively contributed to the decision to join the war on the allies' side at the beginning of April 1917. This was perhaps the most important impact of the Battle of Jutland – the German High Command's conviction that new ways to beat the British had to be found, that unrestricted submarine warfare had to be tried again, despite the virtual certainty of forcing neutrals into the arms of the allies.[5]

In terms of the Royal Navy's response to the submarine problem, a definite step in the right direction had been taken when Jellicoe, shortly after becoming First Sea Lord, formed an Anti-Submarine Division within the Naval Staff to co-ordinate and generate anti-submarine plans which previously had been run by several different staff divisions. It facilitated for the first time concentrated and deliberate thought on how to beat the U-boat. However, many of the suggestions – such as using sound impulses through the water, first essayed against a British submarine in Harwich harbour in the spring of 1918 and not perfected until after the end of the war – would take a great deal of time to develop. Anti-submarine warfare was very much a matter of a large number of cumulative measures in the Admiralty's view.

With the almost unimaginable shipping losses after February 1917 and Jellicoe's deep fears that a solution could not be found, it was clear that something completely different would have to be tried. However, questions were being asked as to whether Jellicoe were the man to lead the Navy in view of his pessimism during the spring and his clear exhaustion from overwork. The First

Lord, Carson, was replaced by Sir Eric Geddes in July 1917 in order to liven up the Admiralty, and in the end Geddes decided that Jellicoe had to go and he was sacked in a most shameful manner on Christmas Eve 1917, being replaced by Admiral Sir Rosslyn Wemyss.[6]

One solution to the U-boat problem was to try convoy – something the Navy and ship owners had been saying for decades was unfeasible as a trade defence measure. Another possibility was to do something about the U-boat and destroyer bases in Flanders, at Ostend, Zeebrugge and Bruges.

Convoy had been suggested as a solution – or at least as part of the solution – to the U-boat problem in October 1916 by the 10th Cruiser Squadron engaged on the northern patrol and by numerous officers in the Grand Fleet in November 1916 when they were asked for ideas, yet at a meeting of the naval staff and ship-owners in late February 1917, it was dismissed. The Admiralty had numerous worries about the proposal, not least that it was thought that there were not enough ships to act as escorts, there was no experience of convoy work (overlooking the fact that they had years of experience in ships sailing in close company with an escort – they just called it the Grand Fleet), and there were too many merchant ships to convoy, an idea which analysis in the Admiralty soon proved to be incorrect.

However, despite its misgivings, the Admiralty had already introduced convoy for the UK–Holland trade route in July 1916 and only three ships had been sunk. Also, the French were so concerned about their coal imports from Britain that in December they had sent a naval officer to set up a system of convoy in conjunction with the Admiralty. The first convoys from this scheme sailed on 6 February 1917, it having been decided in January that the convoys were not to be called convoys in case it provoked the Germans to attack the neutral vessels that made up about half the vessels engaged in the trade – instead the convoys were called 'controlled sailings'. That these controlled sailings occurred after the Germans had already resumed unrestricted submarine warfare at the start of February seems to have been overlooked by the Admiralty.

Perhaps the most significant reason why convoy was not tried earlier was that it was perceived as being defensive; the Navy would have to wait for the U-boats to come to the convoy, rather than seeking out and destroying the U-boats through offensive action (patrols) in a most dashing and satisfying manner.

Finally, on 21 April 1917, a trial of convoy between the Humber and Norway via Lerwick in the Shetlands was agreed. As has been implied, much of the delay over introducing convoy was because the Admiralty feared it did not have the ships to provide escorts and still carry out offensive patrols when in fact the patrols were irrelevant to the problem. But the entry of the USA into the war meant escorts were no longer in quite such short supply. US Navy destroyers could be used to help provide the convoy escorts. Once convoy started its slow introduction, the Admiralty found it did not need as many escorts as it had imagined and that the issue was really one of using resources effectively (or not), rather than having insufficient resources. Far more important was the realisation that the actual number of ocean-going merchant ships which would need to be convoyed each week was not over 2,000, but a far more manageable 120–140. During April the Admiralty was slowly coming round to the idea of a convoy system. On 26 April Rear-Admiral Duff, the director of the Anti-Submarine Division, produced a plan for introducing ocean convoys. Jellicoe approved the plan the next day and the orders to start a convoy from Gibraltar went out almost immediately. Convoy was now part of the Navy's arsenal against the U-boat, three days before Lloyd George visited the Admiralty and claimed to have forced a hidebound Navy to embark on convoying against its wishes. Nothing could have been further from the truth.

Convoy did not, however, end the losses. Indeed, shipping losses only fell slowly for the rest of the year as more trade routes were organised to run on the basis of convoys. But the convoy did help solve one problem: where to find U-boats. In order to sink convoyed merchant ships U-boats had to be within torpedo range of a convoy. The allies could now reduce their search areas from millions of square miles to just a few around each convoy. Instead of being defensive, as had been alleged by many officers since 1870, convoys were actually the basis for anti-submarine forces to take the offensive against the submarines on a ground of their choosing. Escorts, despite not having an effective or reliable means of detecting a submerged U-boat with enough accuracy to make an attack, found that it was now much easier to find U-boats and attack them; aircraft too were more effective and able to concentrate on where U-boats *had* to be if they wanted to sink a merchant ship, rather than on where they might be.

The other course of action – that of doing something about the U-boat and destroyer bases at Ostend, Zeebrugge and Bruges – was also given much thought by the Navy. The desire to close these ports led directly to the decision to mount an operation to block the harbour mouths by sinking old ships which would mean that the canals to Bruges would also be closed. The attack went in on 22–23 April 1918 – St George's Day – and was led by the new commander of the Dover Patrol force, Admiral Keyes. Both Zeebrugge and Ostend had to be blocked if the Germans were to be trapped in Bruges, otherwise they could use the canal network to escape through whichever port remained open. Despite heroic bravery by the landing parties from HMS *Vindictive*, which placed itself alongside the mole or pier, they were not able to silence the gun batteries in the harbours with the result that the block-ships came under heavy fire and were unable to sink themselves in the correct positions. The raid was only a partial success, while the attempt at Ostend was a failure. The attack, however, was a major fillip to British morale, coming as it did at a time when the Army in France was reeling under a series of offensives from the Germans that wiped out all the allied territorial gains of the two previous years.

The other way of doing something about Ostend, Zeebrugge and Bruges and the U-boats based there was to clear the Germans physically from the Belgian coast. From the middle of 1916 the Admiralty was asking the Army to do something to force the Germans back from the Belgian coast. By 1917, with the shipping situation deteriorating, calls for the Army to launch an attack increased. Fortunately for the Navy, the Army was already looking at a plan to make the Belgian coast untenable for the Germans with an attack out of the salient at Ypres in 1917 – the Third Battle of Ypres, or Passchendaele.

Here too, the Royal Navy was involved. On 26 October 1917, in the final phase of the Third Battle of Ypres, the Royal Naval Division (RND) attacked in support of the Canadian Corps' efforts to capture what remained of the village of Passchendaele. The weather had turned and the battlefield was a morass – the drainage systems had broken down under the weight of shell-fire in the Ypres salient and the water could not drain away from the low-lying battlefield area. The conditions were atrocious and very few gains were made in the initial attack and in the assault on 30 October. However, a change of tactics, and the use of night attacks to prevent German pill-boxes from providing mutual support during assaults, facilitated the capture of the immediate objectives over the next four days and without severe losses. On 5 November the RND was pulled out of the line and when the Canadians finally slithered over the last few yards of mud to take and hold Passchendaele village and its ridge on 10 November, the battle was shut down, with the U-boat bases still under German control.

There was another naval dimension to Passchendaele that can be traced back to Jutland and the Royal Navy maintaining its command of the North Sea as well as the German reluctance to continue to try to wear down the Grand Fleet in detail. If the attacks from 30 July onwards were to have been as successful as had been planned and reached the key railway junction of Roulers, it was intended to launch an amphibious assault on the Belgian coast in the vicinity of Middelkerke as part of an assault along the coast from the allied positions on the River Yser north of Ypres. Admiral Bacon, commanding the Dover patrol, provided much of the planning and in the end it was envisaged that the landing would be made by a division supported by tanks. Great efforts were put into developing suitable landing craft that could land the assaulting tanks and infantry quickly, including the development of specialised equipment to allow the British armour to climb over the sea wall – shades of the methods used on D-Day in 1944! The landing was planned for 8 August, but was postponed until 6 September, as the initial 5th Army attack at Ypres made little headway. In fact it seems that the need to conform to the conditions for the landing contributed to Gough's 5th Army rushing its preparations to renew its attacks. The plan for the landing and advance along the coast kept being deferred as the 5th Army attacks, and then from 25 August the 2nd Army, failed to break through the German position and reach Roulers. Finally, on 21 October the division, which had been specially trained for the amphibious attack, left its camp and the plan was abandoned. However, the division in question was the 1st Division, not as might have been expected, the RND, which had been formed back in 1914 for just this sort of operation. Yet had such an attack been mounted, it could only have been contemplated if the Royal Navy could hold off the German High Seas Fleet. Jutland demonstrated to the Germans that they were not prepared to risk their fleet, thus ceding the initiative to the British, and the opportunity to consider amphibious operations was the fruit of this.[7]

The Wider Influence of the Battle

Jutland also had an impact on the air war. The Royal Navy, and the Grand Fleet in particular, was thirsting to get at the High Seas Fleet and achieve their much-anticipated 'second Trafalgar', a desire sharpened by the dissatisfaction over Jutland and the wish to demonstrate that failings had been addressed. However, the German reluctance to risk their fleet and give the Grand Fleet more chances to seize the type of victory they had so hoped for at Jutland presented a problem: how does a fleet destroy an opponent who avoids giving battle? This was not actually a new problem for the Royal Navy. For years in the Revolutionary and Napoleonic Wars the French Navy had been keen to avoid giving the British more victories and had stayed in harbour. Frustrating though this was for the British fleet, all that could be done was to watch and wait and hope that the French would sail, as going into the harbours to attack the French in port was technologically impossible. Now, the British had to watch and wait and hope that the Germans would be rash enough to do so. By the time of Jutland, the British were well versed in waiting and thanks to mines and torpedoes it was again unsafe to risk major British warships in attacks on enemy bases, hence the lamentations that their one opportunity to destroy the High Seas Fleet at Jutland had eluded them. However, there was a new technology which promised to make attacks on an enemy fleet in harbour viable once again: aircraft.

The problems with the early seaplanes that *Engadine* had struggled to launch at Jutland were twofold. First, the ability to hoist out a seaplane onto the water and for it then to get airborne, land on the water afterwards, and be recovered back onto the ship was very weather-dependent – the bigger the waves, the less likely the seaplane would get airborne. Second, the act of taking off or landing on water required large floats. These floats, through their weight and the drag they exerted, meant that the performance of seaplanes tended to be inferior to landplanes of a similar size and engine power.

After Jutland, the numbers of aircraft within the Grand Fleet rapidly increased. At the start of 1917 the Grand Fleet had three seaplane carriers supporting twenty-three aircraft; soon HMS *Nairana* and HMS *Pegasus*, converted ferries, entered service, although Beatty was still unhappy at the level of air support he had available. In March 1917 the fleet was joined by HMS *Furious*, which had been fitted with a flying-off deck on her bow in place of her gun turret and could carry three reconnaissance planes and five fighters. Not only were there more seaplane tenders, but many warships also carried landplanes for anti-Zeppelin work that were launched from runways on top of the gun turrets of the battlecruisers, or the fo'c'sles of the cruisers. The first light cruiser so fitted took her Sopwith Pup to sea on an operational sweep in August 1917, and managed to launch the aircraft in order to attack Zeppelin *L-23*, which was accomplished successfully. By 1 April 1918 seven battlecruisers and ten light cruisers had launching platforms fitted and aircraft embarked. Once the landplanes had carried out their task they would then ditch by their parent ship and the pilot (and sometimes the plane) would be recovered.[8]

A better solution was to find some way of allowing the aircraft to land back on a warship, so that they could be readied for use again. In 1917 Squadron Commander Edwin Dunning RNAS realised that the stalling speed of aircraft like the Sopwith Pup was so low that if a ship were to steam quickly into the wind, the aircraft would to all intents and purposes hover above the deck. On 2 August 1917 Dunning demonstrated that it would be possible to land on the aircraft launching deck of HMS *Furious*. Approaching the ship from astern, he side-slipped round the masts and funnels until he was over the launching deck and then reduced his engine power, allowing his aircraft to sink down onto the deck, where it was held in place by members of the crew. It was the first time an aircraft had been launched from, and landed on, the same ship. It would change naval aviation – and navies – for ever, but sadly Dunning was killed on 7 August when he attempted to repeat his achievement and his plane was blown over the side of the ship by a gust of wind.

HMS *Furious* soon sprouted a landing-on deck on her stern to complement the flying-off deck on her bow, but there still remained the obstacle of her masts and funnels which caused considerable turbulence over the landing area. What was needed was a continuous deck for launching and landing aircraft that was un-obstructed for its entire length. Fortunately, an Italian liner whose construction was halted at the start of the war was purchased by the Admiralty in September 1916 and by March 1918 it had been converted into HMS *Argus*, with a full un-obstructed flight deck. Also at the start of 1918 a new aircraft carrier was ordered, based on the incomplete hull of the battleship that was being built at the Armstrong shipyard in Barrow-in-Furness for the Chilean Navy, while at the same time a new purpose-built aircraft carrier – to become HMS *Hermes* – had been mooted by the Admiralty. In September 1918 HMS *Argus* joined the Grand Fleet and the next month received twelve of the slowly arriving Sopwith Cuckoo torpedo-bombers.[9]

What Beatty, as Commander-in-Chief of the Grand Fleet, wanted all these aircraft for – and more of them too – was to launch an air attack on the German High Seas Fleet in its base at Wilhelmshaven using the new torpedo-bombers, the Grand Fleet having become somewhat exasperated by the refusal of the Germans to come out and fight. The Admiralty had reservations over the resources and time needed to produce a large enough attack force of aircraft and the ships to launch them. When in October 1917 Beatty tried to interest the Admiralty again, the plan was rejected, but with the possibility that it might be considered in the future. By the autumn of 1918 serious and thorough planning was being undertaken into an air attack on the German fleet in harbour, possibly at Christmas or in the New Year. Resources, not imagination, were what the Navy lacked for a successful air attack and only the Armistice arrested the planning.[10]

On 29 October 1918 disturbances rocked the High Seas Fleet. The German fleet was preparing itself for one final sortie against the Grand Fleet, to go down fighting rather than embrace the calls for an armistice that the Army's leaders had successfully pressed for, having lost their nerve at the start of the month. But, thanks in part to the legacy of Jutland, and the fear of being scarified at another such battle just to obtain better peace terms, and also as a result of catastrophic failures in the relationship between German officers and their men, the German sailors had other ideas. By 6 November the sailors were in control of Lubeck, Travemunde, Bremen, Cuxhaven, Wilhelmshaven and Hamburg. The rest of

Germany was in revolt too, led by the mutinous sailors. The German democracy that was created following the Armistice was in part undermined by the nature of the German defeat, an economic defeat – 'the stab in the back' – that was in no small way due to Britain's ability to command the sea after Jutland, while the revolutionary fervour of the sailors in the 1918 revolution and the unwillingness to face another Jutland also influenced the complexion and problems the German government faced in peacetime. It would be far too simplistic, unhistorical even, to claim that the problems of the 1930s and the rise of Hitler originate from issues created by Jutland, but seapower, used well and wisely, casts a long shadow across the land both in war and in the peace that follows.

Conclusion

Jutland is an often misunderstood battle, as people focus on narrow, quantitative methods of analysis – numbers and class of ships sunk, numbers of casualties, emphasising the tactical battle over the more complex operational or strategic issues and their longer-term impact on the conduct of the war. Jutland, by maintaining and confirming British numerical, morale, operational and strategic superiority, gave the allies options to increase the pressure on Germany and its allies until ultimately economic and then political collapse ensued. At the same time Jutland closed off avenues for Germany, forcing her down a road that she had previously rejected owing to the risk of neutrals joining the war on the allied side. In a world of global maritime trading links that feed populations and keep factories working, seapower, correctly used, wins wars.

Notes

1. This account is based on the information in the excellent examination of the battle compiled by Andrew Gordon. See A. Gordon, *The Rules of the Game: Jutland and British Naval Command* (London: John Murray, 2000). For an analysis of the problems of long-range gunnery, see the superb J. Brooks, *Dreadnought Gunnery and the Battle of Jutland* (London: Routledge, 2005).
2. See Gordon, *Rules of the Game*.
3. Scheer, *Germany's High Seas Fleet* (London: UCL Press, 1994), pp. 168–9, quoted in P. Halpern, *A Naval History of World War 1* (London: UCL Press, 1994), p. 328.
4. British Library Add Mss 48992, Jellicoe to Balfour, dated 29 October 1916, ff. 1–74; A. Temple Patterson (ed.), *The Jellicoe Papers*, Vol. 2 (London: The Navy Records Society, 1968), pp. 89, 92; E. Grove, *The Royal Navy* (Basingstoke: Palgrave, 2005), pp. 128–9.
5. Halpern, *Naval History of World War 1*, pp. 328–9, 336–8; H. Herwig, *Luxury Fleet: The German Imperial Navy 1888–1918* (Amherst, NY: Humanity Books, 1987), pp. 194–8, 226.
6. Marder, *From the Dreadnought to Scapa Flow*, vol. 4 (London: Oxford University Press, 1969), pp. 323–49; S.W. Roskill, 'The Dismissal of Admiral Jellicoe', *Journal of Contemporary History*, Vol. 1 (1966), pp. 69–93.
7. A. Wiest, 'The Planned Amphibious Assault', in P. Liddle (ed.), *Passchendaele in Perspective: The Third Battle of Ypres* (Barnsley: Pen & Sword, 1997), pp. 210–11.
8. Grove, 'Air Force, Fleet Air Arm – or Armoured Corps', in T. Benbow (ed.), *British Naval Aviation: the First 100 Years* (Farnham: Ashgate, 2011), pp. 46–7, 51.
9. Ibid., pp. 50–2.
10. Ibid., pp. 50–1; Marder, *From the Dreadnought to Scapa Flow*, vol. 5 (London: Oxford University Press, 1970), pp. 141–2; D. Hobbs, 'The first Pearl Harbor: the attack by British torpedo planes on the German High Seas Fleet planned for 1918', in J. Jordan (ed.), *Warship 2007* (London: Conway Publishing, 2007), pp. 29–38; M. Farquharson-Robert, *A History of the Royal Navy: World War 1* (London: I.B. Tauris, 2014), p. 153.

Suggested Further Reading

Brooks, J., *Dreadnought Gunnery and the Battle of Jutland* (London: Routledge, 2005)

Farquharson-Robert, M., *A History of the Royal Navy: World War 1* (London: I.B. Tauris, 2014)

Goldrick, J., *Before Jutland. Naval War in Northern European Waters, August 1914–February 1915* (Annapolis MY: Naval Institute Press, 2015)

Gordon, A., *The Rules of the Game: Jutland and British Naval Command* (London: John Murray, 2000)

Grove, E., *The Royal Navy* (Basingstoke: Palgrave, 2005)

Halpern, P., *A Naval History of World War 1* (London: UCL Press, 1994)

Herwig, H., *Luxury Fleet: The German Imperial Navy 1888–1918* (Amherst NY: Humanity Books, 1987)

Hough, R., *The Great War at Sea 1914–1918* (Edinburgh: Birlinn, 2000)

Marder, A.J., *From the Dreadnought to Scapa Flow*, vol. 3 (London: OUP, 1966)

Redford, D., *The Royal Navy: A History Since 1900* (London: I.B. Tauris, 2014)

Temple Patterson, A. (ed.), *The Jellicoe Papers*, vol. 2 (London: Navy Records Society, 1968)

Chapter 4

The Trauma of Attrition: Verdun and the Somme

By William Philpott

As the second winter of the war passed into spring, there was no sense of despondency. By 1916 European societies were properly at war, mobilised and committed to the struggle. Participants and spectators had a sense of the momentous events that were likely to unfold as mighty empires engaged a death grip and wrestled in what was expected to be the decisive campaign. In time, nations would have to reconcile themselves with both the ordeals of that year, and the disappointment that by its end the interminable war seemed no nearer a conclusion; indeed it was just getting into its stride as it morphed from a fight for continental hegemony into a truly global ideological conflict. In fact, in 1916 the balance of the conflict shifted firmly towards the allies, as most at the time acknowledged, but at great human, material and emotional cost. The dual motifs of the infantryman's war, of sacrifice and slaughter, which vied with each other in combatants' minds and in societal memory, were in stark juxtaposition during this year of trauma. The war would be over in two years, once allied forces pressed home their ever-growing advantage, but the casualty lists would continue to lengthen, and come 1917 these costs were being questioned, and the consequences disputed.

For a century societies have had to live with 'the weight of the dead on the living',[1] a weight that accrued inexorably during the year of attrition. The twin battles of 1916, Verdun and the Somme, whose prolonged, intense, industrialised killing contradicted traditional concepts of military success and strategic progress, would come down to posterity as the epitome of all that went wrong in the First World War. France and Britain would begin those battles with trauma, and would have to sustain them for months afterwards. Heavy losses brought short-term political repercussions and would, as the years passed, foist a bitter memory of what were actually two ultimately successful battles, centrepieces of a global war of attrition. Germany's traumas were different. More telling in the strategic circumstances of 1916, they proved less vital to posterity since they could have been much worse; and because far worse were to follow.

Winter was always a time for reflection, the interval in which to review the successes and failures of the previous year's campaign and to plan for the next. The winter of 1914 might have been a good time to discuss peace, but already the stakes were too high and the sacrifices too great to allow such thoughts to prevail.[2] Following the huge, costly yet indecisive battles that opened the war and the entrenching of the Western Front, reflection in winter 1914/15 had been unfocused and speculative. Soldiers certainly recognised the sort of attritional conflict that faced armies and nations, and demanded manpower and war material to fight it, yet were unclear about how to do so. Statesmen remained to be convinced, and threw their own hastily drafted alternatives into a strategic free-for-all. Therefore 1915 would be the year in which politicians and diplomats drove strategy. The allies' quest for diplomatic advantages and easy victories away from the main fronts only lengthened the casualty lists while making no appreciable impact on the course of the war. German military initiatives in west and east, while more effective, were on a relatively small scale and did not loosen the allies' grip. The offensives the allies mounted in those theatres were equally indecisive, running out of steam quickly in the face of stout enemy resistance, and at the cost of heavy casualties.[3]

It was planned that things would be different in 1916: no one expected them to be easy. At the French headquarters at Chantilly the allies' military leaders met from 6–8 December 1915 under the presiding influence of General Joseph Joffre, French Commander-in-Chief and *de facto* strategic director of the alliance. There were no politicians present when the experiences of 1915 were digested and a plan for the coming campaign agreed: a good thing in the generals' view since it had been a year in which 'amateur strategists' had held the whip hand. The consequences spoke for themselves. The mismanaged Gallipoli campaign was winding down to an ignominious withdrawal, while the hastily improvised Salonika expedition had failed to save Serbia, had brought down France's government, and was now stalemating like the other land campaigns. Instead, for 1916 Joffre tabled a plan for a 'General Allied Offensive',[4] comprising a large-scale Anglo-French offensive on the Western Front synchronised with attacks on the Eastern and Italian fronts. After a Russian counter-proposal to concentrate effort on defeating Austria–Hungary was vetoed, the allies' military representatives accepted the Chantilly plan. The allied governments would be asked to endorse this scheme – the first concerted strategic plan – individually, rather than collectively. The principles of Joffre's strategy to break the Central Powers were coordination, scale and duration. All the allied armies would attack at the same time, in as great a strength as possible and for as long as was needed to achieve the agreed principal objective, 'the destruction of the German and Austrian armies'. It was a straightforward military objective, if not an easy one given the size of those armies. Implicit in that strategy, but not stated, would be the attrition of the allied armies in their turn. Certainly an attritional phase of operations, which Joffre asked the British and Italian armies to undertake, was expected to precede the main offensive.[5]

General Erich von Falkenhayn, who planned Germany's counterstroke, made that outcome explicit. His own offensive in the west, to be launched against the French fortress of Verdun early in the spring, would bleed white the French Army whose manpower reserves were already declining, and hopefully force France to seek terms before the allies' superior strength proved decisive. It was intended to break the hostile coalition that gripped Germany and her allies in a tightening ring of steel. Should this strategy encourage the allies to counterattack, then so much the better, as the British Army could also be beaten into submission.[6]

Those who prepared 1916's campaign were better experienced, but also chastened by the volatility of politics, the rancour of civil–military relations and the indecisiveness of military operations. For winter was also a time for re-organisation and recrimination. Although the warriors and statesmen of 1914 generally retained their posts into 1915, questions were being raised as to their competence come the second winter of the war. Nations had already started to see ministers removed, ministries reshaped and commanders challenged, a trend that would grow during 1916. By then the soldiers had a better grasp on the conflict while politicians were being marginalised due to 1915's strategic mis-adventures and the governmental and societal restructuring that resulted from mass mobilisation.

The soldiers knew that deciding the war would be costly. Lord Kitchener's New Armies had been raised to kill and to die for their country and were now reinforcing the professional Regulars who had been the mainstay of the British war effort so far. Due to the army's rapid expansion, high rate of casualties and consequent de-skilling, the British Empire's sword was a blunt-edged weapon as the war of attrition got under way in earnest. It was an essential one, however, since 1915's huge battles had thinned the French Army's ranks while the Russian and Italian armies had yet to show much offensive prowess. So in the west, an experienced yet tiring army would have to induct a keen but green allied force into the practicalities of killing Germans if the army that faced them were to be destroyed. That army was proud and professional, and tempered by combat. It had held off all-comers during 1915 and had crushed little Serbia, but had come nowhere near to victory or to breaking the resolve of the allies.

Perhaps Verdun would do that; perhaps the 'General Allied Offensive' would prevail. Either way, come January 1916 preparations were in train for a prolonged trial of strength between the two sides, with thoughts of quick victory abandoned by all but the most naïve. The scene was set for the brutal year that would come to represent the First World War and traumatise its participants for a century. In this year 'modern war machines' would be unleashed to kill and maim men *en masse*, and societies would fracture as mass politics emerged out of mass warfare. The very earth of France would be violated on the twin battlefields of Verdun and the Somme; and the allies would gain the military initiative which would enable them to defeat the invader and liberate the ever-sacred soil to which, thereafter, pilgrims and battlefield tourists would flock to follow in their grandsires' footsteps.

This is not the place to review the preliminaries nor to recount once again the course of the battles that dominated 1916. This has been done many times, and will no doubt be done once more as their centenaries pass.[7] Suffice it to say that Verdun and the Somme were conceived with the same purpose – to decide the war, or at least to decide the western campaign, which in itself was expected to decide the war, by breaking the enemy's army – and would become a single conjoined battle as the Somme offensive shrank and morphed under the force of circumstances into the Verdun counteroffensive while remaining a principal element of the 'General Allied Offensive'.[8] Events at Verdun skewed planning for the Somme. By the summer an offensive conceived to be led by the French and intended to show off the French Army's developing operational skill would become a predominantly British attack that would expose that army's relative inexperience. What happened at the Somme would reverse fortunes at Verdun. There, over the course of a ten-month battle, a gruelling and at times tooth-and-nail French defence would succeed. The struggle would be capped with a striking French counterattack. For this to happen, nearly 2 million men would become casualties. Herein lies the real story and significance of 1916.

By 1916 the armies knew what they were doing, and were better if not fully resourced. Yet what they were required to do seemed inimical to society; war makers appeared increasingly indifferent to the lives of the men in the ranks who were called upon to do their duty. Warfare seemed to have become a mechanised process of slaughter. General Ferdinand Foch, who planned and prepared the Somme offensive, drew a direct analogy between warfare and the industrial process, in which guns were the durable parts and men the perishable components.[9] As the battle raged, Verdun became known as the 'mincing machine' as *poilus* were rotated in along the *voie sacrée* to take their chances under the unceasing rain of German shells: as one *poilu* ruefully recorded, 'to act as standard bearers marking the zone of superiority established by the artillery'.[10] This was not warfare as it had been presented in the heroic fiction and patriotic history books that had prepared soldiers for war. Still, tempering such fatalism with patriotism, men went unquestioningly up the line to do their bit, to kill for their country or to die for it should that be their fate.

When German infantry units launched themselves against the pulverised front lines at Verdun on 22 February, all of France trembled. This smashing attack pushed forwards quickly and captured the key perimeter fort at Douaumont three days later, leading to panic and despondency. This battered strongpoint would be recast first as a symbol of disaster, and then as one of defiance and resurgence, assuming a cultural prominence far outweighing its tactical significance.[11] Thereafter, like all positional operations, the Battle of Verdun settled into steady, grinding attrition, sometimes quicker, sometimes slower. The daily bulletins would record advances or retreats, large when the enemy were on the offensive, smaller when the battle was quiescent – and all essentially insignificant given the scale of the war, merely the bubbles on its surface, in Rudolf Binding's striking metaphor.[12] Nonetheless, for four tension-filled and painful months during the spring and early summer of 1916 Verdun was both the focus of attention and the epicentre of the fighting. What had gone wrong? Had Joffre dangerously weakened the fortress's defences? Was the defence going to collapse? What were the British doing while the French Army bled? Were the enemy going to win?

When Fort Vaux fell in early June those questions seemed overdue for an answer: Joffre's conduct was to be scrutinised by a parliamentary enquiry, while he himself pressured his ally to counterattack on the Somme with France still having reserves left and before it was too late. Although in the tetchy negotiations with General Sir Douglas Haig, the British Commander-in-Chief, over the nature and timing of the attack, the Somme offensive appeared to have become the Verdun relief offensive,[13] Joffre maintained his broader ambition to defeat the enemy that year by concerted pressure despite such tribulations. The fact that

Russian armies directed by General Aleksei Brusilov had attacked the Austrians powerfully and successfully just before Fort Vaux had fallen seemed to be recasting the dice. The 'General Allied Offensive' was belatedly under way and Joffre's winter plan, if much delayed and altered, seemed finally to be coming to fruition. Could a similar blow in the west seize the initiative and decide the war in the current campaigning season?

On Haig's part it had never been his intention not to attack, and to that extent he adhered to the spirit of the agreement reached before he assumed command. However, when and how – and to some extent where – to attack, all remained to be decided as the details of the general offensive and the British Army's role in it were finalised during the spring. In Haig's professional judgement, the later the attack the better, since his improvised armies needed proper training. But, notwithstanding his punctilious and often stubborn negotiations with Joffre over practicalities, Haig always understood the real nature of the military alliance and France's pre-eminent role within it,[14] and as Verdun sapped French strength he could justify the British Army's engagement in terms of the need to sustain and take over from the weakening French.[15] To that extent, it seemed to fall to Haig and his army to fight the battle that might decide the war. Moreover, by the summer of 1916 expectations ran high. The so-called 'big push' that all were anticipating had been cast by journalists and established in popular perception as the fight that would determine the outcome of the war, even though responsible soldiers now knew that on account of Verdun the actual push would be much smaller than originally planned.[16] A gap seemed to have opened between hopes and military feasibility. The allied offensive would mark the start of hard fighting rather than the end: Kitchener, when asked when the war would end, had always said that he did not know, but that it would only start in earnest when the armies he had raised were ready to take the field. But the recently deceased Secretary of State for War was no longer there to quell popular anticipation of a smashing victory.

Although he planned to strike a powerful blow at the start of the offensive, Haig was rather more sanguine than expectant onlookers and gung-ho troops. He stressed that the war would only end when allied troops were across the Rhine, and that, however heavy and effective the blow that would be struck in the summer of 1916, it was potentially only the start of the lengthy process of destroying the German forces that stood between the Somme and the Rhine.[17] For these reasons Haig's actions were hostage to the unrealistic expectations of spectators at home, as well as the unreadiness of his improvised army of citizens led by soldiers to take on the seasoned German Army on equal terms. His offensive would therefore start with trauma, and end with disappointment, because means were inadequate and expectations were unrealistic.

Given this sense of expectation, partial success was problematic. On 1 July 1916 General Sir Henry Rawlinson's Fourth Army's attack struggled almost everywhere, and in places was a complete failure. This tactical catastrophe has set solid in historical memory, obscuring operational realities and the Battle of the Somme's strategic context. It should be noted that the true scale of the disaster did not emerge until years afterwards. A coherent narrative of events and a precise figure for casualties did not appear until official histories were compiled after the war. Nonetheless, the failure to live up to expectations was evident, while the nature of the tragedy could be deduced. To Joffre it was obvious why the British had failed. He noted in his journal on 2 July, 'the causes of their check are to be found in the bad artillery preparation and the failure to mop up the trenches passed by the first waves ... The British don't yet have the "way".'[18] They would have to be taught how to fight and therefore for Joffre the Somme offensive assumed an additional purpose: to oblige and accustom the British to fight.[19] Haig himself tried to gloss over events with the bland generalisation that 'On a 16-mile front of attack varying fortune must be expected!'[20] But such jejune understatement must have masked a sense of disappointment if not of despondency. Haig knew that as yet his armies were 'a collection of divisions untrained for the field', and his warnings to Joffre on this point, brushed aside, had proved prophetic.[21] But he would have hoped for better, not least to put up a good show for the people at home and expectant allies.

By 1916 striking battlefield success was possible with proper preparation, even if it would not be sustainable given the inherent dynamics of military operations. In contrast to the British Army's shambles, the French Army played its part admirably, General Émile Fayolle's Sixth Army taking all its objectives with around 1,600 casualties.[22] To some extent the headlines of 2 July proclaiming a great blow had been struck were apposite. It was the figure for British casualties that later emerged – 19,240 killed and 37,646 wounded – that appals, and which stands today as shorthand for the supposed disaster on the Somme and the assumed futility of attritional trench warfare.

Ex-Cabinet minister Winston Churchill raised with the Prime Minister his concern that the British Army was disproportionally suffering casualties relative to the enemy in July 1916, an anxiety that had validity at the time even if it were of short-term consequence. Yet in his post-war memoir–history, *The World Crisis*, Churchill would go on to use this time-specific observation as the nub of a widely read and influential critique of the battle and the strategy of attrition that it represented, emphasised by one emotive, bloody vignette from 1 July 1916, the decimation of the 8th Division opposite Ovillers.[23] Churchill's 'I told you so' critique transposed a specific complaint into a much broader condemnation, thereby robbing the Somme offensive of proper context and any sense of purpose or military impact. Tapping into a rising post-war swell of disillusionment, Churchill, more than anyone, had thus turned in popular memory the Somme, and the war of which it was the central act, from a consensual sacrifice to mindless slaughter. The framework of reference for histories and popular polemics was set early on; in time, Britain's national trauma would cohere around this one event. The Somme had become, in the emotive words of veteran and historian Basil Liddell Hart, 'both the glory and the graveyard of "Kitchener's Army"'.[24] Kitchener's willing and enthusiastic volunteers, of whom Liddell Hart was one, had been sacrificed to no purpose. By the 1940s, against the background of renewed war with Germany, a casual observation that the British attack of 1 July 1916 was 'typical trench warfare operations' would have raised few challenges, even though it was not even entirely typical of 1 July 1916![25] A cultural memory had formed, grounded in disappointment and separate from the military context of attritional operations and mass warfare. In Britain this signified a point of cultural and historical fracture between the liberal certainties and values of the Edwardian imperial era and the realities of the emerging age of the masses.

There would, in time, have to be recriminations and scapegoats for the disaster. On 2 July, however, the offensive and the war would go on. Over the next few weeks the Empire would add its own traumas to those of the motherland. At Beaumont Hamel Newfoundland was caught up in the disaster of 1 July. Before the month was over, South Africans would sacrifice themselves in a dogged defence of Delville Wood. Australians would be shelled almost to breaking point on the Pozières ridge and massacred at Fromelles in a diversionary attack. Canada would do better in the battle of Flers–Courcelette in September, but before the offensive came to a wintry halt another 360,000 casualties would be added to the army's 'butcher's bill'. To this shocking figure can be added 200,000 French and over 500,000 German losses.

At Verdun between February and December, 700,000 French and German killed and wounded increased 1916's gruesome toll.[26] In Russia and Italy the casualty totals were also huge. Of course these figures only emerged after the war was over, as statisticians and historians tallied the human cost of attrition. At the time, trauma was individual or at least localised: a lost brother or son; a decimated 'pals' battalion; a broken division adding piece by piece to a collective impression of national loss and sacrifice. At the same time, motifs of patriotism, duty and sacrifice still gave comfort to many, combatants and non-combatants, as the grinding process wore on; a comfort that, even post-war and with different values dominant, still sustained some. Although the methods of warfare appalled, few questioned the necessity for it at the time, for there were matters of liberty and existence at stake.

In contrast to Britain, for France the Somme offensive came as a relief, literally and metaphorically. German pressure at Verdun, already slackening as the 'General Allied Offensive' got under way, ended. The French Army was able to mount a counteroffensive there; locally at first as the Somme became the epicentre of fighting and drew away German reserves, and later on a large scale, reversing the traumatic losses of Douaumont and Vaux. On 13 September a mass would be celebrated in the crypt of the fortress's ruined citadel to celebrate Verdun's deliverance. Verdun would not fall, and France would fight on. Were evidence needed, it was provided by Fayolle's successful Sixth Army on the Somme, which, having started the offensive with the most effective blow yet struck by French arms, now followed this up with sustained attrition that brought the German defence to crisis point.[27] While these feats of arms are now long forgotten, French newspapers in the summer and autumn of 1916 were filled with stories of genuine victories, in contrast to the anxious reports of the spring, even if they could not yet report the final victory for which Joffre was pressing. It seemed that the war might yet end in 1916 if France's allies were to match her own effort.

The British were certainly fighting now, although their early progress onto the Thiepval ridge in July had slowed to a crawl during August and seemed to have been contained. Russia was fighting hard, although Brusilov's June success had lapsed into an attritional struggle with the Austrians and had not been followed up with the expected heavy blow against the German Army in the east. The Italians had struck their most powerful blow yet, capturing the town of Gorizia in early August, but again that blow fell on the Austrians not on the Germans. Still, the objective agreed in December 1915 – the destruction of the enemy's main armies – seemed to be progressing on all fronts. A diplomatic coup in early September, the entry of Rumania into the war on the allied side, promised much and impelled intensifying the 'General Allied Offensive'. France committed another army, General Alfred Micheler's Tenth Army, to the Battle of the Somme south of the river on 4 September, stretching the German defence even thinner. On 12 September Fayolle's army broke through into open country at Bouchavesnes. On 15 September the British resumed the offensive in strength, unleashing a surprise new weapon, the tank, in the Battle of Flers–Courcelette. A succession of powerful blows followed in the second half of September, climaxing with the capture of Thiepval, the symbolic bastion of the German defence, on 26 September.[28] This was the high point of the offensive, and the German Army was reaching breaking point. Future German chancellor Franz von Papen, a staff officer with the 4th Guards Division, who on 15 September had improvised a thin defensive line from rear area units, later acknowledged that 'there was not a single reserve company for scores of miles behind us. A complete tactical break-through, the achievement of which the enemy dreamed, had taken place, although they did not seem to realize it. A few dozen administrative personnel were all that stood between the enemy and a major victory.'[29] A similar scenario had occurred three days previously when French troops had seized Bouchavesnes village behind the German third position late in the day. However, French reserves had been unable to press forward quickly enough over the shell-shattered battlefield to exploit this narrow breach before German reserves deployed and closed it.

In fact the very nature of battle – and of victory – was being redefined on the chalk ridges of Picardy along with the belligerents' relationship with the war. Papen noted a tendency in the British troops to fail to exploit success,[30] but all armies faced the same conditions on the battlefield. Deficient communications that hampered command and control reduced the chance of turning tactical successes such as those achieved at Bouchavesnes and Flers into the sort of ground-seizing 'victory' manoeuvre that made newspaper headlines. The British Army had done well on 15 September, but as was normally the case in offensive operations, the troops had exhausted themselves in the process and there was nothing left to throw into the breach even had they known it was there. The sort of reckless cavalry exploitation envisaged by the more obtuse armchair generals and often used as a stick with which to beat 'bungling' First World War generals was no longer an element of the military system. Small units of cavalry might be pushed forward to exploit temporary disarray in the defence and to seize more ground and hold it until the infantry came up, but there was no expectation that a few 'charging' cavalry divisions would turn a tactical success into a decisive victory.[31] This inability to exploit rapidly across shell-shattered ground, exacerbated by deterioration in the weather as autumn rains came, saved the German

Army from breaking on the Somme in the second half of September 1916. From this experience commanders were learning. It was not without reason that Foch, who was to lead the combined allied armies to victory in 1918, chose to have his statue erected at Bouchavesnes. As General Marie-Eugène Debeney, the army corps commander in the sector in October 1916 and later chief of the French Army staff, declared when unveiling the statue in 1926:

> After the Somme [Foch] began to abandon the simplistic idea of obtaining success by breaking a short section of the enemy's front, replacing it with the more fruitful idea, which was to give us victory, of progressively dislocating the various sectors of the front.[32]

Today we dwell on the British Army's traumas from the Somme offensive's start but underplay later successes because these did not immediately move the enemy from in front of them. France's parallel triumphs have until recently been largely forgotten, written out of an Anglo-centric battle narrative and eclipsed in France itself by the contemporaneous tragedy and triumph at Verdun. A patriotic narrative of resistance, with its watchword '*tenir*', proved more serviceable in 1916.[33] It allowed immediate if misguided political capital to be made in 1917, and would later serve the war's veterans better than a story of apparently wasted effort and sacrifice.

Meanwhile, the enemy's own traumas in the grinding *Materialschlacht* imposed upon them by the allies shrank in the telling. Before the Somme, besieged Germany was holding out relatively comfortably; afterwards the defensive walls were crumbling. Makeshift repairs and desperate sallies could only delay their inevitable collapse.[34] Overall, 1916 was a brutal year for Germany, harder than 1914 when the three armies ranged against Germany had been fought to a standstill, and a contrast to 1915 during which the German Army had held the Western Front effectively while driving back the Russians in the east. In that year the allies had expected to win quickly, without having the manpower, munitions and method so to do. Moreover, Germany also had reserves and resources still to mobilise. Come 1916, the allies were ready to win slowly but surely. As well as their agreed and concerted plan, in 1916 the allied armies had deep reserves of men, especially now that Britain's new armies were in the field. They were also benefiting from increasing supplies of munitions and developing the tactical and operational experience needed to conduct a systematic and more cost-effective offensive which would grind down the enemy.

For Germany, by contrast, stretched during 1916 by the competing demands of the trenches and home-front industries, her military manpower reserves had all but reached their limit. Rudolf Binding recorded an army rumour that at the height of the Somme offensive the German First Army's reserves were reduced to a single battalion.[35] There were signs of strategic desperation as the battle wore on. Falkenhayn, who had led the resolute defence since September 1914, was replaced by the victorious commanders from the east, Paul von Hindenburg and Erich Ludendorff. Accustomed to smashing ill-equipped Russian armies in open spaces, the new leaders would be confounded by the tactical and operational constraints in the west. Mass offensives simply did not work. The three fresh but raw divisions they sacrificed under French guns on the Somme in late September 1916 in a vainglorious attempt to reverse the allied success is a long-forgotten incident of the battle, but analogous to the carnage inflicted on elements of the British Army on 1 July 1916.[36]

Germany's battlefield losses for 1916 would total more than 1.4 million, 800,000 of them during the 'General Allied Offensive'.[37] Behind the statistician's aggregate figure lay the stories of individual loss and collective sacrifice. Papen remembered that in three engagements in 'that terrible summer' his division lost 173 officers and 8,699 men. Such losses were no longer sustainable. 'The principal problem in any war has always been to use human lives as sparingly as possible,' Papen noted ruefully. To that extent the German defensive doctrine based on the defence of 'relatively unimportant tactical positions ... to the last' had proved counter-productive.[38] By the end of the year infantry battalion establishments were being reduced and old men and second-grade troops were being combed out to fill their ranks.

The Somme offensive had undermined German morale, even if it had not physically broken the Germany Army. Rudolf Binding, whose division had returned to the Western Front after being sent to help check the Russian offensive in Galicia, felt a sense of apprehension at his next likely destination: 'It is to be hoped that we are not going to be used up on the Somme or at Verdun like any old rubbish; the regiments are too good for that.'[39] It turned out to be the Somme, a name which chilled the marrow. 'In front of me lies a fat packet of papers about experiences in the Somme battle,' Binding noted, 'from which it appears that there are lots of experiences to be had, but not many remedies against the unpleasant ones.'[40] Even to a sardonic veteran with two years' combat experience, the Somme sector proved grim and disheartening. Over the winter Binding lived amid the remnants of the carnage at Bois St Pierre Vaast, where the French advance had ground to a halt:

> The country in front of Bois St Pierre Vaast Wood is a place of horror. I was out there one of the last nights. For days and weeks the earth there has been churned up again and again to its very depths. Dead men and animals, arms and equipment, are tossed about in the mud and slime, splashed up on high, pounded down into the earth again, again thrown up and torn into pieces until they are things without form or shape. Whole batteries of guns and their crews are inextricably kneaded together in the crucible of their gigantic foundry.[41]

Where the front line actually lay was impossible to determine in that empty morass: 'the "blue" line which marked the position on the maps which we took over from the outgoing troops is mere nonsense. There is no "line" out there; there are not and never have been proper posts, dug-outs etc.; not even the usual barbed wire.'

But it was clear to Binding that: 'We are defeated all along the line here.'[42] Amid this general hell, German soldiers suffered a personal nightmare, existing in the mud and cold that characterised the forgotten yet equally atrocious winter phase of the Somme. Physically 'this is the greatest effort of the War', Binding observed.[43] When it came time to move on, to face another battle, Binding's heart was no longer in it; like so many others, to him the war had lost its glory and descended into absurd folly after the Somme. Returning from home leave, he 'visualised to myself [a] thousand and ten thousand times over the useless waste of men's lives in the service of madness'.[44] Withdrawal from the 'hopeless positions' on the Somme offered little comfort: 'our own [helplessness] becomes unpleasantly apparent. Our troops have had no successes; everybody wanted to get away as quick as possible; they were not going to risk fighting … In the meantime there is no sign of the end.'[45]

The decision to conduct a strategic retreat to the newly constructed Hindenburg Line in the centre of the Western Front in the spring of 1917 bought the High Command some time, but it reflected the dual problems that the army could no longer hold its existing defences against resolute French and increasingly effective British attacks, and that there were insufficient manpower reserves to sustain another land campaign like that of 1916. The triumphant entry of Australian troops into Bapaume on 17 March 1917, to be met by a scene of devastation as the retiring German Army implemented a scorched earth policy, attests to the real end point and true outcome of the Battle of the Somme.

When the third winter of reflection arrived, Germany's strategic options were obviously shrinking. Over the winter of 1916/17 there would be deeper mobilisation as the Hindenburg programme of armaments manufacture sought through introducing home-front labour conscription to squeeze more production out of German industry to match allied material predominance. This belated attempt to replace men with machines proved ineffectual: men were hard to come by and women, who were not subject to conscription, were already largely mobilised.[46] Moreover, the political compromises made with trade unions and socialists in order to implement and administer the programme were a sign that the Imperial edifice was starting to crack, on the home front as well as in the field. The army was now firmly in charge, but the people were increasingly fed up – in one area, it might be added, largely with turnips which comprised the mainstay of their diet over the notorious winter of 1916/17.

Military defeat catalysed domestic disaffection, and democrats started to challenge the *status quo*. Chancellor Theobald von Bethmann Hollweg, who sought in vain to preserve Germany's wartime *Burgfrieden* ('social peace'), was forced from office in July 1917, polarising political opinion between pro-war and pro-peace factions. Resorting to a maritime strategy in the spring – the reinstatement of unrestricted submarine warfare – was a sign that the army had given up hope of victory on the battlefield. Russia's steady decline during 1917 would give a respite, but Anglo-French pressure hardly let up, and more breaches in the walls would be forced on the Chemin des Dames, in the Ypres salient and at Cambrai. In 1918 the German Army would have to stake all on a return to the offensive because it could no longer sustain a defensive. Allied predominance in manpower and material would only increase during 1918. Germany's armies were gripped, her warships contained and her people restless. It was better to go down fighting gloriously than to be ground into the dust, Ludendorff believed, but either way the outcome would be the same: military defeat, international humiliation and revolution at home.

In the autumn of 1918 British and French Armies would advance quickly across the old Somme battlefields, on which the enemy had hoped to make a stand over the winter. The final pursuit would last three months, during which the remnants of the German Army would still fight hard – habit and ingrained military discipline determined that. Any British soldiers *re*-crossing those once familiar chalk ridges would have remembered the events of 1916, yet would have felt detached, so much having happened in the interim. Because the German Army had fought on for two more years it seemed increasingly that the struggles on the Meuse and on the Somme were insignificant, even though astute military minds were aware that the victory of 1918, the final destruction of the German Army, was grounded in the effort and sacrifice of earlier years, and achieved with the methods and skills that these battles inculcated.[47] After the war reached its exhausted end, and even more so after a second war renewed the conflict, bringing yet more brutal atrocities and slaughtering a second generation of Europe's young men supposedly to rectify the errors of their fathers, the sacrifice of 1916 increasingly lost its meaning. It came to symbolise the folly of war in general and of the war-makers of 1914–18 in particular, although the generals who managed the industrialised killing emerged with worse reputations than the politicians who had orchestrated it.

To a considerable extent, this fracture between 1916 and what came afterwards would be rooted in the events which ensued immediately after these battles. Short-term political errors in France threw away the military advantages won during 1916. More significantly, wider international developments shifted the parameters of the war away from the nationalistic rivalries of the pre-war era into a globalised ideological struggle between democrats and their political enemies on the left and right. New hope arose in the west as the United States entered the war on the allied side as an Associated Power promoting a populist liberal agenda. This was complemented in the east with the collapse of Tsarist autocracy. Russia was broken by the strain and ultimate indecisiveness of their part in the 'General Allied Offensive'. During 1917 Russia would fight on, broken-backed, while being radicalised by the Bolsheviks' anti-war propaganda which paved the way for their *coup d'etat* towards the end of the year. Quite rightly, at the end of the year the British Prime Minister David Lloyd George identified the rise of America and the emancipation of Russia as two events which would still be significant a century on.[48] These developments made Europe's old imperial squabbles seem rather tangential to wider global issues once the shape of the peace and post-war society became the dominant political theme during 1917. The old war would take its course, but the efforts of the pre-war European Great Powers to determine hegemony on the battlefield seemed increasingly ephemeral now that battle lines were being drawn up for an ideological civil war between autocrats, democrats and anti-capitalists once the armies had exhausted themselves in the trenches.

France, which had contributed and suffered the most up to that point, was to discard hope and pass through despair before resolution returned. The Somme offensive, although far from a failure and disappointment, was to end in anti-climax as the winter set in and operations were reduced to a grim localised struggle in the mud for a few insignificant villages around Bois St Pierre Vaast.[49]

The *poilus* had done their best but were starting to ask whether they had been let down by their allies and their leaders. If the war were to go into another year, could the progress of 1916 be exploited to achieve a decision? Thereafter the field was handed to the British and Australians whose divisions were to hold the line over the grim winter. For that reason France's ally would gain the 'victory' in the spring, following up retreating German forces. So in practice France quickly lost touch with the Somme, physically and emotionally. Yet Frenchmen had not given up hope and expectation that the battered German Army would be overwhelmed once the campaign was renewed, or that one last effort would reward and justify the sacrifice and their faith in Joffre.

A cruel twist of fate was to deny the victors of the Somme their place in history and their due reward. Just as the Somme offensive was winding down, Verdun snatched the limelight. It was the 'victors' of Verdun who were to be the immediate beneficiaries of 1916's efforts. In the reflection over the winter of 1916/17 there was a strong case for maintaining pressure on the German Army until it cracked – this was Joffre's recommendation to the allied governments which their military leaders endorsed. But politics were shifting. Governments seemed to be looking for a way to incite their peoples to yet greater efforts while at the same time rejecting the concomitant sacrifice. For example, Britain's new Prime Minister David Lloyd George talked emphatically of a 'knockout blow' to end the war, rejecting military advice that 'two Sommes at once' were really needed to end the war.[50] French politicians had lost faith in Joffre. A new star was rising: General Robert Nivelle, whose Second Army had retaken Forts Douaumont and Vaux in two effective set-piece offensives towards the end of the Battle of Verdun. This appeared to offer fresh hope, even though, as Fayolle sardonically noted on visiting the Verdun battlefield, Nivelle's success was 'a consequence of the Somme offensive, [and] the result of the methods used on the Somme reconfigured ... [there was] a desire to lower the Somme to make Verdun shine with a brighter light'.[51] French politicians, who did not appreciate that effective tactics were not the same as sound strategy, replaced Joffre with Nivelle, and raised Nivelle's immediate superior, Philippe Pétain, to the post of army chief of staff, *de facto* strategic adviser to the government. The successful Somme triumvirate was temporarily eclipsed. Joffre was appointed Marshal of France and given an advisory position with no real power; Foch was placed at the disposal of the new Commander-in-Chief and for a while became a strategic odd-job man; and Fayolle was moved to a less prestigious army command. Foch and Fayolle would be quickly rehabilitated after Nivelle's over-hyped spring offensive lapsed into further costly attrition, and in 1918, with Pétain, would complete the work started by Joffre. From his office in Les Invalides, Joffre no doubt followed events with vicarious satisfaction, for it was his army led by the men he had promoted to command it which brought his strategy to fulfilment.

This reversion to political and military short-termism would derail the progress made in 1916 and, when Nivelle's offensive failed, induce a rapid shift from elation to despondency, symptomatic of a difficult year of political instability, military mutinies and social unrest during which France had to remobilize and re-engage with the fight for liberation. Perhaps the decision to promote Nivelle over more established commanders and to remove the soldier who had done more than any other to organise and lead the alliance to victory, was redolent of the popular mood in the winter and spring of 1916/17. Galvanised by the intervention of the recently re-elected American President Woodrow Wilson, who in December 1916 asked all the belligerents to state their terms in anticipation of a negotiated settlement, talk was turning from war to peace. What were nations fighting for, why was the sacrifice being made, and if it were to continue what would be the outcome, were the questions statesmen, soldiers and citizens would ask and try to answer during the difficult year following that of Verdun and the Somme.

In response to Wilson's initiative, Germany had offered terms – all the Allies agreed that they were unacceptably bombastic at a time when Germany had lost her earlier advantage – but rejecting Germany's demands did not preclude some concrete counter-proposals to replace the platitudes that had served as allied 'war aims' up to that point.[52] Of course nothing could ultimately be determined until the war had been fought to some kind of conclusion, but perhaps the root of the longer-term traumas that have come down to later generations lies in this mood and its outcomes as much as the events of 1916 themselves. The generation of 1916 was caught in an irreconcilable quandary. What all were agreed on as 1916 moved into 1917 was that the war should be ended as quickly as it could be. At the same time there was no obvious path to a quick end: a negotiated peace, a knockout blow on land or at sea, and renewed and intensified attrition were all mooted and yet the war seemed to be interminable. Now, domestic revolution, an always bubbling undercurrent which threatened to turn into a seething torrent as events unfolded during 1917, seemed to be another way out. As it transpired, it was merely a development that would change the nature of the conflict from that of an international war into that of widespread civil wars.

The campaign in France and Flanders seemed of less significance as events of global import developed. Although Lloyd George could discern the sea-change in geopolitics, he could see no way to bring the old war to an end with honour but without further sacrifice. To win necessitated disabling the enemy until he broke under the strain, his will and his economic and manpower resources depleted beyond repair. Therefore the generals were allowed their freedom of action. The politicians reluctantly accepted that more effort would be required, even if, in their view, for no more tangible purpose than justifying the sacrifice already made. In fact, 1918's sacrifice would be as heavy as that of 1916, although it would not weigh so much on future generations as the war by then seemed to be better conducted, and it was, finally, brought to an end.

Across the Bapaume–Péronne road from the *Souvenir Français* memorial chapel at Rancourt, almost in the shadow of Bois St Pierre Vaast, three quiet cemeteries lie close together – one French, one British and one German. Less visited than the Anglo-French memorial at Thiepval, these contiguous yet contrasting graveyards at the climactic point of 1916's fighting symbolise more than any others the suffering and sacrifice on the Somme. They deserve to be visited by those who wish to reflect upon the real traumas of 1916 and afterwards. Because the Somme, or more accurately the 'General Allied Offensive', did not end the war, it has come down to posterity as a defeat, while it was actually the strategic victory that turned the course and determined the outcome of the war. Both sides appreciated this at the time. Yet the physical and human costs were immense. The cemeteries at Rancourt and dotted across the battle's memorial landscape serve as permanent reminders of that loss to later generations, more poignant as time recedes than the victory monuments erected alongside them.

Perhaps not least more poignant because at the same moment that Europe endured its supreme patriotic sacrifice, the nature and purpose of the war were also changing. Looking back a century later we can see that immediately afterwards the twentieth century's ideological conflicts broke out. Clausewitz identified that war was not just the business of governments and armies, but at its extreme involved popular passions. These were fully mobilised by 1916, among combatants and pro- and anti-war onlookers on the home fronts. Thereafter, war, which for the military was a practical exercise, became for the nations in arms an emotional one that would sweep societies in unexpected directions.

The great battles of 1916 scarred deeply the societies that fought them. In choosing to pursue strategies of attrition to end a stalemated war, peoples were condemned to increased effort and sacrifice in a war that became at the same time more intense and intractable. Germany tried to bring the war to an end by breaking the French Army at Verdun. The allies responded by grinding the German Army down on the Somme. By the end of the year there seemed to be little to show for nearly 2 million casualties. However, although the front lines had moved only a few miles, it was clear that the battles of 1916 on the Western Front marked a turning point in both the course of the war and in the fortunes of the societies that had engaged in them. In 1917 the allies were successful, confident but increasingly fragile, while Germany was exhausted and slipping towards military dictatorship, defeat and civil war. In 1918 the allies would reap the rewards of their effort, Germany would suffer the consequences. Ever after the question of whether it was worth it has exercised societies. Verdun and the Somme became *lieux de memoire* for the belligerents: battlefields preserved physically as sites of memory, and also historical events that have been argued over constantly, cultural fracture points that invite justification or denunciation. A century afterwards, as memory enters a new cycle in which more objective history may finally find its place, it is possible to step back from these deep-rooted and heartfelt traumas to explain and understand these battles as historical events, while also acknowledging their resonance and continued meaning for Britain, France and Germany, the nations that shared the traumas and sacrifices of 1916.

Notes

1. Stéphane Audoin-Rouzeau and Annette Becker, *1914–1918: Understanding the Great War* (London: Profile Books, 2002), p. 1.
2. See Michael Neiberg, *Dance of the Furies: Europe and the Outbreak of World War I* (Cambridge, MA: The Belknap Press of Harvard University Press, 2011).
3. William Philpott, *Attrition: Fighting the First World War* (London: Little, Brown, 2014), pp. 59–193 passim.
4. The title was coined by allied journalists rather than Joffre himself.

5. 'Plan of Action Proposed by France to the Coalition: Memorandum Laid before the Second Allied Military Conference at Chantilly, 6th December 1915', in Brig.-Gen. Sir James Edmonds, *Military Operations France and Belgium, 1916, vol. I: Appendices* (London: Macmillan & Co., 1932), appendix 1, pp. 1–5.

6. Robert Foley, *German Strategy and the Path to Verdun: Erich von Falkenhayn and the Development of Attrition, 1870–1916* (Cambridge: Cambridge University Press, 2005), pp. 183–93.

7. For this author's account see William Philpott, *Bloody Victory: The Sacrifice on the Somme and the Making of the Twentieth Century* (London: Little, Brown, 2009).

8. See William Philpott, 'Why the British were Really on the Somme: A Reply to Elizabeth Greenhalgh', for *War in History*, 9 (2002), pp. 446–71.

9. *Groupe des armées du nord* memorandum, 'La Bataille offensive', 20 April 1916, *Archives de l'armée de terre*, Vincennes, 18N148.

10. Quoted in Hew Strachan, *The First World War: A New Illustrated History* (London: Simon & Schuster, 2003), p. 185.

11. Ian Ousby, *The Road to Verdun* (London: Pimlico, 2003), pp. 85–93.

12. Binding diary, 19 March 1915, in Rudolf Binding, *A Fatalist at War*, trans. I. Morrow (London: George Allen & Unwin Ltd, 1929), p. 55.

13. Philpott, *Bloody Victory*, pp. 81–6.

14. William Philpott, 'Haig and Britain's European Allies', in B.J. Bond and N. Cave (eds), *Sir Douglas Haig: Seventy Years On* (Barnsley: Leo Cooper, 1999), pp. 128–44.

15. 'Sir Douglas Haig's Command? The Image of Alliance in Douglas Haig's Record of the War', *The Douglas Haig Fellowship Records*, 15 (2011), pp. 3–13.

16. Martin Farrar, *News From the Front: War Correspondents on the Western Front, 1914–18* (Stroud: Sutton Publishing, 1998), pp. 97–9.

17. This reflected somewhat contradictory French expectations. In his last briefing to his field commanders Joffre predicted one of two developments depending on the state of the German Army's reserves after Verdun, either a 'rupture' of the front and a return to open warfare, or a long, hard fight before the German defence collapsed. Joffre to Haig, 21 June 1916, National Archives, Kew, 'GHQ General Joffre Correspondence, 21 December 1915–25 June 1916' [WO 158/14]: WO 158/14/124.

18. Joffre journal, 2 July 1916, in Guy Pedroncini (ed.), *Journal de Marche de Joffre, 1916–19* (Vincennes: Service Historique de l'Armée de Terre, 1990), p. 32.

19. Philpott, *Bloody Victory*, p. 218.

20. Haig Diary, 1 July 1916, in G. Sheffield and J. Bourne (eds), *Douglas Haig: War Diaries and Letters, 1914–1918* (London: Weidenfeld & Nicholson, 2005), p. 196.

21. Ibid., 29 March and 29 May 1916, pp. 183, 188.

22. The French never compiled an official figure for losses on 1 July 1916 – there was no need. This figure, '1,590, mostly lightly wounded', was mentioned to Colonel Jack Seely by Foch on 1 July: Rt. Hon. J.E.B. Seely, *Adventure* (London: William Heinemann, 1930), p. 25. Joffre recorded that 3,254 casualties had passed through French dressing stations during the first two days of operations, many lightly wounded: Joffre journal, 2 July 1916, p. 33.

23. Churchill's contemporaneous concerns and his depiction of the Somme in *The World Crisis* are discussed in Philpott, *Bloody Victory*, pp. 319–20 and 598–602.

24. Basil Liddell Hart, *History of the First World War* (London: Pan Books, 1972), p. 231.

25. H.A. de Weerd, 'Churchill, Lloyd George, Clemenceau: the Emergence of the Civilian', in Edward Meade Earle (ed.), *Makers of Modern Strategy: Military Thought from Machiavelli to Hitler* (Princeton: Princeton University Press, 1941), pp. 287–305: p. 290, n. 14. No doubt de Weerd's judgement was based on a reading of Churchill and Liddell Hart.

26. This figure is a broad approximation – casualties at Verdun have never been accurately determined. Estimates vary between 600,000 and 1 million. Ousby, *Road to Verdun*, p. 5, gives a figure of 708,777 casualties of whom 305,440 were killed.

27. Philpott, *Bloody Victory*, pp. 192–282 and 345–84 passim.

28. Philpott, *Bloody Victory*, pp. 349–77.

29. Franz von Papen, *Memoirs*, trans. Brian Connell (London: Andre Deutsch, 1952), pp. 66–7.

30. Ibid., p. 67.

31. For a discussion of cavalry tactics and operations see David Kenyon, *Horsemen in No Man's Land: British Cavalry and Trench Warfare, 1914–1918* (Barnsley: Pen & Sword, 2011).
32. 'Speech on the unveiling of the statue of General Foch', by Debeney, 1926, quoted in Philpott, *Bloody Victory*, p. 441.
33. Ousby, *Road to Verdun*, gives an insightful analysis of the significance of Verdun in France.
34. There are parallels with Germany's situation in 1943–45, during which they would fight hard to delay the inevitable but had no prospect of victory.
35. Binding to his father, 3 April 1917, in Binding, *A Fatalist at War*, p. 157.
36. Philpott, *Bloody Victory*, p. 373.
37. Ibid., p. 602.
38. Papen, *Memoirs*, p. 67.
39. Binding to an anonymous correspondent, 12 November 1916, in Binding, *A Fatalist at War*, p. 138.
40. Binding diary, 2 December 1916, p. 140.
41. Ibid., 8 January 1917, p. 141.
42. Ibid., p. 142.
43. Ibid., 26 December 1916, p. 140.
44. Ibid., 8 March 1917, p. 149.
45. Ibid., 19 and 31 March 1917, pp. 151, 154.
46. Alexander Watson, *Ring of Steel: Germany and Austria-Hungary at War, 1914–1918* (London: Allen Lane, 2014), pp. 378–84.
47. Philpott, *Attrition*, pp. 327–33.
48. 'War Situation: Prime Minister's Review', Motion for Adjournment, 20 December 1917, Parliamentary Debates: Commons, C, 2212.
49. Philpott, *Bloody Victory*, pp. 395–400.
50. Lieutenant-General Sir Henry Wilson, quoted in Philpott, *Attrition*, pp. 249–51.
51. Fayolle diary, 8 January 1917, in Maréchal Fayolle, *Cahiers secrets de la grande guerre*, ed. Henry Contamine (Paris: Plon, 1964), pp. 197–8.
52. Philpott, *Attrition*, pp. 285–7.

Suggested Further Reading

Audoin-Rouzeau, Stéphane and Becker, Annette, *1914–1918: Understanding the Great War* (London: Profile Books, 2008)

Liddle, Peter, *The Somme Reconsidered* (Barnsley: Pen & Sword, 2016)

Ousby, Ian, *The Road to Verdun* (London: Pimlico, 2003)

Philpott, William, *Bloody Victory: the Sacrifice on the Somme and the Making of the Twentieth Century* (London: Little, Brown, 2009)

Philpott, William, *Attrition: Fighting the First World War* (London: Little, Brown, 2014)

Prior, Robin and Wilson, Trevor, *The Somme* (New Haven, CT: Yale University Press, 2005)

Sheffield, Gary, *The Somme* (London: Cassell, 2003)

Sheldon, Jack, *The German Army on the Somme, 1914–16* (Barnsley: Pen & Sword, 2005)

Chapter 5

German Command and Control on the Somme, 1916

By Jack Sheldon

The German Army that had fought the Great War was steeped in the early nineteenth-century writings of Clausewitz. Its military doctrine was firmly planted on the concept of the *Schwerpunkt*, which formed the basis of both German strategic and tactical operational practice throughout the war. Clausewitz had concentrated mainly on the strategic aspects of the idea but, well before 1914, a much developed version had permeated all aspects of military life.

Given that the *Schwerpunkt* was central in German military theory and practice, in order to understand how the Battle of the Somme was prepared and then conducted, it is essential to be aware of the full scope and application of the term. It is a word which translates in several ways, including 'centre of gravity', 'crucial' or 'focal' point, but in the military context it is usually rendered as 'point of main effort', a term which, though correct, barely hints at its all-embracing universality. Every level of command from highest to lowest, every arm and service, has an identified *Schwerpunkt*, which takes priority over all else. This means that often considerable risks are run elsewhere if necessary. It is generally straightforward to determine – at least *ex post facto* – the location of the *Schwerpunkt*. Thus, in 1915 Army Headquarters, *OHL*, placed it firmly on the Eastern Front, allocating to it all twenty-two of the new divisions raised by the spring of that year, the Western Front being placed meanwhile on the strategic defensive.

In 1916 the *Schwerpunkt* was clearly centred on Verdun, with the remainder of the Western Front starved of men and materiel to sustain the attacks in that sector. This had considerable implications for the German Second Army, commanded by *General der Infanterie* Fritz von Below, which was fully engaged in the preparations to meet the major forthcoming offensive astride the River Somme. This was later described by General von Falkenhayn as 'long-expected and hoped-for'.[1] Long expected it may have been, but hardly 'hoped-for'. All Below's requests for permission to launch a pre-emptive attack to disrupt British preparations, and for reinforcements of manpower, aircraft and artillery as the moment of the attack approached, were turned down flat by *OHL*. Earlier there had been certain meagre allocations of troops, most significantly the deployment of the 2nd Guards Reserve Division in May but, although Falkenhayn claimed that this meant that Second Army had been 'materially strengthened',[2] they were dismissed by everyone else as 'a drop of water on a hot stone'.[3]

It was evident that nothing would be forthcoming from the Verdun front and that the reserves held to the north in the Sixth Army sector were not going to be

Between Serre, Thiepval and Ovillers: German determined *Schwerpunkt*, focal point area, north of the River Somme.

made available, so there was nothing else for it but for Second Army and its subordinate formations to make best use of what was available or could be obtained from elsewhere. Once again, determination of the Second Army *Schwerpunkt* is helpful in explaining what was done. The clearest indication that it lay north of the River Somme was the removal of the 10th Bavarian Infantry Division from XVII Corps sector south of the river in mid-June 1916 and its move into XIV Reserve Corps reserve; this despite the fact that an order for the move dated

24 June and issued by Bavarian Reserve Infantry Regiment 8 stated, 'It has been established from reports by agents, that an attack by British and French formations is to be expected shortly on both banks of the Somme.'[4] This left the already relatively weak line south of the Somme even more so, because the ensuing reorganisation meant that the regiments of the remaining three divisions had to take over markedly extended frontages. Infantry Regiment 61, for example, assuming responsibility for the sector of Bavarian Infantry Regiment 16 south of Chaulnes, had to deploy all three of its battalions in the front line, leaving it with no reserves whatsoever.[5]

There appear to be two main reasons why the risk was run. The official appreciation was that the French commitment at Verdun, whilst not totally ruling out French participation on the Somme, would at least mean that it would have to be reduced in scale and scope. This led straight on to geographical considerations. Glib talk of forcing crossings across the Somme was totally unrealistic unless operations could be extended a long way south. The merest glance at the map of the bend of the Somme in this area shows that attempting an opposed assault river crossing south of Péronne and trying to negotiate swamps, marshland and numerous water channels would simply not have been an act of war; it would have stood no chance whatsoever of success. True, German engineers had managed what was regarded as a triumph of construction when they succeeded earlier in building a bridge at Éterpigny, but that took weeks of effort and was achieved out of contact. So, no matter how successful the French might have been south of the river, they would eventually have encountered an impassable obstacle. Events were to bear this out when, at an early stage in the battle, the intensity of fighting south of the river fell away, to be replaced by increasingly desperate attempts by the French Army to turn Péronne from the north.

North of the river, it is clear that the XIV Reserve Corps' *Schwerpunkt* was the 26th Reserve Division sector. The importance for the overall integrity of the defence of the high ground running from Serre to Ovillers had long since been recognised and strenuous efforts continued for two-and-a-half years from October 1914 to make its ridges and spurs as near impregnable as possible. Furthermore, when each division was stripped of a complete brigade headquarters in 1915, so as to furnish command headquarters for new formations, 26th Reserve Division, probably uniquely, was permitted to remain a four-regiment division and to retain both the 51st and 52nd Reserve Brigades, commanded by the experienced *Generalleutnant* von Wundt and similarly experienced *Generalleutnant* von Auwärter, respectively.

Confirmation of its importance is also demonstrated by consideration of the strengthening and reorganisation of the bulk of the German artillery in early summer 1916. That this was possible, despite the refusal of Falkenhayn to release additional resources, leads on to another peculiarity of the forces engaged on the Somme. Contrary to popular belief, there never was an 'Imperial German Army': the navy, yes; the army, no. Instead, it was made up of several contingents; dominated by Prussia, it is true, but also featuring units and formations from the Kingdoms of Bavaria, Württemberg and Saxony, with smaller contributions from other parts of the Reich, including the Grand Duchy of Baden that furnished the 28th Reserve Division, deployed from La Boisselle to Mametz.

This semi-independence, though of course in wartime all owed allegiance to the Kaiser, meant that *Generalleutnant* Freiherr von Soden, commanding the 26th Reserve Division, did not have to rely wholly on a Prussian response. He was able to appeal directly to the Ministry of War of the Kingdom of Württemberg in Stuttgart for the provision of a new artillery regiment (Reserve Field Artillery Regiment 27, formed in June 1916). In addition, he requested the services of a top-class gunner, namely *Generalmajor* Heinrich Maur, to take command of the newly created 26th Reserve Field Artillery Brigade. Maur had been serving on the Eastern Front as Artillery Commander 79th Reserve Division, but he was rushed west and placed in charge of not only twelve organic batteries, but also a further twelve field batteries (Bavarian Field Artillery Regiment 20, complete with three howitzer batteries, 1st Battalion Reserve Field Artillery Regiment 12 and 1st Battalion Field Artillery Regiment 104 from the 52nd Infantry Division). To these were added additional heavy batteries.

On paper, therefore, the *Schwerpunkt* division was supported by twenty-eight and a half field and ten and a half heavy batteries.[6] This sounds reasonably impressive until it is remembered that not only was Maur's command vastly outnumbered by the British artillery, but it was also equipped with a motley collection of obsolescent and even obsolete items, including captured Belgian and Russian equipment, batteries with no horses and 90cm guns and ancient *Ringkanonen* with no recoil mechanisms. That he was able from this unpromising assortment to create and direct centralised control of his firepower and deploy five sub-groups to powerful effect was a defensive triumph. How much easier his task would have been as the offensive opened if he had had modern 210mm howitzers (*Große Gottliebs*) at his disposal, but these fearsome weapons, which spent the war being rushed up and down the Western Front wherever the need was most pressing, had of course been placed in support of the *OHL Schwerpunkt* at Verdun.

As far as infantry firepower was concerned (altogether, spread along the 11km sector were ninety heavy machine guns, including captured weapons, and thirty of the new light machine guns – Danish *Madsens* with a four-man crew and known as *Musketen*), its placement shows that the divisional *Schwerpunkt* lay with Reserve Infantry Regiment 99 in the Thiepval sector and that within that the *Schwerpunkt* of *Schwerpunkts* was the Schwaben Redoubt, located on dominating high ground north of Thiepval village. Small wonder, therefore, that it was reinforced by a company from Bavarian Reserve Infantry Regiment 8 before the battle ever began and that counterattack plans were issued in advance. Small wonder either that its loss to the dash of the men of the 36th (Ulster) Division on the morning of 1 July caused such utter consternation in the German chain of command and set in train the most vigorous countermeasures to restore the situation. Writing after the war, *Hauptmann* Herbert von Wurmb, an officer of Bavarian Reserve Infantry Regiment 8, who received the Knight's Cross of the Military Max Josef Order for his part in its recapture, wrote:

> The Schwaben Redoubt was a point of decisive importance. If the enemy succeeded in establishing himself here on a long term basis, not only would the

whole position of the 26th Reserve Division on the southern bank of the Ancre have been extraordinarily endangered, but also the entire operational viability of the divisional artillery on the northern bank would have been called into question because, from the Redoubt, all the batteries there would have been in full view.[7]

The focus of all defensive attention clear, it is now necessary to consider the means by which the effort in support of the *Schwerpunkt* was directed at the tactical level on 1 July 1916. The point must be made at once that the availability or absence of working telephone links had a significant impact on how events unrolled. At first, once the attacks began, the exact situation north of Thiepval was unclear. The men of the 36th (Ulster) Division had overrun the forward defences with such speed that it took a while before the situation was reported accurately. One initial report to Headquarters 26th Reserve Division, for example, read, 'Our own troops are attacking in the direction of Authuille.'[8] In fact, German prisoners were being despatched rearwards by the Ulstermen. Quite soon, however, a Reserve Infantry Regiment 119 post north of the Ancre saw that the Schwaben Redoubt had been captured.[9]

The information was passed directly to *Generalleutnant* von Soden, who immediately gave orders by telephone for the launch of a counterattack. On the ground, 2nd Recruit Company Infantry Regiment 180 had already spotted what was happening and brought small arms fire down against leading elements from its trenches in the Second Position near Grandcourt.[10] Unfortunately, there was no telephone link available, so the chance of an immediate counterattack went begging. The possibility of such a dangerous development had, nevertheless, been foreseen and *Generalleutnant* von Auwärter had received a warning order on 27 June: 'At 12.00 midday today', noted its log, 'the Brigade received Operation Order No. 2453 from Division that Sector Thiepval North is to be reinforced as necessary. If the enemy gets established there, he is to be ejected at once. Further elements of 1st Battalion Bavarian Reserve Infantry Regiment 8 can be made available to replace troops moved forward out of the Intermediate or Second Position for this purpose ...'[11]

Although it was straightforward on the morning of 1 July to pass orders to brigades, static regiments and the artillery command centres, there were problems with further distribution. There were, for example, no links back from 52 Reserve Brigade in Courcelette to Pys and Irles, where reserve elements of Bavarian Reserve Infantry Regiment 8 were located. However, Reserve *Leutnant* Trainé of the Württemberg Reserve Dragoons was available at Divisional Headquarters for such an eventuality and he took the orders in person.[12] The intention was to counterattack with three tactical groups commanded by the battalion commanders of Bavarian Reserve Infantry Regiment 8. The operation was directed by the Bavarian regimental commander, *Oberstleutnant* Bram.[13] Major Roesch, commander of the 2nd Battalion in Irles, received his orders, typical of the remainder, at 9.55am.[14]

Enemy has forced his way into Schwaben Redoubt. 2nd Battalion Bavarian Reserve Infantry Regiment 8, with 1st Machine Gun Company and one platoon of the Musketen Company, is subordinated to 52 Reserve Infantry Brigade. The Battalion is to move immediately, dealing with any enemy encountered, to the Ancre Valley and is to advance to the Second Position via Stallmulde [Boom Ravine]. Sector South I to South III is to be occupied and held, with main effort on the right flank. 52 Reserve Infantry Brigade will be kept informed from here. Signed: Freiherr von Soden.[15]

Roesch and his men, who had been on full alert since 5.30am, marched off at once but, because of the quantity of British gunfire, such was the weight of artillery directed against the rear areas that it was not until 3.00pm that it even neared Grandcourt. Meanwhile, news having reached Headquarters XIV Reserve Corps, *Generalleutnant* von Stein immediately directed that the attack be expedited and, at 10.45am, an amended divisional operation order was being digested and forwarded by 52 Reserve Infantry Brigade: 'The Corps Commander has ordered that Schwaben Redoubt is to be recaptured at all costs. To that end the arrival of 2nd Battalion Bavarian Reserve Infantry Regiment 8 is not to be awaited. Rather the attack is to be launched with forces from the Second Position.'[16] Five minutes later *Generalleutnant* von Auwärter passed his own order to 1st Battalion Bavarian Reserve Infantry Regiment 8:

> The British have forced their way into the Hanseatic Position and Schwaben Redoubt. Major Prager, with Companies Schmeißer, Schnürlen, Hudelmeier and Engineer Company Schofeld, together with 1st Machine Gun Company of Reserve Infantry Regiment 119 and Sharp Shooter Troop 89, is to conduct this attack from the right flank of the Second Position. Major Beyerköhler will advance on Schwaben Redoubt from Hill 153 with three companies.[17]

More time was then lost as orders were passed on and the troops moved with great difficulty towards their start lines. *Oberstleutnant* Bram did not reach Stuff Redoubt to control the operation until 2.00pm, almost three hours after he had received his orders from *Generalleutant* von Soden. Due to heavy fire, he had had to walk from Pys, via Courcelette, where he had received fresh orders from *Generalleutnant* von Auwärter. However, because of multiple problems, the troops were still not correctly placed and some never arrived in time at all. Instead there were various attacks by different groups, but the hoped-for synergy was not achieved.[18] Established at last in Stuff Redoubt near Grandcourt, *Oberstleutnant* Bram's attempts to grip the situation were made harder due to battlefield obscuration, but urgings from on high, reports arriving and his own observations made the overriding need for speed clear, so he directed that the counterattack was to begin at 4.00pm. Fortunately he was able to speak personally to one battalion commander and also to *Hauptmann* Graf Preysing, from Reserve Field Artillery Regiment 26, who was coordinating the artillery support for the counterattack.[19] As it transpired, because of the earlier initiative of another of his battalion commanders, 2nd Recruit Company Infantry Regiment 180 launched forward at 3.40pm and other elements, taking this for H-Hour, set off as well. This, coupled with a false report that the Schwaben Redoubt had already been recaptured, prejudiced effective artillery preparation so, despite numerous acts of heroism and severe losses, progress was slow and was soon threatening to grind to a standstill.[20]

Generalleutnant von Soden, himself under pressure, then despatched an order demanding fresh impetus be given to the attack.[21] Relayed at 5.02pm via Goat Redoubt by 52 Reserve Infantry Brigade, it read:

> The Adjutant [Oberleutnant Grabinger], 3rd Battalion Bavarian Reserve Infantry Regiment 8, is to despatch, immediately, two patrols bearing written orders to Oberstleutnant Bram in Stuff Redoubt, stating that the Division expects and expressly orders Bavarian Reserve Infantry Regiment 8: to recapture the entirety of Schwaben Redoubt, to occupy it and to bring relief to the hard-pressed parts of Reserve Infantry Regiment 99. This is a direct order.[22]

There was no doubt what had to be done and *Oberstleutnant* Bram, making best use of his resources as reinforcements trickled in, managed to make further progress during the next two hours. Remaining in close touch with *Hauptmann* Graf Preysing, Bram settled on a plan to complete the recapture of Schwaben Redoubt. General von Auwärter, linking with the divisional commander and also *Generalmajor* Maur, finally informed Bram at 9.27pm that he could expect a one-hour bombardment by every battery within range from 10.00pm.[23] Right on cue, Maur's guns brought down fire for effect on the redoubt and, on the stroke of 11.00pm, the Bavarian Reserve Regiment 8 survivors, commanded by *Hauptmann* Wurmb, combining with a group from Reserve Infantry Regiment 99, attacked in the pitch-black night, cleared out Schwaben Redoubt, poured fire at the remnants of the 36th (Ulster) Division as they pulled back to Thiepval Wood and then went into hasty defence.[24] In so doing they had captured about a hundred prisoners and numerous machine guns. 'The British corpses of 700 courageous members of the Ulster Division littered the Redoubt, every foot of which was soaked in blood.'[25] Rigid concentration on the *Schwerpunkt* by all concerned within 26th Reserve Division had enabled them to remain focused on the need to stabilise the situation, to exploit to the full the means of command and control at their disposal and to overcome their numerous communications problems. It had been a close-run affair, but they had prevailed. Not to have done so could have spelled disaster for the defence.

So much for the tactical level as the battle opened, but the best efforts of the troops *in situ* would not have determined its eventual outcome, so the higher direction of the German defence must now be considered. This is a subject that is inextricably associated with the performance of the General Staff and its relationship to both higher commanders and the troops subordinate to them. The Great General Staff occupied a dominant position in the German Army during the Great War; dominance which may be traced right back to the earliest days of the Prussian Reformers. Aware that commands would frequently be given to men by virtue of their royal or aristocratic connections, rather than because of any inherent or acquired military ability, they set out to create a permanent, self-sustaining structure that would neutralise this problem. Scharnhorst, choosing his words carefully, expressed it thus:

> Normally it is not possible for an army simply to dismiss incompetent generals. The very authority which their office bestows upon generals is the first reason

for this. Moreover, the generals form a clique, tenaciously supporting one another, all convinced that they are the best possible representatives of the army. But we can at least give them capable assistants. Thus the General Staff officers are those who support incompetent generals, providing the talents that might otherwise be wanting among leaders and commanders.[26]

In order to give substance to this aim, processes developed which ensured that the General Staff became the preserve of a very small minority of highly motivated men, who had dedicated themselves to the study and practice of their profession and were possessed of military talent and a huge capacity for work. There was always an overtly arrogant exclusiveness about its approach to its duties, which was a source of both strength and resentment amongst others, who felt that its frequently high-handed approach was at times inappropriate. One particular manifestation and area for criticism was the system of dual command that was developed in its most extreme form on the static Western Front.

The commander at each level bore overall responsibility for the decisions taken, but he would be steered towards a particular course of action by his chief of staff. One such example occurred in the wake of the British attack, supported by tanks on 15 September 1916, when Commander First Army contemplated a withdrawal. Loßberg, his chief of staff, recorded the incident as follows:

> General von Below, who temporarily considered withdrawing the left and right wings of the army into positions to the rear, which were partly complete and partly still under construction, decided, under my influence,[27] to continue resistance along the current line of battle.[28]

Of course the commander did not have to follow staff advice but if he chose not to there were two consequences. First, his own decision would be entered into the war diary in full, followed by the dissenting decision of the chief of staff, so as to record the fact that the decision had been taken against 'professional' advice and, second, the telephone wires would be humming as the chief of staff reported what was happening up the staff chain of command. Given that the chiefs of staff at army and army group level had access twenty-four hours per day to, first, Falkenhayn and later Ludendorff,[29] who effectively had the ultimate say in these matters, this consideration must have borne heavily on any commander tempted to go his own way.

Ironically, it was the availability of the telephone, the essential means of exercising command, which enabled the General Staff to exercise tight control over much of the detail of the defensive battle and which drew the most criticism from the rest of the army and elsewhere. Post-war, one civilian critic, a member of the Reichstag, complained:

> The army was split into two sharply differing parts, that had almost nothing in common. On the one hand there was the battlefront, the officers and men who actually fought the war; on the other was the staff ... who knew nothing of the true needs of the front. The front and staff were divided by an opaque, impermeable wall.[30]

It was in response to this type of stinging criticism that General Hermann von Kohl, chief of staff successively to First Army, Sixth Army, then Army Group Crown Prince Rupprecht, rushed into print a defence of the General Staff with his book *Der deutsche Generalstab in Vorbereitung und Durchführung des Weltkrieges*. However, prominent officers in the army were quite often of the same opinion. *Generalleutnant* von Moser, commander during the Battle of the Somme of the highly successful 27th Infantry Division, which defended Guillemont for several weeks, and later of XIV Reserve Corps, was quite convinced – and stated as much in his post-war memoirs, based on his diaries – that the staff used the telephone system not only to improve working efficiency but also to manoeuvre behind the backs of commanders. He wrote subsequently:

> I had the feeling that misuse of the telephone system was in full swing ... It appeared to me that one of my General Staff officers was more than keen to participate in this. The officer had occupied exactly the same position since the beginning of the war. As a result, his attitude to all around him and, indeed, to the fighting troops, was insufferably high-handed. He had become accustomed to thinking that he was quite infallible. I discussed this matter in serious terms with my chief of staff and directed that this officer was to be posted without delay to a front line unit ... Quite rightly, the endless retention of totally fit and able unwounded General Staff officers in the higher level staffs was the source of much ill-feeling in the army.[31]

It was not just individuals apparently abusing their positions which angered him, but the entire way of day-to-day working within the staff chain of command:

> ... the most important tactical matters dealt with from army chief of staff down to the General Staff officer of a division, are often thrashed out totally over the telephone, or so arranged that, when the commander gets to hear about them subsequently, he can hardly do other than agree to what has been decided ... The climate of mistrust, the patronising system and the way the General Staff operates, unavoidably damages the authority of the corps and divisional commanders ... Complaints about this are general because it encourages the impression, in fact it is often expressed, that, as far as tactical operations are concerned, not only is this not exclusively the responsibility of the commander; rather it is due in equal, if not greater, measure of the General Staff officer.[32]

Regardless of ill-feeling on both sides of the alleged divide, the fact remains that the Battle of the Somme was controlled by the General Staff, much of it by one single officer, namely *Oberst* Fritz von Loßberg. Loßberg first came to real prominence when, after making an excellent impression during his time on the staff of *OHL*, he was posted from there at the Kaiser's personal command at the end of September 1915 as chief of staff Third Army at the height of the autumn battle in Champagne. Thereafter he was sent successively to Second (later First) Army on the Somme, Sixth Army at Arras and Fourth Army in Flanders, on each occasion being despatched to solve a major defensive crisis. Possessed of an iron will, great stamina and the constitution of an ox, he was a staff officer of great ability. His analytical skills enabled him to get straight to the heart of a problem, reduce the most complex matters to manageable proportions and to act boldly and decisively. As was always the case in the German Army, it was his appointment, rather than his relatively junior rank, which gave him his authority and he did not hesitate to use it; always demanding and being granted full powers of decision by the generals he served and insisting up the chain of command that he be given all the resources in men and materiel he required for the fulfilment of his task. He also expected the full and unqualified support of all the heads of the various staff branches in his headquarters, regardless of their rank and, invariably, he received this; the individuals concerned knew perfectly well that he would have no hesitation in securing their removal should it be necessary.

Loßberg was posted at no notice to the Somme front in the wake of the 2 July visit to St Quentin by General von Falkenhayn when *Generalmajor* Grünert, chief of staff Second Army, was sacked for agreeing to a request from *General der Infanterie* von Pannewitz to shorten his line along the front of XVII Corps near Herbécourt, by permitting the 121st Infantry Division to withdraw under French pressure.[33] Admittedly this did expose the left flank of VI Reserve Corps, but the dismissal was controversial. Crown Prince Rupprecht devoted a diary entry on 3 July to the subject:

> Quite apart from the fact that it is inappropriate to change a Chief of Staff at a moment of supreme crisis, such a measure also amounts to lack of confidence in the relevant commander, who does in fact bear the ultimate responsibility for any decisions which are taken. This, in turn, diminishes the commander in the eyes of his subordinates. As I have already noted, the blame for what happened lies at the door of OHL itself, which did not arrange in time for reinforcements to be allocated to Second Army.[34]

Regardless of these objections, the die had been cast and Loßberg was driven through the night to meet Falkenhayn at Mézières, arriving there at 1.00am on 3 July and launching into a long statement of requirements, during which presentation to Falkenhayn, who was in bed, he listed the need for large-scale reinforcements, additional artillery, aircraft and other supplies and stated that it was essential to break off the attacks at Verdun with immediate effect. According to Loßberg, after he pressed the case, Falkenhayn finally shook hands with him in agreement. However, Loßberg later noted, 'General von Falkenhayn did not keep to his agreement. Instead he continued the offensive at Verdun right up until he was relieved as Chief of the General Staff of the Field Army on 28 August 1916.'[35]

Lest he be thought overbearingly arrogant and bullying, it must be stated clearly that he sought always to achieve harmonious working relationships wherever he went, realising only too well that such an approach led to efficiency and that the pressures of the frequently grave situations left no room for time-wasting squabbles. Furthermore, if he expected much of his subordinates, he granted all his branch chiefs automatic access to himself day and night,[36] did away with unnecessary, time-consuming staff rituals and drove nobody harder than himself. The only sleep he got during the night of 2/3 July was in the back of the car as he was chauffeured north, then, having arrived at St Quentin, he embarked immediately on a full tour of inspection of the front, followed by endless other commitments. It was a full forty-eight hours later before he lay down to sleep.

> From the morning of 3 July my duties demanded a great deal of work. Following the night drive from Vouziers via Mézières to St Quentin, I next got to bed for three hours during the night of 5/6 July. My nightly rest throughout the entire Battle of the Somme was very seldom much longer. However, I had the ability to snatch naps during any spare moment; I could even catch up on lost sleep during car journeys. My strong constitution enabled me easily to survive all the strain which lasted for months.[37]

The 'great deal of work' which occupied Loßberg and the higher staffs during the early part of July for the most part comprised rushing forward as soon as they arrived all and any reinforcements, often at regimental or even battalion level, to plug gaps in the line. There was, however, one exception. Fricourt, outflanked, had to be evacuated early on 2 July. Pressure built up on Reserve Infantry Regiment 110, defending La Boisselle, and, following intense fighting, the village was lost a day later. This was a serious crisis, because had any more ground been lost and had the southern shoulder of the vital Thiepval–Serre ridge crumbled, there was a real threat to the integrity of the defensive *Schwerpunkt*. At the tactical level, *Generalleutnant* von Soden reacted at once. At 5.10pm on 2 July 26th Reserve Division issued an order by telephone to its left forward regiment: 'Reserve Infantry Regiment 110 [28th Reserve Division] is pulling back via La Boisselle. Infantry Regiment 180 is to hold Ovillers to the last man.'[38] This was followed by the arrival of a written order at 9.30pm: 'Infantry Regiment 180 is to defend Ovillers to the last man. It is not to take a single step backwards from its current positions without a written order from division ...'[39]

At Army level, there was equal awareness of the threat to the vital ground and, so as to reinforce the *Schwerpunkt*, Loßberg played the strongest card he held at that time. Ignoring other problem areas and demands for additional forces, on 3 July he deployed the outstanding 3rd Guards Division, complete, to shore up the Ovillers–Pozières sector. There, over the next few days, the élite *Lehr* Infantry, Fusilier Guards and Grenadier 9 Regiments bled to death in the cause; but they saved the situation. There could hardly be a greater contrast with the attitude of the British commander, as recorded in his diary following a tense meeting with General Joffre during the afternoon of 3 July:

> Joffre pointed out the importance of our getting Thiepval Hill ... I was considering the desirability of pressing my attack on Longueval ... at this General Joffre exploded in a fit of rage. 'He could not approve of it'. He 'ordered me to attack Thiepval and Pozières' ... The truth is the poor man cannot argue, nor can he easily read a map.[40]

The real truth is that Joffre could indeed 'read a map', and could spot a *Schwerpunkt* when he saw one, but was not in a position to order General Haig to do anything. So, from that moment on, the French and British armies effectively fought two separate battles. Coordination was poor and there was an almost total lack of synergy. The Germans, who had been fearing a repetition on the Somme of the long-drawn-out attritional battles around the Butte de Tahure in Champagne the previous autumn, had been thrown a lifeline by the British. For this they were extremely grateful, especially when the British Army began to concentrate its efforts on an area of the battlefield dotted with woods that was particularly favourable for defence. So, while the British Fourth Army spent the period 2–13 July launching no fewer than forty-six narrow-front attacks, which cost 25,000 casualties,[41] in preparation for the assault on the German Second Position from Bazentin le Petit to Longueval, the staff at Second Army worked flat out to stabilise the situation, introduce a coherent system for the absorption of reinforcements and develop counterattack plans.

The counterattack plans never came to anything. They were contingent upon sufficient reinforcements of all kinds being made available and they never were. Loßberg raised the subject on several occasions with Falkenhayn, but his responses were always evasive.[42] More progress was made in adapting the command arrangements to changing circumstances and the arrival of reinforcing formations. Key to this was the redesignation of the various corps headquarters as 'Groups', named after their commanders. Thus XIV Reserve Corps became Group Stein. The Groups were charged with the provision of continuity of command over particular sectors whilst infantry formations rotated through them. Occasionally these higher headquarters were themselves relieved, but this was a fairly rare occurrence. By mid-July the span of command had become so great that responsibility for the Somme front was split between First Army (General von Below), chief of staff *Oberst* Loßberg, and Second Army (General von Gallwitz), chief of staff *Oberst* Bronsart von Schellenberg, with Gallwitz in overall command. There were several implications, but just two days prior to this change came disturbing news.

In the early hours of 15 July reports arrived at Second Army from two different headquarters north of the Somme, both unanimous, that there had been a British breakthrough between Bazentin and Longueval and that they were marching on Flers. What happened next gives a clear insight into how Loßberg coped with emergency situations. Immediate orders went out to the 5th Infantry Division and the 8th Bavarian Reserve Division to the south, and the 8th Division (which was in the process of conducting a relief in the Sixth Army area) to the north, to march at once, making maximum use of trucks, to the Flers area, there to launch converging attacks on the force that had broken through. That done, he then despatched two liaison officers forward in motor cars to examine the areas to the north and south and to report back to him by telephone. Despite several phone calls to subordinate headquarters during the night it was not until about 10.00am on 15 July that matters were clarified.

It then transpired that the 'enemy penetration' was in fact a group of 500 prisoners being escorted to the rear. 'A huge weight was lifted off my shoulders', wrote Loßberg, 'as it was also from those of the army commander and General von Falkenhayn, to whom I passed an immediate report.'[43] A furious Loßberg attributed the misleading information to exaggerated reporting in a tense and confused situation and he launched an immediate, but unsuccessful, enquiry into how it had happened. It might be thought, given the situation, that the reserves summoned to the scene would have been retained, but not a bit of it. Some elements of the 8th Division did become involved in a counterattack but, once Loßberg heard that the front had settled down along the line Pozières, northern edge of Longueval, western edge of Guillemont to the eastern edge of Harde-court, he considered that the immediate crisis was over and he released the 5th Infantry Division and the 8th Bavarian Reserve Division at once for deploy-ment elsewhere. His attention was already moving onto other pressing matters, especially because it was quite apparent that the British Army was now thrusting at 90 degrees to the original axis of advance and was thus drifting even further away from its French allies.

Most of those in senior appointments viewed with dismay the simultaneous placement of General von Gallwitz as both commander of Second Army and in overall coordination of both armies engaged on the Somme, seeing it as yet another example of Falkenhayn's increasingly erratic decision-making. In a measured response, *Generalleutnant* von Kuhl, chief of staff to Crown Prince Rupprecht, described it as, 'just as unprofitable as the subordination at the beginning of the war of Kluck's First Army to Generaloberst von Bülow, com-mander Second Army'.[44] The Crown Prince, for his part, made a robust entry in his diary on 17 July and increased his already extensive manoeuvring against Falkenhayn:

> General von Below is justifiably sickened by this slight. The guilt for the reverses his army has suffered lies with OHL and not with him. They ignored his reports and took no account of his requests for reserves. When, at long last, reserves did arrive, it was too late. They arrived in dribs and drabs and had to be deployed immediately to plug gaps. As a result there has been such a mixing of formations, that nobody knows what is happening.[45]

Inevitably, it was not long before friction increased and then there was a major clash between the army commanders in the wake of a dispute over manpower. It is of course true that one of the continuing problems was the fact that so few reserve formations were made available to the Somme sector. On arrival for his initial meeting with Falkenhayn on 17 July, Gallwitz had presented a proposal for a major counterattack into the right flank of the French Army, which had switched its primary focus to offensive operations north of the Somme. Rejecting the plan, Falkenhayn allegedly sent him on his way with the words, 'Hold on, hold on – that is the only thing that matters!'[46]

Following the reorganisation, command of the Somme battlefield was divided so that each army had three subordinate corps. For First Army these were initially: Group Stein (XIV Reserve Corps), northern army boundary to the Ancre; Group Armin (IV Corps), Thiepval to Guillemont via Ginchy; and Group Goßler (VI Reserve Corps), south to the Somme then east to Cléry. Second Army commanded Group Quast (IX Corps), from the Somme south to a point near Vermandovillers; Group Pannewitz (XVII Corps), south to Soyencourt, north of

Balâtre; and, finally, Group Plettenberg (Guard Corps), extending down to the army boundary south of Noyon.

Given the predominance of allied thrusts in the northern sector of the battle-field, it is no surprise that First Army gradually assumed command of additional Groups as senior headquarters were relieved and frontages reduced. These pressures led to further increased tension between Below and Gallwitz. Finally, this came to a head in the wake of serious fighting in early August around Maurepas that caused heavy losses to the 1st Bavarian Reserve Division. General von Below arranged for its relief on 13 August by the 1st Guards Division, then in reserve to Gallwitz's 'army group'. Gallwitz, who had overall control of manpower reserves, despatched a sharply worded and, frankly, unjustified written reprimand to Below, accusing him of deploying the Guards prematurely. A seething Below was persuaded with some difficulty by *Oberst* Loßberg not to institute the formal complaints procedure and, riding to the rescue, he arranged to meet Falkenhayn.

Following his discussions with Loßberg, Falkenhayn spoke at length on the telephone to Below, then met him for an extended one-to-one interview at a prearranged place to the east of St Quentin. According to Loßberg,[47] this defused the situation. Be that as it may, it was an unnecessary, time-wasting diversion of effort at a critical moment and symptomatic of poor judgement by Falkenhayn, when he failed to establish a suitable senior command structure the previous month. By now Falkenhayn was running out of time in any case. He had lost the respect of his senior subordinate commanders and at a conference of all army chiefs of staff on 14 August at Mézières, he made a 'very painfully embarrassing' impression on his audience, who contrasted unfavourably his current demeanour with his 'unjustified optimism' when he briefed his plans for the attack on Verdun earlier.[48] His own staff described how he 'was visibly losing his calm and security'[49] as August wore on, and then came the final straw. On 27 August Romania declared war on Austria-Hungary, the Kaiser lost confidence in Falkenhayn and sent for Hindenburg and Ludendorff.

One of the first acts of the new duumvirate was to hold a major conference at Cambrai on 7 September to take stock of events and to determine a durable way forward. In a totally positive atmosphere all the armies were given the opportunity to brief their situation and to make recommendations. There was a general air of confidence that matters would improve following the removal of Falkenhayn, though of course the overall situation, both on the Somme and elsewhere, was far from ideal and the ability of *OHL* to make dramatic changes in the short term was out of the question. After the conference Ludendorff noted that,

> The requests of the various participants culminated in urgent demands for increases in artillery, ammunition, aircraft and balloons, together with improvements in the system of reliefs, by means of increased and more timely deployment of fresh divisions and other troops. Halting attacks at Verdun made this somewhat easier, but even there we had to reckon on significant wearing down of forces due to local circumstances.[50]

It did prove possible gradually to improve the situation for the hard-pressed defenders. The second part of the battle, for example, was fought with a considerable increase in German aircraft in the skies, coupled with changes to artillery allocations and tactics, but it was perhaps in the area of reliefs and replacements that the biggest difference was achieved in the short to medium term. With receipt of his Prussian field marshal's baton, Crown Prince Rupprecht, appointed army group commander with a coordination role over First, Second and Sixth Armies, had all the authority he needed to allocate manpower and resources to his subordinate commanders, being required only to keep *OHL* informed of his decisions. This led to an immediate improvement in this important area and, given the constant dialogue between the staffs, there were never any unpleasant surprises, especially because it was the declared aim of Ludendorff, despite pressures elsewhere, to put an end to the need for the defenders on the Somme to be 'living from hand to mouth' in this respect.

Despite these changes and a slightly more relaxed attitude to trading space for reduced casualty lists, throughout September and October the battle remained, in Ludendorff's words, 'balanced on a knife edge'. The ground-holding divisions had almost universally gone over to crater field defence in depth, causing the allies, lacking clearly defined trench lines to engage, to waste gigantic quantities of shells in an attempt to suppress them, though there was a price to be paid in terms of problems of resupply, local command and the organisation and coordination of counterattacks. Nevertheless, the loss rates dropped, which was just as well in view of the fact that the 1897 class of recruits had already been called up the previous July, fifteen months ahead of time, whilst overall losses were still extremely high.[51] Ludendorff was later to write:

> The demands on commanders and troops were extraordinary. The reliefs planned at Cambrai and the overall plan for the Western Front could not be adhered to. Divisions and other troops had to be thrown into the Somme front in ever more rapid succession and there hold out for longer. The nervous tension at Pleß [location of OHL] was terrible ... Everything depended on Generals von Gallwitz, Fritz von Below and von Kuhl, together with Obersts von Loßberg and Bronsart v Schellendorf displaying nerves of iron and not losing their heads, in order that they might put to best use the reinforcements as they arrived and, despite all setbacks, keep their eyes fixed firmly on restoring the situation. Above all it relied on the [efforts] of the German soldiers.[52]

In this assessment he was of course absolutely correct. There were still too many demands on resources to permit anything other than a hard-fought delaying action to be continued until a combination of bad weather and Allied exhaustion ruled out further attacks that year. However, the system of command and control developed and finally perfected following the change in command at *OHL* proved to be sufficiently robust to meet all challenges as the battle ground on. The French Armies under Foch exerted immense pressure around Rancourt, Bouchavesnes and Sailly Saillisel in September and October without managing to break the defence – despite coming close at times, whilst the many British attacks were always contained, if not with ease and speed, nevertheless before any advances could be expanded into major territorial gains. In a post-war summary, *Oberst* von Loßberg wrote:

> All the time that General von Falkenhayn was chief of staff, command and control of the battle from OHL through every level down to platoon commander was extremely problematic. During the first part of the battle reinforcements were only made available at the very last minute to continue the heavy fighting. This meant that our fighting divisions were bled so dry that they could only recover very slowly once they had been withdrawn. At hardly any time during Falkenhayn's time did First Army have access to a usable army reserve. The then OHL even considered – admittedly only temporarily – whether it could withdraw troops from the Somme front. Once Hindenburg and Ludendorff were placed in command, the situation changed instantly. Reserves were always available in a timely manner to permit reliefs to take place. The artillery was strengthened from central army reserves, permitting defensive fire widths to be reduced from 400 to 200m per battery. This meant considerably improved support for the front-line troops in the defence and especially for counterattacks. In the final part of the battle the allocation of aircraft spotting for the artillery and a squadron of fighters in every divisional sector led to a decisive improvement in the performance of our guns.[53]

The German defenders had been hard-pressed throughout the months of campaigning but, despite the high losses, the fighting spirit and endurance of the troops, directed by an efficient system of command and control in skilful hands, had enabled them to hold on in the face of great odds. It ought to have been celebrated as a great defensive performance, but the cost had been too high.

In the battle area of the Somme it did not quieten down until the onset of wet weather began to transform the ground into bottomless mud. The millions of shell holes filled with water and became graveyards. For neither of the opposing sides was there talk of the joy of victory. Over everything lay the appalling, oppressive weight of this battlefield which, in its grim desolation, seemed to surpass even that of Verdun.[54]

Notes

1. Falkenhayn, General Erich von, *General Headquarters 1914–1916 and its Critical Decisions* (London: Hutchinson, 1919), p. 262.
2. Ibid., p. 238.
3. Grote, Hans Henning Freiherr, *Somme* (Hamburg, 1941), p. 25.
4. *Kriegsarchiv Munich*, BRIR8 Bd 3.
5. Keiser, Oberstleutnant von, *Geschichte des Inf.-Regts. v.d. Marwitz (8. Pomm) Nr. 61 im Weltkriege 1914–1918* (Privately published, 1928), p. 158.
6. Soden, Freiherr von, *Die 26. (Württembergische) Reserve-Division im Weltkrieg 1914–1918 I. Teil* (Stuttgart: 1939), p. 96.
7. *Kriegsarchiv Munich*, HS 1984.
8. *Kriegsarchiv Munich*, HS 2205.
9. Soden, Freiherr von, *Die 26. (Württembergische) Reserve-Division*, p. 110.
10. *Kriegsarchiv Munich*, BRIR8 Bd 4.
11. *Hauptstaatsarchiv Stuttgart*, M43/19 RIR 99.

12. Klett, Fritz, *Das Württembergische Reserve-Dragoner-Regiment im Weltkrieg 1914–1918* (Stuttgart: 1935), p. 100.
13. *Kriegsarchiv Munich*, HS 2205.
14. All timings are German, i.e. one hour ahead of allied time.
15. *Hauptstaatsarchiv Stuttgart*, M410 Bu 239.
16. Ibid.
17. Ibid.
18. Ibid.
19. Wurmb, Herbert Ritter von, *Das K.B. Reserve-Infanterie-Regiment Nr. 8* (Munich: Verlag Max Schick, 1929), p. 70.
20. *Kriegsarchiv Munich*, HS 1984.
21. Soden, Freiherr von, *Die 26. (Württembergische) Reserve-Division*, p. 111.
22. *Hauptstaatsarchiv Stuttgart*, M410 Bü 239.
23. Ibid.
24. Ibid.
25. *Hauptstaatsarchiv Stuttgart*, M410 Bü 260.
26. Quoted in Hohn, Reinhard, *Scharnhorsts Vermächtnis* (Bonn: 1952), pp. 312–13.
27. Author's emphasis.
28. Loßberg, Fritz von, *Meine Tätigkeit im Weltkriege 1914–1918* (Berlin: 1939), p. 254.
29. Kohl, H. von, *Der deutsche Generalstab in Vorbereitung und Durchführung des Weltkrieges* (Berlin: 1920), p. 195.
30. Gothein, Georg, *Warum verloren wir den Krieg?* (Deutsche Verlags-Anstalt: 1919), p. 33. Quoted Kohl, H von, *Der deutsche Generalstab*, p. 200.
31. Moser, General Otto von, *Feldzugsaufzeichnungen als Brigade- Divisionskommandeur und als kommmandierender General 1914–1918* (Stuttgart: 1923), pp. 306–7.
32. Ibid., pp. 308–9.
33. The opinion of General von Falkenhayn concerning rigid retention of terrain is quoted in the German Official History, *Der Weltkrieg 1914 bis 1918,10. Band. Die Operationen des Jahres 1916*, p. 355 as follows: 'The first principle of positional warfare has to be not to yield a single foot of ground and if a foot of ground is lost, to launch an immediate counterattack with all forces, down to the last man.' This was a policy he referred to constantly in his *General Headquarters 1914–1916 and its Critical Decisions*, notably at pp. 35–8.
34. Rupprecht, *Kronprinz, In Treue Fest: Mein Kriegstagebuch: Erster Band* (Munich: 1929), p. 495.
35. Loßberg, Fritz von, *Meine Tätigkeit im Weltkriege*, p. 215.
36. Ibid., p. 223.
37. Ibid., p. 224.
38. Soden, Freiherr von, *Die 26. (Württembergische) Reserve-Division*, p. 113.
39. Vischer, Alfred, *Das 10. Württ. Infanterie-Regiment Nr. 180 in der Somme-Schlacht 1916* (Stuttgart: 1917), p. 21.
40. Gary Sheffield and John Bourne (eds), *Douglas Haig War Diaries and Letters 1914–1918* (London: 2005), p. 198.
41. Robin Prior and Trevor Wilson, *The Somme* (London: 2005), p. 127.
42. Loßberg, Fritz von, *Meine Tätigkeit im Weltkriege*, pp. 222–3.
43. Ibid., p. 229.
44. Kuhl, General d.Inf. a.D. Hermann v, *Der Weltkrieg 1914–1918 Band I* (Berlin: 1929), p. 493.
45. Rupprecht, *Kronprinz*, p. 503.
46. Kabisch, *Generalleutnant* a.D. Ernst, *Somme 1916* (Berlin: 1937), p. 64.
47. Loßberg, Fritz von, *Meine Tätigkeit im Weltkriege*, pp. 240–1.
48. Ibid., p. 243.
49. Tschuppik, Karl, *Ludendorff: The Tragedy of a Specialist* (London: 1932), p. 57.
50. Ludendorff, Erich, *Meine Kriegserinnerungen 1914–1918* (Berlin: 1919), p. 210.
51. *Bundesarchiv – Militärarchiv Freiburg*, RH61/51716 *Kriegsministerium M.J. 14864/16. A.1. Geheim*, dated 17.7.16.
52. Ludendorff, Erich, *Meine Kriegserinnerungen*, p. 217.

53. Loßberg, Fritz von, *Meine Tätigkeit im Weltkriege*, p. 268.
54. Hindenburg, *Generalfeldmarschall* von, *Aus, meinem Leben* (Leipzig: 1934), p. 160.

Suggested Further Reading

Hirschfeld, Gerhard, Krumeich, Gerd and Renz, Irina, *Die Deutschen an der Somme 1914–1918* (Essen: 2006); available in translation as *Scorched Earth* (Barnsley: Pen & Sword, 2009)

Philpott, William, *Bloody Victory: The Sacrifice on the Somme and the Making of the Twentieth Century* (London: Little, Brown, 2009)

Sheldon, Jack, *The German Army on the Somme* (Barnsley: Pen & Sword, 2005)

Sheldon, Jack, *The Germans at Beaumont Hamel* (Barnsley: Pen & Sword, 2006)

Sheldon, Jack, *The Germans at Thiepval* (Barnsley: Pen & Sword, 2006)

Chapter 6

Soldiers and Politicians in Strife: The Case of Henry Wilson in 1915

By Gary Sheffield *and* John Spencer

The clash between the politicians or 'Frocks' and the generals or 'Brasshats' is central to traditional accounts of British politics and strategy in the First World War.[1] The poisonous and sometimes confrontational relationship between David Lloyd George, a leading member of the Cabinet throughout the war and Prime Minister from late 1916, and Douglas Haig, commander of the British Expeditionary Force (BEF) from December 1916, is the most notable example. Another critical figure was Henry Wilson, who held a number of important posts before becoming Chief of the Imperial General Staff, the professional head of the British Army and senior adviser to the government, in February 1918. Wilson was a divisive and controversial figure. He was intensely and overtly political in a way that set him aside from his peers; a bowdlerised version of one senior officer's assessment was that 'whenever he came within a mile of prominent politicians he suffered from a sexual disturbance'.[2] Wilson acquired a reputation as an intriguer, a ruthless, devious individual determined to gain and exercise power, a general who was more of a political animal than a fighting soldier, a reputation which has continued down to the present day. Indeed, one biographer even speculated that his assassination in 1922 forestalled Wilson's emergence as dictator.[3] This chapter seeks to redress the balance by examining, 'in the round', Wilson's activities during the year 1915. He put his undoubted political skills to use – not just in intriguing with politicians, but also in liaising with the French Army. In the first part of the chapter, Wilson's career is placed in the wider context of civil–military relations in Britain during the First World War. After a sketch of the historical context, the major flashpoints of the uneasy relationship between the Frocks and the Brasshats are addressed. With the background in place, the second part is devoted to a study of Henry Wilson's career in 1915.

Civil–Military Relations in Britain[4]

Modern models of civil-military relations in liberal democracies are founded upon the supremacy of the civilian political authority. Politicians give orders to soldiers, not the other way round. Senior officers are supposed to steer clear of political controversy, especially if this were to involve taking sides in party politics. In reality, senior officers have considerable influence, and have a share in the making of policy and strategy. The convention is that they are entitled to express their views to government and civil service, provided certain rules are followed; debates, for instance, should not be conducted in public. If a general were to disagree with a decision so fundamentally that he must publicly disassociate himself from it, he has the option to resign – in the sure knowledge that his successor will do the politicians' bidding. By 1914 the United Kingdom, which was a liberal democracy, albeit an imperfect one, had developed civil–military relations which broadly followed this pattern.

The seventeenth century cast a long shadow.[5] The English experience of military government during the Protectorate of the 1650s, and the role of the army in the coup of 1688, dignified by the title of the 'Glorious Revolution', had helped produce a political culture in which the military was subordinate to civilian government. The Mutiny Act, renewed annually until well into the nineteenth century, provided the legal basis upon which the army existed. The fact that Britain lacked a military caste along the lines of the Prussian Junkers also contributed to the establishment of this political culture. Officers were typically drawn from a narrow socio-economic group, but this same class also provided politicians, clergy and other 'establishment' roles. Thus Ivor Maxse, a Coldstream Guardsman, who rose to command a corps in the course of the Great War, was the brother of the influential right-wing journalist Leo Maxse. Although a number of military families, generation after generation, provided officers for the army, British officers were not an exclusive club, isolated from wider society.

The army, and indeed the Royal Navy, lacked a tradition of overt involvement in party politics, as opposed to the involvement of individual soldiers or sailors. This is not to argue that the armed services were – or are – apolitical. Although some people are horrified at the notion,[6] by its very nature the British Army is a political organisation. To make a success of running an army in peace and war, which involves regular interaction with ministers, parliamentarians and civil servants, senior officers have to be adept at politics. However, Victorian and Edwardian Britain had no equivalent of a General Boulanger, ambitious for political power beyond his military sphere. The relatively small size of the army, when compared to its French, German or Russian counterparts, and the fact that much of it was routinely deployed overseas as imperial garrisons, were also of importance in determining its political role. The strongly tribal nature of the army, with much of it organised into fiercely independent infantry and cavalry regiments, militated against it acting as a cohesive political force, as did the fact that senior officers were by no means an homogenous body. Cliques were formed, such as the Victorian army's Roberts and Wolseley 'rings' and their Edwardian successors. Finally, it is worth noting that there is a negative reason for good civil–military relations in that, generally, governments did not pursue policies that the officer corps, or important factions within the officer corps, believed threatened their vital interests. When this situation changed, as in the case of the 1914 Curragh Incident, so did the political role of the army.

Whatever the theory, serving and retired soldiers had long played a political role in Britain.[7] Especially in the eighteenth and early nineteenth centuries, sizeable numbers served as Members of Parliament or sat in the House of Lords. This tradition had by no means disappeared by the time of the First World War. Lieutenant-General Sir Aylmer Hunter-Weston won a seat at a by-election in October 1916. The Duke of Wellington, who from the 1790s had combined a military and a political career, sat in the Cabinet, including spells as Prime Minister from 1828 to 1830, and briefly in 1834. Even after Waterloo, technically, Wellington was a serving soldier, as field marshals never retire, and thus provided a precedent for Field Marshal Earl Kitchener of Khartoum to sit as Secretary of State for War in 1914–16. Another field marshal, the Victorian military hero Lord Roberts, had a high profile political role in the years immediately before the Great War as President of the National Service League, a pressure group seeking compulsory military training. He was opposed by General Sir Ian Hamilton, a rare Liberal among this group of Unionist (i.e. Conservative)-inclined soldiers, who wrote a book attacking 'compulsory service'.[8] If the Prime Minister, H.H. Asquith, had carried out his threat of a mass creation of peers to override the Unionist-dominated House of Lords' veto of the 1911 Parliament Bill, Hamilton might well have sat on the government benches in the upper chamber of parliament. And of course in the War Office, senior soldiers worked closely with ministers and civil servants. Major-General Douglas Haig played a major role during the Haldane reforms. Haig, who by instinct was a Conservative, acted as Richard Burdon Haldane's military lieutenant, becoming a staunch admirer of the great Liberal Secretary of State for War in the process.[9]

Thus, long before the Great War, there was considerable military involvement in politics. The outbreak of war in August 1914, and subsequent political decisions, brought about a huge increase in the size of the army and made it a central factor in Britain's waging of total war. As a consequence, key senior officers were propelled from the periphery of British politics to its centre. Kitchener, as Secretary of State for War, was arguably the most important figure in government in 1914–15.[10] Generals Sir William Robertson and Sir Henry Wilson, successive Chiefs of the Imperial General Staff from late 1915 until the end of the war, were important actors in national politics, far more so than their predecessors. With Brasshats being thrust unexpectedly into the political limelight, it was inevitable that there would be tension with the Frocks. What gave the relationship a particular edge was the fact that the greatest crisis in British civil–military relations since the seventeenth century took place shortly before the outbreak of war with Germany.

In 1912 H.H. Asquith's Liberal government, reliant on the votes of Irish Parliamentary Party MPs to stay in power, introduced a bill to grant Home Rule to Ireland. This proposal of a limited form of devolved government met with such fierce opposition from Ulster Unionists that Ireland was on the brink of civil war by the beginning of 1914. A group of Anglo-Irish army officers, centred around 3 Cavalry Brigade stationed at the Curragh camp outside Dublin, threatened to resign their commissions rather than lead their troops north to coerce Ulster into accepting Home Rule. The crisis divided the officer corps but was ultimately defused. It had raised the spectre of at least part of the leadership of the British Army refusing to obey the orders of the elected government. What differentiated the Curragh Incident from previous political crises was that the generally even tenor of civil–military relations was disturbed because government policy touched directly on the interests of an important group within the British officer corps. That this potential defying of the orders of an elected government had occurred so recently doubtless acted as an unspoken influence on civil–military relations during the Great War.[11]

Strains in the relationships between politicians and generals were not confined to Britain. In France Marshal Joseph Joffre wielded enormous power in the Zone of the Armies (a classic study of French civil–military relations refers to 'military dictatorship'[12]) and the elected government in Paris spent much of 1915 trying to assert its authority. France maintained a front based around the Greek port of Salonika from the end of 1915 (to which their British allies were reluctant contributors) in part because of the need to provide an independent command for the politically powerful General Maurice Sarrail.[13] Under Hindenburg and Ludendorff German high command was, by the end of 1916, exercising a 'silent dictatorship' over the state. While civilian politicians remained in the public eye, real political power rested with the generals.[14] This wider European context is important in assessing the state of civil–military relations in wartime Britain. On most occasions British generals recognised that in matters of politics there was a line that should not be crossed.

The fact that a serving soldier was appointed as Secretary of State for War in August 1914 immediately raised the likelihood of civil–military clashes. One problem was that although Kitchener held a civilian Cabinet post, he behaved as if he were also Commander-in-Chief of the British Army. This was a position which had actually been abolished ten years before, to be replaced by that of Chief of the Imperial General Staff, but until late 1915 Kitchener worked with a series of weak men in this position whom he was able to dominate. Kitchener was not well suited for collective Cabinet government, and his secretive and imperious ways annoyed and even infuriated many of his civilian colleagues.[15] Nonetheless, there is no evidence that Kitchener deliberately set out to subvert civilian government. Towards the end of 1915, dissatisfaction with Kitchener's performance, and a desire to reduce his enormous power, led to General Sir William Robertson being appointed as CIGS. An ex-ranker with an intellect and a personality that were equally powerful, Robertson negotiated the terms on which he agreed to take the job. The key was that he was recognised as the sole source of military advice to the government, often attending Cabinet meetings. This had the effect of clipping 'K of K's wings, but at the price of making Robertson a very influential actor on the political stage'.[16] Robertson's role as CIGS with greatly enhanced power was to become a major bone of contention when Lloyd George became Prime Minister.

Whatever his personal misgivings, Robertson staunchly defended Haig's attritional strategy against its critics in London. Lloyd George was horrified by Haig's methods but, as a Liberal reliant on Unionist support to keep him in Number 10, he could not move directly against either man. Robertson's positioned weakened during 1917, not least because he forfeited Haig's confidence, and Lloyd George effectively forced him into resignation in February 1918. This could have led to a major clash – Robertson was in contact with Asquith, now the Leader of the Opposition, and also with right-wing journalists, who publicly touted him as a potential prime minister. That the crisis did not escalate, either in February 1918 or during the Maurice debate in May (see below), was largely due to Robertson himself. He fought his corner stubbornly, but in spite of Lloyd George's accusations that Robertson sought the post of 'virtual dictator', evidence for this is singularly lacking. David R. Woodward has commented 'Britain was no Germany, and it is absurd really to think that Parliament would tolerate a military dictator or that Robertson wanted to become one'. Robertson went quietly to the backwater of Eastern Command. Although he hoped to be restored as CIGS, and maintained contacts with his allies in politics and the press, Robertson did not get actively involved with 'any military–political cabal'.[17]

Robertson was replaced by Henry Wilson, who initially was more to Lloyd George's taste as CIGS. Wilson, however, did not inherit all his predecessor's powers, the post of CIGS being trimmed back. In spite of Lloyd George's assertions, in reality Robertson, while robustly defending his position and carving out a novel role, essentially behaved properly towards his political masters. Lloyd George, by contrast, damaged any attempt to establish a fruitful working relationship with Robertson and Haig. In 1916, even before he became Prime Minister, as Secretary of State for War he angered Haig by privately asking French generals their opinions of their British counterparts. Inevitably, stories soon reached GHQ, with utterly predictable results.[18]

Lloyd George's behaviour contrasted strongly with that of his predecessor as Prime Minister. H.H. Asquith had been generally content to leave the generals alone, which of course endeared him to Douglas Haig. This 'hands-off' approach had contributed to a rough political consensus concerning the military conduct of the war enduring from August 1914 to the end of 1916. It had come under some strain; for instance in 1915 within the Coalition cabinet some Unionists voiced opposition to the Dardanelles campaign. Famously in August 1916 Winston Churchill, recently returned to the back benches from self-imposed exile as a battalion commander in France, managed to circulate a memorandum to the Cabinet which was highly critical of the conduct of the Somme offensive. Robertson denounced it as a 'damnable paper'.[19] However, it was not until Lloyd George replaced Asquith as Prime Minister in December, shortly after the end of the Battle of the Somme, that the political consensus over strategy and operations unravelled.[20] In 1917 Lloyd George sought to undermine Haig. In Lloyd George's Calais plot, the Prime Minister conspired with French generals to have the BEF placed under French command, with operational control of British forces in France and Flanders removed from Haig. This was a maladroit gambit, which failed to achieve its objectives and destroyed any lingering trust and respect that Britain's senior soldier had for his political master, and gravely weakened Lloyd George's hand in dealing with generals.[21]

Ironically, if anything, thereafter the government exercised less control over strategy on the Western Front, rather than more. In part this was the consequence of Haig concealing plans from London for fear of intervention – for instance, those for what became the Battle of Amiens in August 1918. But Lloyd George and his colleagues showed a curious lack of interest in operations. During the Third Battle of Ypres, or Passchendaele (July–November 1917), a campaign that Lloyd George denounced at length and with great passion in his post-war

war memoirs, operations in Belgium were rarely discussed in the War Cabinet and there was certainly no attempt to halt Haig's offensive.[22]

Lloyd George's relationship with the generals hit another low point on 7 May 1918, when he was publicly accused by Major-General Sir Frederick Maurice, a close lieutenant of Robertson's, of misleading Parliament over the number of troops available on the Western Front before the great German Offensive of 21 March 1918. Maurice knew that by writing to the press he had gone beyond what was acceptable and it marked the end of his military career. This could have prompted a major crisis in civil–military relations, as the 'Maurice Debate' in the House of Commons became a vote of confidence in Lloyd's George's government. However, the Prime Minister triumphed, not only because of his virtuoso display of oratory, but also because the prospect of the return of Asquith to the premiership marshalled many MPs into the government camp. Maurice's action was prompted by concern for the well-being of the army, not by the desire to bring down the government and replace it by military rule. Significantly, Robertson, who might have returned as CIGS as a result of the crisis, kept his distance from any conspiracy and held his counsel. Moreover, many of Maurice's fellow generals, even the highly politicised Henry Wilson, disapproved of his actions even if they applauded his motivations. Maurice had made 'a grave mistake', Haig wrote to his wife: 'No-one can be both a soldier and a politician at the same time.'[23] Unlike his diary, Haig's letters to his wife were not for wider circulation so one can safely assume that this represents his true views. Haig was no stranger to political activity, but clearly he regarded intervention in party politics, and certainly any attempt to supplant the civilian government, as beyond the pale. In this, Haig reflected the ethos of the British officer corps. As Hew Strachan has correctly argued, the Maurice Debate demonstrated 'that the urge to intervene [in politics] prompted by military professionalism was contained within reasonably tight limits'.[24] This assessment speaks volumes about the state of civil–military relations in Britain during the Great War.

There is one important exception to this rule of generals adhering to a self-denying ordinance. Field Marshal Sir John French, Haig's predecessor as C-in-C of the BEF, conspired with Charles à Court Repington, a former army officer and the military correspondent of *The Times*, to attack the government. The context was the failure of the BEF's offensive at Aubers Ridge on 9 May 1915. French sought to deflect the blame by drawing attention to the lack of shells available to the attacking force. It is likely that French had his enemy, Kitchener, in his sights, rather than Asquith and the Liberal government, although he may not have greatly cared if either of the latter sustained collateral damage. Armed with information supplied by French, on 14 May an inflammatory article was published in *The Times*. This was followed seven days later by another piece in a second paper owned by Lord Northcliffe, the *Daily Mail*, headlined 'The Shells Scandal: Lord Kitchener's tragic blunder'. On 17 May the Liberal government had fallen, shortly to be replaced by a Liberal–Unionist coalition headed by Asquith. In his post-war memoirs, French boasted that he had brought the government down in the national interest: 'For my unprecedented action I claim that no other course lay open to me. To organise the nation's industrial resources upon a stupendous scale was the only way if we were to continue with success the great struggle which lay before us, and I feel that the result achieved fully warranted the steps I took.'[25] This was untrue. In reality, French's intervention was one of a number of factors that triggered the formation of the coalition, not least that for various reasons it suited Asquith to bring the principal Opposition party into government. Nonetheless, the significance of the most senior British Army officer on the Western Front actively intriguing with the press, and with both Unionist and Liberal MPs to destabilise the elected government, should not be underestimated and makes a telling contrast with the circumspection of other generals. Douglas Haig for one took a very different view of the conspiracy. On discovering that French's 'personal Staff are mixed up in it', he called it a 'most disgraceful state of affairs'. All this added to Haig's disillusionment with French, a man 'of a very jealous disposition'. In the field of the constitutional relationship of senior soldiers to the government, just as in many other areas of life, John French lacked sound judgement.[26]

Henry Wilson in 1915

Major-General Henry Wilson had become closely associated with French in 1914, serving as Sub-Chief of Staff to the BEF during the first stage of the war, but he appears to have had little direct involvement with the shells scandal conspiracy, noting that 'Sir John is in very bad odour at home'.[27] This might have surprised some of his contemporaries, as Wilson's reputation was indeed, as in Lord Beaverbrook's words, 'a schemer and intriguer both'.[28] Haig settled for that of an 'intriguer'. Field Marshal Sir Henry Wilson, as he became, was assassinated in 1922 by Irish Republicans before he was able to put his side of the story, as he almost surely would have done, in the so-called 'war of the memoirs'. Until recently, his image in the historiography has been that painted by C.E. Callwell's biography, the result of judicious garnering from Wilson's private diaries and letters – sadly now lost – to his wife.[29] Callwell cherry-picked the diaries for the more sensational outbursts to which Wilson was prone when letting off steam at the end of a long day. In fairness to Callwell, unguarded remarks and instant judgements on events and on those he encountered come thick and fast in the diaries, and in his private correspondence. They are highly entertaining. Their selection though, at the expense of Wilson's extensive operational, strategic and political musings, helped paint a one-dimensional picture of an untrustworthy bandwagon jumper whose only real talent was a silver tongue.[30]

Until Keith Jeffery's recent work, which provided a more rounded view of a complex and intelligent soldier, Wilson was condemned as much by his jottings as by his actions.[31] He was a divisive character, loved by some, hated by others, but recognised by all as a man who revelled in politics with both a big and small 'p'. As Jeffery has pointed out, other senior officers were also capable of plotting and 'politicking' when it suited them; the difference was:

> ... merely one of degree. Wilson was a blatant gossip who chattered incessantly about the war and its management. Not for him the silent communion

of strong, characterful men. Therein lay much of his attraction to civilian politicians, many of whom thrived on his knockabout, apparently well informed, conversation.[32]

However, as his activities in the year 1915 demonstrated, there was much more to Wilson than that. He was a substantial figure who played a significant, if generally unsung, role in the British war effort.

When Wilson became Britain's Principal Liaison Officer with the French at the end of January 1915 he was, in some ways, merely formalising a long-term arrangement. Indeed, it could be argued that helping develop, preserve, protect and, where possible, enhance Anglo-French relations was Wilson's key role in Britain's senior command structure both before and during the war. It was certainly the area in which he was most effective. In early 1915 relations between the French and British military high commands were, as might be expected in coalition warfare, often fragile and sometimes strained. French losses in the first five months of the war had been enormous.[33] Although British forces on the Western Front were increasing, with Kitchener's 'New Armies' expected by the summer, France thought her ally could and should do more. Britain's senior soldiers sometimes struggled to hide their irritation with what they considered to be unreasonable French expectations. Unfortunately for both countries, the BEF's Commander-in-Chief, Sir John French, was a difficult character who found it easier to fall out with friends than to adapt to fighting an industrialised coalition war.[34] The appointment of the Francophile Wilson to smooth the rocky road of Entente relations was, in this respect, inspired. Unfortunately for Wilson, it was not the job he wanted. Nonetheless, he held the post for almost the whole of 1915, a year of costly disappointments for the allies, and found his gift for diplomacy put to the test regularly.

Henry Wilson had spent the four years leading up to the outbreak of the Great War as Director of Military Operations (DMO) at the War Office. During this period he had devoted considerable effort to strengthening Anglo-French military understanding and developing the British Army's deployment contingency plans in the event of war with Germany. In essence this meant the immediate dispatch of the BEF to fight alongside the much bigger French Army. Wilson's meticulous planning meant that when put to the test in early August 1914 the scheme went like clockwork. When the senior command of the BEF was confirmed, Wilson, after some wrangling, was appointed Sub-Chief of Staff to Archibald Murray.[35] Murray's performance during the retreat from Mons in late August was disappointing. At one point he broke down under the pressure. Over time, Sir John's confidence in Murray waned while his opinion of the more self-assured Henry Wilson grew. The unfortunate Murray was, according to a recent monograph, 'an able, honourable, dedicated man who was in the wrong job, with the wrong commander, in the wrong place, at the wrong time'.[36]

In late January 1915 Murray was 'kicked upstairs' as Deputy Chief of the Imperial General Staff (DCIGS).[37] Before Murray was replaced, French had told Wilson, with whom he had been friendly for many years, that the Chief of Staff post was his. However, not everybody shared Sir John's high opinion of

Wilson. If 'intriguer', in late Edwardian Britain, were to have meant an inveterate gossip to whom deference to office, military or political (in private at least), was anathema, and a personality generously larded with an eye for the main chance, Wilson fitted the bill. His career suffered as a consequence. Most damaging was his role in the Curragh Incident of March 1914. Although based in London, Wilson was seen by the Prime Minister as cheer-leader for the group. Asquith got his revenge by ensuring Wilson was denied the Chief of Staff post, one he had 'worked for and dreamt of for many years'.[38] On 25 January 1915 William Robertson, who had acquitted himself well as Quartermaster General to the BEF, became its Chief of Staff.[39] Wilson was made the BEF's Principal Liaison Officer with the French Army headquarters, the *Grand Quartier General* (GQG). Putting on a brave face, he wrote, with characteristic bravado, to his wife: 'My duties will be pretty much what I like to make them, and will, in point of fact, be much what they have been, but with additional rank, which will, of course, in due course give me additional power.'[40]

Callwell's assessment was that even before this appointment Wilson had been combining his Sub-Chief role with that of 'principal intermediary between GHQ and GQG', where he was already '*persona grata*'. When he took up the new posi-tion, the French Commander-in-Chief, General Joseph Joffre, told him he was 'the best known and best beloved officer to the French Army'.[41] Jeffery observed that 'as the "political dimension" became increasingly significant in the wider prosecution of the war, so too did the value of his talents'.[42]

'Wully' Robertson quickly brought administrative rigour to the Chief of Staff function. Lord Esher wrote that the Commander-in-Chief '... likes Robertson's methods. French gives his general instructions. Robertson comes in with a few questions on half a sheet of note paper. They are answered, and everything goes forward.'[43] Wilson was thus free to concentrate on improving relations between the British and French commanders and their staffs: a much-needed function. The French had a negative opinion of their ally, he noted, because of 'our want of enterprise ... this hostility must be stopped'.[44] Wilson's pre-war work had seen him build a network of valued relationships with French colleagues. The most important was with General Ferdinand Foch, in 1915 commander of the French Northern Army Group, fighting alongside the BEF. Their friendship began when Wilson was Commandant of the Staff College and the Frenchman his opposite number at the *Ecole Supérieure de Guerre*.[45] They met at least eleven times between December 1909 and May 1914, and, when war came, this famili-arity meant 'they were able to communicate honestly with each other'.[46] Such frankness stood them in good stead throughout 1915.

In his biography Callwell portrayed Wilson as a kind of unofficial Chief of Staff, a rival to Robertson 'unhampered by responsibility, whose relations with Sir John were especially close and cordial' and who in 1914 'had actually been more in Sir John's confidence than any member of the Head-quarters Staff'.[47] This image of Wilson as Svengali to an impressionable Sir John French has per-sisted in the historiography. Those who encountered him were often disarmed by his easy charm and carried away by his rhetoric. As Douglas Haig's intelligence chief, John Charteris, wrote of an early encounter:

> At GHQ itself things are very unsatisfactory. Sir J French seems altogether in Wilson's pocket. Wilson lives with French, and Robertson in another mess altogether. I came out in the same boat as Wilson on Thursday and we talked all the way across – rather he talked and I listened. He is an extraordinarily amusing and interesting conversationalist. I can easily understand how he fascinates those who do not know him well. But it all leads nowhere.[48]

Wilson certainly talked, but, in his diary at least, it appears that Johnnie French ignored the advice as often as he took it up. All too often he complained that his chief went his own way. He had access, but the BEF's commander was too inde-pendent a character to dance to the ministrations of others. There is no doubt that Sir John French, like so many others, enjoyed Wilson's company and in April 1915 invited him to join him in his mess.[49] In his memoirs, Robertson, who was excluded, made light of the snub, but it must have rankled and meant that as time went on and Sir John's star dimmed, Robertson was one of those happy to see him go.[50] In fact, Wilson's influence with the French, especially Foch and to some extent Joffre, was far more important.

The year was dominated by a series of large, and costly, French offensives in support of which the BEF fought four battles of its own, Neuve Chapelle (10–13 March), Aubers Ridge (9–10 May), Festubert (15–25 May) and Loos (25 September–16 October). In addition, the allies took a mauling at the Second Battle of Ypres in the last week of April. Each of these encounters, to a greater or lesser extent, exposed the BEF's shortcomings in terms of manpower and materiel, particularly heavy artillery and high explosive shells. In the words of the Official Historian, shortages of all kinds meant that French and his commanders 'never had the means to conduct defence or undertake offence with reasonable confidence'.[51] Wilson concerned himself directly with the tensions surrounding these actions, shuttling between the BEF's headquarters at St Omer and Joffre's at Chantilly and acting as unofficial translator for the two Commanders-in-Chief during their occasional meetings to discuss future operations.

The events leading up to the Battle of Neuve Chapelle provide a good illus-tration of the type of work Wilson did in 1915, and its often frustrating and dis-appointing outcome. Mutual distrust between Sir John French and Joffre meant that apart from agreeing on the primacy of the Western Front, their relationship was bad.[52] On 19 February, with Wilson fresh into the liaison role, Joffre asked the BEF to take over additional line by relieving Foch's IX Corps near Ypres.[53] This had been agreed in principle the previous month and the French needed the men for an offensive against the Vimy heights around Arras. The attack was planned for March and the British intended a supporting offensive further north in the area of La Bassée. Wilson was sympathetic to the principle of taking on more line, but dismissed the extent of the proposal, that it should be completed by the end of February, as 'impossible'.[54] Ever sensitive to perceived slights, Sir John appeared to have been as much offended by the tone of the French request as its content, and he made clear he would not comply, citing lack of troops. Wilson condemned Joffre's letter as 'a stupid one, inaccurate in some important details and rather hectoring in tone'.[55] Nonetheless, it wouldn't do to refuse to help 'in the face of the reinforcements, giving a total of 36 Batt[alion]s, exclusive of the Canadians who have just finished arriving'.[56] He met Foch on succeeding days in an effort to find a solution but Sir John was adamant that he would do nothing to relieve the French until 1 April, at the earliest.[57] Anxious to avoid a major rift in Anglo-French relations, Wilson and Foch worked hard to intercede between their respective commanders:

> I asked Foch as a personal favour to me to write to Joffre at once … begging Joffre not to be angry, but to write a private line (through me) to Sir John, saying how disappointed he was, and begging him to reconsider and to help if he could, as success at Arras depended upon it. Foch promised to do this at once.[58]

The note had no effect and on 27 February French was told the regular 29th Division he was expecting to come to France would instead go to the Dardanelles for the upcoming Gallipoli campaign.[59] Sir John's response was that not only would he not take over IX Corps' trenches but that he now also wanted the French to relieve some of his cavalry units. Wilson broke the bad news to Foch and drafted an explanation for Joffre to the effect that Secretary of State for War Lord Kitchener, unaware that the 29th Division was earmarked to relieve French forces massing for a major offensive, had decided to send them elsewhere. Understandably exasperated, Wilson wrote in his diary: 'I cannot do any more, and this is our last chance. Sir John has not told Kitchener about the projected attacks, beyond the vaguest outlines, so it is possible that when Kitchener realises all this he may change.'[60] Sir John's failure to communicate with Kitchener would blight British policy throughout 1915.[61]

In fact, all that changed was that Joffre, unmoved by Wilson's creative attempt to explain away Sir John's obduracy, postponed his proposed Arras offensive, citing the BEF's failure to relieve his forces.[62] As a result, the British attack, originally intended as a supporting effort, went ahead on 10 March. The Battle of Neuve Chapelle began positively but quickly ran out of steam as a result of limited artillery and a shortage of reserves.[63] Foch provided some artillery support but was constrained in what he could do because 'Joffre had been so angered by Sir John's refusal to relieve the French that he gave strict orders that Foch should not undertake any action around Arras'.[64] As the battle was coming to an end, Foch offered eight batteries of heavy guns and wanted to know where to send them. Wilson's diary recorded that: 'Sir John would not tell him anything, said he wanted to keep his moves and Haig's secret. As far as I can judge, our fight at Neuve Chapelle is finished. We have neither infantry nor gun ammunition to go on with it. This is a disappointing business.'[65]

In the coming weeks Wilson worked hard and with some success to mend relations with the French, as ever using Foch as both sounding-board and, when necessary, as an intermediary, with the French Commander-in-Chief. Foch likewise used his close friendship with Wilson to remain at least on reasonable terms with Sir John French, if not to be able to control him.[66] Wilson's diplomatic skills came to the fore again in late March when the French Commander-in-Chief told him that he intended writing to his British counterpart and telling him bluntly that he was doing far too little to help. Knowing only too well Sir John's likely reaction to such a tone, Wilson persuaded Joffre to 'look at the picture in a different way'. By listing the many trials and tribulations facing French, 'I got Joffre round to quite a different frame of mind. I told him to give us orders, but without appearing to do so, not to refer to our numbers or dispositions but to refer to Sir John's loyalty and to leave the rest to his good heart – and me.'[67] Thanks to Wilson's undoubted diplomatic skills, while he was in post, relations between the two allies never again reached the nadir of February–March 1915; this, in itself, was a noteworthy achievement.

As if the challenges posed by its German adversaries were not enough, things were made worse for the BEF by the often dysfunctional relationships between its senior commanders and their political masters. Sir John French's relationship with Field Marshal Lord Kitchener got off to an infamously poor start in 1914 and went from bad to worse the following year.[68] Wilson succeeded in crossing swords with 'K of K' before the Expeditionary Force even left for France, over a meeting he had had with the French liaison officer Colonel Victor Huguet. Wilson condemned Kitchener as a 'd[amned] fool' in his diary and the two were on unfriendly terms thereafter.[69] It meant that Wilson was in no position to pour balm on the fractious relationship between Kitchener and French, although this relationship did improve marginally as the year progressed.[70] As we have seen, the debilitating feud had reached its climax in May, with the shells scandal.

In the summer the French began discussions with their British allies for another offensive. Wilson recognised the need for the BEF to play its full part and told Robertson: 'One thing was clear – if the French were left under the impression that a serious attack was going to be made, and then it was not made, it would lead to serious trouble.' He repeated his concerns to Sir John, stressing the need to inform the French of his intentions, and that 'a serious attack was essential ... I rubbed in the danger of failing the French'.[71] The result was the Battle of Loos, which began on 25 September in support of a much larger French offensive to the south.[72] Insufficient artillery support meant Haig, who was commanding the British forces, had been forced to use gas in the hope of clearing the German trenches. The tactic failed and the British, despite some early localised success, suffered heavy losses. Haig blamed the failure on the handling of the reserve force, laying responsibility with the Commander-in-Chief. Four days before the offensive Wilson wrote presciently:

> Apparently Haig thinks he will catch them 'quiet' at 5am and does not want to disturb them! The fact is that Haig is unfit to 'mount an attack'. He has failed every time and this is crowning folly. Having based his attack on gas he is not able to see the difference if he can't use it ...[73]

On 29 September he summed up the situation thus:

> Haig claims if he had had command of these [reserves] a day or two before he would have pushed in ... and smashed the line. Rawly[74] evidently thinks so. I imagine Robertson says so and thinks so and I think he is working all he can to get rid of Sir J and put in Haig. My own opinion is that Haig's attack was a

muddle[d] business, that he was to a great extent depending on gas and XI Corps which was Sir John's Reserve which he had no right to depend on, and that Sir J ought to have made this clear to him.[75]

Wilson's own *bête-noir* was the Prime Minister. Antipathy brought about by Asquith's apparent vetoing of his Chief of Staff ambitions grew throughout 1915 with Wilson regularly condemning 'Squiff' in both diary and private correspondence. At the heart of his criticism was the shortage of men and material for the Western Front. Wilson believed the reasons were the failure to bring in conscription, Asquith's refusal to treat the war seriously, and the government's diversion of resources to other theatres. He was not alone in opposing the Gallipoli campaign, condemning it as 'madness' and adding that 'Winston [Churchill] ought to be and must be *dégomme* for this'.[76] The failed landings at Suvla Bay in August 1915 meant the Gallipoli campaign was 'a vile and dangerous mess'.[77] He was even more opposed to the allied campaign in Macedonia and was clear who he thought responsible for both 'sideshows': 'It is an awful thing for a great country to be governed, at a time of crisis, by knaves and fools, and these only of the second order.'[78]

As the year progressed, Wilson's diary and correspondence became increasingly critical of the inconsistent and essentially *ad hoc* nature of allied policy-making. He witnessed at first hand the misunderstandings, disagreements and self-interested initiatives of the French and British high commands, and the lack of political direction at home. If the politicians were not able to provide clarity and structure, he believed, soldiers such as he himself needed to come up with some answers. In October he sent the first of a series of letters to the Conservative Party leader and colonial secretary Andrew Bonar Law, proposing the establishment of a 'Committee of Six' to coordinate Anglo-French strategy. It would be comprised of the two countries' foreign ministers, their war ministers and commanders-in-chief, and neither government would embark on 'any enterprise' without this group being consulted:

> I don't want to be in the least alarmist but I do want to impress on you the fact that we are running into serious difficulties and difficulties which can and <u>must</u> be avoided if we want to win this war … We have now reached the point when neither country is going to be so lenient to the other's faults, and it is a very short distance from where we now stand to the point where both countries will be positively on the watch for each other's mistakes. Therefore I am uneasy and if my solution is not acceptable let some other be discovered, but I beg you to be under no illusion about the dangers that lie ahead of us, or about the disasters that are sure to come if we are content to drift.[79]

Despite his lobbying, neither politicians nor soldiers had the will or wherewithal to take up Wilson's idea.[80] He would have to wait another two years for the creation of the Supreme War Council, with himself as its leading light, before genuine, structured strategic policy-making came into being.

Reviewing Wilson's role it is clear that he had both access to and influence over Sir John French, but that influence should not be overestimated. William

Robertson was a resilient and efficient Chief of Staff who gained authority as Sir John's declined. Wilson was increasingly anxious about 'Wully' and the rise of his influence. In a jibe about Wilson's apparent Francophilia: 'Robertson blurted out that he thought I ought to be at Chantilly! [Joffre's HQ] That's it. R[obertson] told me this morning that K[itchener] had told him that he was going to recast the Gen Staff at W[ar] O[office] as they did not know their business but he did not know who to move in as C[I]GS.'[81]

Wilson hoped that the post would be his, but it was not to be, as he predicted on 2 December: 'Esher now in favour of Robertson succeeding Murray. I seem to have dropped out of his picture! How amusing these fellows are.'[82] At the end of the year Sir Douglas Haig was appointed Commander-in-Chief and Robertson became CIGS. Wilson accepted the consolation prize of command of IV Corps; his final diary entry for 1915 read:

> I part from 1915 with no regret. To me, personally, it has been an unkind year, commencing with the offer by Sir John of C[hief of]G[eneral]S[taff] and [which] Squiff refused to allow, finishing with Robertson getting CIGS which at one time it looked as though I was certain to get, whether when Murray got it, or later, before Robertson got it. So long as we keep that cynical callous blackguard Asquith as PM we have a serious chance of losing the war. Wars cannot be won by INDECISION.[83]

That the alliance survived the stresses of 1915 is at least in part due to Wilson's efforts and his excellent relations with the French in a difficult year. Arguably his greatest failure was his inability to persuade the allied commanders and the politicians in London and Paris that much closer liaison, planning and ultimately unity of action were essential elements in achieving victory. For that he had to wait until the close of 1917, when he at last found an audience able to do more than simply applaud and encourage from the sidelines.

Notes

1. The phrase comes from the politician's frock coat, the sartorial equivalent of the modern-day lounge suit, and the gold braid on the general's headgear. One biography of Wilson alludes to the latter nickname: Basil Collier, *Brasshat: A biography of Field-Marshal Sir Henry Wilson* (London: Secker & Warburg, 1961).
2. Sir Sam Fay, *The War Office at War* (London: Hutchinson, 1937), p. 100.
3. Bernard Ash, *The Lost Dictator: Field-Marshal Sir Henry Wilson* (London: Cassell, 1968).
4. For a useful short comparative overview of civil military relations, with suggestions for readings, see D. George Boyce's article in Charles Messenger (ed.), *Reader's Guide to Military History* (London: Fitzroy Dearborn, 2001), pp. 107–10.
5. For an overview of constitutional developments affecting the army, see Correlli Barnett, *Britain and her Army 1509–1970* (London: Allen Lane, 1970).
6. See John Keegan's review of Hew Strachan's *The Politics of the British Army* in the *Times Literary Supplement*, 24 July 1998, p. 26.
7. By far the best study of the political role of the British Army is Hew Strachan, *The Politics of the British Army* (Oxford: Oxford University Press, 1997), to which the authors are indebted.
8. Ian Hamilton, *Compulsory service, a Study of the Question in the Light of Experience* (London: John Murray, 1910).
9. Gary Sheffield, *The Chief: Douglas Haig and the British Army* (London: Aurum, 2012 [2011]), pp. 59–60.

10. George H. Cassar, *Kitchener's War: British Strategy from 1914 to 1916* (Dulles, VA: Potomac Books, 2004).
11. I.F.W. Beckett (ed.), *The Army and the Curragh Incident, 1914* (London: Bodley Head for the Army Records Society, 1986).
12. Jere Clemens King, *Soldiers and Politicians: Conflict between France's High Command, Parliament and Government, 1914–18* (Westport, CT: Greenwood Press, 1971 [1951]), chapter 2.
13. David Dutton, *The Politics of Diplomacy: Britain and France in the Balkans in the First World War* (London: I.B. Taurus, 1998).
14. Martin Kitchen, *The Silent Dictatorship* (London: Croom Helm, 1977).
15. Cassar, *Kitchener's War*, pp. 28–31.
16. J.M. Bourne, *Britain and the Great War* (London: Arnold, 1989), p. 146.
17. David R. Woodward, *Field Marshal Sir William Robertson: Chief of the Imperial General Staff in the Great War* (Westport, CT; Praeger, 1998), pp. 209–10. See also Strachan, *Politics*, pp. 137–8.
18. Sheffield, *The Chief*, p. 191.
19. David French, *British Strategy and War Aims 1914–1916* (London: Routledge, 2014 [1986]), p. 205.
20. Brock Millman, *Pessimism and British War Policy 1916–1918* (London: Routledge, 2001), p. 26.
21. Sheffield, *The Chief*, pp. 204–8.
22. Robin Prior and Trevor Wilson, *Passchendaele: The Untold Story* (New Haven, CT: Yale University Press, 1996), pp. 141–4, 185–90.
23. Gary Sheffield and John Bourne (eds), *Douglas Haig: War Diaries and Letters 1914–1918* (London: Weidenfeld & Nicolson, 2005), p. 411.
24. Strachan, *Politics*, p. 141. See also Woodward, *Robertson*, pp. 209–10.
25. Sir John French, *1914* (London: Constable, 1919), p. 360.
26. Strachan, *Politics*, pp. 130–1; Richard Holmes, *The Little Field-Marshal: A Life of Sir John French* (London: Cape, 1981), pp. 289–91; Haig diary, 26 May 1915, in Sheffield and Bourne, *Douglas Haig*, pp. 126–7.
27. Imperial War Museum (hereafter IWM), Wilson diary, 30 May 1915. (Wilson's diary for 1915 is catalogued as: HHW 1/24/1–2.)
28. Lord Beaverbrook, *Politicians and the War, 1914–1916* (London: Oldbourne, 1960), p. 192.
29. C.E. Callwell, *Field-Marshal Sir Henry Wilson: His Life and Diaries*, two vols. (London: Cassell, 1927).
30. Haig diary, 26 January 1915, in Sheffield and Bourne, *Douglas Haig*, p. 96; Lord Beaverbrook, *Politicians and the War 1914–1916* (London: Oldbourne Book Co., 1960), p. 192.
31. Keith Jeffery, *Field Marshal Sir Henry Wilson: A Political Soldier* (Oxford: Oxford University Press, 2006).
32. Ibid., p. 154.
33. French casualties for 1914 have been estimated at 300,000 killed, 600,000 wounded, missing or captured: Alistair Horne, *The Price of Glory: Verdun 1916* (London: Penguin, 1993 [1962]), p. 19. British casualties for the same period were 89,864 killed, wounded, missing or captured: Brig.-Gen. James E. Edmonds, *History of the Great War Based on Official Documents: Military Operations France and Belgium, 1914*, II (London: Macmillan, 1925), p. 469.
34. Holmes, *Little Field Marshal*, pp. 5–6.
35. Jeffery, *Wilson*, pp. 132–3.
36. John Bourne, 'Major General Sir Archibald Murray', in Spencer Jones (ed.), *Stemming the Tide: Officers and Leadership in the British Expeditionary Force 1914* (Solihull: Helion, 2013), pp. 68–9.
37. Murray was appointed Chief of the Imperial General Staff (CIGS) on 26 September and was replaced by William Robertson on 23 December 1915.
38. IWM, Wilson diary, 30 January 1914.
39. Jeffery, *Wilson*, pp. 140–1.
40. Wilson to wife, 31 January 1915, quoted in Callwell, *Wilson*, p. 204.
41. Callwell, *Wilson*, p. 204.
42. Jeffery, *Wilson*, p. 144.
43. Churchill Archives Centre, Hankey Papers (HNKY 4/7), Esher to Hankey, ? March 1915 (precise date obscured by hole punch in original notepaper).
44. IWM, Wilson diary, 2 February 1915.

45. Wilson was appointed Commandant of the British Army Staff College at Camberley at the end of 1906; Jeffery, *Wilson*, pp. 64–6.
46. Elizabeth Greenhalgh, *Foch in Command: The Forging of a First World War General* (Cambridge: Cambridge University Press, 2011), pp. 10, 81.
47. Callwell, *Wilson*, p. 205.
48. Brig.-Gen. John Charteris, *At GHQ* (London: Cassell, 1931), 24 April 1915, p. 87.
49. Jeffery, *Wilson*, p. 147.
50. Sir William Robertson, *From Private to Field-Marshal* (London: Constable, 1921), p. 222; Robertson's predecessor Archie Murray had suffered similar treatment, once again in favour of Wilson. See Bourne, 'Murray', p. 65.
51. Brig.-Gen. James E. Edmonds and Capt. G.C. Wynne, *History of the Great War Based on Official Documents: Military Operations France and Belgium, 1915*, I (London: HMSO, 1927), p. 3.
52. Greenhalgh, *Foch*, p. 100.
53. Holmes, *Little Field Marshal*, p. 269.
54. IWM, Wilson diary, 20 February 1915.
55. Ibid., 21 February 1915.
56. Ibid., 20 February 1915.
57. Ibid., 21, 22 February 1915.
58. Ibid., 22 February 1915.
59. Edmonds, *Official History, 1915*, I, p. 72.
60. IWM, Wilson diary, 28 February 1915.
61. John Spencer, 'Friends Dis-United: Johnnie French, Wully Robertson and "K of K"', in Spencer Jones (ed.), *Courage Without Glory: The British Army on the Western Front 1915* (Solihull: Helion, 2015).
62. Edmonds, *Official History, 1915*, I, p. 73; Holmes, *Little Field Marshal*, p. 270.
63. Edmonds, *Official History, 1915*, I, pp. 74–156.
64. Greenhalgh, *Foch*, p. 102.
65. IWM, Wilson diary, 13 March 1915.
66. Greenhalgh, *Foch*, pp. 106–9.
67. IWM, Wilson diary, 23 March 1915.
68. See Holmes, *Little Field Marshal*, esp. pp. 231–5.
69. IWM, Wilson diary (HHW 1/23), 7 August 1914.
70. Callwell, *Wilson*, vol. 1, p. 161.
71. IWM, Wilson diary, 15 August 1915.
72. For the full story of the battle see Nick Lloyd, *Loos 1915* (Stroud: The History Press, 2008).
73. IWM, Wilson diary, 21 September 1915.
74. Henry Rawlinson, a close friend of Wilson, commanded IV Corps at Loos.
75. IWM, Wilson diary, 29 September 1915.
76. Ibid., 7 April; '*dégomme*': to be dismissed.
77. Ibid., 11 September 1915.
78. Ibid., 10 October 1915.
79. Parliamentary Archives, Bonar Law papers (BL 51/4/31), 27 October 1915, Wilson to Bonar Law; see also (BL 51/5/34), 19 October 1915, Wilson to Bonar Law, and (BL 52/1/10 and BL 117/1/27), 3 December 1915, Wilson to Bonar Law.
80. William Philpott, 'Squaring the Circle: The Higher Co-Ordination of the Entente in the Winter of 1915–16', *English Historical Review* (vol. 114), No. 458 (Sep. 1999), pp. 875–98.
81. IWM, Wilson diary, 24 September 1915.
82. Ibid., 2 December 1915; Lord Esher had no formal governmental portfolio but was influential in both the Asquith and Lloyd George administrations.
83. IWM, Wilson diary, 31 December 1915.

Suggested Further Reading

Callwell, C.E., *Field-Marshal Sir Henry Wilson: His Life and Diaries*, two vols. (London: Cassell, 1927)
Cassar, George H., *Kitchener's War: British Strategy from 1914 to 1916* (Dulles, VA: Potomac Books, 2004)

Collier, Basil, *Brasshat: A biography of Field-Marshal Sir Henry Wilson* (London: Secker & Warburg, 1961)

French, David, *British Strategy and War Aims 1914–1916* (London: Routledge, 2014 [1986])

French, David, *The Strategy of the Lloyd George Coalition* (Oxford: Oxford University Press, 1995)

Holmes, Richard, *The Little Field-Marshal: A Life of Sir John French* (London: Cape, 1981)

Jeffery, Keith, *Field Marshal Sir Henry Wilson: A Political Soldier* (Oxford: Oxford University Press, 2006)

Jones, Spencer (ed.), *Stemming the Tide: Officers and Leadership in the British Expeditionary Force 1914* (Solihull: Helion, 2013)

Sheffield, Gary, *The Chief: Douglas Haig and the British Army* (London: Aurum, 2011)

Spencer, John, 'Friends Dis-United: Johnnie French, Wully Robertson and "K of K"' in Spencer Jones (ed.), *Courage Without Glory: The British Army on the Western Front 1915* (Solihull: Helion, 2013)

Strachan, Hew, *The Politics of the British Army* (Oxford: Oxford University Press, 1997)

Woodward, David R., *Field Marshal Sir William Robertson: Chief of the Imperial General Staff in the Great War* (Westport, CT: Praeger, 1998)

Chapter 7

Integration, Stabilisation and Aggression: The Royal Flying Corps, the Western Front and the Control of the Air in 1915 and early 1916[1]

By James Pugh

On 15 June 1915, in his eighth despatch as Commander of the British Expeditionary Force (BEF), Sir John French declared that, '[t]he Royal Flying Corps [RFC] is becoming more and more an indispensable factor in combined operations'. Praising the aggressive spirit of the Corps, French noted that by attempting to seize control of the airspace over the Western Front, the RFC was enabling the BEF to gain the benefits of aerial reconnaissance and artillery observation whilst denying such benefits to the German Army.[2] Similar sentiments were expressed in French's ninth despatch of October 1915, and he praised the aggressive and proactive manner in which the RFC fought to establish the control of airspace.[3] For the RFC, the need to utilise armed aircraft to fight for control of the air had been articulated prior to the First World War and was bound in a culture and doctrine that saw the Corps adopt an aggressive, offensively minded approach to such activities.[4] The result, an extended attritional struggle for control of the air, has been widely criticised in the historiography because of its heavy cost in terms of both men and materiel.[5] While academic debate about the RFC is active, with scholarship by Michael Molkentin challenging these critical interpretations, popular perceptions of control of the air during the conflict, illustrated by the dominant mythology of a contest between 'aces and aircraft', remain entrenched.[6]

Indeed, Michael Paris lamented the tendency to 'dwell at great length on the romantic icons of that first war in the air'.[7] The names of Albert Ball, James McCudden and Mick Mannock, three of Britain's leading aces of the conflict, are now immortalised in popular history, but, as Molkentin observed, these individuals are not representative of the wider cohort of those that took part in aerial fighting.[8] The word 'contest', often used to describe such fighting, subconsciously and consciously manifests the sporting and chivalric qualities attributed to air power during the conflict. For John Morrow, these qualities, captured in a 'Knights of the Sky' narrative, have done much to obscure the 'genuine ... significance' of air power during this period.[9] Moreover, our understanding of air power is complicated by the central importance of technology to the evolution of aviation roles and capabilities, and, as John Buckley argued, the ability to control airspace was dependent on the technologies necessary to deploy truly effective fighting aircraft. Peter Gray supported this contention, arguing that ideas relating to the control of airspace far outstripped the technological capability to put such ideas into practice.[10] A focus on aces and aircraft, whether justified or reflecting an inherent fixation with the fusion of human and machine, can serve to prevent a fuller understanding of the ideas, doctrine and practices relating to the control of airspace: a facet of air power that Peter Dye argued was an important enabler of three-dimensional warfare during the conflict.[11]

Such issues are also shaped by wider historiographical trends relating to the First World War and, as Gary Sheffield and Spencer Jones have suggested, our knowledge of 1915 – the historiographical 'black hole' of the conflict – lacks depth.[12] Situated between the 'comic-opera' aerial fighting of the first year of the conflict and the sustained and attritional struggle that defined air power from mid-1916 onwards, the period of 1915 and early 1916 illustrated these wider trends.[13] The centenary has provided both the impetus and the opportunity to redress this balance, demonstrated by Peter Hart's chapter on the RFC in 1915 in Spencer Jones' edited volume, *Courage without Glory*.[14] Of the studies that scrutinise the RFC during 1915 and early 1916, including the British and Canadian official histories and the work of Malcolm Cooper, there is a tendency to understate the importance of the period by offering the characterisation of the Corps as passing through a phase of both experimentation and transition. Whilst this characterisation is persuasive, it is vital to consider the importance of the period in terms of shaping the RFC's understanding of, and approach to, control of the air.[15]

Accordingly, this chapter seeks to explore how the RFC approached the task of controlling the airspace over the Western Front in 1915 and into 1916, concluding before the Corps began its preparations for the Somme campaign and at the point where military aviators were given increased responsibility for the air defence of the United Kingdom.[16] This has to be set within the wider strategic and operational contexts of British air policy and the British Expeditionary Force more specifically. These contexts include the increasing and tangible importance of air power to the BEF in 1915 and the influence of the aggressive culture/ doctrine of the British Army. As John Terraine noted, the Corps 'was part of the Army and did not pretend to be anything else'.[17]

The period also saw a wider struggle between Britain's military and naval aviators for the control of resources, set against the backdrop of efforts to defend the airspace of the United Kingdom against strategic raiding by German airships, the latter in the harsh glare of Britain's baying press. Indeed, 1915 was a challenging year for the RFC in which command difficulties threatened the stability of the Corps.[18] When taken in combination with the growing effectiveness of German aviation at the battlefront, this period had the potential seriously to disrupt the RFC's ability to control the airspace over the Western Front.

While the historiography suggests that 1916 was a crucial year for the RFC in terms of establishing the technologies, doctrine and practices for the effective control of airspace, the author of this chapter argues that 1915 was also a highly significant year in which a series of factors aligned to provide the foundations from which the RFC was able to make a significant contribution to the centre-piece of Britain's military strategy during 1916: the Somme campaign.[19] These factors included the evolution of doctrine, the development of operational and tactical practices, liaison with, and learning from, allies, the creation of a stable command environment within the RFC and the articulation and presentation of a coherent vision for the control of airspace. It should be added that technological evolution, explored in some depth by Richard Hallion, was an important factor during this period too, but it will not be a focus of this chapter.[20]

These facets, which enabled the RFC to continue with the successful integration of air power into the BEF, were also shaped by understanding the importance of an offensive and aggressive approach to warfare: values at the core of the British Army's ethos and practice during the period.[21] In turn, in running battles over policy and the control of air power assets during 1915 and into early 1916, the RFC, possessing a coherent and focused vision for the application of air power, was able to outmanoeuvre its naval colleague, the RNAS, arguing that the priority in terms of human and material resources should be in supporting military operations on the Western Front.[22] By examining the evolution of the RFC's ideas and approaches to the control of airspace in 1915 and early 1916, an attempt will be made to illuminate aspects of the rich and complex history of air power during this period.

In setting the wider context of 1915, it is important to recognise that Britain was fighting as part of a coalition in which it was very much the junior member. Whilst the BEF lacked sufficient supplies of both men and materiel, the British were compelled to take the offensive during the year in order to demonstrate their willingness to assume a proactive role in the expulsion of German forces from French territory.[23] These strategic motivations were combined with considerations at the lower level in which senior commanders in the BEF believed in the importance of shifting to the offensive in order to boost the morale of British forces that had suffered heavy casualties in 1914. For example, in February 1915 Sir John French issued a memorandum that stressed the importance of 'constant activity and of offensive methods in general in dealing with the enemy opposed to us'.[24] Such instructions were in keeping with the aggressive values at the core of Field Service Regulations (1909), a document, which emphasised that, '[d]ecisive success in battle can only be gained by a vigorous offensive', facilitated by 'a firmer determination in all ranks to conquer at any cost [emphasis in original]'.[25] This wider context set the operational tone for the RFC during 1915 and into 1916, and it is not a coincidence that during February 1915 the RFC forwarded a report to French which emphasised that, '[t]he principle of attacking hostile aircraft whenever and wherever seen … has been adhered to and has resulted in the moral fact that enemy machines invariably beat immediate retreat when chased'.[26]

This aggressive approach to control of the air was captured and codified in the RFC's doctrinal publication, the *Training Manual*, published on the eve of war in June 1914.[27] This document, written before the RFC possessed the equipment and technology to seize control of the air, was significant because it attempted to ensure that RFC personnel conducted operations in keeping with the wider aggressive ethos of the British Army.[28] As evidence from the first year of the conflict indicates, the RFC was held back not by a lack of offensive intent, but by a lack of fighting aircraft, a factor reflected in repeated calls from the front for machines capable of fighting for the control of airspace.[29]

More specifically, the coalition context played a direct role in the manner in which the RFC came to conceptualise the control of airspace. For example, Dye demonstrated the close practical and intellectual ties that existed between the RFC and their French counterparts during the First World War.[30] Further research into British aviation in 1915 indicates that links between the RFC and their French colleagues, which had been established in the pre-war period, were actively developed during the year. For example, in September 1915 arrangements were made with the French Air Service to include liaison personnel with the RFC's First and Second Wings, building on an existing arrangement with the Third Wing.[31] In turn, the RFC had already started to receive reports and operational guidance from the French, including an example from mid-September 1915 in which French ground units were issued with instructions to assist French aviation units taking part in fighting in the air.[32] During the winter of 1915/16 even closer ties were developed between British and French aviators and senior commanders with both services meeting regularly to discuss the conceptual and practical approaches required to facilitate control of the air over both British and French sectors.[33] This included the regular exchange of reports during the battles around Verdun, with the British utilising such information directly to inform and shape their approach to the control of airspace during the lead into the Somme offensive. In many respects, the close and functional relationship that existed between British and French aviators during the conflict, including conceptual and practical discussions that shaped doctrine and operational/tactical practices, serves to challenge the interpretations of Elizabeth Greenhalgh, who is generally critical of the cooperation between the British and French Armies, especially in the winter of 1915/16, during the Verdun campaign and on into the summer of 1916.[34]

With regards to the evolution of doctrine, 1915 proved to be crucial for the RFC because the organisation had gained the experience necessary to reflect and expand upon its pre-war doctrine. In addition, it had officers in place with the necessary staff training to distil the lessons from aerial combat combined with a culture that stressed the importance of formally disseminating operational and tactical lessons. In particular, Robert Brooke-Popham, the Commander of the RFC's Third Wing, an officer who attended the British Army's Staff College in the pre-war period, took the time to write a short paper on the growth of aerial fighting. Brooke-Popham emphasised the need to develop both offensive and defensive tactics, which maximised the ability to deliver concentrated fire.[35] Given that air power tactics developed during the conflict from duels between individual aircraft into large multi-aircraft engagements, this report was vital in recognising the benefits that came from massing fighting aircraft to seize control of the air. While such aircraft would not be available in sufficient quantities until the Somme campaign, Brooke-Popham's report was influential in building upon the RFC's existing doctrine.

The report, widely disseminated within the RFC down to flight commander level, served to supplement the *Training Manual* and provided impetus to revise the latter during the second half of 1915. The amendments made to the *Training Manual* during this process, following the Corps' now standard method of disseminating proof copies to senior squadron commanders for comment, included the rebalancing of the document to embrace a greater emphasis on the theory and practice of fighting in the air.[36] This small, but natural expansion – some 7 per cent of the document was now devoted to fighting in the air – was effectively a *verbatim* reproduction of Brooke-Popham's February 1915 report. This example demonstrates that, as with the wider BEF, the RFC was a reflexive organisation that took time to analyse its battlefield experience. However, as Neville Parton has acknowledged, this administrative process often led to a time lag between evolving operational practice and the recommendations and guidance offered in publications such as the *Training Manual*.[37] As with earlier renditions of RFC doctrine, the important aspects at this stage were not so much the tactical advice or detail, but rather the spirit in which air power operations were to be conducted. On this point the RFC was consistent and emphatic throughout the conflict, emphasising the importance of a sustained and aggressive offensive against German air power. This approach was entirely in keeping with the wider operational ethos of the BEF.

From an operational and tactical perspective, 1915 saw significant developments in terms of the RFC's ability to control airspace, and, as an Air Historical Branch history noted, it was the year in which 'the foundations of aerial fighting were laid'.[38] A pre-war discussion in the Corps focused on the overall structure of squadrons, with a debate over the benefits of heterogeneous multi-purpose squadrons versus the creation of homogenous units utilising a single aircraft type.[39] The conclusions of such debates, which led to the creation of heterogeneous squadrons, were driven by considerations relating to the flexibility of the Corps. However, the decision was also shaped by the limited availability of aircraft, which meant the RFC was unable to field whole squadrons made up of the same type of machine.[40] Yet, as the contribution of air power continued to grow, recognised in the expansion of the RFC during the winter of 1914/15, the ability to ensure freedom of action for friendly aircraft was increasingly important for the BEF.[41] To give some quantitative perspective, the RFC expanded from some 1,200 officers and men in August 1914 to more than 7,000 a year later. By the end of 1915 the RFC had some 15,000 personnel with a front-line strength of 161 aircraft on the Western Front, a rise of some 100 per cent since March of that year.[42]

The desire to expand the RFC at such rate was given significant impetus by the role and performance of the Corps in the planning for the Neuve Chapelle offensive in March 1915. Air power played a central part in gathering intelligence which was subsequently utilised to create detailed trench maps around which the offensive was planned.[43] To secure and maintain this freedom of action, the RFC began the processes that led to the deployment of Britain's first homogenous fighter unit, No. 11 Squadron, which deployed to France in July 1915.[44] Indeed, the formalisation of fighting patrols to seize control of the air began during the time of the Neuve Chapelle offensive, with orders first issued to squadrons in the RFC's First Wing during March 1915. Additional orders in April and May paved the way for the standardisation of such operations for the rest of the war.[45]

These developments in the air were influenced, at both a practical and a conceptual level, by wider developments on the Western Front. Obliterating any notion that the war would be 'over by Christmas', the winter of 1914/15 saw the conclusion of fluid, manoeuvre warfare and the rise of attrition as the cornerstone of operational practice.[46] Shaped by the fragility of contemporary aircraft, their limited number and wider concepts relating to the decisiveness of manoeuvre warfare, pre-war RFC doctrine stated that control of the air would be established in a total and decisive fashion. This approach, reflected in the use of the term 'complete command of the air', did not survive 1915 and with increasing numbers of reliable and specialist fighting aircraft the RFC came to understand that control in the air would not be established in an absolute fashion.[47] The nature of air power, its impermanence, its flexibility and the vastness of the skies meant that control of the air had to be renewed on a daily basis. As such, rather than writing in terms of 'command', RFC doctrine, based on Brooke-Popham's insightful analysis of operational practice in early 1915, moved to focus on ideas of 'superiority in the air'; a term that reflected the expansive, attritional and impermanent nature of air power.[48] Thus, operational orders to First Wing, emphasising the continuous requirement to renew control in the air, demonstrated the practical influence of this doctrine. This process also captured the wider stabilisation of the Western Front, which meant that an element of routine could be introduced to air power practices.

From French's despatches of 1915, the manifestations of this doctrine, fighting to facilitate both reconnaissance and artillery observation for British forces while denying such benefits to German forces, were very clear. Expressed in the consistent and aggressive language of the BEF, it is evident that such despatches were written for public consumption in Britain and around the world.[49] However, analysing these despatches in greater depth reveals an aspect of what S.L. Gordon has referred to as the 'historical process of challenge and response'.[50] Given the intended audience, it is unsurprising that the despatches painted a picture of an RFC dominant in the air during this period, but as Brooke-Popham noted in a letter written in July 1915 to the Corps' Administrative Wing based in Britain, '[t]he German aeroplanes are becoming far more active and are making a regular habit of attacking our machines when on reconnaissance, and we are now having to fight for all our information'.[51] As French was to record in his despatch of June 1915, '[s]ince my last despatch there has been a considerable increase both in the number and in the activity of German aeroplanes in our front'. Reassuring his readers that such activity had taken place over or behind the German lines, further indicating the correct aggressive spirit of the RFC, French could not disguise that a shift in the balance of aerial power was beginning.[52]

Compounding this situation was the arrival at the front of the German *Fokker Eindecker*, a specialist monoplane fighter with a machine-gun synchronised to fire through the propeller. This gave the pilot of the aircraft the ability to deliver accurate fire by 'aiming' the entire plane – an improvement on a fighter armed only with a flexibly mounted gun. While the influence of the *Fokker* has perhaps been overstated, especially as so few of the type were actually active on the Western Front during 1915 and early 1916, the appearance of the aircraft did serve to embolden Germany's Air Service into more aggressive action.[53] As French was to write in this despatch of October 1915, '[t]he volume of work performed steadily increases; the amount of flying has been more than doubled during this period. There have been more than 240 combats in the air, and in nearly every case our pilots have had to seek the enemy behind his own lines.'[54]

As the RFC's own statistics make clear, there was a significant rise in RFC casualties during the latter half of 1915, demonstrating the tangible impact of the *Fokker*, its effects on the morale and aggressiveness of the German Air Service and the wider growth of air power activity during the period. The RFC clearly saw improved technology as a fundamental requirement, and a wing commanders' conference of August 1915 focused on the desire for improvement of existing aircraft while developing and deploying dedicated fighting aircraft alongside multi-role aircraft capable of projecting a bubble of aerial control around their operations.[55] However, lacking aircraft capable of challenging the *Fokker* on its own terms, the RFC demonstrated a tactical flexibility that, given the consistent aggressive rhetoric of the Corps, is often downplayed in the historiography. Building on Brooke-Popham's paper of February 1915, the senior commanders in the RFC noted the importance of conducting reconnaissance operations by utilising pairs or flights of aircraft – three to four machines – to provide mutual support and security.[56] This was a sensible precaution until effective fighting aircraft were available to allow the RFC to regain the initiative in the air in the run-up to the Somme offensive, and the practice of escorting reconnaissance machines and formation flying was formalised during early 1916.[57]

While it is possible to characterise the language of French's despatches as shaped for consumption by a public audience, an examination of the RFC's own combat reports from the latter half of 1915 indicates that its pilots expressed themselves in similarly high-spirited and offensively minded language. Significantly, the combat report as a vehicle by which to gather knowledge and analyse the ongoing evolution of aerial fighting was only formalised in the RFC during 1915. For example, such reports only began to be submitted in April 1915, and a standard pro forma to record combat reports appears only to have been created in June 1915.[58] These reports had another function and, as Christopher Cole has written with regard to the introduction of official RFC communiques during the summer of 1915, '[a]ny rapidly expanding organisation sooner or later reaches a point where its component units become out of touch with the overall aims and achievements. Enthusiasm, efficiency and morale can obviously be raised if this situation is remedied.'[59] The narrative aspects of the combat report were featured regularly in RFC communiques, which were issued on a weekly basis by the RFC's headquarters.

In examining the combat reports for No. 11 Squadron, giving 'chase' or 'pursuit' to German machines was a linguistic feature during the latter half of 1915, and it is clear from this evidence that while an offensive ethos was being fostered on squadrons of the Corps via the RFC's own doctrine and the wider ethos of the

British Army, its pilots also embodied these values.[60] Of course, from a practical standpoint, the aircraft possessed by No. 11 Squadron, the Vickers Fighter, lacked the speed necessary to catch many German aircraft types and so the squadron spent much time 'chasing' rather than 'catching'.[61] By circulating such reports within the Corps, the RFC was able further to cement these offensive/ aggressive values whilst sharing the latest knowledge and evolving tactical prac- tices. The latter became particularly important as the RFC's control of airspace came to be contested in a serious manner in the winter of 1915, and tactical advice filtered through in reports and communiques as encounters with the *Fokker* became more frequent.[62] Also significant was the moral value of com- muniques, which served to help strengthen the resolve of the RFC when faced with its first serious test in terms of the control of airspace.

Another pressure on the RFC during this period was the ongoing struggle over resources and air policy, which Alfred Gollin traces to pre-war arguments regard- ing responsibility for the air defence of the United Kingdom.[63] While Admiralty and War Office discussions over such policy are well documented by Ferris, by Cooper and by the official historian, this process had the potential to derail the RFC's ability to control the air at the battlefront as calls for aircraft to protect British airspace could only come at the expense of resources to support the BEF in France.[64] As H.A. Jones, the Official Historian, commented, 'it has never been the British way for one service to hold anything back when another service was giving all', and the RFC provided support to the British Army in keeping with this mantra.[65] Importantly, the coherence of RFC doctrine and its integration into the BEF by mid-1915 meant that it could resist calls for the Corps to assume a more central role in home defence duties. Such calls only grew in frequency and intensity as the inadequacy of Britain's air defences were demonstrated by German airship raiding against cities in northern England during mid- to late 1915, a situation inflamed by the hysterical tone of the Northcliffe press.[66]

The result, which saw an extended administrative battle during the latter half of 1915 and into early 1916, with the Admiralty keen to reduce significantly its responsibilities, was that the RFC was compelled to take over such duties in February 1916.[67] However, even after this stage the RFC continued to argue that the priority for both men and materiel should remain the Western Front and the Corps continued to resist calls to divert significant resources to such duties. Much force was lent to the RFC's case because of the emphatic and unrelenting argument it was able to put forward based around the importance of controlling airspace over the battlefront and the support the Corps gained from key figures inside the British Army, including Sir Douglas Haig, who would come to replace French in command of the BEF. As such, air defence schemes created between March and July 1916 were frequently watered down so as to keep defensive resources to a minimum while ensuring that the strength and capabilities of the RFC in France continued to grow during the year.[68] Naval aviators were not in a position to challenge the growing hegemony of the RFC because they experi- enced a largely dysfunctional and unproductive relationship with their parent service and, in marked contrast to the RFC, did not possess a coherent vision for the application of naval air power. Indeed, at the same time that Sir John French was praising the 'indispensable' qualities of the RFC, senior figures within the British government were criticising the Naval Air Service for being too 'aerial' and insufficiently 'naval'.[69]

It is important to note that what became clear during this period was that considerations relating to the control of airspace were not exclusively bound in military terms. While Ferris is right to conclude that German strategic raiding made little, if any, military difference during this period, it did provoke a public and political response that indicated the importance of providing at least some localised air defences.[70] While figures within the British Army and RFC resisted such thinking on the grounds that it diminished their ability to control airspace over the Western Front, at least some cosmetic steps were required to placate the British press and public. This included the transfer of already obsolete aircraft to defensive duties, coupled with a natural improvement in air defences based around the very limited capabilities of German airships. Fortunately for the RFC, air defence threats remained low until the summer of 1917, when the limitations of Britain's defensive system against more effective German strategic bombers would be highlighted in sharp relief.[71] Yet the winter of 1915/16 was crucial because it demonstrated two important points: first, that air power at the strategic level was intimately connected to air power at the tactical level. By applying pressure at the tactical level it was possible to have an effect at the strategic level and vice versa. Second, and closely linked to this concept, the RFC had stressed the important principle of utilising air power in an offensive fashion to compel an opposing force to devote resources to defensive duties, thus reducing the latter's offensive capabilities.

Beyond refining doctrine, modifying operational and tactical practices and drawing closer to their French allies, 1915 was a crucial year for the RFC because it saw a highly significant change in command and this led to a period of great stability within the Corps. As Cooper emphasised, 1915 saw difficulties at the senior command level of the RFC as Sir David Henderson, who came to command the RFC in the field during 1914 and early 1915, was first posted to 1st Division in December 1914 before returning to the Corps in early 1915, suffering with frequent bouts of ill-health during this period.[72] That Henderson was balancing two posts – he held the role of Director General of Military Aeronautics (DGMA) at the War Office – was problematic, but he had an able deputy and ample support from Lord Kitchener as Secretary of State for War.[73] With Henderson transferred to the temporary command of 1st Division and then sidelined by ill-health, the command of the RFC passed to his Chief of Staff, Frederick Sykes, a talented and driven officer who had commanded the RFC prior to the war and had played an instrumental role in developing the Corps' doctrine and infrastructure before August 1914.[74] This would not have been a problem except for the potentially dysfunctional relationship that existed between Sykes and his senior wing commander, Hugh Trenchard, who took charge of First Wing from the winter of 1914.[75]

The origin of the dispute between Sykes and Trenchard is impossible to ascertain as their respective memoirs and subsequent biographies have taken an unsurprisingly partisan line. Whether based on a clash of personalities, a lack of inter-personal skills or a more genuine grievance, it is clear that the intensity of feelings only grew in the years following the First World War.[76] The exact timings of Sykes' command of the RFC are unclear, although evidence exists of orders issued by Sykes in this role during April 1915.[77] However, the consequence of this period saw Sykes transferred to the Royal Naval Air Service to provide support for ongoing operations in the Dardanelles. The motivation for this posting is unclear, but Ash suggested that Henderson was unhappy with Sykes for criticising Henderson's dual role as both commander of the RFC and DGMA.[78] For Henderson, this period saw his return to the War Office to focus his energies exclusively on his role as DGMA, leaving Trenchard to take command of the RFC in August 1915.

Trenchard was not an original thinker, nor did he play a pivotal role in shaping RFC doctrine to this point. As both Ash and Cooper have pinpointed, Trenchard merely applied the RFC's existing doctrine, a doctrine crafted by both Henderson and Sykes and other figures in the Corps such as Brooke-Popham.[79] However, as Ash suggested, 'Trenchard's forte was in repeating and enforcing strategic concepts expressed by others, and then fighting tenaciously and successfully for them'.[80] Thus, Trenchard was already equipped with a coherent and sensible vision for the control of airspace based around the use of fighting aircraft to secure freedom of action, and it was this vision that guided his actions during his time as the commander of First Wing. In turn, he took the practices he helped develop during his time as a wing commander and applied them across the RFC during the remainder of the war, including calls for specialised training for aircrew relating to fighting in the air.[81]

Henderson may have lacked the robust qualities needed to sustain operational command during this period, but he set an important precedent in establishing a close working relationship between the RFC, HQ and the BEF's GHQ, which was based around a strong personal relationship between the organisation's senior commanders.[82] Trenchard followed this model, developing a close and functional relationship with Haig, Commander of First Army and, from the winter of 1915, Commander-in-Chief of the BEF. Trenchard and Haig had first worked together in an extended fashion during the preparation for the Neuve Chapelle offensive and it was clear that both men shared views on key matters – not least the importance they attached to offensive action – and they possessed common physical and spiritual attributes – stamina and endurance, so vital in coping with an attritional conflict on an unprecedented scale.[83] In Haig, Trenchard found a powerful sponsor who was willing to support the expansion of the RFC throughout the remaining years of the conflict. Significantly, this period saw the continued growth of the RFC, including a focus on deploying more fighting aircraft able to facilitate control of the air. By February 1916 an additional three squadrons were deployed to France, each with aircraft types that were superior to the *Fokker*.[84] This expansion and an increase in fighting aircraft allowed Trenchard to apply the RFC's existing offensive doctrine on a scale previously unimagined, placing the RFC in a position of dominance in the period leading to the Somme.

In drawing the chapter to a conclusion, it is apparent that 1915 into early 1916 was a key period in the growth of British air power on the Western Front. The developments discussed during the chapter help to demonstrate the complex evolution of air power and the central importance of the control of airspace during 1915 and early 1916. These matters are indeed too often overshadowed by an 'aces and aircraft' narrative. They were driven by the increasingly important role played by the RFC in providing support to the BEF, especially in terms of reconnaissance and artillery observation, which was dependent on fighting to establish control of the air.

The need to fight to control airspace had been recognised during the pre-war period and was captured in RFC doctrine published on the eve of war, but 1915 saw the crucial codification of operational experience, demonstrating the impermanent nature of control of the air and the need to apply attritional principles to secure and maintain supremacy. This included the instigation of fighting patrols and the use of formation flying, two factors that came to characterise the war in the air during the latter half of the conflict. That this approach, articulated in emphatically aggressive and offensively minded language, mimicked the wider ethos and doctrine of the BEF on the Western Front is no coincidence. These organisational/doctrinal factors combined with operational and tactical considerations to shape the evolution of RFC concepts and practices during this period. In turn, when faced with an emboldened German Air Service, the RFC held to the aggressive rhetoric at the core of its doctrine, but the consistency with which such language was used should not disguise the flexibility with which the RFC developed operational practices to ensure freedom of action in the air. It is also important to acknowledge that such concepts and practices were developed within a coalition context. The RFC built close connections – practically and intellectually – with their French colleagues during this period.

The period also saw the rise of Hugh Trenchard, an individual now synonymous with the RFC's much-criticised approach to the control of airspace. Building a close working relationship with Haig and possessing the stamina necessary to see the Corps through an unprecedented attritional struggle, Trenchard utilised the RFC's already clearly defined and forcefully articulated doctrine to expand the provision of aerial support to the BEF. This included a focus on the deployment of homogenous squadrons dedicated to the practice of fighting in the air. Of course, the growth of air power also reflected its increasingly important influence at the battlefront, but Trenchard helped to cement the position of the RFC as an intrinsic component of the BEF. This process also helped the RFC to resist calls to divert resources to the air defence of Britain during this period, and both human and material resources were prioritised for the Corps on the Western Front.

Notes

1. While based on original research, this chapter also draws on aspects of the author's PhD thesis. See J.N. Pugh, 'The Conceptual Origins of the Control of the Air: British Military and Naval Aviation, 1911–1918' (PhD Thesis, University of Birmingham, 2012), chapters 2, 4 and 5.
2. *London Gazette*, Supplement 29255, 10 July 1915, p. 6794.
3. Ibid., Supplement 29347, 1 November 1915, p. 10759.
4. Pugh, 'Conceptual Origins', chapter 2.

5. For example, see S.F. Wise, *Canadian Airmen in the First World War, The Official History of the Royal Canadian Air Force*, Vol. I (Toronto, CA.: University of Toronto Press, 1980), pp. 571–5.

6. M. Molkentin, *The Centenary History of Australia and the Great War; Volume I: Australia and the War in the Air* (Oxford: Oxford University Press, 2015), chapters 4, 7 and 9. Also, see J. Pugh, 'Conceptual Origins', chapter 5.

7. M. Paris, *Winged Warfare: The literature and theory of aerial warfare in Britain, 1859–1917* (Manchester: Manchester University Press, 1992), p. 2.

8. Molkentin, *Australia and the War in the Air*, pp. 160–1.

9. J. Morrow, *The Great War in the Air: Military Aviation from 1909–1921* (Washington: Smithsonian Institution Press, 1993), p. xv. For a scholarly biography that moves beyond an 'aces and aircraft' narrative, see A. Smith, *Mick Mannock, Fighter Pilot* (Basingstoke: Palgrave MacMillan, 2015).

10. J. Buckley, *Air Power in the Age of Total War* (London: Routledge, 1999), pp. 50–2; P. Gray, *Air Warfare: History, Theory and Practice* (London: Bloomsbury, 2015), p. 51.

11. P. Dye, *The Bridge to Airpower: Logistic Support for the Royal Flying Corps on the Western Front, 1914–18* (Annapolis, M.D.: Naval Institute Press, 2015), p. 139.

12. J. Bourne, 'Series Editor's Foreword', in *Early Trench Tactics in the French Army: The Second Battle of Artois, May–June 1915* (Farnham: Ashgate, 2013). Also, see S. Jones, 'Introduction: The Forgotten Year', in S. Jones (ed.), *Courage without Glory: The British Army on the Western Front 1915* (Solihull: Helion, 2015), pp. xxiv–xxx.

13. M. Cooper, *The Birth of Independent Air Power: British Air Policy in the First World War* (London: Allen & Unwin, 1986), p. 19.

14. P. Hart, 'The BEF Takes Off: The Royal Flying Corps, 1915', in Jones (ed.), *Courage without Glory*, pp. 125–45.

15. Wise, *Canadian Airmen*, chapter 12; H.A. Jones, *The War in the Air: Being the Story of the part played in the Great War by the Royal Air Force (WIA)* Vol. II (Oxford: Clarendon Press, 1928), chapters 2 and 3; Cooper, *Independent Air Power*, chapter 3.

16. J. Ferris, 'Airbandit: C3I and Strategic Air Defence during the First Battle of Britain, 1915–18', in M. Dockrill and D. French (eds), *Strategy and Intelligence: British Policy During the First World War* (London: Hambledon Press, 1996), pp. 23–66.

17. J. Terraine, 'World War I and the Royal Air Force', *Journal of the Royal Air Force Historical Society*, No. 12 (1994), p. 13.

18. M. Cooper, 'A House Divided: Policy, Rivalry and Administration in Britain's Military Air Command 1914–1918', *Journal of Strategic Studies*, Vol. 3, No. 2 (Summer 1980), pp. 178–201.

19. On the Somme campaign, see C. Duffy, *Through German Eyes: The British and the Somme, 1916* (London: Weidenfeld & Nicolson, 2006); W. Philpott, *Bloody Victory: Sacrifice on the Somme* (London: Abacus, 2010); G. Sheffield, *The Somme* (London: Cassell, 2003).

20. R.P. Hallion, *Rise of the Fighter Aircraft, 1914–1918* (Baltimore, MD.: Nautical and Aviation Co., 1984).

21. For example, see General Staff, War Office, *Field Service Regulations, Part One: Operations*. Reprinted with amendments, 1912 (London: HMSO, 1912), p. 135. (Hereafter *FSR*.)

22. Cooper, *Independent Air Power*, p. 18.

23. E. Greenhalgh, *Victory through Coalition: Britain and France during the First World War* (Cambridge: Cambridge University Press, 2005), chapter 2; R. Holmes, *The Little Field Marshal: A Life of Sir John French* (London: Weidenfeld & Nicolson, 2004 [1981]), pp. 256–8.

24. J.E. Edmonds and G.C. Wynne, *Military Operations: France and Belgium, 1915*, Vol. I (London: Macmillan & Co., 1927), p. 33.

25. *FSR* (1912 amendments), p. 126.

26. The National Archives, Kew (hereafter TNA), Air Ministry Files (AIR) 1/1176/204/1/2595 – Royal Flying Corps (RFC) Chief of Staff to General Headquarters (GHQ), British Expeditionary Force (BEF), 2 February 1915, p. 2.

27. General Staff, AP 144, *Training Manual, RFC (Military Wing)*, Part II (June 1914).

28. J. Pugh, 'Oil and Water: A Comparison of Military and Naval Aviation Doctrine in Britain, 1912– 1914', in M. LoCicero, R. Mahoney and S. Mitchell (eds), *A Military Transformed? Adaptation and Innovation in the British Military, 1792–1945* (Solihull: Helion, 2014), pp. 132–5; N. Parton, 'The

Evolution and Impact of Royal Air Force Doctrine, 1919–1939' (PhD Thesis, University of Cambridge, 2009), chapter 2.

29. For example, see TNA, AIR 1/118/15/40/36 – Précis of remarks, Commander of RFC in the Field to Deputy Director of Military Aeronautics, War Office, 9 September 1914; TNA, AIR 1/824/204/5/99 – Letter, Director General of Military Aeronautics to the Aircraft Manufacturing Company, London, 2 November 1914.

30. P. Dye, 'France and the Development of British Military Aviation,' *Air Power Review*, Vol. 12, No. 1 (Spring 2009), pp. 1–12.

31. TNA, AIR 1/920/205/5/884 – Minutes, Wing Commanders Conference, 9 September 1915.

32. TNA, AIR 1/920/205/5/885 – Translation of French GQG Order 12149, 20 September 1915.

33. Jones, *WIA*, Vol. II, pp. 164–6.

34. Greenhalgh, *Victory Through Coalition*, passim; Pugh, 'Conceptual Origins', pp. 241–8.

35. TNA, AIR 1/746/204/3/22 – Report, Commander, RFC Third Wing, 'Fighting Hostile Aeroplanes in the Air', 1 February 1915.

36. TNA, AIR 10/180 – General Staff, *Training Manual, Royal Flying Corps, Part II (Military Wing)*, Provisional 1915; reprinted with amendments 1916, pp. 71–2; TNA, AIR 1/1273/204/9/152 – 'Training Manual Part II', proof copy 1915.

37. Parton, 'Evolution and Impact', pp. 39–40. On British Army doctrine during the latter half of the First World War, see J. Beach, 'Issued by the General Staff: Doctrine Writing at British GHQ, 1917–1918', *War in History*, Vol. 19, No. 4 (November 2012), pp. 464–91.

38. TNA, AIR 1/688/21/20/11 – Air Historical Branch, 'No. 11 (Bombing) Squadron', p. 1.

39. TNA, AIR 1/119/15/40/69 – Letter, Commander, RFC to Director General of Military Aviation, War Office, 30 October 1913.

40. On the supply of machines and air power logistics, see Dye, *The Bridge to Airpower*.

41. Paper, GHQ, BEF 15 January 1915, 'Notes on Air Reconnaissance,' copy in F. Sykes, *From Many Angles: An Autobiography* (London: G.G. Harrap & Co., 1942), pp. 525–6.

42. War Office, *Statistics of the Military Effort of the British Empire during the Great War* (London: HMSO, 1922), p. 227; Jones, *WIA*, Vol. II, appendices I, II and III.

43. Jones, *WIA*, Vol. II, pp. 99–100; Edmonds and Wynne, *Official History, 1915*, Vol. I, pp. 85–6; D. Jordan and G. Sheffield, 'Douglas Haig and Air Power', in P.W. Gray and S. Cox (eds), *Air Power Leadership: Theory and Practice* (London: HMSO, 2002), pp. 270–1.

44. TNA, AIR 1/2148/209/3/199 – Letter, RFC HQ to HQ, Third Wing, 24 July 1915. Also, see TNA, AIR 1/688/21/20/11 – Air Historical Branch histories of No. 11 Squadron.

45. TNA, AIR 1/1252/204/8/7 – First Wing, RFC Operation Orders, Jan–Jun 1915. Orders of 29 March, 1, 7 and 12 April and 7 May 1915.

46. On the evolving concepts and practices of attrition, see R.T. Foley, *German Strategy and the Path to Verdun: Erich von Falkenhayn and the development of attrition, 1870–1916* (Cambridge: Cambridge University Press, 2006); W. Philpott, *Attrition: Fighting the First World War* (London: Abacus, 2015 [2014]).

47. *Training Manual, RFC (Military Wing), Part II*, pp. 47–9.

48. TNA, AIR 10/180 – *RFC Training Manual*, 1915, p. 71.

49. For example, see *London Gazette*, Supplement 29128, 14 April 1915, p. 3676.

50. S.L. Gordon, 'Air Superiority in the Israel–Arab Wars, 1967–1982', in J.A. Olsen (ed.), *A History of Air Warfare* (Washington, DC: Potomac Books, 2010), p. 153.

51. W. Raleigh, *WIA*, Vol. I, (Oxford: Clarendon Press, 1922), p. 446.

52. *London Gazette*, Supplement 29255, 10 July 1915, pp. 6794–5.

53. Molkentin, *Australia and the War in the Air*, p. 66.

54. *London Gazette*, Supplement 29347, 1 November 1915, p. 10759.

55. TNA, AIR 1/920/204/5/884 – Wing Commanders Conference, 2 August 1915.

56. Raleigh, *WIA*, Vol. I, p. 446.

57. TNA, AIR 1/521/16/12/2 – Letter, Commander of RFC to BEF, GHQ, 9 March 1916.

58. TNA, AIR 1/1216/204/5/2634 – Combat Reports, No. 1 Squadron, April 1915–October 1918; TNA, AIR 1/1217/204/5/2634 – Combat Reports, No. 5 Squadron, April 1915–September 1918; TNA, AIR 1/1216/204/5/2634 – Combat Reports, No. 3 Squadron, May 1915–October 1918.

59. C. Cole (ed.), *RFC Communiques, 1915–1916* (London: Tom Donovan, 1990), p. 11.

60. TNA, AIR 1/1219/204/5/2634 – Combat Reports, No. 11 Squadron, 1 August 1915–October 1918.
61. AIR 1/688/21/20/11 – Air Historical Branch, 'No. 11 (Bombing) Squadron', p. 4.
62. For example, see Cole, *RFC Communiques*, pp. 110–13.
63. A. Gollin, 'A Flawed Strategy: Early British Air Defence Arrangements', in R.J. Adams (ed.), *The Great War, 1914–1918: Essays on the Military, Political and Social History of the First World War* (London: Macmillan, 1990), pp. 31–7.
64. Ferris, 'Airbandit'; Cooper, *Independent Air Power*, chapter 4; H.A. Jones, *WIA*, Vol. III (Oxford: Clarendon Press, 1931), chapters 2 and 3.
65. H.A. Jones, *WIA*, Vol. VI (Oxford: Clarendon Press, 1937), p. 557.
66. Jones, *WIA*, Vol. III, pp. 105–7. For a typical example of press reporting from this period, see the *Daily Mail*, 22 October 1915.
67. Jones, *WIA*, Vol. III, pp. 153–7.
68. TNA, AIR 1/511/16/3/60 – Air Defence Instructions, March–July 1916; Jones, *WIA*, Vol. II, pp. 456–9.
69. S.W. Roskill (ed.), *Documents Relating to the Naval Air Service: Vol. I, 1908–1918* (London: Navy Records Society, Vol. 113, 1969), p. 209. Letter, M. Bonham-Carter, Prime Minister's Private Secretary to M. Hankey, Secretary of Committee of Imperial Defence, 6 June 1915. More generally, see Pugh, 'Conceptual Origins', chapter 6.
70. Ferris, 'Airbandit', pp. 60–2.
71. The result saw calls for the creation of an independent air service capable of defending Britain and striking directly at Germany. On this, see the two Smuts reports: TNA, Cabinet Files (CAB) 24/20 – G.T.1451, 'Committee on Air Organisation and Home Defence against Air Raids. First Report', 19 July 1917; TNA, CAB 24/22 – G.T. 1658 – 'Committee on Air Organisation and Home Defence against Air Raids. Second Report', 17 Aug 1917.
72. Cooper, 'House Divided'; J. Pugh, 'David Henderson and Command of the Royal Flying Corps', in S. Jones (ed.), *Stemming the Tide: Officers and Leadership in the British Expeditionary Force 1914* (Solihull: Helion, 2013), pp. 281–5.
73. On Henderson's deputy, see N. Macmillan, *Sir Sefton Brancker* (London: William Heinemann, 1935), pp. 57–69.
74. E. Ash, *Sir Frederick Sykes and the Air Revolution, 1912–1918* (London: Frank Cass, 1999), chapter 2; M. Baring, *R.F.C. H.Q.* (London: Bell & Sons, 1920), pp. 85–6.
75. Ash, *Sir Frederick Sykes and the Air Revolution*, p. 62.
76. On Sykes and Trenchard, see F.H. Sykes, *From Many Angles: An Autobiography* (London, G.G. Harrap & Co., 1942); Trenchard Papers (TP), Royal Air Force Museum, Hendon (RAFM), MFC 76/1/61 – Trenchard's Autobiographical Notes; A. Boyle, *Trenchard* (London: Collins, 1962); Ash, *Sir Frederick Sykes and the Air Revolution*.
77. TNA, AIR /2148/209/3/199 – RFC HQ, Routine Orders, 25 April 1915.
78. Ash, *Sir Frederick Sykes and the Air Revolution*, pp. 194–6.
79. Ash, *Sir Frederick Sykes and the Air Revolution*, p. 42; Cooper, *Independent Air Power*, pp. 19–20.
80. E. Ash, 'Air Power Leadership: A Study of Sykes and Trenchard', in Gray and Cox (eds), *Air Power Leadership: Theory and Practice*, p. 167.
81. TNA, AIR 1/138/15/40/281 – Letter, Commander of RFC to Deputy Director of Military Aeronautics, 25 October 1915.
82. Pugh, 'David Henderson and Command of the Royal Flying Corps', in Jones (ed.), *Stemming the Tide*.
83. Trenchard Papers, MFC 76/1/61 – Autobiographical Notes, pp. 72–3; Jordan and Sheffield, 'Douglas Haig and Air Power'.
84. TNA, AIR 1/1/4/3 – Memo, RFC HQ, 'Organization of the British Royal Flying Corps in the Field', 10 Feb 1916; Jones, *WIA*, Vol. II, pp. 158–60.

Suggested Further Reading

Ash, E., *Sir Frederick Sykes and the Air Revolution, 1912–1918* (London: Frank Cass, 1999)
Cooper, M., *The Birth of Independent Air Power: British Air Policy in the First World War* (London: Allen & Unwin, 1986)

Molkentin, M., *The Centenary History of Australia and Great War, Volume I: Australia and the War in the Air* (Oxford: Oxford University Press, 2015)

Morrow, J.H., *The Great War in the Air: Military Aviation from 1909–1921* (Washington DC: Smithsonian Institution Press, 1993)

Raleigh, W. and Jones, H.A., *The War in the Air: Being the Story of the part played in the Great War by the Royal Air Force*, Vols I–VI and Appendices (Oxford: Clarendon Press, 1922–37)

Wise, S.F., *Canadian Airmen in the First World War: The Official History of the Royal Canadian Air Force*, Volume I (Toronto, CA: University of Toronto Press, 1980)

Chapter 8

The Indian Army and the Mesopotamian Campaign, 1914–1918

By Robert Johnson

At Kut al Amara, after the intense fighting at the commencement of the Ottoman Army's investment of the town on the Tigris, the Indian Army had endured a bleak and dull winter in 1915/16, with the slow and relentless deterioration of food stocks interrupted by periodic shelling, sniping and raiding. It had been amusing to watch 'Johnny Turk' being forced hastily to evacuate his forward trenches when the annual flooding got under way, but there was precious little else for cheer. By the end of that winter the rations of the Indian infantrymen, the *sepoys*, who made up the majority of the garrison, had become meagre because they had been surrounded and cut off for weeks. To alleviate their hunger, some had taken to gnawing their leather equipment. The horses and mules were slaughtered, but the meat was tough because the animals too had been starved for so long. The weather had been particularly hard to endure with frequent storms of rain and intense cold. Casualties had been heavy in the battles that had pitched them back from Ctesiphon in the first weeks of the campaign, but the fetid conditions and lack of medical supplies made death by disease even more prevalent than through combat. Machines of the Royal Flying Corps had managed to drop a few cases of supplies, but there was too little to sustain a force of 11,000.

More heart-breaking still was the fact that, in the spring, a relief force had been heard battling its way up the Tigris to the town. It had been checked on several occasions, losing a staggering 23,000 men in the attempt to relieve the beleaguered garrison.

Then, in late March, it appeared that the relieving force under the command of Lieutenant-General Fenton Aylmer VC might break through the Ottoman lines, but even where they managed to get into the enemy trenches, they were thrown back by determined Ottoman counterattacks. In one last forlorn effort, the river steamer *Julnar*, packed with 240 tons of food, tried to force a passage up the river. She got to within a few miles but became stuck on a sand bar, and her crew was cut down by machine-gun fire from the banks.

After this failure, the commander at Kut, Major-General Charles Townshend, knew that he had no choice but to surrender, which he did at the end of April 1916. The two world wars of the twentieth century offer but two comparisons in the scale and significance of this defeat of British arms: first, that of the 2nd British Expeditionary Force in France in 1940 and second, more appropriately by reason of there being no 'Dunkirk' escape for the defeated, the surrender at Singapore in 1942. The prisoners taken at Kut were to be treated little better than the hapless Allied troops in South-East Asia a generation later.

The drama of the surrender at Kut was matched by the equally theatrical opening to the campaign. It had all begun so well for the British and Indian force. Having landed and secured Basra in the first few weeks of the war, in order to protect the terminus of the oil pipelines and the oilfields of southern Persia, they had repulsed Turkish counterattacks, and then pursued the Ottoman forces northwards. Although outnumbered at Shaiba in the spring of 1915, they had seen off and then enveloped a Turkish and Arab irregular army twice their number. Townshend had even chased the retreating Turks up the River Tigris in a flotilla of river boats known as 'Townshend's Regatta'. The British government in India had approved the penetration of Mesopotamia on the basis that it protected the approaches to Basra, and therefore increased the security of British possessions. Townshend's advance seemed irresistible and held out the possibility that Baghdad could be secured. This would represent a triumph for Britain, and assist in the diminishing of the prestige of the Ottoman Sultan, a crucial point because of the Caliph's call for a *Jihad* amongst all Muslims within the British Empire.

In his advance, Townshend's force had always been dangerously overstretched, and critics felt that he had courted disaster, even before Kut. His transport system was totally inadequate and even crucial medical arrangements were neglected. He had too few troops to fulfil his objectives so that by the time he reached Ctesiphon, just short of Baghdad, he was outnumbered by the Ottoman defenders. Even though there were reports of Turkish reinforcements *en route*, Townshend ordered his men to attack from the line of march. In a confused battle, British and Indian troops actually broke into the defences and compelled the Turks to withdraw. However, the commanding officer knew that he could proceed no further. He retreated to Kut, was pursued and besieged. When the relief force failed to reach Townshend in time, and with his supplies exhausted, he had little choice but to seek terms.

Throughout the summer of 1916 Lieutenant-General Sir Frederick Stanley Maude, who replaced the previous commander at Basra, had the opportunity to build up his forces, improve training, develop port facilities and river transport, construct a railway to supply his forward troops and prepare for further operations. He was the model of a thorough approach to warfare. By contrast, the Turkish commanders of Sixth Army, initially Nurud'din and then Khalil Pasha, deprived of any reinforcements, were forced to disband one division, the 38th, in order to reinforce the other three local formations. In short, they were thrown into more *ad hoc* arrangements.

In December Maude was finally authorised to resume the advance up the Tigris. Neutralising fortifications one by one, he adopted a methodical, combined arms approach, then switched axis in order to bypass the strongest defences to the south of Kut. The manoeuvre unhinged the Ottoman position and caused a precipitate withdrawal. Kut was taken. A similar approach was used at Diyala, where the Turks hoped to screen Baghdad.

On 11 March 1917 British troops entered the fabled city, but also captured 15,000 Ottoman troops who had failed to escape in time, leaving Khalil Pasha with just 30,000 men between Baghdad and Mosul. At this point Maude called a halt, largely to improve his logistical lines of communication and to avoid movement at the hottest part of the year. Maude died suddenly that November, but his replacement, General Sir William Marshall, pushed on towards Mosul in February 1918. Despite being reinforced, the Ottomans were driven out of Hit and Tikrit, often retreating before the British could bring their forces to bear. At Khan Baghdadi the Ottomans were enveloped by a mobile column and resistance collapsed. Marshall was then compelled to release troops to the Palestine Front and to Persia, which ended any further advance until the autumn of 1918. At Sharqat the remnants of the Ottoman Sixth Army were enveloped and defeated, and Khalil Pasha was forced to capitulate at the armistice, although Mosul was secured a few days later.

The Indian Army on Campaign

The Indian Army had begun its existence as the auxiliary 'Native' contingents of the contracted army of the Honourable East India Company in the 1740s, and in the nineteenth century there had been three separate, geographically based 'Presidency Armies', with the troublesome northwest frontier region under the direct control of the Governor-General. After calls for amalgamation, there was a period of reform between 1895 and 1903, and a single Indian Army was created by Lord Kitchener, the then Commander-in-Chief, India. Old 'presidency' titles were, in theory, abolished, but various names and nicknames survived. Crucially, and in the question of food, essentially, units retained religious practices, traditions and customs to reinforce their identity and regimental *esprit de corps*.

To stiffen the Indian Army, and provide it with heavy and field artillery, British regiments were brigaded with two or more Indian ones. The arrangement was known as the Army in India. The proportions of British and Indian troops, and the long-standing article of faith that Indian troops should be equipped only with light mountain guns, were legacies of the Indian Mutiny. It was considered a sensible precaution not to equip Indian units too powerfully.

In 1908, to ease administration, the Indian Army was divided into northern and southern armies, but the strength of the force lay in its ability to garrison every part of the subcontinent, despatch troops to pacify the frontiers and, if necessary, deploy independent brigades overseas. Before the Great War there were 39 regiments of cavalry (not including contingents of bodyguards), 95 single-battalion regiments of infantry, 12 single-battalion Pioneer regiments, and 11 double-battalion regiments (39th Garwhals and the ten Gurkha regiments).[1] There were three units of Sappers and Miners for engineer operations, mountain artillery, ordnance units, logistics teams, medical units and administrators. *In extremis*, especially on the frontier, there were Imperial Service Troops, local auxiliaries trained for the most part to a standard acceptable to the Indian Army. There were also militias, levies and scouts, who provided some regional security, especially to British Political Officers and constabulary. There was a pool of European and Anglo-Indian Volunteers who could be called on to protect installations such as the railways, and there were also sizeable private armies directed by the Princely States, such as the Hyderabad Contingents, the Central India Horse, or the local units of Malwa, Erinpura and Deoli, where the quality varied between anachronistic retainers to more modernised troops.

The legacy of the nineteenth century was not limited to titles and organisation, but also influenced the source of manpower. The Mutiny of 1857 effectively ended recruitment from Bengal, where the revolt had begun, and by reason of contemporary assumption fuelled by prejudice, men from the rural south were not considered particularly energetic or 'martial'. By contrast, Bombay and the mountainous north seemed to produce especially warlike groups, and the Indian Army recruited them extensively. Thus, for example, while there were just 5,588 Madrassis and 3,000 Tamils from the south in the army in 1904, there were 31,000 Sikhs, 32,000 Punjabis, 14,000 Gurkhas and 11,000 Rajputs.[2]

The other peculiarity of the Indian Army was the organisation of the officers. Each infantry battalion had 12 European officers; subordinate to them, regardless of experience, were 17 Indian officers carrying the Viceroy's Commission. Together they commanded 729 men in the ranks and 42 civilian 'commissariat' followers. In the cavalry the proportions were the same. Of course there were obvious cultural differences between British and Indian Army units and in the composition of the officer corps.[3] In the Indian cavalry the legacy of being 'irregular' and under the personal command of pioneering individuals gave rise to an attitude that praised initiative, carried disdain for parade ground precision (while exhibiting pride in the most splendid Indian uniforms) and cherished the horses and men – *sowars* – above all else. The fact that troopers, by the *sillidar* system, owned their own mounts and equipment made the men particularly responsible.

Of the Indian infantry, the later Field Marshal the Lord Auchinleck described a similar atmosphere of respectful relations between officers and men: 'there was no question of ordering them about – they were yeomen really and that made all the difference'.[4] Viceroy's Commissioned Officers, despite their subordination to the British officers holding the King's Commission, were the most respected of all, and guided young British officers in their role. They were referred to as 'God's Own Gentlemen'. In contrast to most European armies which expected their 'native' soldiers to learn the respective European language, in the Indian Army every officer had to learn to speak to his soldiers in their vernacular, not least because he was regarded as the neutral arbiter in any local disputes.[5] The emphasis on personal leadership imposed an obligation to lead from the front in combat, but that had its own attractions for young British officers. The appeal of command in the Indian Army was so high that in 1913, twenty of the top twenty-five cadets at the Royal Military Academy, Sandhurst, opted to join the Indian Army.[6]

The motivation of the *sepoys* and *sowars* of the Indian Army was initially not in doubt. A hierarchy of prestige, based on 'fighting quality' and physique, ran through the ethnic groups that constituted the army, and each was eager to assert its martial prowess.[7] This competitiveness existed between units recruited on the basis of territorial demarcation as much as on ethnicity, and it was common in 'mixed' units where companies were made up of a particular 'class'. The 6th Bengal Lancers, for example, consisted of one Muslim squadron, one Hindu and one Sikh, with the headquarters squadron made up of troops from all three 'classes'.[8] Half of the Regular army was drawn from the Punjab, and even regiments designated with particular regional titles might actually contain a cross-section of more competitive groups.[9] However, there was also a trait amongst some groups to enlist for the 'fight' rather than identity *per se*.

At the tactical level, certain experienced regiments of the Indian Army were highly accomplished, able to use field-craft and the skilled deployment of fire to defeat guerrilla fighters on the frontiers. However, units with little experience of mountain warfare were unsuited to the modern conditions of combat. As early as 1885, when large-scale manoeuvres were undertaken, the dispersed skirmishing techniques required of the infantry exposed the army's weaknesses in control, movement, direction and junior leadership, especially amongst Indian officers.

At the higher command level, a General Staff was created in 1903 to manage the complexities of training, military policy, operations, plans, intelligence and deployments. However, while relieving the Commander-in-Chief India of many tasks, the General Headquarters had still to manage a high volume of minor administrative matters and there was no clear chain of command to divisional level. Moreover, the Commander-in-Chief had to combine the duties of Military Member of the Viceroy's Council (1906) and Military Supply (1909). Divisional commanders were burdened with administering not only their three infantry brigades, a cavalry regiment and their artillery and pioneers, but also all the additional formations in their area of responsibility, including militias and volunteers, even though these would not be the units under their command in wartime. Indeed, when a divisional headquarters was deployed, these other units were simply abandoned, with no plan for continuity in such an eventuality. Moreover, while there was a surplus of this additional manpower, there was a paucity of vital ancillary services, including medical and administrative staff. Worst of all, there were far too few staff in each headquarters. In 1906 'A' staff of the General Branch, directed by the Chief of Staff, was concerned with training, discipline and personnel, while 'Q' staff was concerned with equipment and supply. The following year a Staff College was established at Quetta, ending older systems of patronage or dependence on the British Staff College at Camberley. The only tragedy of this excellent reform was that it came too late to produce senior staff-trained officers before the outbreak of war in 1914.

The Indian Army of 1914 was a long-service professional force but one of its fundamental flaws was that it lacked sufficient trained reserves to be able to regenerate itself in the event of significant casualties. Frontier fighting had required well-trained units with the cohesion to withstand demoralising insurgency, but casualties had, on the whole, been light.[10] The fighting had offered sufficient hazard to reinforce one's personal *izzat* (honour) or sense of fate, demonstrate attachment to one's officer and unit, and earn decorations and promotion without a high probability of death. The Afghan and Pashtun tribes' habit of murdering the wounded and mutilating the dead meant that heroic efforts were always made to recover casualties, which again reinforced cohesion.

Service in Indian regiments tended to deter the rapid turnover of personnel and therefore it was hard to generate a large cadre of reservists. To qualify for a pension, soldiers had to serve twenty-five years. By contrast, three-year short service men, who could take opportunities for periodic retraining, were few and far between and in any case insufficiently trained to be useful. Often, sickness and civilian employment rendered ex-soldiers unfit for further military service. The result was an army of some experience in mountain warfare, cohesive, with a strong sense of its exclusive identity, but without any notion of formation level operations or high-intensity 'European type' war, and unable to draw on a large pool of trained reservists.

In India, despite all the concerns about the loyalty of Indian subjects in the nineteenth century, there was particular enthusiasm for Britain's cause at the outbreak in 1914. When the Viceroy declared war on India's behalf, unfashionable though it may seem today, there was a sincere response from many Indian leaders and organisations: the All India Muslim League, the Punjab Provincial Congress, the Princely States and many thousands of individuals expressed their loyalty to the British Empire. Gandhi, not yet well known across the sub-continent, tendered a resolution to the Indian National Congress for unconditional service to the Empire. Offers of money, horses, medics, hospital ships and ambulances were made, and twenty-one of the twenty-seven princes' Imperial Service Troops contingents were mobilised. The Nizam of Hyderabad committed his troops to the war effort and gave 60 lakhs of rupees (£400,000). The Maharajah of Mysore gave a further 50 lakhs (£333,000). Enthusiasm and cohesion were not in doubt: the Jodhpur Lancers, for example, were even commanded by their septuagenarian Regent-Maharajah, Major-General Sir Pratab Singh.

Four expeditionary forces were mobilised, far more than had been planned. It was to the credit of the pre-war planners that the Indian Army had a scheme for mobilisation and deployment in place, with specialist equipment, when the war broke out. India had two infantry divisions and one cavalry brigade available for immediate operations.[11] But the requirement to expand this deployment so rapidly caused disruption and overwhelmed the depots. The Lahore and Meerut Divisions (Force 'A') were assembled and despatched urgently to France. Indian Expeditionary Forces 'B' and 'C', barely at brigade strength, went to East Africa, ostensibly to secure the coast and neutralise the German naval threat to shipping in the Indian Ocean but also to protect the British railways into Kenya for which there was insufficient manpower for defence.

Indian Expeditionary Force 'D' was despatched to the Persian Gulf in October 1914 with orders to protect the oil installations at Abadan and in southern Persia. The motive for the subsequent landings was also to maintain British prestige among the local sheikhs of the Gulf, many of whom enjoyed British protection in return for an allegiance that gave Britain hegemony in the region. Within the government of India there was anxiety that the invasion of what were, in terms of sovereignty, Ottoman domains would be 'provocative' and might precipitate belligerence, but, urged on by the India Office in the British government, the 16th Infantry Brigade of 6th (Quetta) Division was diverted from Force 'B' bound for East Africa, which perhaps contributed to the failure of operations there that November.[12] Initially the objective for Force 'D' was simply to assert a military presence at the Shatt al-Arab river at the head of the Gulf and it landed at Fao on 6 November 1914.[13] However, once war had been declared by the Ottoman Empire, following its aggression against Russia, Force 'D' was ordered to advance northward towards the town of Basra, which it captured on 21 November.

To cover its expanding area of control, the 16th Infantry Brigade was soon augmented by the arrival of the 18th Brigade, while a third brigade arrived in January 1915. In due course another infantry division would be deployed, as proposals were made for an advance up the River Tigris towards Baghdad, particularly when operations in the Dardanelles stalled in the summer of 1915.[14]

The government of India had no mechanism for long-term planning, and, as far as the campaign in southern Mesopotamia was concerned, the piecemeal approach to deciding on objectives meant improvisation for every phase of operations. There has been much criticism of this situation since the publication of the Mesopotamia Commission Report in 1917, but the context is crucial: the British government was struggling to manage its resources and make the transition to a war economy.[15] It had long been established that, in the event of a crisis in the Middle East, British expeditionary forces would form the bulk of the military effort in that region. In other words, no one had foreseen that it would be the Indian Army that would lead a full-scale invasion of Mesopotamia and of Palestine, and thus, in effect, bear the brunt of the fighting against Ottoman Turkey.

In late 1914 the Indian Army proceeded with some caution. A single brigade of 4,182 men did not have the firepower to seize Basra in a *coup de main* and it was estimated that the defences of the area might be considerable, including the blocking of the river on which all substantial movements depended. But the surprising success of the 16th Brigade in enveloping the Turkish defences at Saihan and the hurried Ottoman evacuation of Basra, leading to a collapse of law and order there, drew Force 'D' forward. Order was restored by the British and Indian troops, and economic activity resumed, boosted by the presence of the soldiers.

A series of operational successes continued to lure the Indian Army deeper into the interior. The rapidity of Townshend's advance offered the hope of seizing Baghdad, but the equally urgent withdrawal to Kut, and the subsequent fall of the town, while not threatening Basra, nevertheless carried significant strategic implications.

At the time there was a deliberate attempt to play down the significance of Kut. The British authorities in India were anxious that this defeat in Mesopotamia might encourage Muslim soldiers (who made up a significant proportion of the Indian Army) to mutiny. The Singapore Mutiny of 1915, in which an Indian battalion had killed its officers and run amok, was an indication that this was a serious and real danger. Perhaps, because of the attempt to reduce the importance of the fall of Kut, the subsequent assumption was that this theatre was relatively unimportant. Even though there had been a feeling in 1915 that the Central Powers of Germany, Austria-Hungary, Bulgaria and the Ottoman

Empire could be defeated by 'knocking away the props', by 1916 the prevailing view was that the allies should focus only on the war's centre of gravity – and that meant defeating the German Army in Europe. This view continued to hold sway in the following year, as exemplified by the British Prime Minister Lloyd George referring to the lesser importance of 'the side issues' of Africa and the Middle East, in relation to the overwhelming significance of the struggle against Germany.

The official Mesopotamia Commission Report (1917) stated that the fall of Kut had been the result of inadequate logistics, mismanagement in India, and poor decision-making by particular individuals, especially General Sir John Nixon who was in command at Basra and had permitted Townshend to go forward to Baghdad.[16] The judgements of the Commission have influenced subsequent histories considerably.[17] In essence, the Commission assisted in producing the orthodoxy that bad leadership could explain the setbacks. Townshend was singled out as an overambitious general who had taken unacceptable risks with his logistics and strategy in his headlong rush to take Baghdad. It was through hubris that early victories in 1914–15 were interpreted as Turkish cowardice, and this meant that, even when faced by greater enemy numbers at Ctesiphon, Townshend foolishly thought he could win. Arrangements over the casualties were singled out as particularly shocking. The dash up the Tigris meant that there were not enough casualty evacuation facilities and some wounded men were left untreated as they were sailed downriver for fourteen days to Basra. Other wounded men were not collected from the battlefields by the relief force, with the consequence that they either died of their wounds or were murdered by Arab irregulars sent out at night.

However, subsequent histories have acknowledged to a far greater degree than did the Commission the particularly trying conditions inexorably to be endured by soldiers and commanders in Mesopotamia. The Viceroy of India, Lord Hardinge, had gone so far as to assert that with better leadership the relieving troops would have 'easily' broken through the Turks to reach Kut.[18] The testimony of the soldiers, British and Indian, tells a very different story of floods, water-borne diseases, extreme temperatures and long distances over difficult terrain without any infrastructure at all and with limited riverine transport. After the war it was understandable, as many struggled to come to terms with the sheer scale and cost of the war they had just endured, that there was an inevitable search for scapegoats. Few seemed able to grasp that the war had occurred at a particular junction in military evolution. Whilst the range, rate of fire and accuracy of weapon systems had developed rapidly after 1870, the means of manoeuvre on the battlefield, in Europe and in Mesopotamia, had not changed at all. It was still necessary to cross open ground to close with the enemy on foot or on horseback, which left the assaulting forces vulnerable to very high casualties from modern, rapid-firing weapons. Railways, telegraph, telephone, barbed wire, preserved food and other products of the industrial revolution, when they were available, actually enhanced the power of troops in defensive positions. The configuration of rivers and deserts in Mesopotamia channelled the Indian Army into a narrow axis of advance, further intensifying the effectiveness of the Turkish defence.

But some criticisms are still valid when it comes to the conditions the soldiers endured, most particularly concerning the lack of adequate provision for the reception, treatment and safe evacuation of casualties. Townshend chose to campaign in the very hottest part of the year, which meant that troops had to toil on foot for weeks to reach their enemies. That said, Mesopotamia was unforgiving at any time of year. The relief force for Kut had to wade through spring floods, had their trenches flooded and were alternately frozen or soaked in the cool season.

Perhaps the chief criticism of the leadership was that Mesopotamia was a campaign theatre at all. The decision to launch an offensive up the Tigris in early 1915 was not the result of a clear and coherent plan, but a policy of 'drift', or, to use a modern expression, of 'mission-creep'. Instead of sticking to the defence of the coastal oil installations, close to the source of resupply and reinforcements, and also of intelligence sources and sympathetic local tribes, the British allowed themselves to be drawn into the interior. This was not, as some suggest, a war for oil, because the British already possessed the Anglo-Persian Oil conglomerate, but rather a situation where the strategic imperative was badly defined.[19] The acquisition of one position seemed to necessitate the protection of its approaches and therefore the seizure of another position further upstream. As late as 1918 some advocates of a 'forward defence' still believed that Mesopotamia would only be safe if the headwaters of the Tigris and Euphrates were also in British hands, a view that implied that the Caucasus should also be annexed. It is still a matter of debate as to whether Mesopotamia was of any strategic value to the outcome of the war. Major-General G.F. Gorringe felt the campaign was 'a side show and nobody's child'.[20] Cyril Falls later echoed Basil Liddell Hart's assessment that the campaign had not contributed to winning the war, but, on the contrary, the diversion of resources had merely helped to produce 'its dreary and bloody prolongation'.[21]

Under-resourced, over-extended and in too few numbers to achieve their objectives, it seems even more remarkable that the British and Indian troops still won most of their engagements in the first two years of the war. It is probably fair to say that the military performance of the 6th Poona Division neither deserved the defeat at Kut in 1916, nor the terrible conditions of captivity its men endured after their surrender.

Less well known is the story of the Indian Army's recovery and counter-offensive. In 1916 Maude proceeded methodically, reforming the medical and supply arrangements before attempting any operations. There was a modernisation of staff work, intelligence collection and processing, and productive development of air operations. Reinforcements were introduced, including a stronger ratio of artillery. Basra was redeveloped as a port, greatly increasing its capacity to handle large volumes of stores and munitions. A railway was constructed, and vehicles introduced to speed up the supply system. Depots were opened up along the route to the front, and a scientific approach was adopted towards the entire question of logistics.

Operational and then administrative responsibility for the campaign was placed in the hands of the War Office in London in February and July 1916 respectively, while India was relegated to the supplying authority.[22] On 1 October

1916 General Charles Carmichael Monro assumed overall direction of the theatre, integrating it into the strategy of the Middle East and the rest of the war effort against the Central Powers. This offered the opportunity for truly coordinated action against the Ottoman Empire. Monro, who had commanded the Mediterranean Expeditionary Force in the closing stages of the Gallipoli campaign, was served by an experienced staff.[23]

By October 1916 Maude had under his command 150,000 troops, consisting of the original III Indian 'Tigris' Corps and the 13th (Western) Division of the British Army, but it took weeks to ensure that medical and transport arrangements were in place and permissions had been given in London for the anticipated offensive. On the night of 13/14 December Maude opened the assault with two corps advancing in parallel up both banks of the Tigris. Heavy rain impeded progress but it was Maude's concern to minimise casualties and proceed methodically from one objective to the next that slowed the force. The process worked and Kut was retaken. After a pause north of Kut, Maude resumed his offensive on 5 March 1917 and it took just three days to reach the Diyala river, where the Ottomans had prepared defences at the confluence with the Tigris. On 9 March the initial British probing attacks were repulsed and Maude opted to outflank the river positions and threaten Baghdad. His force then assaulted the Diyala defences and overwhelmed them.

The Ottoman troops were then chased closely with the result that Baghdad fell without resistance. Some 9,000 enemy soldiers were captured in the confusion, while local residents, anticipating great destruction, greeted the peaceful British occupation with relief. Maude issued a Proclamation a week later, claiming that the British were not conquerors or occupiers but liberators. Maude was, nevertheless, the military governor of the entire Tigris plain down to Baghdad and this gave him the authority to preclude any realisation of the Governor General of India, Lord Hardinge's ambition to include the administration of the occupied provinces within the remit of the government of India.[24] (In the aftermath of the surrender at Kut, Hardinge's encouragement of a forward military policy towards that political end was roundly castigated.)

Part of the reason for Maude being authorised by Whitehall to exercise such military governance over civil affairs was that London was eager to extend control across Mesopotamian clans and tribes to prevent a costly breakdown of order. As a result, military detachments accompanied by Political Officers radiated across the region, demanding supplies and local manpower, mainly for logistical work. Only the Shi'ite holy shrine towns of Najaf and Karbala were exempted from the comprehensive policy of extraction and flag marches. Such exemptions were very largely for reasons of political and religious sensitivity: the above-named settlements were administered through local sheikhs, although they still came under British supervision. A new Directorate of Local Resources, and Supply and Transport Officers, organised the labour flows. Nevertheless, the process was something alien to many local tribes, who had little experience of centralised authority. If conditions were not maintained to their liking, resentment would stir.[25]

Maude's primary concern was to prevent the remainder of the Ottoman Army north of Baghdad joining with the 15,000-strong corps that was withdrawing from Persia under Russian pressure. The solution was to seize the rail junction at Samarrah, some 130km to the north. Marching out with 45,000 men, Maude planned four short attacks; his first objective was to prevent any attempt to flood the Euphrates plain and thus render British operations impossible; the secondary objective was to secure the western approaches to Baghdad. The first thrust was resisted strongly but the British drove the Ottomans back 35km to the Adhaim river. Maude's force took Fallujah on 19 March. However, an attempt to encircle the Turks was checked, and an attack had to be put in at Dogameh, where, despite severe losses, the two enemy forces were prised apart. The Ottomans consolidated on the Adhaim river, but the British drove them out of their positions on 18 April.

When his enemy withdrew to a much stronger series of prepared defences at Istabulat, which lay between the Tigris and the Ali Jali Canal, Maude initiated a series of attacks along the defensive lines on 21 April, and some positions changed hands several times in close-quarter fighting. The Ottomans were eventually pushed out, and occupied a low ridge some 10km from the Samarrah railway junction. The attacks were maintained and when the Turkish commander realised his position could no longer be held, Samarrah, the British objective, was secured.

Maude was confronted by the classic strategic dilemma of reaching a culminating point: although he had begun the offensive in December 1916 with an overwhelming numerical advantage, the steady attrition of casualties through combat and sickness, the need to despatch columns to carry out pacification around Baghdad, the requirement to garrison Baghdad and secure its western approaches, and the security needs of the long lines of communications back to the coast had reduced the available forces to something approaching parity with his opponents. Furthermore, the balance was tipping out of his favour.

The Turkish objective was to retake Baghdad with strategic reserves released from Anatolia but the Ottomans knew they would first have to ensure the security of Jerusalem and Palestine before moving on towards Baghdad, lest the allies break through and threaten their lines of communications in Syria.

Meanwhile, the Indian Army was endeavouring to consolidate its hold. In July 1917 an attempt to defeat the Turkish divisional garrison at Ramadi had ended in failure. In September another attempt was made. The combined effects of surprise, an envelopment and a rapid encirclement by armoured car units threw the defenders utterly off balance. Their effort to escape was cut off by cavalry and the remaining forces had to surrender the following morning.

When operations were resumed in March 1918, the 15th Indian Division took Hit without resistance, as the garrison gave way in its path. Some 300 lorries were used to add mobility to the infantry for the next phase. Cut-off groups were deployed and dug in along the anticipated line of withdrawal. As expected, the Turks offered some resistance to the conventional assault and then started to withdraw. However, they soon came under fire from the blocking groups and discipline collapsed. In a relatively short time the entire force had surrendered. The victory was so complete that, in following up, the mobile force overwhelmed the enemy supply base some 46km in the rear, and captured its personnel, including the German advisers there.

The final phase of the Mesopotamia campaign, commanded by Maude's successor, Sir William Marshall, was the result of the British government's direction that Mosul, and its valuable oil resources, should be in British hands at the end of the war. This was to be a vital diplomatic advantage for London in any peace negotiations, for it was anticipated that with Bulgaria now out of the war and an Ottoman peace overture imminent, the war would soon be at an end. Screening Mosul was the *Dicle Grubu* (Tigris Group), a remnant of the Ottoman Sixth Army. Confronted by Marshall's much stronger command of two divisions and two cavalry brigades, Hakki Bey withdrew a further 100km upriver. However, the British 11th Cavalry Brigade caught and pinned down the Turks, while the 17th Infantry Division came up in support. Through numerous delays, the British cavalry came under sustained shelling and took the decision to mount their own assault on the high ground where the Turkish guns were positioned. Arriving on horseback, the 11th Hussars dismounted and assaulted the hill, capturing the guns. The incident, when combined with news that negotiations to end the war were already under way, convinced the Turks to surrender, and so, on 30 October 1918, resistance came to an end. The British pressed on to Mosul, securing the city just after the announcement of the armistice.

Deductions from the Campaign

Criticisms of military leadership, a common aspect of First World War studies, seem more valid when the 'lessons' of previous operations are not learned. Successful armies require an ethos of 'professional learning', and some candour in appreciating what went wrong. Remarkably, the evidence suggests that the Indian Army did indeed recognise its structural and organisational weaknesses and set them right whilst on campaign, and then continued to review its approach to operations in the 1920s with a work aptly entitled *The Critical Study.*[26]

By an unhappy coincidence, Mesopotamia lay at the junction of responsibilities of government in London and the Viceroy's Council in India, and the British government's indifference to the Persian Gulf before 1914 meant that responsibility for the region fell to the under-resourced Indian authorities. The Indian Army, which provided the bulk of the personnel, had only been reconfigured in 1903 for large-scale operations outside India. While Indian Army detachments had served in East Africa and East Asia in the nineteenth century, and there had been preparations for fighting the Russians and Afghans across the northwest frontier, the forces from the subcontinent were not prepared for the demands of a simultaneous commitment to Mesopotamia, East Africa and France at the outbreak of war, and then later, Gallipoli too. There were critical shortages in transport and medical provision, and the logistical arrangements were inefficient. Having prepared before the war for the deployment of just three brigades, in 1914 the Indian authorities had to find three times that number and the demand continued to rise steeply throughout the conflict. Despite a mobilisation plan, the expansion and the shortage of officers, particularly Staff officers, meant that those who were given a staff appointment had little experience of their roles and had not served together. Intelligence collection was geared towards the frontier and central Asia, with too few personnel to manage the workload required in

Mesopotamia. Indian Army units lacked heavy artillery and, whilst many units were adequate for frontier skirmishes and garrison duty, they lacked the training for sustained operations against the modernised Ottoman Army.

Remarkably, these shortcomings in the pre-war army were overcome in the course of the Mesopotamian campaign. There were increases in the manpower available, improvements in logistics and river transport, more artillery, improved staff work, increased intelligence collection, the improvement of combined arms operations (including integration of the new air arm), and the import of ideas from the Western Front.[27] Maude commanded a very different army in 1917 from that available to Townshend in 1915. More proficient in combat, more efficient in supply and arguably more realistic about their capabilities and limits, the British and Indian forces in Mesopotamia were far more effective in 1917 but, sadly, the analysis of this achievement receives little acknowledgement.[28]

Given the Army in India's return to peacetime garrison duties and the perennial security problems of the northwest frontier, there was considerable debate in India about the need to 'modernise' the Indian Army whilst, at the same time, being able to fulfil the demands of internal security and frontier policing. Central to this debate was the role of cavalry and light infantry, and the discussion about appropriate force structures, training and tactics continued throughout the 1930s and 1940s.[29] The tendency in military history until recently has been to regard colonial warfare and imperial armies as anachronistic compared with the modern, industrial wars of Europe,[30] but the Indian Army commanders had not been unaware of the shortcomings of their army. However, colonial campaigners had tended to put considerable emphasis on traditional concepts of boldness and rapid offensive action, and frequently made do with *ad hoc* arrangements with their logistics. Townshend's drive up the Tigris fits this ethos exactly.

The Mesopotamian campaign was just as 'modern' as the fighting on the Western Front in Europe and subject to many of the same problems. The inadequate artillery bombardments of the Kut relief force in 1916 resulted in the same problems that were encountered on the Somme that year. Thick cloying mud was just as much an obstacle at the Hanna as it was in the Ypres Salient in 1917, leaving troops almost immobile and exposed to the high rates of fire of machine guns and field artillery. On 6 April 1916 the 7th Meerut Division attacked in daylight on a narrow front hemmed in by marshes. They lost 1,200 men in twenty minutes. When in 1917 Maude set out to take Kut, his men dug saps and fought for each enemy trench exactly as the allies did in Europe. Artillery was timed to drop a curtain of fire just in front of the advancing Indian infantry. At Khan Baghdadi in March 1918 a mobile blocking force was deployed in the rear of the Turkish Army by a fleet of 300 motor lorries, armoured cars and a cavalry brigade. Their success mirrored the achievements of similar motorised and cavalry forces in Europe later that year. In every respect, then, the fighting in this theatre was as 'modern' as in any other.

On the other hand, this was a campaign that illustrated important continuities of warfare. The gradual attrition of disease, casualties and climate add to the difficulties of manpower numbers and resupply until the attacking army reaches a 'culminating point'. This is the moment at which the advantages switch to the defending army. The concept certainly applied to Townshend's advance on Baghdad. It was Maude's determination to avoid a repeat of this problem that led to his more methodical approach in 1917. However, it is always a temptation to focus on manoeuvre as the solution to successful campaigning when simply 'concentrating', and being able to resupply the right number of troops *en masse*, is just as important to the outcome. Townshend had 12,000 men for his task; Maude and his successors could command 300,000 for theirs. The Mesopotamian campaign shows that our frequent obsession with the new aspects of 'modern warfare' can obscure significant continuities. Morale, mass, appropriate tactics and training were just as important as new technology and firepower.

Despite the existence of intelligence officers and consular officials across the Persian Gulf region, intelligence on Mesopotamia was limited. The predictions of Major-General Sir Percy Cox, the Resident and Chief Political Officer of southern Persia, who had first been despatched to the area in 1904, to the effect that Arabs would welcome British intervention against the Turks, proved disappointingly inaccurate.[31] Many Arabs simply remained neutral, and a few thousands actively assisted the Turks. As a result, it proved more difficult to get information on the strength of Ottoman forces facing the British Indian advance on Baghdad than expected.

Until 1920 the peoples of the Ottoman provinces of Basra, Baghdad and Kurdish Mosul had believed they would gain their independence from the British. Maude's proclamation of Baghdad in 1917 certainly indicated that Turkish rule would not be reimposed. However, when it was announced that Britain would administer the new state of Iraq under a League of Nations Mandate, there was widespread rioting.[32] The fighting quickly got out of hand, and Indian reinforcements had to be deployed.[33] Aircraft were used to bomb Iraqi groups and, at the height of the crisis, some consideration was given to the idea of using poison gas, although this was soon dismissed. Many Iraqis were furious with the British suppression of the revolt and they had a sense that the promises of 1917 had not been fulfilled. Significantly, the wellspring of Iraqi nationalist resistance was the army officer corps, suggesting a continuity not often acknowledged.

The threat posed by the declaration of *Jihad* by the Caliph in 1914, which the government of India could not ignore, indicates that we should measure the success or failure of the Indian Army's operations in Mesopotamia on the basis of how far German and Turkish strategic plans, particularly the attempts to bring down the British Empire by subversion and revolt, were frustrated.[34] A severe check was suffered by the army at Kut al Amara but the defeat was not on the scale of that of Gallipoli. Indeed, the fact that the Indian Army went on to capture Baghdad, and then drove into the Kurdish north in 1918 demonstrates a successful strategic outcome.

Despite the criticism that the British should never have embarked on the campaign, Britain felt compelled to secure its 'national interests' in the region, which equated to resources and assets like the Imperial Bank of Persia and Anglo-Persian Oil. Nor should we underestimate the importance of loyalty of Muslim subjects of the British Empire in India and Egypt and how sensitive Britain was to upholding prestige as a factor in its imperial power.[35] It is easy to overemphasise this aspect when considering the strategic motivating forces of the campaign, but, while maintaining the indefatigable image of the empire being achieved partly through bluff, it also required the willingness to demonstrate its power.[36] Indeed, it was not really a concern to acquire oil that drove the British deep into the interior in Mesopotamia, but the far older, pre-war anxieties of regional, particularly Russian, influence that Britain needed to forestall during the war and after.[37] The 'Great Game' had dominated British thinking about the region in the late nineteenth century, and the emergence of the Bolshevik threat ensured continuity in this area of policy.[38]

What emerges from these deductions is that the strategy the British developed was, in part, a reaction to the plans of the Central Powers, but combined the need to maintain the idea of imperial cohesion with some more pragmatic priorities about resources and security.

Studies of this theatre of operations have often focused on the early stages of the campaign, and there has been a particular emphasis on the failures of leadership and logistics. Less importance has been placed on the latter stages of the fighting, on the evolution of combined arms operations and on aspects of Arab resistance. In order to give due weight to the achievements of the Indian Army in the Mesopotamia campaign, we should use a more comprehensive assessment. We might also acknowledge that the conditions under which the operations were conducted were particularly gruelling and as harsh as any experienced on the Western Front in Europe. Understanding the full array of factors which shaped the operations, including the myriad constraints, the power of the contemporary armaments when ranged in defence, and the relative strengths of the belligerents, gives us a better appreciation of the courage, endurance and achievements of all those who took part.

Notes

1. The National Archives (hereafter TNA): Redistribution of the Army in India, 1904, Committee of Imperial Defence 58-D, CAB 6/2.
2. Caste Returns, 1 January 1904, L/Mil/7/17084, India Office records, British Library, London.
3. George Morton-Jack, *The Indian Army on the Western Front: India's Expeditionary Force to France and Belgium in the First World War* (Cambridge: 2014), p. 3.
4. Charles Allen, *Plain Tales From the Raj* (London: Andre Deutsch–Penguin, 1975), pp. 239–40.
5. There were two examinations, with further training in specialist languages as required.
6. Incidentally, Auchinleck succeeded; Montgomery failed. Charles Chenevix Trench, *The Indian Army and the King's Enemies, 1900–1947* (London: Thames & Hudson, 1988), p. 25.
7. There is an extensive literature on the martial races, but a clear explanation is given in David Omissi, *The Sepoy and the Raj: The Politics of the Indian Army, 1860–1940* (London: Macmillan, 1994). For a contemporary view, see George MacMunn, *The Martial Races of India* (London: Sampson Low, 1933).
8. Francis Ingall, *The Last of the Bengal Lancers* (London: Leo Cooper, 1988), p. 5.
9. The 129th Baluchis, for example, despite the title, contained no Baluchis but was made up of Pashtuns, Mahsuds and Punjabis. In Wilde's Rifles there were companies consisting of Dogras, Pathans, Punjabis and Sikhs.
10. The most significant losses of the frontier wars occurred in the 1897–98 Pathan Rising. On the Tirah expedition some 287 were killed and a further 853 were wounded, but this was exceptional. Captain H.L. Nevill, *Campaigns on the North West Frontier* (London: 1912), p. 301.

11. A further five cavalry brigades could be deployed with sufficient notice. Indian Expeditionary Force A, War Diary, Simla, October 1914, p. 136. BL, India Office records, L/Mil/17/5/3088.

12. Charles Townshend, *When God Made Hell: The British Invasion of Mesopotamia and the Creation of Iraq, 1914–1921* (London: Faber & Faber, 2010), pp. 3–4.

13. Kristian Coates Ulrichsen, *The Logistics and Politics of the British Campaigns in the Middle East, 1914–22* (Basingstoke: Palgrave Macmillan, 2010), p. 33.

14. Ghassan Atiyyah, *Iraq: 1908–1921. A Socio-Political Study* (Beirut: The Arab Institute for Research and Publishing, 1973), p. 41.

15. TNA, CAB 19/2–27: War Cabinet Commission on the Mesopotamia Campaign (1917); Stuart Cohen, 'The Genesis of the British Campaign in Mesopotamia, 1914', *Middle Eastern Studies*, XII (1976), pp. 119–32; V.H. Rothwell, 'Mesopotamia in British War Aims, 1914–1918', *Historical Journal*, 13, 2 (Jun 1970), pp. 273–94.

16. F.J. Moberly, *The Campaign in Mesopotamia, Official History* (London: HMSO, 1924–27), p. 48.

17. Andrew Syk, 'The Mesopotamia Commission: Britain's First Iraq Inquiry', *RUSI Journal*, 154, 4 (2009), pp. 94–101. See also Paul K. Davis, *Ends and Means: The British Mesopotamian Campaign and Commission* (London: Associated University Presses, 1994).

18. Hardinge to Sir Percy Cox, 14 March 1916, cited in Syk, 'Command and the Mesopotamia Expeditionary Force', p. 5.

19. Marian Kent, *Oil and Empire: British Policy and Mesopotamian Oil, 1900–1920* (London: Macmillan, 1976).

20. Mesopotamia Commission, Statements of Evidence, TNA CAB 19/8, p. 127.

21. Cyril Falls, *The Great War* (New York: 1959), p. 179.

22. *Memorandum on India's Contribution to the War in Men, Material, and Money: August 1914 to November 1918*, L/MIL/17/5/2381 India Office records, British Library; Coates Ulrichsen, *Logistics and Politics*, p. 65.

23. George Barrow, *The Life of General Sir Charles Carmichael Monro* (London: Hutchinson, 1931), p. 132.

24. David Fromkin, *A Peace to End All Peace: The Fall of the Ottoman Empire and the Creation of the Modern Middle East* (New York: Henry Holt & Co., 2001).

25. Memorandum from Arnold Wilson to the Chief of the General Staff, GHQ, 17 September 1918, L/P&S/10/619, India Office records, British Library, London.

26. *Critical Study of the Campaign in Mesopotamia up to April 1917: Compiled by Officers of the Staff College, Quetta, Oct–Nov 1923* (Quetta, 1925). An analysis of the *Study* can be found in Edwin Latter, 'The Indian Army in Mesopotamia, 1914–18', *Journal of the Society for Army Historical Research*, 72 (1994).

27. Kaushik Roy, 'The Army in India in Mesopotamia from 1916–1918: Tactics, Technology and Logistics Reconsidered', in I.W.F. Beckett (ed.), *1917: Beyond the Western Front* (Boston: 2009), pp. 131–58.

28. This is also the verdict of E.A. Cohen and J. Gooch, *Military Misfortunes: The Anatomy of Failure in War* (2006), pp. 156–63.

29. T.R. Moreman, *The Army in India and the Development of Frontier Warfare* (London: Macmillan, 1998); Kaushik Roy, 'Modernisation or Demodernisation of the Army in India: Cavalry from the First World War to the Third Afghan War, 1914–1919', paper presented at the First World War Studies Conference, Imperial War Museum, 11 September 2009.

30. This is challenged by Kaushik Roy, 'The Historiography of the Colonial Indian Army', *Studies in History*, 12, 2 (1996). See also the longer studies T.A. Heathcote, *The Military in British India: The Development of Land Forces in South Asia, 1600–1947* (Manchester: 1995) and Daniel Marston and C.S. Sundaram (eds), *A Military History of South Asia: from the East India Company to the Nuclear Era* (2008).

31. Philip Graves, *The Life of Sir Percy Cox* (London: 1941).

32. See Peter Slugett, *Britain in Iraq, 1914–32* (London: Ithaca, 1976); A.L. Macfie, 'British Intelligence and the Causes of Unrest in Mesopotamia, 1919–21', *Middle Eastern Studies*, 35 (1999), pp. 165–77.

33. Aylmer Haldane, *The Insurrection in Mesopotamia* (London: 1921)

34. David French, 'British Strategy and Winning the Great War', in B.A. Lee and K.F. Walling (eds), *Strategic and Political Rationality: Essays in Honour of Michael I. Handel* (London: Routledge, 2003), p. 207; Hew Strachan, *The First World War: A New Illustrated History* (London: Simon & Schuster, 2003), pp. 674–5.

35. John Darwin, *Britain, Egypt and the Middle East: Imperial Policy in the Aftermath of War, 1918–22* (London: Palgrave Macmillan, 1981), p. 144.

36. David French, 'The Dardanelles, Mecca and Kut: Prestige as a Factor in British Eastern Strategy', *War and Society*, 5, 1 (1987), p. 45.

37. S.A. Cohen, *British Policy in Mesopotamia, 1903–1914* (London: Ithaca, 1976; republ. 2008), p. 308.

38. Robert Johnson, *Spying for Empire: The Great Game in Central and South Asia, 1757–1947* (London: Greenhill, 2006), pp. 218–22; Keith Neilson, '"For Diplomatic, Economic, Strategic and Telegraphic Reasons": British Imperial Defence, the Middle East and India, 1914–1918', in G. Kennedy and K. Nielson (eds), *Far Flung Lines: Essays on Imperial Defence in Honour of Donald Mackenzie Schurman* (London: Routledge, 1996), pp. 103–23.

Suggested Further Reading

Johnson, Robert (ed.), *The British Indian Army: Virtue and Necessity* (Cambridge Scholars Press, 2014)

Moberly, F.J., *The Campaign in Mesopotamia, Official History* (London: HMSO, 1924–27)

Rogan, Eugene, *The Fall of the Ottomans* (Oxford: Oxford University Press, 2015)

Syk, Andrew, 'The Mesopotamia Commission: Britain's First Iraq Inquiry', *RUSI Journal*, 154, 4 (2009), pp. 94–101

Townshend, Charles, *When God Made Hell: The British Invasion of Mesopotamia and the Creation of Iraq, 1914–1921* (London: Faber & Faber, 2010)

Ulrichsen, Kristian Coates, *The Logistics and Politics of the British Campaigns in the Middle East, 1914–22* (Basingstoke: Palgrave Macmillan, 2010)

Chapter 9

Reluctant Warriors: America, 1914–17 – The President, his Men and his Circumstances

By James Cooke

In 1915, following the sinking of the liner *Lusitania*, there were demands by many Americans that this outrage should be the last straw and that the United States was well justified in declaring war against Germany. A few weeks before the 7 May event, the German government warned that any passengers sailing on British ships into the war zone did so at their own risk, but the torpedoing cost the lives of 1,200 civilians, including 128 Americans, many in the toll being children. Woodrow Wilson, the progressive, reformist President of the United States, was in a state of indecision, but with an election looming a year away he had to say something. He did, stating that: 'There is such a thing as a man being too proud to fight.' His Secretary of State, William Jennings Bryan, argued that the Germans had every right to sink British ships that were carrying contraband items, and to claim that the presence of Americans aboard those ships should prevent an attack was akin to an army using women and children as a cloak for their real purpose.

That the President spoke so forcefully did not mean that everyone around him held the same opinion. The war in Europe was less than a year old and the terrible cost in human life and in the dislocation of countless civilians had yet to be made clear. America's slow movement towards a declaration of war on 7 April 1917 involved a set of complex personalities and events. The United States was a patch-work of many ethnic groups, and some, like the Irish-Americans, opposed any help for Britain. On the other hand, there were older families, many rich and influential people, who were Anglophile. In the American South the painful memories of the Civil War had an impact on politicians who in consequence spoke of 'a rich man's war, a poor man's fight', and who exhibited distrust of northern banking and business interests. Across the old Confederacy there was opposition to entering the war in Europe. The Southern states were solidly Democrat, and President Wilson, himself a Southerner, could not alienate those states, especially since the presidential election in 1916 promised to be very close.

However, in an age when letters to newspapers and 'correspondent's reports' meant a great deal, information on the war in Europe was coming from Americans in France as ambulance drivers or witnesses from other viewpoints. For example, noted writer and literary figure Edith Wharton published books depicting the fighting and the effects on French society. She openly favoured the allied cause.

The British recognised early in the war that America was basically an Anglophone nation and that a serious propaganda campaign could and would be effective if it were to focus on the historic links between Britain and America, and on the needless destruction caused by German troops. The German conduct in Belgium and in eastern France gave grist to the mill, and the reports of mass killing of civilian men, women and even children in Dinant opened the door for a propaganda campaign. On 25 August German troops began the destruction of the city of Louvain. The shooting of civilians was followed by the burning of historic buildings including the renowned University Library, with irreplaceable manuscripts being lost. Berlin refused to condemn these actions, thereby conferring a gift for British propaganda now convincingly able to portray the acts as a symptom of the dark, heartless nature of the 'Hun', the savage barbarian. The aim of British propaganda in the United States was, of course, to end America's position as a neutral and to enlist her colossal potential manpower and industrial resource to the allied cause.

At the commencement of the war there had been a general opinion that war in Europe was none of America's business. Speakers recalled the admonition of George Washington that the United States should engage in no 'entangling alliances'. For most Americans, if they thought about it at all, this was indeed old Europe with its entangling alliances. Wilson, the politician, understood Democratic Party constituencies, relying on Italian, German and Irish voters as well as a solidly Democratic South where politicians denounced the outbreak of war as sheer madness. As a child he had seen the devastation of the Civil War in Richmond, Virginia. One of his fondest childhood memories was standing beside General Robert E. Lee. As a staunch Southern Presbyterian, Wilson carried with him a love of order and simplicity, morality and reformism, and as President of Princeton University he made a name for himself as a progressive reformer which carried him into the governorship of New Jersey, then into the White House in 1912. Two years later, this very complex man, with memories of the horror of war, a doctorate from Johns Hopkins University, an author, and a serious politician who had serious questions about the American system of national government, now had to formulate a policy for a neutral United States when, beyond her borders, a widening war engulfed the world.

In early August 1914 Wilson officially proclaimed American neutrality, and then in mid-August called on the people to be 'impartial in thought as well as in action'.[1] This sounded good, but the reality was that Americans were already taking sides.

To pay a political debt, Wilson selected William Jennings Bryan as his Secretary of State. Bryan was a Democratic Party stalwart with precious little experience in foreign affairs. Wilson had needed Bryan's many populist followers in his bid for the presidency in 1912. Bryan was a devoted pacifist who began to negotiate a series of agreements entitled 'Treaties for the Advancement of Peace', which called for arbitration by a neutral power. He tried to interest Germany in negotiations, but with little to show for his efforts. Most foreign diplomats in Washington disdained dinners at the State Department because Bryan, a vocal prohibitionist, served water or grape juice rather than wine, giving rise to the term 'Grape Juice Diplomacy'. It was good fortune for the United States that Bryan spent much time away from Washington attending prohibitionist and fundamentalist religious rallies. He was obviously not the man to occupy the position as Secretary of State when war broke out in Europe in 1914. The President spent very little time reading any communication from Bryan and, in fact, Bryan was seldom called to the White House for meetings. Basically foreign policy was directed by the President and his advisers and not by the Secretary of State. The final break between Wilson and Bryan came when Wilson sent two notes to Germany over the sinking of *Lusitania*, the first a protest over the sinking, the second a strong condemnation of Germany's actions. It was the second note that caused Bryan to resign his position because he felt the President's strong words could bring the United States close to war.

Wilson immediately nominated Robert Lansing to become the new Secretary of State. Lansing was a prominent lawyer from New York, a conservative Democrat, and a strong supporter of Wilson for President in 1912. He was well known as an expert in international arbitration, and he participated in a series of negotiations over Alaskan borders and fisheries in the Bering Sea. He was more than a superior lawyer; in 1906 he was instrumental in the founding of the American Society of International Law, and in 1909 was prominent at the inception of an academic journal devoted to international law. His reputation and expertise in foreign negotiations brought him to Washington as Counselor to the State Department, and in 1914 he advocated a 'benevolent neutrality', though his basic sympathies rested with Britain. Despite this, he was firm in protest over British blockades, arguing that they violated the freedom of the seas. As a cabinet member in 1915, he advised Wilson, privately pointing out that America had more in common with Britain than with Germany or Austria. However, Lansing was a realist in politics and wanted nothing to upset Wilson's re-election prospects.

Lansing would be a different Secretary of State from Bryan and, given his stature as an expert in international affairs and litigation, his memoranda to the President could not be ignored. There was a problem, however, in that Wilson had come to rely on old favourites such as Colonel House for opinions on the war in Europe. Lansing had to be careful in dealing with such people.

The American ambassador with the most difficult task was James Watson Gerard in Berlin. Gerard was a prominent New York lawyer but with a National Guard army background. A strong, well spoken, progressive Democrat, Gerard attracted Wilson's attention during the 1912 presidential election, and in 1913 he was appointed as the United States Ambassador to Germany. Gerard was a non-career appointee, often outspoken to the distress of his career underlings. His friendship with the British Ambassador to Germany was quite obvious. In late August 1914 Gerard and the American Embassy accepted responsibility for British interests in Germany. He and his career colleagues were appalled by German brutality in Belgium. His communiques to Lansing, and eventually to Wilson, manifested his disgust and were of special interest to Wilson, the academic scholar. Gerard had an audience with Kaiser Wilhelm II and was handed a telegram which he stated should be personally delivered to President Wilson. In it, the Kaiser argued that Germany's invasion of neutral Belgium was based on 'strategical grounds', and Wilson was asked to intercede with the Belgians to allow German troops to pass through their country, – which, in fact, they were doing – and to offer the payment of an indemnity to Belgian civilians. The neutral United States would not become involved in such proposals.

As the war dragged on beyond the time Gerard and others in prominent positions anticipated, the British government asked Gerard to look at conditions under which British prisoners of war were confined. Gerard's inspection led him to make strong protest and the German military authorities took steps to alleviate some of the problems which existed.

From the beginning of his tenure as Ambassador to Germany it was clear that Gerard did not care for the German officials with whom he had to deal and still less for their policies. The German government was aware of this and the situation got worse with the sinking of *Lusitania*. Lansing knew that Gerard's dispatches from Berlin reflected a growing anti-German bias, but Gerard was correct that there were differences of view within the German military over a declaration suspending U-boat warfare in September 1915. In January 1917 the German government simply asked Gerard to leave Germany. Three months later Wilson went before the American Congress and asked for a declaration of war against Germany.

Gerard's observations and information about Germany were interesting, but the American ambassadors in England and France sent dispatches which were similar in nature in that both were becoming advocates for Britain and France rather than maintaining a strict neutrality. The most interesting of the ambassadors was Myron T. Herrick, a republican of Ohio who had been appointed by President William Howard Taft. With Taft's defeat in 1912, Herrick submitted his letter of resignation to the newly sworn-in Wilson, who in turn indicated that he had selected William F. McCombs for the position of Ambassador to France. McCombs had been the energetic campaign manager for the now President of the United States of America. Herrick was of course aware that a new administration would select ambassadors from the party now in power, and he assured Wilson he would help the incoming ambassador. Oddly, Wilson did not respond to Herrick's letter of resignation, and when McCombs finally did arrive, the United States had, in fact, the confusion of two functioning ambassadors. This extraordinary situation arose because McCombs was not a man of personal wealth and would have to rely on an income quite insufficient for the obligatory drinks and dinner parties for which there was no funding in the embassy budget. McCombs wanted the post, but his financial situation simply did not allow him to accept it. Why Wilson had selected him when he knew that his former campaign manager had inadequate resources for the post seems a reasonable question.

With Myron Herrick in Paris as ambassador, Wilson now nominated William Graves Sharp, a Democratic congressman with experience on the House of Representatives Committee for Foreign Affairs, as the new Ambassador to France. Wilson had yet to respond to Herrick's letter of resignation, and consequently the United States still had two ambassadors at the same time. Sharp stated that it would be several months before he could take over his duties. He thought that it would be the second week of August before he could be in Paris. Herrick confided later, 'As I look back on it, I realize that I have never had such a carefree time in my life as during those first seventeen months as ambassador under the Wilson administration.'[2]

Reacting to the military situation in the war during this extraordinary ambassadorial circumstance in the early weeks of the war, the French government moved to Bordeaux and the roads out of Paris were jammed with fleeing civilians. General Joseph Gallieni prepared to defend Paris and US Ambassador Herrick became a rock of stability for Americans and for the French too.

Paris was saved by the so-called 'miracle of the Marne' and the American replacement diplomat duly took up his post. However, Secretary of State Lansing was not finished with related problems – he had Walter Hines Page, America's Ambassador to the Court of St James! In the long run the question remains: did Page represent American policies to the British, or was he an agent of British interests? Page was born in North Carolina during the Civil War and was a committed Confederate. His mother even had their white picket fence repainted to resemble a Confederate flag, and young Walter once told a Union officer that he would rather eat with the pigs than with Yankees. After a solid traditional education, Page opted for a career in journalism and literature. In 1882, while working in Atlanta, he befriended a young lawyer by the name of Woodrow Wilson, and they found each other to be a congenial conversationalist. They would meet again when that young lawyer was Governor of New Jersey and was being mentioned as a possible candidate for the Presidency of the United States.

In 1882 Page returned to North Carolina and helped to found the Raleigh (NC) *States Chronicle*, which was noted for its positive stand for education for all North Carolinians, including African-Americans. After leaving North Carolina for New York, he worked for a number of prominent magazines, and became a partner and vice-president of Doubleday, Page & Co., destined to become one of America's great publishing houses. During this time Page renewed his relationship with Woodrow Wilson, who had been selected to head the Democratic Party in the 1912 presidential election, and Page campaigned for Wilson using the skill of his pen and the depth of his purse.

In May 1913 Page took a telephone call from Colonel House, who told him that after a dinner at the White House Wilson had said: 'I've about made up my mind to send Walter Page to England. What do you think of that?' House agreed and was directed to call Page in the morning which he did.[3] It is interesting that it was Colonel House calling to offer Page the ambassadorial position and not the Secretary of State. During the war years Page continued sending letters to House, which contained much sensitive information. Needless to say, the relationship between Britain and the United States was a vital one, and Page saw himself as an Anglophile to the hilt, a position taken up when he was but a schoolboy. Both Page and Wilson had an affinity for Britain and the British form of government, but Page, as ambassador, went beyond being just an American Anglophile who enjoyed afternoon tea. In the season he was invited to join shooting parties on the great landed estates; he was liked by the British upper classes and by the public in general. They recognised in the American ambassador a true ally who saw a prospective German victory as a devastating blow to the expansion of democratic institutions.

Following the sinking of *Lusitania*, Page became an open advocate for America to join the war. In a letter to Colonel House he wrote: 'I see no possible way for us to keep out, because I know the ignorance and falseness of the German leaders. They'll drown or kill more Americans – on the sea or in America. They may at last even attack one of our own passenger ships ... [Here Page refers to possible German sabotage teams which would attack vital installations.]'[4] Page's official correspondence and dispatches to Washington became a constant litany about the unwillingness of the American leadership to recognise that the only course of action should be a declaration of war against Germany. Page had been a journalist, a first-rate writer for influential journals and newspapers. He should have recognised that Wilson faced a re-election campaign in 1916.

Wilson would run on a platform of peace, and no intervention in a foreign war. He needed the American South, where there was no enthusiasm for war, and he would do nothing to alienate the Irish-American and German-American voting blocs. Wilson and the Democratic Party wished to paint the Republican candidate, Charles Evans Hughes, as an advocate for entering the war on the side of the British and French. Much to Page's distress, Wilson's campaign stressed such slogans as 'War in Europe, Peace in America, God Bless Wilson', 'Peace with Honor, Wilson, preparedness', and 'He proved the pen is mightier than the sword', and tens of thousands of postcards extolling Wilson, saying 'Woodrow Wilson's Wisdom Wins', staggered the United States Postal Service. It fell to Page to try to explain an American political campaign to the British government and people – no easy task even for the popular Page.

In August 1915 a German U-boat had torpedoed the British passenger ship *Arabic*, killing a number of civilians including Americans. British propagandists described the sinking as '[o]ne more atrocity to add to the number which makes the whole German nation stink in the nostrils of all Christian nations', and during the election of 1916 an embarrassed Page tried to defend America's neutrality. Lansing, like Wilson, stopped opening Page's correspondence.

Lansing had another ambassadorial problem – finding an ambassador for Russia. Wilson initially offered the post to Henry L. Pindell, a Democratic stalwart of Illinois, but he declined. Months passed and Wilson offered the job to George Thomas Marye Jr, a well respected banker from San Francisco, who accepted it with some reservations. His dispatches were clear: Russia was falling apart, with rumours of the nobility moving to Paris and London with their riches, the royal family under the pernicious influence of Rasputin, the Russian war effort collapsing with poor leadership, troops with almost nothing to eat, continual and disastrous shortages of weapons and ammunition, and non-existent medical care. Czar Nicholas II had failed as a military commander, and it was clear that a revolution was near. Ambassador Marye left Russia in March 1916, and was replaced by Davis R. Frances, a professional Democrat politician, a former mayor of St Louis and Governor of Missouri. He was to observe the collapse of Russia.

When Lansing came to the State Department he had a general idea that Wilson relied on his confidants like Colonel House, but as time passed he saw just how much the President depended on his close associates. In the autumn of 1915 House and Wilson had lengthy conversations over the military situation in Europe which had evolved into stalemate in France and Belgium and a fearful casualty rate.

House put forward the idea that perhaps the time was right for a conference to end the war with no winners or losers. It appeared to House that he had Wilson's agreement, and the ever-energetic Texan brought the outline of a plan to Lansing, who agreed that it might work. On the other hand, Lansing did not envisage what House actually planned, which included lengthy stays in Britain and many long sessions with Sir Edward Grey, Britain's experienced Foreign Secretary.

A surprising addition to Wilson's circle was the mayor of Cleveland, Ohio, Newton D. Baker, as Secretary of War in 1916. The President was displeased with the aggressiveness of Lindley Garrison, his previous Secretary of War, who firmly believed that sooner or later war would come to America and the military forces of the United States, army and navy, should be enlarged and prepared to fight. This did not fit in with what Wilson declaimed in the campaign which would decide if he were to secure a second term. Wilson had met Baker, the younger man, when they were at Baltimore's John Hopkins University. Baker shared Wilson's views on reform in government. As President, Wilson's appointment of Baker to replace Garrison came as a shock because Baker had a reputation as a pacifist as well as a progressive reformist mayor.

One of Baker's first tasks was to oversee the 1916 punitive expedition into Mexico. Both Regular Army and National Guard were sent to the border to maintain order, and Regular Army troops crossed over the border to chase Pancho Villa, the Mexican leader, who brought his forces into Columbus, New Mexico. For Baker, the Mexican operation showed that the United States Army and the National Guard were in dire need of both hard training and modernisation of weapons and equipment. For example, the United States Army had only one aero squadron to deploy to the border, and that squadron had obsolete aircraft which were unfit for modern warfare. Newton Baker set out to implement major changes within the confines of limited preparedness. He also identified Brigadier-General John J. Pershing as the officer to command American forces if war were to come to the United States, a decision he kept to himself.

To complete the cast of Washington characters around the President, we must now turn to Colonel Edward House of Texas and New York. House had no military experience, but in many of the states of the old Southern Confederacy those who served on the staff of the governor, or contributed generously to his election campaign, were designated a 'Governor's Colonel'.

House was born in Texas, and became an intelligent, wealthy man, ready to dip into his deep purse. He was active in Texas Democratic circles, serving and advising four governors. Feeling that he had done all he could in Texan politics, House moved to New York City. In 1911 he met Woodrow Wilson, the then Governor of New Jersey, and, in House's style, made himself a confidant of

Wilson. House had an affinity for Britain and was an admirer of David Lloyd George and his historic progressive reforms. Wilson used House on diplomatic missions to Europe, and House saw for himself the scale of the British and French battlefield toll. He judged that the United States would be drawn eventually into the war on the side of the 'democracies', – it would be a question of numbers needed to prevent German victory. Much to the irritation of many of Wilson's 'insiders', House's unassailable position as his major adviser covered a full range of issues including foreign affairs.

Returning to the European scene as witnessed by Americans, Edith Wharton wrote in 1915:

> The tone of France after the declaration of war was the white glow of dedication: a great nation's collective impulse (since there is no English equivalent for that winged word, elan) to resist destruction. But at that time [1914] no one knew what the resistance was to cost, how long it would have to last, what sacrifices, material and moral, it would necessitate. And for the moment baser sentiments were silenced ...[5]

Wharton and others were writing for that class of Americans who were already Anglophiles or Francophiles and who followed the war through friends and associates in England or France or from what appeared in highly literate magazines. The masses of Americans did not subscribe to *Scribner's Magazine* or other high-priced journals for that matter. Local newspapers had more to do with moulding American public opinion, and many of them were openly opposed to American entry into the European war. Readers, whatever their opinion on war, were, however, engrossed by the courtship of President Wilson and Edith Bolling Galt.

The loss of American lives in the torpedoing of *Lusitania* and *Arabic* presented problems to the President and Lansing with the 1916 election looming. There was a growing national irritation towards Germany as a result of such actions and, no less, incredulity over the decision to execute a woman, the British nurse Edith Cavell. British propaganda had been given three field days and then another with the capture of German nationals who had carried out a serious plan of sabotage in the States. Among Wilson's strongest supporters were those who opposed any action which would cause the United States to enter a conflict now spreading across the world.

Lansing had made it clear to the German ambassador, Johann von Bernstorff, that the patience of President Wilson and the American people had grown weary of German U-boats sinking passenger ships, and the suggestion that the U-boat, in the case of *Arabic*, was responding to the latter's attempt to ram, was simply neither realistic nor acceptable. After consultations with Berlin, von Bernstorff put forward what was in effect an apology for the sinking of *Arabic*, stating that the German government 'regrets and disavows this act', and offered an indemnity for the American lives lost.

On 24 March 1916 a U-boat torpedoed the passenger ship *Sussex*. No American lives were lost but anger over this latest attack reached a high level in the United States, even among those immigrant groups who had been opposed to any military participation in the war. The *Sussex* attack also forced President

Wilson to consider the necessity of preparedness if and when the United States entered the war. Even with these challenges, Wilson preferred negotiations to breaking relations with Germany, and he turned to Colonel House, sending him to Europe on a peace mission. On the other hand, in a public statement Wilson warned that the United States could break off diplomatic relations with Berlin. The German response was a pledge that it would end a policy of 'unrestricted submarine warfare', something which occasioned divisive debate in the German High Command.

In the autumn of 1915 the American administration decided on an increase of the Regular army from 108,000 officers and enlisted men to 141,707, and the creation of a reserve army of around 400,000 men. The National Guard was overlooked, as a poorly trained force, rent with local politics. These actions by the Wilson administration began a major and contentious debate over American military policy. Wilson was accused by many former supporters of introducing a militarism which would lead America into war. Church groups visited the White House to urge Wilson to abandon this policy of preparedness and return to prayer and negotiations. Wilson's staff could well point out that opposition and support for 'preparedness' was about equal, and in Congress Wilson could count on the vast majority of Democrat congressmen and senators as well as a number of Republican politicians.

The loudest complaints came from the National Guard, and in looking at the plan it is clear that the state guards received a small increase in funding, but that was all. There had been a constant tension between the small Regular army and the larger militias of the states. The Regular army looked on the National Guard as a disorganised, poorly trained group of men subject to political involvement where a governor of a state could appoint officers who had no military training but who had contributed to the election or re-election campaign of the state's chief executive. For example, it was possible that a bank president could be commanded by one of his cashiers. All too often the Guards' armouries were more usually considered a site of social gatherings in the smaller towns.

Much of this was true, but the Guard could point out that it had the troops which would expand the number of fighting soldiers by tens of thousands, and could also refer to the fact that during the Civil War Pennsylvania alone contributed over 200 regiments of infantry to the war effort, while Massachusetts contributed even more, including a well trained, battle-worthy regiment, the 54th Regiment of Infantry, which was made up of African-American soldiers. The Guard took pride in pointing out that the first official muster of the militia was in 1636 in the colony of Massachusetts and it was militia soldiers who fought at Lexington and Concord. The militia National Guard took every opportunity to point out that the citizen-soldier had never failed to heed the call of the nation, so why would the country ignore him now?

The debate over military preparedness brought to the fore two men whom Wilson would have preferred not to have in the limelight: Theodore Roosevelt and General Leonard Wood. Former President Roosevelt had been a vocal advocate for 'the vigorous life' – a life of physical activity and military service. During the Spanish American War this 'cowboy', as his detractors called him, helped to raise and then to command the 1st Volunteer Cavalry. He gained national fame by fighting up Kettle Hill and then leading his troops in an assault on San Juan Heights. The victory opened the road to Santiago and made an impact on the settlement ending the war. President William McKinley had selected this national war hero as his Vice-President, and when McKinley died as the result of an assassin's bullet in September 1901, Roosevelt became President. By 1915 Roosevelt had become a supporter of Wilson's reserve or continental army. Perhaps there would be a place for such a man, an officer, a proven leader, a man who had charged up Kettle Hill and San Juan Heights?

New Hampshire-born Leonard Wood studied medicine at Harvard and received his degree through Boston City Hospital in 1884. A year later he signed on as an army contract surgeon. During the campaign to capture Geronimo, he was awarded the Medal of Honor. In 1891 Wood was promoted to the rank of captain and was assigned to Army Headquarters in Washington. There he came into contact with senior officers and his experience included caring for the President of the United States. In an unusual move for a medical officer, Wood was appointed to the rank of colonel of the 1st Volunteer Cavalry, better known as 'the Rough Riders'. His second-in-command was Colonel Theodore Roosevelt. Both men were aggressive and both had political ambitions. After Wood was promoted, Roosevelt took command of 'the Rough Riders' and, as we have seen, rose to national prominence. After service in the Philippines, Wood was named Army Chief of Staff and served in that position from 1910 to 1914. In 1915 Wood joined with Theodore Roosevelt in supporting the 'preparedness' movement despite the fact that both men were members of the Republican party.

The debate over 'preparedness' was lengthy and fiercely fought, with Garrison, on occasion, clashing with the various committees in Congress. The biggest bone of contention was over the concept of the continental or reserve army of about 400,000 men. Many southern congressmen and senators worried that African-Americans would be enrolled and form units within the reserve force. As the debate ran on, it became clear that a new law would be put in place, and that the National Guard would be a part of the nation's defence. Garrison's relationship with Congress deteriorated during the debates and it appeared that 'anti-preparedness' forces were gaining strength. He tendered his resignation as Secretary of War, which Wilson gladly accepted and then appointed Newton Baker to fill the post.

Baker's personality eased the bad relationship with Congress. Both Roosevelt and Wood were vocal over the shifting opinion in Congress that the National Guard should have a larger role in the nation's defence. The National Guard was under-estimated as to its potential with solid training and good leadership. In due course, when the first four divisions were sent to France, two were National Guard – the 26th Yankee Division and the 42nd Rainbow Division – and both served at the front with ability, discipline and gallantry.

As with the Regular army, training and leadership would make or break those divisions and support troops which made up the American Expeditionary Forces (AEF). The army establishment in Washington went to Capitol Hill in force every day to fight to keep the 400,000 reserve force, or the 'continental army', as some called it, in any new bill. Leonard Wood proclaimed that '[The National Guard] will be solid and effective in only one line, and that will be in a raid on the federal treasury', and Theodore Roosevelt stated that the new bill was 'a bit of flintlock legislation'.[6] Numbers of officers realised that the National Guard divisions would need leadership that was up-to-date as far as training methods and experience were concerned. Where would this leadership come from? In the event, it came from Regular army officers who could very well find themselves generals overnight.

The word 'preparedness' meant that the United States had to expand its military establishment. The war in Europe had left the US far behind the combatants technologically and with regard to doctrine and organisation. To understand what faced the United States military in 1914–1917 if it were seriously to consider entering into the European War, it is helpful to look back at what the American armed forces faced at the turn of the century. The American Civil War had cost the nation over 600,000 lives, and a large portion of the south lay in ruins. The war produced heroes on both sides but that did not translate into enthusiasm for increasing the peacetime military budgets for the army or navy. The army remained at about 100,000 officers and men with the majority engaged in keeping the peace on the frontier and enforcing policies regarding native Americans.

For military thinkers there were two American truths: first, the US had to develop new tactics that reflected lessons learned from the Civil War, and second, that it was unthinkable that the American Army would ever fight on foreign (European) soil. The massive frontal assaults based on European/Napoleonic tactics that produced the terrible losses at Fredericksburg in 1862, Gettysburg in 1863 and Cold Harbor in 1864 would, in the minds of the army's thinkers, never be repeated. Up to the Spanish-American War of 1898, American soldiers trained in small units and placed great emphasis on marksmanship.[7] Seldom did American regiments train as a full battlefield unit.

The Spanish-American War of 1898 showed that all the thinking and writing since the Civil War had not addressed fundamental weaknesses in the structure of the army. Army logisticians, for example, lost control of the flow of supplies: railway trains full of needed supplies for the troops departing for Cuba were simply lost; transportation for infantry, cavalry and artillery was inadequate, with many cavalry units forced to leave their horses behind; some food staples such as hardtack (army bread) arrived full of mould, bug-ridden and unfit for human consumption. General Rufus Shafter, commanding V Corps, was ridiculously obese, had difficulty mounting his horse and remained very close to his headquarters. Medical services were abysmal, with fever felling more Americans than the Spanish did, even with their more modern infantry and artillery weapons.

The final battle of the war had, as the ultimate objective, the taking of the city of Santiago. The Spanish commander fortified the high ground and placed modern breech-loading cannon using smokeless powder to sweep the ground where the Americans had to assemble for their assault. To add to American miseries, the Spanish infantrymen had the new 7mm Mauser rifle with smokeless powder. Despite thirty years of American military thinking a direct frontal assault was ordered, and while San Juan and Kettle Hills were taken and the road to Santiago opened for the final victory, casualties were high.

Despite the outpouring of patriotic support for the troops who fought in Cuba and those soldiers who were on the way to the Philippines, the poor American performance in relation to logistics, tactics and leadership was clear. The Secretary of War, Elihu Root, a well known New Yorker, turned his attention to serious reform of the United States War Department. His goal was to change the army into a modern organisation equal to any military force in Europe. Developments in killing power on the battlefield dictated that an army must be anchored on both modern weaponry and sound tactical doctrine. The latter could only be achieved through study and professional application within the various branches of the army. Root organised the Army War College to train those officers of intelligence and ambition to study all aspects of war and its effects on a modern nation state. Under Root's guidance, the first American General Staff was formed, and the first Chief of Staff was authorised by congressional legislation. While Root himself had no military experience, he understood that promotion by merit rather than by seniority was essential in building a modern, professional army.

There was of course anger among many in the army at such root and branch reform, but Root continued to restructure the army with the support of President Theodore Roosevelt, who had seen the chaos in Cuba. If the army were to be professionalised then it would be wise to start at the beginning with the officer corps at the United States Military Academy at West Point. The number of cadets was increased and the courses of study placed emphasis on the professional nature of being an officer. During his tenure as Secretary of War, Root dealt with the new American colonies, especially Cuba and the Philippines. Troops would be needed to fight an on-going Philippine revolt, and Root angered anti-imperialists in the United States with the vigorous suppression of the rebels. American soldiers had a new, effective weapon in the 1903 Springfield rifle based on the German Mauser design (Model 98), a weapon that the Spanish had used with effect in the 1898 war. As it happened, so similar was the new design that a substantial royalty payment had to be made to the German firm.

For all the progress made by the spring of 1917, the army was still underfunded, undersupplied and woefully short of both trained officers and noncommissioned officers. When the United States declared war on Germany there was a critical shortage of the fine Springfield rifle, and all too often newly inducted soldiers had to learn the manual of arms with broomsticks. However, despite public apathy and congressional underfunding, the Root reforms began the process of bringing the army up to date.

Unsurprisingly, the cost and implication of modernisation fuelled 'antipreparedness' forces in Congress and Wilson himself was far from comfortable with what in a later age would have been called the rearmament programme placed before him.

In the spring of 1916 Baker, the pacifist mayor-turned-Secretary of War, drafted legislation which would create a civilian-staffed agency to study the economic and human resources available if the nation were to enter the war. What

Baker wanted was an agency that would be prepared to go into action alongside the military. Wilson discussed the bill which Baker presented to him and accepted it with enthusiasm. The bill, with an absurdly long name, went to Congress, where the Senate changed the name to the more manageable 'Council of National Defense'. In the late summer of 1916 this far-reaching piece of legislation was passed. It included an army appropriations bill and Wilson nominated seven well known and respected leaders to its council. For various reasons this bill attracted little attention, despite the power which was granted to the council. A second bill, also with far-reaching consequences, was the 'Shipping Bill' of 1916, passed by an indifferent Congress and ignored by the press. Complex in its nature, the bill, as one historian noted, 'marked the rebirth of the American merchant marine'[8] by a series of regulations issued by a commission which would be independent from political or private shipping companies. For all the transformative nature of such legislation, Wilson also kept his eye on foreign affairs, especially with a breakdown of relations with Mexico.

By 1916 he had reached the conclusion that, despite divisive issues, war with Mexico was not in America's best interests but the situation was dramatically changed on 9 March 1916 when a hundred soldiers of the famed guerrilla leader Francisco 'Pancho' Villa attacked Columbus in New Mexico, engaging a detachment of the 13th US Cavalry, burning a large section of the town, and seizing horses and military equipment. In the process eighteen Americans were killed, together with a large number of Villa's irregulars. Wilson was greatly angered and ordered General Frederick Funston to send 5,000 soldiers to the Columbus area to prepare for a punitive expedition against 'Pancho' Villa. The officer selected to command this expeditionary force was Brigadier-General John J. Pershing, who moved quickly and sent the famed 7th US Cavalry south into Mexico. Despite the fact that Villa's guerrillas had crossed over the border to attack, and that eighteen American citizens were killed, Wilson was deluged with letters and petitions urging that the affair should not result in military action, but Wilson's patience had reached its limit.[9]

It was clear that the army was too small and too inexperienced to handle large operations such as the punitive expeditionary force. Wilson then sent to Congress a bill to expand and modernise the army. After bitter debate, the National Defense Act of 1916 was passed and signed by the President. The Regular army was expanded to 175,000 officers and men and the National Guard increased to 450,000 officers and men. The sum of $17 million was allocated to purchase more than 300 aircraft and an air division was created with its headquarters at Langley, Virginia. The bill also included the creation of the Reserve Officers Training Corps (ROTC) to be established at colleges and universities, a move which angered the 'anti-preparedness' faction who described the establishment of the body as the road to militarism and dictatorship.

One of the most important sections of the act authorised the President to federalise the National Guard in times of internal crisis or war. With that authority Wilson called to the colours a number of National Guard units which were sent to the Mexican–American border, where they trained and stood guard over hastily built military camps and American towns. No observer could have imagined the impact that sending the National Guard to the border would have in less than a year. After a period of confusion, units began training under military discipline with officers and non-commissioned officers learning how to command the men entrusted to them. Training was rudimentary and there was no realistic introduction to the machine gun units or the artillery which would support the infantry if the United States were to enter the European war. In the event, both the National Guard and the Regular army would have to correct those problems in France in just over a year.

As troops began to leave the Mexican border area, the lessons learned were clear: the 1st Aero Squadron had shown to Pershing and to the staff in Washington that air reconnaissance vastly expanded an overview of the battlefield; the use of trucks and other forms of motor transport added speed to the logistics flow; the wireless telegraph enhanced the decision-making process for both the intelligence and the operations sections. There was a definite feeling of confidence among officers and men.

It needs to be remembered that the above may well be the case but in the background was Wilson's strong showing in the 1916 presidential election featuring his stance on peace. Lapel buttons, postcards, pennants and all the cheaply produced campaign material featured one appealing thought: *Peace*. However, there were many around President Wilson who firmly believed that war was drawing near. There was less uniformity in the anti-war opinions held within the Irish-American and German-American communities as men joined the units that served on the border and experienced the local acclaim given them.

Meanwhile, in the corridors of the American State Department there were serious discussions over the possibility of revolution in Russia, and the likelihood of Russia leaving the war. If that were to happen – and from the American Ambassador's dispatches it appeared quite possible – it would allow Germany to transfer thousands of troops to the Western Front against hard-pressed France and Britain. How could they match such an increase in German military power? There was only one country capable of supplying healthy young men – the United States – and certainly Berlin was aware of this.

It might appear that it would take years for the United States to be in a sound enough military position to engage in the European War which was raging in 1917. Inadequacies had been strikingly revealed by the Mexican War, though some of the better prepared officers who had been educated in the mode of the German General Staff considered it was worth the risk of engaging in the European War. The solid foundation of any army, or so the General Staff officers thought, was the officer corps, but the American Army was exceedingly short of experienced officers. Furthermore, as seems to have been overlooked, all officers, even those who had graduated from West Point, were inexperienced until they went into battle for the first time.

The Germans were aware of the 'anti-preparedness' movement in the United States. Very important personalities opposed military training, and, as Henry Ford said, one had to be a lazy person with no sense of hard work if one wished to be a soldier. Wilson was clearly opposed to war. His attempts by negotiation to end the bloodshed in Europe were well known and well received by the progressives who supported him financially and by the ballot. He urged the American people to be neutral, and advocated a policy of peace without victory, but it fell on deaf ears in London and Paris.

Despite surface appearances that the United States was broadly committed to neutrality, there were those who firmly believed that the nation was seriously underprepared for any major crisis. As has been made clear, Theodore Roosevelt and General Leonard Wood were the most prominent advocates for expansion of the army and navy. Wilson was suspicious of the motives of both men, believing that Roosevelt wanted to use the 'preparedness' movement to enhance his position as a former President whose main mission in life was to convince the nation that peace and security came only through military strength. Wood looked forward to a possible run for the presidency in 1920 by securing the nomination as the candidate of the Republican party. These two powerhouses were joined by Henry Stimson and Elihu Root, both former Secretaries of War, and both having been careful not to oppose Wilson's neutrality position in 1914. What these leading figures wanted was a training programme for volunteers, a programme that became known as the 'Plattsburg Movement'.

The supporters of Plattsburg did not want to be seen as extremists, advocating such causes as universal military training (that is, 'conscription'). In their writing and speeches they argued that economic power and military strength accomplished much more than Wilsonian ideals of mass democracy and national self-determination.

In 1915 the army issued an order which would allow a training camp to be set up for qualified young men, mainly young professionals, to attend, as long as they paid for it. The government, specifically the War Department, had no financial responsibility for this camp which opened in 1915 near the New York State town of Plattsburg. The first training class of 1,200 young, physically fit men looked like the pages of *Who's Who in America*, with almost every important family having a member enrolled for the ninety days of training. For example, Theodore Roosevelt Jr was a '90-day wonder', and went on to fight with the 1st Infantry Division in the Great War. The Plattsburg camp continued to turn out a large number of leaders, but it was exclusive because of the cost. As its popularity grew, further camps were established. In March 1917 *The Plattsburg Manual: A Handbook for Military Training*, written by Captains O.O. Ellis and E.B. Garey, was published. It became required reading for those entering the three-month programme or for those contemplating attending the programme. Although it reads today as if it were written exclusively for the well heeled – 'Travel light, don't bring a trunk' and 'Bring a pair of sneakers or slippers, they will add greatly to your comfort' – it should be noted that half of Pershing's officers in France during the war had been trained at the Plattsburg camps.

Events that would make the Plattsburg training meaningful were close at hand. On 11 January 1917 a telegram was sent by Germany's Foreign Minister, Arthur Zimmerman, to Heinrich von Eckardt, German Ambassador to Mexico, proposing a military treaty between the two countries if the United States entered the war against Germany. If that were to happen, Von Eckardt was authorised to offer 'generous' financial aid to Mexico, and to urge Mexico to begin military

.. Chief advocate of the Dardanelles/ Gallipoli venture, the Rt Hon. Winston S. Churchill MP, First Lord of the Admiralty. (US Library of Congress, George Grantham Bain Collection, photograph dated 1908)

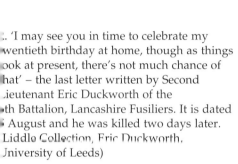

.. 'I may see you in time to celebrate my twentieth birthday at home, though as things look at present, there's not much chance of that' – the last letter written by Second Lieutenant Eric Duckworth of the 6th Battalion, Lancashire Fusiliers. It is dated 5 August and he was killed two days later. (Liddle Collection, Eric Duckworth, University of Leeds)

Gallipoli.
August 5. 1915

Dear brother,

Little enough did I think 12 months ago to-day that on the anniversary of mobilisation I should be writing you from a hole in the Gallipoli Peninsular, not having seen you for 0/2 months, and to the tune of 75ᵐᵐ guns. However you never know your luck, and I may see you in time to celebrate my 20ᵗʰ birthday at home, tho as things look at present, there's not much chance of that.

3. Sapper Eric Wettern in his Cape Helles dugout which he named 'the Pigstye'. (Liddle Collection, E.F. Wettern, University of Leeds)

4. Officers of the Dorset, the Berks, and the Bucks Yeomanry study orders for the imminent attack on 21 August on Scimitar Hill. (Museum of the Dorset Yeomanry – Wingfield Digby Estate)

5. A painting of the evacuation from Helles by Lieutenant R.C. Perry, attached to the 4th Battalion, Worcester Regiment. The painting was completed in hospital in Egypt as Perry recovered from dysentery. (Liddle Collection, RC Perry, University of Leeds)

6. The British 4.7-inch gun, a weapon of Boer War vintage which proved inaccurate and inadequate in the First World War. However, shortage of artillery necessitated its widespread employment in 1915. (Spencer Jones)

7. A dramatic portrayal of Captain Woolley of the 9th London's throwing a Hand Grenade No. 1 in the midst of ferocious close combat at Hill 60 in April 1915. The picture clearly shows the unusually long wooden handle of the grenade and the complex percussion detonator. Woolley won the Victoria Cross for his part in the action. (Spencer Jones)

8. A carefully posed photograph of a Bavarian gun crew and their *minenwerfer* (mine thrower). Powerful mortars such as these provided the Germans with impressive close-range firepower which the British were unable to match for much of 1915. (Private collection of Jens Neumann)

9. HMS *Queen Mary* exploding. HMS *Lion* is on the left, surrounded by shell splashes. Photograph taken from HMS *Lydiard*. (NMRN)

10. HMS *Vindictive* seen after the raid on Zeebrugge. The mass of mangled metal on the centre of the ship is the remains of the special gangways built to allow the landing force to get up onto the mole or pier and attack the German guns. (NMRN)

11. HMS *Caroline,* a C class light cruiser, with an aircraft and launching platform fitted above the forward gun turret. HMS *Caroline*, having fought at the Battle of Jutland, was converted into a Royal Naval Volunteer Reserve Drill Ship in the 1920s. She performed this until the early twenty-first century before being preserved for the nation in Belfast as the last surviving ship from the Battle of Jutland. (NMRN)

12. Field Marshal Joseph Joffre, French Commander in Chief 1914–16 (Wikimedia Commons)

13. A midnight service in Fort Douaumont during the Battle of Verdun. (US Library of Congress)

14. British Mark 1 Tank, named C-15, near Thiepval, 25 September 1916. The tank is fitted with a wire grenade shield on top and a steering tail. (Wikimedia Commons)

15. A British wiring party with un-barbed concertina wire near Hamel on the Somme in September 1916. (US Library of Congress)

16. *Generalleutnant* Freiherr von Soden, Commander of the German 26th Reserve Division. (Public domain)

18. Field Marshal Sir John French, in command of the BEF until December 1915. (US Library of Congress, Harris and Ewing Collection)

17. *Oberst* Fritz von Loßberg, Chief of Staff, German First Army. (Public domain)

19. Field Marshal Lord Kitchener, Secretary of State for War, soldier in political command. (US Library of Congress, George Grantham Bain Collection)

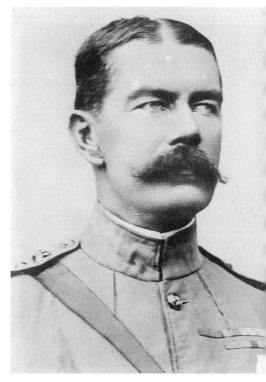

20. General Sir Douglas Haig, in command of the BEF from December 1915 and subsequently the principal target of Lloyd George's conviction and personal animus over the way the war was being waged in France. (US Library of Congress)

21. General Sir Henry Wilson, the most 'political' of generals but deserving credit for his handling of the difficult role liaising between British and French high military command in 1915. (US Library of Congress, Bain Collection)

22. The Rt Hon. David Lloyd George MP, Chancellor of the Exchequer from the outbreak of war and, from December 1916, Prime Minister. He was the leading critic of the 'Brasshats'. (US Library of Congress, George Grantham Bain Collection)

23. Major-General Frederick Sykes in the initial Royal Air Force uniform, 1918. Sykes succeeded David Henderson in command of the Royal Flying Corps in early 1915 but was in that year transferred to the Royal Naval Air Service, amalgamated with the RFC into the Royal Air Force in April 1918. (Wikimedia Commons)

24 (*left*). Major-General David Henderson, in command of the Royal Flying Corps in 1914 and early 1915. (US Library of Congress, George Grantham Bain Collection)

25 (*right*). Major-General Hugh Trenchard, who succeeded Frederick Sykes in command of the Royal Flying Corps and, in parallel with Sir Douglas Haig during the 1916 Battle of the Somme, was convinced that only attritional measures would win the war in France. (Public domain)

26 (*below*). 'An unarmed *Fokker Eindecker c.*1915. While the history of air power during the period is too often shaped by a technologically driven narrative, the appearance of the *Eindecker* with a machine-gun synchronised to fire through the propeller did serve to present the Royal Flying Corps and its aggressive doctrine with its first serious challenge.' (James Pugh)

27 (*right*). Royal Flying Corps Christmas card, 1915, demonstrating the importance of aerial fighting and the offensively minded and aggressive corporate image of the Corps during this period. (James Pugh)

28. Indian cavalry in the desert near the Tigris. (US Library of Congress, Bain News Service)

29. Indian troops manning a 6-pounder Hotchkiss gun mounted in a railway wagon on the military railway between Basra and Nasiriya. Such armed wagons were used to protect troops and supply trains from attacks by bands of hostile Arabs in 1917/18. (Captain Charles Henry Weaver – www.mespot.net)

30. Quite a mix of troops from the Indian sub-continent and British troops in Mesopotamia. (Wikimedia Commons)

31. 'Sinking of the Lusitania – the last plunge': a British propaganda postcard prepared for an American audience. (James Cooke)

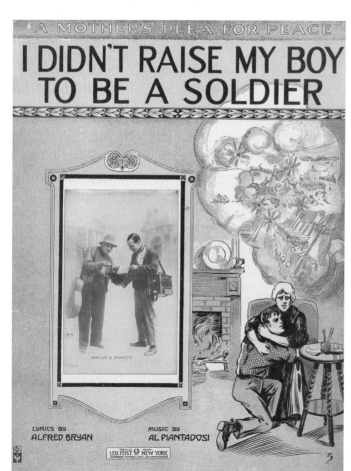

32. 'I didn't Raise my Boy to be a Soldier': the sheet music for a very popular song in America, 1915 to early 1917. (James Cooke)

33. William Jennings Bryan (*left*) and President Woodrow Wilson. As Secretary of State in May 1915, and as a convinced pacifist, Bryan was in disagreement with the strongly worded protest the President sent to Germany following the torpedoing of *Lusitania.* The incident was to lead to Bryan's resignation. (James Cooke)

35. Former President Theodore Roosevelt and General Leonard Wood of the Plattsburg Movement, a movement financed by those in support of 'Preparedness'. (James Cooke)

34. Colonel Edward House (*left*), hugely influential with President Wilson. (James Cooke)

36. The Pacifist former Mayor of Cleveland, now US Secretary of State, Newton Baker, visiting the trenches in France. It may be noted that he is wearing a British steel helmet. (James Cooke)

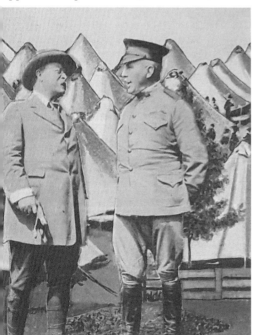

37. J.J. Mulroy cartoon highlighting what was seen as the selfish attitude of 'the slacker'. (*Halifax Courier*, 8 May 1915)

38. J.J. Mulroy cartoon reflecting on the forthcoming National Registration. (*Halifax Courier*, 14 August 1915)

39. J.J. Mulroy cartoon humorously reflecting on the problems facing military recruitment. (*Halifax Courier*, 6 November 1915)

THE TENNIS SEASON HAS COMMENCED.

Sportive Slacker : " Service."

Passing Tommy : " Yes, but who's—yours or the country's ? "

REGISTRATION.

The Stout Party : " I offered to go nursing. Collectin' bloke asks me if I'd had experience ; Me wots 'ad ten and buried eight ! Ever know sich cheek ? "

" If you are the man I think, you 'ave the 'eart of a lion, plenty o' grit, and the real fighting spirit,—ready ter shed yer blood for yer Country."

"Sorry. I can't ; I'm anæmic !"

40. A postcard making a joke of a civilian applying to a Military Service Tribunal for exemption from conscription. (Tony Allen Collection:

"And what work are you doing of National Importance?"
"Why, I'm rearin' eight children an' helping to make airyplanes!"

41. End of War Open Day in one of the munitions workshops at the Campbell Gas Engine Company, Halifax. (Stephen Gee Collection)

42. Machine tools essential for industry: an armour drilling machine at Asquith's, Halifax. (Grace's Guide, 1913)

43. Picric acid workers at His Majesty's Explosives Factory (HMEF) Greetland, near Halifax. (Stephen Gee Collection)

44. Willis & Bates lantern advert showing the basic tin hat shape. (*Halifax, a Commercial and Industrial Centre*, Halifax Chamber of Congress Booklet, 1915)

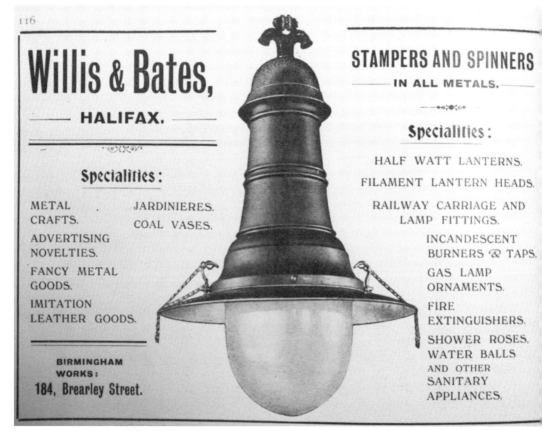

Willis & Bates,

— HALIFAX. —

Specialities:

METAL   JARDINIERES.
CRAFTS.   COAL VASES.

ADVERTISING
NOVELTIES.

FANCY METAL
GOODS.

IMITATION
LEATHER GOODS.

BIRMINGHAM
WORKS:
184, Brearley Street.

STAMPERS AND SPINNERS
— IN ALL METALS. —

Specialities:

HALF WATT LANTERNS.

FILAMENT LANTERN HEADS.

RAILWAY CARRIAGE AND
LAMP FITTINGS.

INCANDESCENT
BURNERS & TAPS.

GAS LAMP
ORNAMENTS.

FIRE
EXTINGUISHERS.

SHOWER ROSES.
WATER BALLS
AND OTHER
SANITARY
APPLIANCES.

15. Harold Gillies in 1915. (British Association of Plastic, Reconstructive and Aesthetic Surgeons' archive, London)

16. Pastel portrait and diagram of Lieutenant Grinlington, AIF. (Royal College of Surgeons, London)

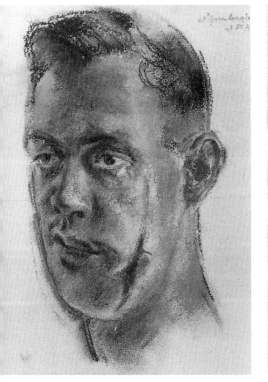

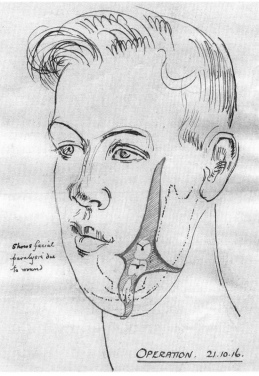

Shows facial paralysis due to wound

OPERATION. 21.10.16.

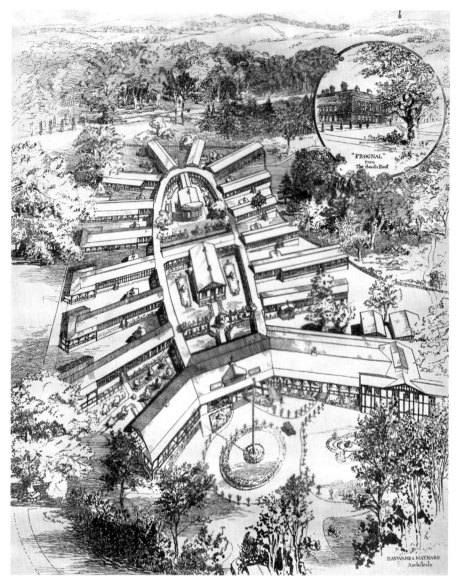

47. Architect's drawing of the Queen's Hospital, first phase. (Andrew Bamji)

48. Upper lip reconstruction using a flap taken from within the hairline. (Royal College of Surgeons, London)

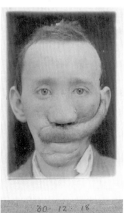   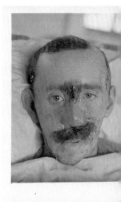

9. Queen's Hospital, Ward 5: Christmas photograph. (Andrew Bamji)

0. Private Thomas, Cheshire Regiment, on admission (6.11.18) and final appearance in 1924. (Royal College of Surgeons, London)

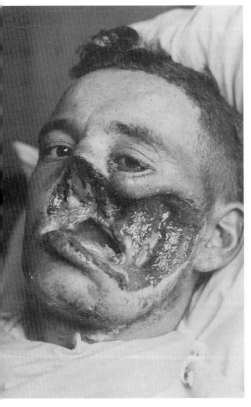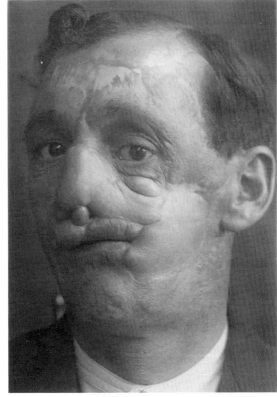

51. Joseph Lamb, Mary Anne's husband, 1915. (Andrea Hetherington)

52. Postcard printers were quick off the mark to exploit the market of the married couple with the husband off to serve in the trenches. (Andrea Hetherington)

Devotion

Darling, my heart beats fast for you,
Darling, my love is sincere, fond and true,
Though we are far apart to-day,
My love is yours and lasts for aye.

3. Joseph and Mary Anne Lamb's eldest son, also called Joseph, shown here with his grandfather in Trimdon Colliery, c.1911. (Andrea Hetherington)

4. The only known photograph to exist of Mary Anne Lamb, now Mrs Britton. She is second from the left in this 1954 family wedding photograph. (Andrea Hetherington)

55. Acting Captain Alfred Pollard, MC* DCM, is decorated with the Victoria Cross by HM King George V on 21 July 1917. (Chown family)

56. The gates of Armoury House, which opened at about 11.30am on 8 August 1914 and admitted Alfred Pollard to the Artillery Garden and Armoury House. (N.S. Nash)

57. Lieutenant Alfred Pollard, aged 23 in 1916 (*left*), and aged about 60, in 1953 (*right*). (Chown family)

58. Pilot Officer A.O. Pollard, VC MC** DCM. A photograph taken in 1924 on his being commissioned into the Royal Air Force. (Chown family)

59. Armoury House, the home of the Honourable Artillery Company. (N.S. Nash)

60. A young munitions girl working on a 60-pounder shell. (From Hall Caine, *Our Girls: Their Work for the War* (Hutchinson, 1917))

61. Field Marshal Sir William Robertson, deservedly credited for his role in the creation of young soldier training battalions in 1917. (From W. Robertson, *From Private to Field Marshal* (Constable, 1921))

62. Lieutenant Walter Ogden, Tank Corps, aged 19. He was mortally wounded at Cambrai in November 1917. (*Harrogate Advertiser*, 2015)

63. 'When they came to us they were weedy, sallow, skinny, frightened children – the refuse of our industrial system – and they were in very poor condition because of wartime food shortages. But after six months of good food, fresh air and physical exercise, they changed so much their mothers wouldn't have recognised them.' (W. Robertson, *From Private to Field Marshal* (Constable, 1921))

64. Young lads at Swan Hunter and Wigham Richardson's Shipbuilding yard on the Tyne. (Max Arthur, *The Faces of World War I* (Cassell, 2007))

65. Officers in training at the Royal Military College, Sandhurst, 1917, relaxing in the lounge before the start of a rugby game. (Max Arthur, *The Faces of World War I* (Cassell, 2007))

56. A cutting from the Florence Lockwood diary advertising an anti-conscription rally in Huddersfield. (Liddle Collection, Florence Lockwood, University of Leeds)

57. 'Refusing to be made a soldier' – an example of Richmond Castle conscientious objector graffiti. (Photograph: Clive Barrett)

58. 'If you take a sword' – Richmond Castle conscientious objector graffiti citing J.R. Lowell's Hosea Biglow. (Photograph: Clive Barrett)

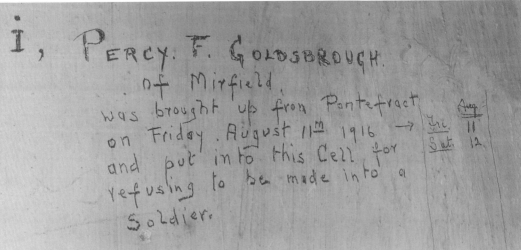

National Council Against Conscription.

YORKSHIRE
DEMONSTRATION

In ST. GEORGE'S SQUARE, HUDDERSFIELD

SUNDAY, JULY 16th, at 2-45 p.m.

Speakers:

Councillor MARGARET ASHTON,
F. W. JOWETT, M.P., H. SNELL,
W. PICKLES, FRED BRAMLEY.

If wet, in the Friendly and Trades Hall and I.L.P. Rooms.
13—7

I, PERCY. F. GOLDSBROUGH.
of Mirfield,
was brought up from Pontefract
on Friday. August 11th 1916 →
and put into this Cell for
refusing to be made into a
soldier.

Fri. 11
Sat. 12
Aug.

If you take a sword & dror it
to run a fellow through
The government asn to answer for it
God will send the bill to you
Ernest Lawson
July 14th 16

69. Richmond Castle keep and cell block in which conscientious objectors were held. (Photograph Clive Barrett)

70. Conscientious objectors sent to France, a photograph annotated by Norman Gaudie. (Liddle Collection, Norman Gaudie, University of Leeds)

71. Letter from Adrian Hill to his mother, 22 September 1916. (Liddle Collection, estate of Adrian Hill, University of Leeds)

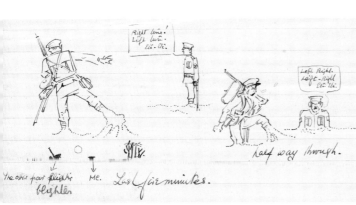

72. Letter from Adrian Hill to his parents, c.20 September 1916. (Liddle Collection, estate of Adrian Hill, University of Leeds)

73. HAC advance, Adrian Hill, c.1917. (Reproduced with kind permission of the Honourable Artillery Company)

74. German 'O.P.' outside Lille, Adrian Hill, 1917. (Reproduced with kind permission of the Honourable Artillery Company)

75. Beaumont Ridge – 1917, Adrian Hill, 1917. (Reproduced with kind permission of the Honourable Artillery Company)

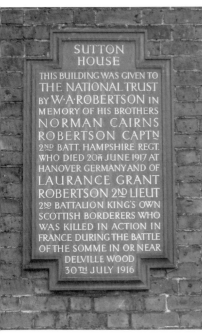

76 (*left*). Memorial plaque at Sutton House, Hackney. W.A. Robertson donated the building to the National Trust in honour of his two brothers who died in the Great War. (Photograph: Lucy Oldnall and Rachael McMillan)

77 (*right*). Barnet and Nazeing Pilot Study volunteers undertaking Great War field investigation around Nazeing Church. (Emily Glass)

78. Grove House in King Street, Newcastle-under-Lyme, which was registered as a War Supply Depot in 1915. (Photograph: John Mason Sneddon)

79. The Great War air-raid shelter constructed for watercress workers at Waltham Abbey Gardens, Mrs Julia Pryor adjacent to the entrance. (Waltham Abbey)

80. Interior of Cordite Press House No. 5 at the Royal Gunpowder Mills, Waltham Abbey. The cordite expansion dates from 1916. (Photograph: Len Stuart)

operations to regain territory in Texas, New Mexico and Arizona lost to the Americans after defeat in the Mexican War. There were those who believed the telegram to be a hoax, but Zimmerman acknowledged that he sent it. Many in the United States were angered by the telegram, but perhaps an equal number thought that the idea of a Mexican army conquering American territory was quite a joke. Wilson found neither the action nor the text a joke and the Zimmerman telegram became another step towards a break between the United States and Imperial Germany.

Both President and people were losing conviction in the stand they had taken. Within the Wilson administration pressures were building to take a stronger line against Germany because, as many argued, it was just a matter of time before Germany would move to break the British naval blockade which was causing severe hunger, close to starvation, for its civilian population. It was becoming difficult to feed the troops in the trenches too and to supply them with the necessary sinews of war. Kaiser Wilhelm was very much aware that his admirals and generals favoured a return to unrestricted submarine warfare, even if meant that the United States entered the war on the side of the allies. From reports, it seemed that if America declared war it would take quite some time before the troops could be raised, trained, transported and sent to the trenches. The Kaiser's advisers argued that there was no large, trained, viable American officer corps to command the number of troops that would be needed to make a difference on the Western Front. Besides, the generals posited, there was considerable opposition to conscription led by prominent men such as Henry Ford and William Jennings Bryan. In their calculations, it would take such a measure to fill the ranks of a large American Army. Furthermore, did an American Army not spend nearly a year chasing Pancho Villa, without success?

On 31 January the German Emperor made the fateful decision that on the following day unrestricted submarine warfare would be resumed. For Wilson, and for many in the peace movement, this was the final straw and the President, who had tried so hard to avoid confrontation, severed diplomatic relations with Germany. This move was dramatic, but it did not mean automatically that a state of war existed between the two countries. Much to the frustration of Britain and France, and of course to Ambassador Walter Hines Page, there were still a few things that Wilson could try before resorting to war. After a few non-lethal losses by U-boat attack in February, Wilson on 12 March issued an executive order to arm American merchant ships. It stated: 'We stand firm in armed neutrality.' The US Navy placed sailors aboard merchant ships to man the guns now installed on merchant ships. Word reached the White House that on 12 March the American steamship *Algonquin* had been fired upon by a U-boat, and after a twenty-round bombardment German sailors boarded the ship, placed explosives and sank her. Two days later the cargo ship *Vigilancia* was hit by a torpedo with the loss of six American sailors. *City of Memphis* was sunk by torpedo on 17 March, and on the next day *Illinois* was destroyed. Just before the end of March the tanker *Healdton*, bound for Rotterdam, was hit by several torpedoes, killing seven American sailors. With the support of his cabinet and advisers, Wilson finally decided to address Congress on 2 April, to set forth the reasons for a declaration of war. It had taken a long time for him to ask them to do their constitutional duty to declare war. He had procrastinated not least because Colonel House had been giving him such 'poor advice during those critical weeks, perhaps a victim of wishful thinking'. As historians have pointed out, House believed that his old friend could still bring peace between the warring nations after three years of monumental carnage.[10] Now, not even House could save Wilson from the collapsing foundations of his ideals. The question of America's entry into war belonged to the Congress of the United States. The President spoke about a 'war against mankind', calling out for the need to fight to make 'the world safe for democracy', and with his voice rising to personify America and the decision for war, he declaimed: 'God helping her, she can do no other.' On 6 April 1917 the United States went to war against Imperial Germany. Finally, indeed 'she could do no other'.

Notes

1. D. Clayton James and Anne Sharp Wells, *America and the Great War, 1914–1920* (Wheeling, IL: Harlan Davidson, 1998), p. 3. See the well received but controversial Justus D. Doenecke, *Nothing Less Than War* (Lexington, KY: University of Kentucky Press, 2014). It was thought that the many ethnic groups would embrace neutrality, and many Americans and Europeans thought the numbers of groups was a weakness if the United States went to war. This proved not to be the case. See Nancy Gentile Ford, *Americans All: Foreign-Born Soldiers in World War I* (College Station, TX: Texas A&M Press, 2001); James J. Cooke, *The All-Americans at War: The 82nd Division in the Great War* (Westport, CT: Praeger, 1999); and John S.D. Eisenhower, *Yanks: The Epic Story of the American Army in World War I* (New York: The Free Press, 2001).
2. Colonel T. Bentley Mott (ed.), *Myron T. Herrick: Friend of France* (New York: Doubleday, Doran & Co., 1929), p. 117.
3. Burton J. Hendrick (ed.), *The Life and Letters of Walter H. Page*, Vol. 1 (London: William Heinemann, 1922), pp. 130–1.
4. Ibid., Vol. 2, p. 16: undated letter from Page to House.
5. Wharton's articles were published in book form. See Edith Wharton, *Fighting France: From Dunkerque to Belfort* (New York: Charles Scribner's Sons, 1917). This book became a bestseller in the United States. Also of interest is Arlen J. Hansen, *Gentlemen Volunteers: The Story of the American Ambulance Drivers in the Great War* (New York: Arcade Books, 1996). This work details the work and letters (some published) from highly educated, articulate members of the American upper class who disagreed with Wilson's neutrality in 1914 and went to France to serve.
6. See Arthur S. Link, *Wilson: Confusions and Crises, 1915–1916* (Princeton: Princeton University Press, 1964), p. 332. Professor Link devoted his scholarly life to writing a complete biography of Wilson. The volumes contain a vast amount of detailed information, often unravelling a number of historical knots.
7. Perry D. Jamieson, *Crossing the Deadly Ground: United States Army Tactics, 1865–1899* (Tuscaloosa, AL: Alabama University Press, 1994), pp. 1–4.
8. Link, *Wilson*, pp. 340–1.
9. For a well researched recent work, see Charles H. Harris III and Louis R. Sadler, *The Great Call-Up: The Guard, the Border and the Mexican Revolution* (Norman, OK: University of Oklahoma Press, 2015). Other current studies are: John S.D. Eisenhower, *Intervention! The United States Involvement in the Mexican Revolution, 1913–1917* (New York: W.W. Norton, 1995) and James W. Hurst, *Pancho Villa and Black Jack Pershing* (Westport, CT: Praeger Publishing, 2007). Also consult Richard Slotkin, *Lost Battalions: The Great War and the Crisis of American Nationality* (New York: Henry Holt, 2005).
10. Meirion and Susie Harries, *The Last Days of Innocence: America at War, 1917–1918* (New York: Random House, 1997), pp. 72–3.

Suggested Further Reading

Clifford, J. Garry, *The Citizen Soldier: The Plattsburg Training Camp Movement 1913–1920* (Lexington, KY: University of Kentucky Press, 2014)

Cooke, James J., *The All-Americans at War: The 82nd Division in the Great War* (Westport, CT: Praeger, 1999)

Doenecke, Justus D., *Nothing Less than War* (Lexington, KY: University of Kentucky Press, 2014)

Eisenhower, John S.D., *Yanks: The Epic Story of the American Army in World War I* (New York: The Free Press, 2001)

Ford, Nancy Gentile, *Americans All: Foreign-Born Soldiers in World War I* (College Station, TX: Texas A&M Press, 2001)

Harris III, Charles H. and Louis R. Sadler, *The Great Call-Up: The Guard, the Border and the Mexican Revolution* (Norman, OK: University of Oklahoma Press, 2015)

Hurst, James W., *Pancho Villa and Black Jack Pershing* (Westport, CT: Praeger, 2007)

Slotkin, Richard, *Lost Battalions: The Great War and the Crisis of American Nationality* (New York: Henry Holt, 2005)

PART TWO

Chapter 10

How Committed was Halifax to the Great War?

By David Millichope

Harold Lasswell argued that no nation could hope to win a total war unless it could obtain the support of the majority of its populace.[1] Nowhere is this better illustrated than when studying the experiences of local communities such as Halifax. Viewed from the twenty-first century, the Great War is often represented as a pointless conflict in which the populace had to suffer untold misery and privations in pursuit of trivial objectives. Yet how could this be? Are we to believe, as some would have it, that the Great War was a massive confidence trick fuelled by the manipulative propaganda of the establishment? Propaganda and censorship certainly existed. What war could be successfully pursued without presenting a positive and selective view of its purpose and conduct? The crucial questions become: Did the populace believe the message they were receiving?, Were they in a position to make a fair judgement as to its veracity? and perhaps most important of all, How did they respond? For the first time in Britain's history all of her local communities were important for the prosecution of a war. It was not a war that belonged to someone else or to certain sections of society. Given this unique situation, how readily did local communities such as Halifax see it as 'their' war and fully embrace its implications?

With hindsight, we all know that the war became total, involved massive mobilisation of industry and required conscription to achieve the necessary army size. None of this was apparent to the average man or woman on the Halifax streets in August 1914. It was something they came to experience by degrees, often with a lot of difficult soul-searching. On the outbreak of war, Halifax followed a pattern which seems to have been repeated at local level throughout the country.[2] At first the town saw no reason for Britain to be involved in a general European war and was even alarmed that jingoist tendencies were misguidedly propelling the country in that direction. This was followed by mixed bewilderment at unfolding events and then a complete u-turn that viewed the war not only as necessary but as a fight to the death. Following Kitchener's appeals for his 'New Armies', Halifax was ready enough to supply a goodly number of volunteers but apparently well short of expectations set by army recruitment officers. The arrival of conscription and the military service tribunals revealed many interesting new dimensions. Local socialist groups represented a significant minority who were not going to play the game at all, but of more importance was a sizeable section of the male population who were apolitical yet had little or no intention of becoming soldiers. Perhaps here there was an ambivalent attitude to total war.

Yes, the war was necessary and broadly they supported it, but rather than become soldiers their preferred options lay elsewhere. Because there was an industrial base in Halifax, many turned to making munitions and other war material. Halifax was, after all, a 'town of a thousand trades'.

Today Halifax is a part of the Metropolitan Borough of Calderdale. In 1974 this was formed by the merger of the existing county boroughs of Halifax, Brighouse and Todmorden, with the urban districts of Elland, Hebden Royd (which included Hebden Bridge), Ripponden, Sowerby Bridge, Queensbury (part) and Shelf (part) and Hepton Rural District. In terms of population size, Halifax is by far the largest of these districts, and arguably has always been the district's focus. This account will concentrate on the borough of Halifax but it must be borne in mind that it had strong links with these outlying districts.

Halifax was a significant industrial town but not one of the great conurbations of the United Kingdom. Apart from the Halifax Barracks, an establishment which led a relatively isolated existence, Halifax did not have any significant association with the armed forces. There were no Portsmouth docks, Tyneside shipbuilding or even a Woolwich Arsenal. It was a northern mill town with a variety of trades of which engineering and textiles were the most significant. For our purposes, its very 'ordinariness' is a positive feature, because it reminds us that we should not take London, or any of the other higher profile cities, as the sole marker for British popular opinion.

One of the problems with the current British public's perception of the Great War is that it has been greatly influenced by accounts written some time after the war or by eye-witness accounts delivered some distance from the actual events. The danger here is that the accounts have become coloured too much by subsequent events. It becomes necessary to revisit what people wrote down during or in the immediate aftermath of the war to gain a reasonably authentic picture of how people felt about the war at the time. In this respect a careful examination of contemporary provincial newspapers delivers a much more honest impression of life during the war. Yes, there are dangers. Whose voice are we listening to? How honest and representative were the reports? And of course we have to contend with propaganda and censorship. Despite these qualifications, there are numerous reasons why provincial newspapers deliver an unexpected authenticity. First, they read like diaries. Accounts of the voluntary recruitment campaigns in 1915 are not, for example, coloured by the inevitability of conscription. Accounts of the events of 1 July 1916 have no knowledge of the rest of the Somme campaign, of Arras or of Passchendaele. Second, part of a reporter's trade was the use of shorthand, so meetings or events were often recorded verbatim (or at least very nearly). In many cases we are hearing the actual words used at the time. Third, there is the detail. The two local newspapers, the *Halifax Courier* and the *Halifax Guardian*, were both broadsheets packed with an ocean of minute print. They are formidable to read but within them is a mass of everyday life recording thoughts, opinions and accounts. It must also be borne in mind that most provincial newspapers tended to reflect what the local community was thinking. We can be fairly sure that it was not at odds with its readers. The papers depended on sales and this was not just to a local elite. Most people who bought their local news-paper would have been members of the working class.

It is often thought that the content of provincial newspapers was so distorted by government censorship as to be a useless primary source. Adrian Faber dis-putes this, saying how difficult it would be continually to police the vast number of provincial newspapers.[3] If the papers were indeed policed, then it is difficult to understand some of the papers' candour. What is more likely is that the Halifax newspaper editors were broadly in agreement with government aims, were clear in their support of the war and willingly cooperated with guidelines sent to them. There is, for example, correspondence between the *Halifax Courier* and the government-controlled Press Bureau over how an anti-conscription meeting should be reported. Significantly it is the *Halifax Courier* which seems to be lead-ing the discussion, not the Press Bureau. Although many and various sources were used in this account of Halifax, it is the content of the two local newspapers which provides most of the narrative. In the process more than a few of the classic Great War myths were laid bare. For the record, the *Halifax Guardian* was the borough's Tory newspaper and the *Halifax Courier* its Liberal counterpart.

In early August 1914, as the European crisis was moving towards a general European war, the non-interventionist argument held most sway in British news-papers.[4] Typical of this was the editorial of the *Halifax Courier* on 1 August:

> It is lamentable to see efforts being made in this country to embroil us should there be a general war ... Are we to be rushed by jingoes into active inter-ference? Let our countrymen beware![5]

Within a week, the editor of the *Halifax Courier* had performed a remarkable about-turn:

> ... the unscrupulous action of the Germans, their complete disregard of the neutrality of Belgium and Luxembourg ... has developed the situation terribly ... For us it is a life and death struggle with Germany.[6]

The turning point, of course, had been the invasion of neutral Belgium. At a stroke this united the interventionists with the fence-sitters as well as a consider-able number of those who had been non-interventionists. From this point on the British public, including in Halifax, was convinced of the moral necessity of going to war with Germany. It was a belief that gathered momentum with each new German outrage and formed the bedrock of the British public's support for the war. It is quite remarkable how consistent this message was in the local news-papers throughout the war. As the *Halifax Courier* pronounced, 'For us it is a life and death struggle'.

When a group of Belgian refugees arrived at Halifax station on 14 October 1914 to be greeted by a reception party, a more immediate reason for war soli-darity was evident. What the Germans were doing in Belgium spoke volumes for what would be in store for any defeated nation. The mayor declaimed a message to the people of Halifax: 'we promise to stand by the Belgian people and to fight the cause until we have put down this military tyrant who has infested Belgium and would do the same with England'.[7] The government could not have put it better.

One of the myths of the Great War has been that the country was eager for a war with Germany and displayed an enthusiasm bordering on hysteria when it was declared. None of this was evident in the pages of the Halifax papers. There were no reports of jingoistic crowds gathering in public places to wave flags or sing patriotic songs. William Henry Stott of West Vale noted in his diary entry of 5 August, '11 O'clock last night war was declared against Germany, the greatest excitement prevails',[8] but the *Halifax Guardian* reports such excitement as tension, certainly not unrestrained bellicose fervour: '... the tension upon the public spirit was great, and yet it was discreetly held within bounds. It was more of an emotional excitement ... a resignation and brave submission to the inevitable'.[9]

Several reports exist of exuberant or excited crowds gathering to give a send-off to departing troops but the prevailing mood was more of support than jingoism. All of this sits very comfortably with the studies of people such as Adrian Gregory[10] and Catriona Pennell,[11] who argued for a more nuanced view of the British response to the war's outbreak.

This contrasts with what James Parker (Independent Labour Party and one of the two MPs for Halifax) experienced in London:

London is back in Mafficking mood and the blood lust has gripped its people ... I wish I could blot from my memory the scenes of the last three days ... I confess I was appalled with the light-hearted recklessness of my fellow men and women. Judging by the demonstrations of the crowd it might have been a picnic the nation was entering upon instead of the greatest crisis of a century – shouting, singing, cheering mobs beside themselves with blood lust and war intoxication ... Inside the House of Commons there was a recklessness and enthusiasm for war that was horrible to witness. ... The Tories cheered wildly. They wanted a fight with Germany ...[12]

This was not a retrospective account by a Bertrand Russell[13] or a David Lloyd George.[14] This was written within twenty-four hours of the event. James Parker is clear. Jingoism did exist on the streets of London but we must remind ourselves that London was not representative of the whole of Britain. Halifax, and one may suppose many other provincial towns and cities, did not react in this way.

Part of the reason for a lack of enthusiasm was a sober realisation that this war would mean a lot of casualties. The *Halifax Guardian* declared on the eve of war:

War is hateful, atrocious, bloody. It means on the present scale at any rate, an intensity of suffering which nobody for the time being can actually imagine. There will be heavy financial losses, but that is small to the enormous toll that will be paid in human life.[15]

A few days later, when the realisation was sinking in of what had happened, the *Halifax Guardian* continued:

Britain at the present time is plunged into a more bitter war than the existing generation has ever imagined would be the case. Those of us who have lived a little have heard of the France-Prussian War, the Crimea, and the Napoleonic struggles. All these pale into insignificance compared with what is happening today.

This runs counter to another myth, that the British public was totally naive about the potential severity of the war. It is true that few understood the real horror of modern war and probably none could have soundly anticipated its ultimate cost and duration, but there was at least an appreciation that it was going to bring severe loss and would be traumatic in its effect.

The *Halifax Courier* also has some interesting things to say about the anticipated length of the war. The classic belief has been that nearly everyone believed it would be a short war which would be 'over by Christmas'. This has been expanded in some quarters to imply that the belief was deliberately generated by the government. The latter has little basis because it is well documented that the Secretary of State for War, Lord Kitchener, projected that this would be a war of about three years. Stuart Halifax has long since discredited the simplicity of the 'over by Christmas' myth,[16] and the evidence of the local Halifax newspapers conforms closely with his analysis. If we look at the *Halifax Courier* in the first months of the war there is little reference to it being 'over by Christmas'. The general tone is that preparations must be implemented to counter the expected casualties and social distress caused by the war. Everything suggested this would be a while, although no specific timescale was ever mentioned. The tone changed by late 1914 and early 1915 when there was increasing talk that the worst was over (Germany having been checked) and the allies' superior strength would soon bring Germany to her knees. The belief that the current year would be the one in which the war would end persisted even up to 1917. The very few references to 'over by Christmas', and they are few, are found in soldiers' letters to the *Halifax Courier* or in the replies sent to them. This is a clue as to where this iconic belief may have originated. There was a tendency for all soldiers going off to war to say they would soon have the job done; 'over by Christmas', in fact. It served to reassure the families back home and at the same time it was a coping mechanism for the soldiers themselves. It is also possible that recruiting sergeants were not above using the phrase in an effort to encourage enlistment. Writing in October 1914, the *Brighouse Echo* made a telling distinction: 'What and when the end will be no one can say. Soldiers speak of Christmas, but experts are talking about twelve months hence, and some further away still.'[17]

With the war came the famous Kitchener 'call to arms' and the first real test of how committed the local communities were to the war effort. Here lay an immediate problem. Local communities in Britain existed under a system which was quite unlike those of her continental neighbours, who all lived with national service as a means quickly to mobilise vast armies. With certain exceptions, militarism was not part of the social fabric of the local communities of Britain. It is true that Halifax had the depot for the Duke of Wellington's (West Riding) Regiment, but it did not have as strong an association with its local residents as might be thought. For the rest of this account I shall refer to this regiment by its simpler title of the West Riding Regiment.

The Halifax depot was the headquarters for the 33rd Recruiting District, which covered many other West Riding areas including Huddersfield, Keighley and Skipton. Halifax was nominally home to four battalions. The 1st and 2nd Battalions alternated between home and foreign service and were in Halifax only infrequently. Its complement consisted of no more than 50 per cent who could claim to be from Halifax and the surrounding areas. The 3rd Battalion was a training battalion and again posted away from Halifax. In 1914 it was on garrison duties in northeast England. The 4th Battalion had perhaps the strongest local flavour because it was a territorial unit based on drill halls in Halifax (Prescott Street), Sowerby Bridge, Elland, Brighouse and Cleckheaton. This battalion, therefore, consisted of men living locally, but these were part-time soldiers required for home defence in the eventuality of an emergency. There was thus a lack of any strong ethos of militarism in the Halifax area. This will be a theme that runs continuously through Halifax's recruitment story in the Great War.

Kitchener's declaration that this would be a long war and would require Britain to raise a mass army completely bucked the trend of Britain's historical way of going to war. Britain simply did not have the infrastructure for recruiting, training and equipping hundreds of thousands of men. Not surprisingly, it raised practical problems. One was a need for more officers, including those who would be required to deal with recruitment at local levels. The partial answer was 'dugouts' – men who had retired from the army but had the necessary military experience. One such person was Lieutenant-Colonel Hayden Douglas Thorold, one-time commander of the 1st Battalion West Riding Regiment. He was tasked with raising the 'New Army' battalions for the West Riding Regiment. Local newspaper accounts give an impression of Colonel Thorold as a hugely enthusiastic and energetic man with a direct and somewhat theatrical approach to recruitment. Whether his style went down well with local men we can only guess. Typical of his approach was this early appeal on 13 August 1914:

> Roll up, Yorkshire lads, men of Halifax, Brighouse, Cleckheaton, Skipton, Keighley and old Huddersfield. Rally to your regiment which has for more than 200 years fought for you in every quarter of the world … Yorkshire mothers and fathers, do not hold your children back – your country needs them to learn to defend their homes.[18]

There was no instant response in these early weeks of the war, a pattern repeated around the country. A few days later, on 17 August, Colonel Thorold had to bang the drum again: '1,000 men have to be raised within 21 days for the defence of Yorkshire homes, to serve as long as the war lasts … At present only 10 have come forward in the large 33rd Recruiting Area, in response to my appeal.'[19]

Colonel Thorold appealed to clergymen 'to preach the right of every man to defend his own home' and implored private motor car owners 'to lend your motor cars … there is not a village which will not give their quota of men if visited and the men brought back at once'. The *Halifax Courier* also alluded to an issue that was to become something of a theme over the 1914–15 recruiting campaign: the response in Yorkshire was not as strong as elsewhere:

> The statement that only 10 men have come forward up to the present does not rebound to the credit of Yorkshiremen and it is to be hoped Col. Thorold will be able to report to the government that the new battalion has been filled by Yorkshiremen.[20]

However, by the Saturday edition of the *Halifax Courier* on 29 August, the news-paper was able to report the beginning of a surge which had started round about 25 August: 'The recruits for Kitchener's Army increased in a very short period (3 days) from 45 to 620 and on Thursday [27 August] 350 men were enlisted.'[21] The timing suggests that the initial trigger for this surge was the trickle of news beginning to arrive from about 25 August suggesting that all was not going well for the British forces on the continent. This began to firm up over the next few days into a British retreat. It seems that the message was finally getting through and the efforts and exhortations of Colonel Thorold's many meetings were beginning to achieve an encouraging response. Gratifying though this was, it highlighted an embarrassment for the military authorities. The Halifax Barracks could not cope:

> Victoria Hall ... is now given over to the war spirit. Commandeered by the military authorities from Wednesday it will be the sleeping place of hundreds of soldiers ... The men brought here to relieve the overtaxed Halifax Barracks will stay until called for special training.[22]

More than three weeks after the declaration of war, non-militarist Halifax and other areas in the 33rd Recruiting Area now appeared to be making some adjust-ment to the new realities that this war was going to need a lot of men. This became the proverbial 'rush to the colours' and was further fed by Kitchener's second appeal for more recruits. At the urging of Colonel Thorold, and possibly on the heels of a strong hint from the *Halifax Courier* that mayors around the country were getting involved,[23] a huge recruitment rally was convened by the mayor of Halifax for the Victoria Hall on 3 September. It was a pivotal moment. With the recruitment bandwagon finally rolling, and the civilian authorities getting involved, it was a prime opportunity for Halifax's local dignitaries to remind its citizens of why the country was at war. As grist to their mill the speakers were able to point to the alarming developments on the continent, now laid bare in the newspapers by the recently published 'Amiens Dispatch'. With British troops retreating from Mons and pursued by what appeared to be a German monolith, it was a clear case of the enemy at the gates.

J.H. Whitley, Halifax's Liberal MP and future Leader of the House, delivered the keynote speech:

> There had been an impression in some quarters that too many people did not understand the nature of the crisis and why it was necessary for as many men as possible to enlist. We were in it for liberty ... the action of Germany gave us no option ... with France perhaps beaten to her knees ... where would England be? We should be but waiting for our turn for the same thing ...[24]

Halifax's other MP, James Parker (Independent Labour Party), spoke of his con-version from 'man of peace' to his present position as a supporter of the war:

> As circumstances have come along he was heartily glad that their efforts for reduction in armaments had been unsuccessful ... glad that there was a bigger navy protecting our shores ... It was not an easy thing for him to talk like that

for war to him was a horrible and devilish thing. But there was a price at which peace could not be purchased – the sacrifice of truth, honesty and personal honour.[25]

James Parker's 'conversion' is a remarkable comment on the myth that the Great War was 'pointless'. Here was a man of the radical left who was a member of the Independent Labour Party which was pacifist in outlook, yet he was moved by the circumstances of the war not only to support its necessity, but consistently to advocate that it should be prosecuted to the bitter end. This was no blood lust on his part but a belief that the future peace of Europe depended on a dictated peace to Germany. He was later disappointed that conscription was necessary and deeply saddened by the waste and losses of the war, but never lost his conviction that, regrettably, the war was necessary.

The meeting was 'crowded to overflowing' and it took place soon after Lord Derby had delivered his famous speech in Liverpool on the concept of recruiting 'Pals' battalions – units in which men from common backgrounds and even the same workplace could enlist, train and serve together. Colonel Thorold opened proceedings and was 'enthusiastic in his praise of the "Pals" companies and assured his hearers that if they should join in bodies of fifty or one hundred he would make it his duty to see that they were not separated'.

The Pals concept is usually attributed to either Sir Henry Rawlinson or Lord Derby,[26] but it is such a logical and compelling approach to take when trying to convert civilians into citizen soldiers that it must surely have originated in the minds of many recruiting officers throughout the land. Colonel Thorold himself seemed to be thinking along these lines when he had said on 15 August: 'If practicable, I want to organise the new battalion so as to keep all men from the same district together, under the command of officers who know them …'[27]

Despite his advocacy, Halifax never did form a 'Pals' battalion in the strictest sense of the word. Several 'New Army' battalions were initially raised in Halifax, such as the 8th, 9th, 10th and 11th Service Battalions for the West Riding Regiment and later the 21st Battalion (Wool Textile Pioneers) for the West Yorkshire Regiment. The 8th, 9th and 10th Service Battalions moved out of the district in the early months of the war, and completed their complement elsewhere. They maintained a Halifax contingent but casualty returns suggest a fairly wide geographical spread of recruits. The 11th Battalion was 'cancelled' by the War Office because it had failed to reach its recruitment target and instead became part of the 3rd Reserve Brigade, which did not serve abroad. The Wool Textile Pioneer Battalion moved to Skipton fairly soon after its initial establishment and its Halifax connection may well have waned.

The newspapers frequently referred to 'Chums' or 'Pals', particularly in connection with the 4th Battalion West Riding Regiment and its reserve battalion. This was probably a reflection of how pockets of enlisted Halifax soldiers viewed themselves rather than as a consequence of any official designation.

There were two proposals, which initially at least seem to have matched the ideal of a 'Pals' unit. Under the column headline 'Pals Corps idea', the *Halifax Courier* of 6 September reported on a meeting in the Old Cock Hotel to form a battalion of businessmen.[28] The suggestion that it might be available if conscription came did not really square with the Pals concept. Thereafter any further mention of it disappeared from the local newspapers. The following week, under the heading 'Halifax Pals Battalion' in the *Halifax Courier* of 12 September, the ever-enthusiastic Colonel Thorold also proposed a battalion based on the grammar and secondary schools of Halifax.[29] Initially, the expectation was that they could join the territorial 4th Battalion but its numbers had been completed, so Colonel Thorold suggested they should become the nucleus of a Halifax Pals battalion in Kitchener's 'New Armies'. This also never materialised but it may have been that they were drawn into the Reserve 4th Battalion which was raised shortly afterwards.

This reserve battalion was the one that most closely corresponded to the 'Pals' concept. Its companies were recruited during the war and on markedly local lines. Four were from Halifax and the others from Brighouse, Elland, Sowerby Bridge and Cleckheaton. It was in many respects not unlike the Accrington Pals, who were drawn from Accrington, Chorley, Blackburn and Burnley. The difference was that the 4th Battalion West Riding Regiment was the reserve for a territorial battalion, not a 'New Army' battalion. It did not see service abroad until 1917, by which time its Halifax composition had become diluted. It is, however, still frequently referred to as the 'Halifax Pals' in many local sources.

In common with most of the rest of the country, Halifax experienced a boom period of recruitment at this time. The *Halifax Courier* noted the success of the recruitment rally and reported that Halifax Barracks was now processing 2,000 men a week.[30] On Monday, 7 September 1,100 recruits in Kitchener's 'New Army' battalions were marched from the Barracks through the town and dispatched to their training camps. Two days later a Civilian Recruiting Committee was set up to help the military authorities in their recruiting campaigns. It must have seemed that the bandwagon was finally rolling and the dream of a volunteer mass army was becoming a reality. It was never to be as good again. In the last two weeks of September the pace slackened and by October Colonel Thorold was being regularly quoted in the local newspapers as saying that recruitment was lax and too many eligible men were avoiding their duty:

> For the present, recruiting in the district is slack ... supplying members for Lord Kitchener's Army, this district, Col. Thorold feels, has been somewhat lagging ... authorities express great disappointment with the response of Halifax and district ... we have a superabundance of hesitants.[31]

The newspapers give an impression that recruitment was poor but by the end of 1914 the 33rd Recruiting District had processed 10,000 men. Relatively speaking, this was better than other cities and towns in Yorkshire, such as Leeds, Bradford, Sheffield and Hull.[32] The negativity was perhaps being generated by the frustrations of recruiting officers who could see many eligible men who were simply taking no notice of any appeals. Voluntarism had the built-in expectation that very nearly all eligible men would 'do their duty'. If this were not to be realised, then the 'New Armies' would not reach the numbers that could meet

Kitchener's projections for something like seventy divisions. In 1915 this was the big concern.

In the first few months of 1915 recruitment returns were fairly brisk, if not as heady as in the days of late August and early September 1914. The constant gifting of propaganda opportunities to Britain by Germany's crass acts of ruthlessness no doubt helped things along. The atrocities committed by the German Army in Belgium and the naval bombardment of Scarborough (a favourite coastal resort for Halifax residents) had galvanised public opinion in 1914. In 1915 this was reinforced by reports of terror bombing by Zeppelins and the sinking of non-naval ships such as merchantmen. With a knack of doing things in the full glare of the world's publicity, German U-boats were also sinking large passenger liners such as *Lusitania*. What really filled the Halifax newspapers with outrage was the German use of gas on the battlefield. The local 2nd Battalion West Riding Regiment suffered horribly in May 1915 and the papers carried numerous personal accounts from soldiers who graphically witnessed the appalling agonies of men asphyxiated by gas:

> Then the most terrible scene I have ever remembered began ... the poor beggars were staggering along the trench choking and gasping. Some dropped but were walked over by chaps endeavouring to get out ... when the gas gets into the system it terribly weakens the limbs.[33]

Even after the war, the disgust is evident in the published history of the battalion:

> ... a cynical and barbarous disregard of the well-known usages of civilised war, and a flagrant defiance of The Hague Convention ... On came this terrible stream of death, and before anything could be done, all those occupying the front line over which it swept were completely overcome, the majority dying at their posts ... The battalion suffered over 300 casualties that morning, large numbers dying as a result of this barbarous gas.[34]

Despite these provocations, it was evident by the summer that the recruitment trend was downward. Typical of this were the comments of recruiters at an indoor meeting in the Albert Theatre, Brighouse, on 22 May. The *Halifax Guardian* reported that 'the Germans' latest outrages should have convinced everyone that it was not only the Army and Navy which was at war but the whole people ... It was only a question of getting them to see that it was their duty to go.'[35]

One speaker referred pessimistically to a 'barrier of complacency' which had been much in evidence lately'. What exactly were the root causes of this 'barrier of complacency'? One consideration was that Britain was not a militarist society. Once the men who had, for a variety of reasons, already enlisted had done so, you were left with a large body of men for whom soldiering held no appeal. It was not just the understandable fear of the dangers involved, or a growing familiarity with what it was like at the front. It could also be for the very practical reason that family or economic circumstances made it difficult for them to leave home. Much of this would surface later in the military service tribunals from 1916 onwards. One stumbling block to recruitment was a concern amongst workers that enlistment would lead to a loss of their jobs when the war was over. One of the paradoxes of the war was that industrial centres like Halifax were booming with well paid jobs linked to government work. Sir George Fisher-Smith, a former mayor of Halifax, speaking at the Halifax Chamber of Commerce, believed:

> It was becoming increasingly difficult to get recruits in Halifax because, comparatively, there are few to enlist. In Halifax they were engaged to a considerable extent upon the manufacture of war munitions.[36]

One recruiting officer was less charitable in his verdict: 'There are hundreds of young fellows in the town slinking behind a badge of some description.'[37]

We must not discount that there may have been a genuine belief (although many might say excuse) amongst some eligible men that making munitions was just as patriotic to the war effort as taking up arms. Indeed, 1915 was a year in which there were two demands being placed on manpower, which in many respects were pulling against each other. On the one hand was Kitchener's drive to fill his 'New Armies' and on the other was Lloyd George's insistence on mobilising the workforce to make more munitions and other necessities of war. Which claim was the more valid? It was a conundrum for the government and one which demanded a plan to rationalise the nation's manpower resources. The government acted, and passed the National Registration Act on 15 July 1915. Its requirement was that every person between the ages of 15 and 65 was required to register details of their age, marital status, where they lived, their occupation and if they had any secondary skills. Cynics believed that the ultimate aim was to find the men who could and should be soldiers.

The day for collection of registration was set for 15 August and it was to be organised and administered on a local basis before the data was finally sent to central government. A rumour began circulating, later established as fact, that 'pink forms' were being compiled containing the names of all eligible men who had not enlisted. As always, the *Halifax Courier* put a soothing spin on this idea:

> We see there is mention of pink forms (we have not seen one) on which, it is said, the names of men of military age are to be afterwards written, for submission to the officers commanding regimental depots. We know nothing about these pink forms, but trust there is no suggestion of their use in some form of indirect compulsion. The voluntary system is the one under which the country is working, and there must be no departure from it without Parliamentary sanction.[38]

On the first anniversary of the war in August, Halifax staged a week-long recruitment jamboree. It began with a huge procession involving twenty-six vehicles filled with wounded soldiers, veterans and nearly 800 soldiers' children 'transformed by an artistic treatment of posters' appealing to the consciences and manhood of the un-enlisted of Halifax. Boy scouts, local bands, boys' brigades and the Volunteer Training Corps all pitched in. The *Halifax Guardian* commented: 'This demonstration ... was, in a manner, symbolic of the authorities going on their bended knees and begging the enlistable [sic] young men to come to a sense of duty.'[39]

On the Saturday evening the local rugby football ground was host to a military tattoo:

> The spectacle of 400 torches forming fantastic figures was one of bewildering brilliancy. To swinging martial music ... the air of the ancient Roman amphitheatre ... National Anthems of our French, Belgian, Russian and Italian Allies ... massed bands ... the mournful note of the 'Last Post' ... grand display of aerial fireworks ... gymnastic display ... bands of the two regiments.[40]

The contrast with September 1914 was stark. Then, thousands had come forward. Now it was a paltry twenty-nine. The well had dried up. The *Halifax Guardian* was rueful: 'True this is a munitions area ... but we cannot close our eyes to the fact that to many young men the appeal has gone out in vain. The general excuse is that they have good jobs ...[41]

Nationally, the September monthly recruitment figure fell below 100,000. By the end of the month Lord Derby had been appointed as Director-General of Recruiting to try one last attempt to energise voluntary recruitment and avoid the need for conscription. Armed with the information from the 'pink forms', the Halifax Civilian Recruiting Committee was instructed to organise a canvas of all un-enlisted men. The tactic was for the canvassers to confront every one of them face to face and ask them directly if they were willing to enlist. Those who agreed to enlist would then be required to 'attest' at a local recruiting office and would be placed in groups according to age and marital status. They would then be allowed to return to their normal civilian work until called up. Unmarried men were to be called up first. The local newspapers advertised appeals for men to come forward to assist the Recruiting Committee by being canvassers. Once in place, the process began on 1 November and continued throughout the month.

In theory, the canvassing was to be done 'without bullying' but the opportunities for abuse were obvious. The *Halifax Courier* gave the impression that it was all a very good-natured exercise, but we cannot discount that this was a propaganda ploy to make the job of the canvassers more acceptable.[42] By the second week in November the word 'voluntary' had become very flexible. Lord Derby had issued a warning: 'If single men do not come forward voluntarily before November 30, then measures to compel them would be taken.'[43]

Familiar conflicts still existed. The military recruitment process did not want men who were 'indispensable to any business of national importance' or who were involved in 'any business conducted for the general good of the community'. But who was the arbiter? Yet again, this role fell to the local authorities, who were instructed to set up 'tribunals' with 'adequate provision for dealing with special or exceptional circumstances'. The Halifax tribunal was appointed by the Halifax Town Council to hear applications for exemption at the town hall. The military commanding officer of the district was to have the right to appeal against any exemption granted. Thus, the essential framework was already in place for the 'infamous' military service tribunals that had to deal with applications for exemption from compulsory military service in 1916–18.

The Derby Scheme was later extended up to 12 December and a specially equipped and more central recruiting office was set up under the auspices of the

Civilian Recruiting Committee in the York Café (Alexandra Buildings, which later housed the Halifax Building Society), located more conveniently in the centre of Halifax. The *Halifax Courier* reported a last-minute rush as the deadline arrived,[44] and on occasions many of these attested men joined parades around the streets of Halifax, probably as a gesture of support for the voluntary principle.[45]

As an attempt to boost voluntary recruitment, Lord Derby's Group Scheme was reasonably successful, but it was still not achieving its fundamental aim of drawing the large mass of men who had apparently decided that they did not wish to be soldiers. Halifax's missing legions were not going to go easily. The government reluctantly recognised that the scheme was not meeting the needs of the army so it deemed the Derby Scheme 'unsuccessful'. Voluntarism had thus become the pipe-dream that many people had predicted. At this point, the conscription debate became highly charged.

We must not run away with the idea that the reluctance of large numbers of men in Halifax to volunteer equated to politically motivated resistance to state militarism. Most of the non-volunteers were apolitical and, although we have no hard statistics, it was probably a case of 'For Gawd's sake don't send me'. Nevertheless a hard core existed which *was* politically motivated and was prepared to take a robust stand against any attempt at compulsory military service. This should not be surprising as socialist groups, who were opposed to conscription and many to the war itself, were well represented in the West Riding. Nearby Bradford was the birthplace in 1893 of the Independent Labour Party, which had strong pacifist tendencies, and its first treasurer was John Lister of Shibden Hall, Halifax. In the 1918 General Election nearly 20 per cent of the Halifax voters were willing to send a revolutionary socialist, Arthur McManus, to Westminster to represent the town.[46]

Nationally, the No-Conscription Fellowship (NCF) was set up in London on 27 November 1915. The secretary of the local Halifax branch was William Richard Stoker. Its argument was that compulsory military service was defeating the very thing for which the country was supposed to be fighting. Britain had entered the war to defend liberties and to resist the militarism of Prussia, yet here she was becoming a mirror image of Prussia. The NCF's objective was to stem the drift towards conscription by means of public meetings. Some measure of the mood of the times and the heat generated by these meetings can be discerned from reports of one held by the Halifax Friendly and Trades Club at the Odd Fellows Hall, Halifax. The *Halifax Guardian* made no attempt to disguise where it stood on conscription:

> Halifax is no place for anti-conscriptionists. Prattlers on peace at any price can keep their distance. This fact was forcibly impressed on would-be speakers at a meeting ... convened by the National Citizen Party ... Conspicuous in attendance were a dozen or so local soldiers, members of the 4th Battalion of the Duke of Wellington's Regiment ... They occupied the front row of seats, and they early made their presence felt.[47]

At the sound of a whistle the soldiers surged forward and occupied the platform waving a Union Jack as they went. A minute later 'the chairman was on the ground' and then, with some of the other speakers, he was bundled out through an exit. One of the soldiers mounted the chairman's table and continued the flag waving. One soldier shouted: 'We want men for the Army. We are fighting for the women and children of Old England. We want no anti-conscriptionists here.'

Other meetings at Todmorden and Hebden Bridge were similarly over-whelmed and another at the Friends Meeting House in Halifax was seriously dis-rupted. The Liberal *Halifax Courier* also did everything it could to obstruct and discredit this meeting. Along with the *Halifax Guardian* it refused to run any advert for it and was in correspondence with the government Press Bureau over whether it should even report on it.

On 8 January 1916 the Military Service Bill began its journey through Parlia-ment and by 29 January it was law. From 1 March 1916 all eligible males between the ages of 18 and 41 were deemed to have enlisted in His Majesty's forces. From 2 March the call-up of single males would begin. Even at that point 'compulsion' was not absolute. Exemption could be granted on grounds of health, family or business difficulties and employment in work which was essential to the com-munity or was of national importance. At the instigation of two Quaker MPs, an additional exemption was included in the Bill for cases of conscientious objection to combatant service. All cases were to be adjudicated by the tribunals which were already in place to help sort out the employment issues for the Derby Scheme.

The work of the military service tribunals was arduous and varied. The vast majority of cases were, as with the Derby Scheme, to do with employment issues. Any review of their activities tends to allocate a disproportionate amount of attention to the cases of conscientious objectors, even though they represented something like only 2 per cent of all cases.[48] Nevertheless, the issues involved were at the heart of attempts by a central government to compel non-militarist communities such as those of Halifax to accept compulsory military service. Conscientious objectors could be exempted from 'combatant service', but the wording of the Bill provided only two alternatives – either to undergo military non-combatant duties or to be engaged in other types of work which 'in the opinion of the local tribunal is of national importance'. This largely satisfied the religious groups (although by no means all of them), whose objection was based on their refusal to kill their fellow men of whatever nationality.[49] What the government had not anticipated was the large number of socialists who were to confront the military service tribunals with secular arguments of conscience.[50] The most difficult to resolve were those of the 'absolutists' – religious, political, moral and ethical – who believed that it was wrong to help the war effort in any shape or form. This type of appeal excluded non-combatant work (with the military) and even work of national importance. The Bill gave the military service tribunals no escape strategy for dealing with these cases. As the tribunals were held in public (and reported in the local newspapers), the result was a high-profile legacy of difficult dealings with 'absolutist' conscientious objectors.

The tribunal panels were made up of civic-minded individuals who were basically amateurs struggling with the legalities of a complex Act. They were being tested by applicants who were often a mixture of people not entirely sure of the legal grounds of their appeal or who were presenting cases for which the

Act had made no real provision. Looking at the local newspapers in the early months of 1916 it is easy to believe that the predominant application was one of conscience. It is likely that selective reporting of the 'more interesting' cases contributed to this. Nevertheless, research by Cyril Pearce places Halifax above the national norm for numbers of claims on conscience grounds relative to its male population.[51] This should come as no surprise because, as noted previously, the West Riding of Yorkshire was home to a large number of socialist organisations and was a particular stronghold of the Independent Labour Party (ILP).

At the outbreak of war, the ILP represented an important component part of the 'Parliamentary Labour Party'. This was not a single party but an electoral pact between the trade unions, socialist societies and parties whose aim was to gain greater representation of the working man in council and parliamentary elections. The ILP was also a staunchly anti-war organisation and its executive body, the National Administrative Council, declared that it and its branches would not help recruit volunteers for the war. This created problems not only for some of its members but also for several of its elected MPs, including the Halifax MP James Parker. He broke with the ILP policy of non-cooperation with the recruitment campaign by tirelessly recruiting not only in Halifax but all around the country. This was not received favourably by his ILP political masters and he was constantly being censured by them. By the end of the war the National Administrative Council of the ILP decided it could no longer recognise James Parker as an ILP MP.[52]

ILP non-supporters of the war included Fenner Brockway, the editor of the ILP's newspaper, *Labour Leader*. He maintained the traditional ILP party line:

> I am not one of those who believe this to be a war against war, a militarist uprising against militarism, a spiritual strife over civilisation. I believe it to be a war of jealousy and fear, the inevitable result of the devilries of designing diplomats and the machinations of armament mongers.[53]

The local ILP branches acted as a focus for various levels of war resistance, including support for the No-Conscription Fellowship and the activities of conscientious objectors. In April 1916 a bitter debate spilt over into the local Halifax newspapers over the arrest of a group of conscientious objectors. On the one hand was John Selwyn Rawson, the military representative for the Sowerby Military Service Tribunal, and on the other was William Richard Stoker, ILP member and secretary of the Halifax No-Conscription Fellowship.[54] These two individuals represented the opposite poles of the conscription argument.

Stoker and the Halifax No-Conscription Fellowship had passed a motion objecting to the arrest of a group of conscientious objectors who had defied their call-up. Rawson made no attempt to disguise his feelings and wrote with clear anger to Stoker:

> ... the childish and senseless resolution passed by a few irresponsible renegades does not interest me. I am content to leave the cases of any self-styled 'Conscientious Objectors' in the hands of the Local Tribunals believing that they are quite able to deal in a proper manner with cowards and traitors who

skulk behind the hypocritical garb of religion and my only regret is that steps have not already been taken to bring to justice members of a body who are a disgrace to the country which allows them that protection and liberty to which they have no moral right ... PS If you wish to send copies of this correspondence to the press by all means do.

And this is what he did. Stoker's reply appeared in the *Halifax Guardian* on 14 April 1916 alongside Rawson's original:

> ... the general tone proves that all the Huns are not in Germany and that had our own Military Representative had a free hand without any restraining influence of such organisations such as ours the people of this country would have no need to look to Germany and Russia for undisguised brutality. They would find it in their midst ... it proves to me that militarism and brutality are inseparable. Mr Rawson leaves our cases ... to the mercy of the Tribunals. Their operation and abuse of the act have been a scandal and even the President of the Local Government Board admitted in the House last month 'that in certain cases respecting conscientious objectors, the Tribunals had taken a wrong view both of the Act and of the regulations' ... we are fighting the extension of the very militarism at home which so many have died to destroy in Prussia. In our different ways our members are working for a system of society where wars would be impossible ... through an attempt to introduce by constitutional means an International Socialist Republic.[55]

The use of the word 'cowards' by Rawson was unhelpful, because the conscientious objectors were certainly no cowards. On the other hand, the activities of the conscientious objectors were arguably helping Germany's war effort rather than Britain's. This was of no relevance to Stoker, whose allegiance appeared to be rooted in internationalism. From the practical point of view, the logical outcome of Stoker's position, if it were universally applied, was that Britain would lose the war and Germany could then impose its militarism on Europe. That was something that people like James Parker MP and the majority of Halifax had long since decided should not be allowed to happen.

There is no concrete evidence available which can tell us whether this hard core of socialist anti-war activity had any great influence on the large body of men who had refused to volunteer for the armed forces. As has been previously argued, there were many reasons for men not to volunteer, often to do with employment, and it is interesting to try to put some sort of quantitative estimate on how many of this group applied to the military service tribunals for exemption. Adrian Gregory's view was that applications to the tribunals were the norm rather than the exception.[56] He even went so far as to suggest that in nearby Huddersfield applying to the tribunals was possibly the 'automatic response to being called up'.[57] Figures for Halifax suggest a similar picture. The Halifax Book of Remembrance contains 2,064 names.[58] This equates to about 16,000 Halifax men in the army. We don't know how many of these were volunteers but nationally it was roughly half. This leaves us with a figure of about 8,000 from the Borough of Halifax who would have been conscripted. We now need to estimate the number of Halifax men who passed through its tribunal system. The total number of cases heard by the Halifax tribunals was 18,971.[59] Figures quoted in Adrian Gregory's research indicate that we need to halve the number of cases to get an approximate figure for the number of men appealing to the tribunals.[60] This gives us a total just short of 10,000. We must deduct the 1,974 exempted men[61] from this figure to give us about 8,000 Halifax men who passed through its tribunal system before entering the army as conscripts. If this were the case, then, like Huddersfield, it seems that application to the tribunals was the 'automatic response to being called up'.

In summary we could say that only half of Halifax's eligible men joined the armed forces with any degree of enthusiasm. The other half not only held back but took several positive steps to prevent it happening. Not only had they resisted the many campaigns to get them to enlist voluntarily, they had publicly refused to enlist when canvassed by the Derby Scheme and then put considerable effort into gaining exemption through the military service tribunals. Was the spirit of non-militarism in Halifax alive and kicking after all? The response of Halifax to the Great War may well have been solid in the supportive sense[62] but roughly half of its eligible men seemed to have had little intention of translating this into active battlefield participation.

Notes

1. Lasswell, H.D., *Propaganda Technique in the World War* (University of Michigan, 1927, repr. 1938, 1971).
2. See, for example, Pennell, C., *A Kingdom United* (Oxford University Press, 2012).
3. Faber, A., *The Provincial Press During The First World War: A Case Study of the 'Wolverhampton Express and Star' between January and March 1918* (Dissertation submitted as part requirement for the degree of MA in British First World War Studies at Birmingham University, 2006).
4. The big exception to this was, of course, the Northcliffe press.
5. *Halifax Courier*, 1 August 1914, p. 6.
6. *Halifax Courier*, 8 August 1914, p. 6.
7. *Halifax Courier*, 17 October 1914, p. 3.
8. William Henry Stott Diaries 1872–1935 (5 August, 1914). Unpublished (Stephen Gee private collection).
9. *Halifax Guardian*, 5 August 1914, p. 6.
10. Gregory, A., *The Last Great War* (Cambridge University Press, 2008).
11. Pennell, *Kingdom United*.
12. *Halifax Courier*, 8 August 1914, p. 4.
13. Russell, B., *The Autobiography of Bertrand Russell: 1914–44*, vol. 2 (London: 1968), p. 16. Quoted in Gregory, *Last Great War*, p. 10.
14. Lloyd George, D., *War Memoirs*, vol. 1 (London, 1938), p. 39. Quoted in Gregory, *Last Great War*, p. 10.
15. *Halifax Guardian*, 4 August 1914, p. 6.
16. Halifax, S., 'Over by Christmas. British Popular Opinion and the Short War in 1914', *First World War Studies*, Issue I, no. 2 (2010), p. 104.
17. *Brighouse Echo*, 16 October 1914, p. 3.
18. *Halifax Courier*, 15 August 1914, p. 7.
19. *Halifax Courier*, 17 August 1914, p. 3.
20. *Halifax Courier*, 17 August 1914, p. 3.
21. *Halifax Courier*, 29 August 1914, p. 3.
22. Ibid.
23. *Halifax Courier*, 17 August 1914, p. 3.

24. *Halifax Guardian*, 5 September 1914, p. 7.
25. Ibid.
26. See, for example, Simkins, P. *Kitchener's Army: The Raising of the New Armies 1914–1916* (Barnsley: Pen & Sword, 1988), p. 83.
27. *Halifax Courier*, 15 August 1914, p. 7
28. *Halifax Courier*, 6 September, p. 2.
29. *Halifax Courier*, 12 September, p. 5.
30. *Halifax Courier*, 5 September 1914, p. 2
31. *Halifax Courier*, 17 October 1914, p. 6.
32. Spiers, E.M., *The Public Response to the National Crisis.* Paper delivered to the Weetwood Hall Conference, Leeds, 28 July 2014.
33. Letter from Lance-Corporal Greenwood in the *Halifax Courier*, 22 May 1915.
34. Bruce, C.D., *History of The Duke of Wellington's Regiment (1st and 2nd Battalions)* (Medici Society, 1927; repr. The Naval and Military Press, 2002).
35. *Halifax Guardian*, 22 May 1915, p. 7.
36. *Halifax Courier*, 29 May 1915, p. 11.
37. *Halifax Guardian*, 14 August 1915, p. 5.
38. *Halifax Courier*, 14 August 1915, p. 4.
39. *Halifax Guardian*, 7 August 1915, p. 3.
40. Ibid.
41. *Halifax Guardian*, 14 August 1915, p. 5.
42. *Halifax Courier*, 6 November 1915, p. 5.
43. *Halifax Courier*, 13 November 1915, p. 6.
44. *Halifax Courier*, 18 December 1915, p. 3.
45. *Halifax Courier*, 1 January 1916, p. 2.
46. The poll result was John Henry Whitley (Liberal), 22,136, Arthur McManus (Socialist), 4,036. McManus later became the first chairman of the British Communist Party.
47. *Halifax Guardian*, 4 December 1915, p. 11.
48. Adrian Gregory estimated that about 2 per cent of all tribunal cases were of conscientious objectors. Gregory, *Last Great War*.
49. In Halifax the religious group most represented at the tribunals as conscientious objectors was the Christadelphians.
50. McDermott, J., 'The Work of the Military Service Tribunals in Northamptonshire 1916–18' (PhD Thesis, Northampton University, 2006).
51. Cyril Pearce has produced an 'index of conscientious objectors' which is calculated from the total number of identified conscientious objectors divided by the eligible male population in 1911. Presentation by Cyril Pearce given at Bankfield Museum (Calderdale Museums Service), Boothtown, Halifax, 21 February 2015. This is to be included in a future publication, *Communities of resistance: patterns of dissent in First World War Britain*.
52. In 1918 he successfully contested the Cannock Chase constituency as a Labour candidate.
53. *Labour Leader*, 10 September 1914.
54. This often referred to itself as the Anti-Conscription Council for Halifax.
55. *Halifax Guardian*, 14 April 1916.
56. Gregory, *Last Great War*, p. 101.
57. Ibid., p. 102.
58. Hornshaw, T.R. and Fowler, M.W., *Calderdale War Dead: A Biographical Index of the War Memorials of Calderdale* (Calderdale Libraries and Information Services, 1995).
59. *Halifax Courier*, 25 January 1919, p. 9.
60. See figures for Bristol. Gregory, *Last Great War*, p. 101.
61. *Halifax Courier*, 25 January 1919, p. 9.
62. The pages of the *Halifax Courier* and *Halifax Guardian* were full of numerous and diverse committees which raised money, collected a huge range of goods and made all manner of garments to provide support for soldiers and sailors in training camps, hospitals, prisoner-of-war camps and at the front. Many 'auxiliary hospitals' were opened to provide convalescence facilities for servicemen, using buildings which were loaned, staffed in the main by volunteers, and supported

financially by public fund appeals. Additionally, there were fund-raising appeals for Belgian Refugees, Belgian Famine Relief, Serbian Relief and Blind Soldiers and Sailors.

Suggested Further Reading

Crawford, M., *Going to War: People of the Calder Valley and the First Weeks of the Great War* (Hebden Bridge Local History Society, 2013)

Gregory, A. *The Last Great War* (Cambridge University Press, 2008)

Halifax, S., 'Over by Christmas. British Popular Opinion and the Short War in 1914', *First World War Studies*, Issue I, no. 2 (2010), p. 104.

McDermott, J., *British Military Service Tribunals, 1916–1918: 'A very much abused body of men'* (Manchester University Press, 2011).

Millichope, D., *Halifax in the Great War* (Barnsley: Pen & Sword, 2015)

Pearce, C., *Comrades in Conscience* (London: Francis Boutle Publishers, 2001)

Pennell, C., *A Kingdom United* (Oxford University Press, 2012)

Robbins, K., *The Abolition of War* (Cardiff, University of Wales Press, 1976)

Simkins, P., *Kitchener's Army: The Raising of the New Armies 1914–1916* (Barnsley: Pen & Sword, 1988)

Chapter 11

The Mobilisation of Halifax Industry

By David Millichope

Kitchener's famous prediction that, against general expectation, the war would last at least three years implied not just an unprecedented need for manpower but a relatedly unprecedented demand for industrial performance. His campaign to raise the 'New Armies' of millions in order to match those of the continental armies is well documented.[1] The need to supply this army and the means by which it was to be achieved were integral to adequacy in an immensely challenging circumstance. The way in which the British government was able to reorganise a peacetime economy into that of wartime in such a relatively short space of time and with such far-ranging consequences must command the utmost respect from any historian wishing to understand how Britain was able fully to contribute to the defeat of so formidable a foe as Germany.

It must be remembered that on the outbreak of war it was the War Office and the Admiralty which were responsible for handling the requirements of the armed forces for both men and materials. It should also be borne in mind that the circumstances of this war were to prove quite different from previous wars. Apart from Lord Kitchener, no one in office foresaw either the length or the worldwide extent of the war. Initially, the War Office and the Admiralty wished to obtain their supplies by dealing directly with the small group of well known and expert armament manufacturers who had served them in the recent past. Consequently, emphasis was on expanding the capabilities of these existing armaments firms.[2] The early thinking was to recruit as many skilled men as possible into the established firms from the non-armaments companies, and then to subcontract some of the work to smaller firms. The big armaments companies began actively recruiting for skilled engineering men in such places as Halifax, Leeds, Hull and Sheffield.[3] The engineering firms in these places, which were not involved in armaments production, were already facing a reduction in their workforce due to the call-up of reservists. This had been followed by further losses due to random voluntary enlistment of the country's manpower into the services. Now it seems, they were being asked to lose more men and many firms faced the possibility of having to close. Not surprisingly, they began voicing their concerns. The protests of the local employers can be illustrated by this resolution passed in early 1915:

At a meeting of the Halifax Association of Engineering Employers held on 12 January 1915, great complaints are made regarding the sending of representatives from Sir W.G. Armstrong, Whitworth and Co., and Vickers Ltd to entice the men from our shops. The meeting strongly protests against this unjustifiable means of robbing us of our employees, as practically the whole of the shops in this district are fully occupied on work for war material. The unanimous feeling of the meeting is that Labour exchanges are being used for a purpose for which they were never intended, viz, for recruiting centres for armament firms.[4]

However, in December 1914 the War Office and Admiralty were already having delivery problems with the established armament firms, in many cases owing to difficulties with subcontractors.[5] The War Office did not consider this was a deficiency in the system itself and invited the Board of Trade to help it gather more information and communicate its needs more widely through the country. In March 1915 the Board of Trade, operating through the Labour exchanges, began touting for more men and also conducted a 'census of machinery' with the intention of relocating as much of this as possible to the existing armaments companies. It was during this process that the Board of Trade became aware of the discontent and protests from firms around the country. Many did not see why they should disadvantage their own businesses so that armaments companies could make even bigger profits. At this point we begin to see something of a dichotomy. On the one hand the Board of Trade began exploring the possibility of using existing engineering firms to tender directly for contracts. On the other hand the War Office and Admiralty persisted in wanting to use what they regarded as the tried and tested channels of the existing armaments companies. Interestingly, a Cabinet mission had already visited France at the beginning of the war to see how the French handled armaments production and had found that many of the existing non-armaments companies had formed co-operatives and adapted their machinery to armaments production. The War Office was, however, averse to this idea.[6]

While the Board of Trade was proceeding with its enquiries, there was an important development in Leicester which brought into focus many of the arguments surrounding the two different approaches. When the Leicester Labour exchange had contacted the Leicester Association of Engineering Employers with a demand for 30,000 skilled men to be drafted into the armament firms, the request met with considerable resistance. It was pointed out that removing men would leave local plant idle and men would be less productive under new conditions and with unfamiliar machines. The report that went back to the government recorded that Vickers' action in going to Leicester to recruit men had 'set the local employers ablaze'.[7] They considered it would make more sense to take advantage to the fullest extent of the facilities already existing in the district. Whilst very few firms had all the necessary skills and equipment for making whole shells, it was possible to share the work amongst several of the local firms who could collectively produce complete shells. Significantly, instead of individual firms tendering for contracts, it would be the whole group that tendered. Thus was born the Leicester Co-operative group and, as we shall see later, it was this pioneering model that would eventually be applied to many areas, including Halifax. It was also, of course, a ringing endorsement of the French approach.

In 1915, as the search continued to increase production of war materials, Kitchener and the War Office still persisted with their emphasis on the existing armaments firms. On 31 March 1915 Kitchener set up and chaired the 'Armaments Output Committee'. Anyone who had been following the arguments arising from the Board of Trade investigation would have been shocked to discover that its brief was confined to taking 'the necessary steps to provide such additional labour as may be required'. At this stage it was only an advisory committee. Nevertheless, here were the small beginnings of a central control body looking at the problem of armaments production, albeit following War Office policy on how this should be done. On the committee was George Macaulay Booth, who had initially been called in as an expert adviser to the Director of Army Contracts.[8] Booth must be regarded as one of the unsung heroes of Britain's progress towards the great success story we now know as the Ministry of Munitions. He brought to the Armaments Output Committee a belief that armaments production, particularly shells, depended on 'a reorganisation of the industry on the basis acceptable to the manufacturers themselves and adjusted to local conditions'.[9] Significantly, he brought with him the experience of helping in the formation of the Leicester Co-operative group. By 29 April he was already fundamentally changing the policy of the Armaments Output Committee and bridging the gulf between the War Office and the Board of Trade, declaiming in a speech:

> Every district will have its own methods ... I advocated ... that the country should be divided up in this manner – that the big shop was best, but that the country had thousands of small shops, and that you could not move them more than a certain amount, and therefore must take the work to them.[10]

Before examining how this was applied to Halifax, we need briefly to tie up a few loose ends in the story which tells us how industrial mobilisation was going to be organised and executed in this country.

A 'Munitions of War Committee' was set up by the Treasury on 9 April and was chaired by David Lloyd George. This new committee was the beginning of a recognition that policy-making should be detached from the War Office and the Admiralty. The logic behind this move was that the structure and traditions of the two service departments had evolved under conditions in which the need for total industrial mobilisation had not existed. Thus, in April 1915 the country had two government committees examining essentially the same problem. George Booth was invited to serve on this new committee also, and was thus able to bring about the important bridging of the two service departments with the civilian Board of Trade. Booth was the classic example of a 'push and go' businessman that Lloyd George promoted to help drive the British war effort.

As Booth considered that the harnessing of surplus engineering capacity for munitions production was to take place locally, it was deemed necessary that areas would form 'Local Armaments Committees' – often called 'Munitions Committees', as in the case of Halifax – to deal with War Office and Admiralty contracts.[11] However, Sir Percy Girouard, a member of the Munitions of War Committee, had visited the committees at places such as Leeds and Birmingham and was of the opinion that co-operatives were unworkable because of the difficulties with competent inspection. His proposed solution, delivered to a meeting of the Munitions of War Committee on 26 April, was to create new 'National

Shell Factories' where all the processes were under one roof.[12] This proposal dismayed local munitions committees, including the ones at Halifax, Nottingham, Hull and Wakefield, which were already in the process of organising co-operative schemes. Others such as Bradford and Keighley had even been interviewed already by the Armaments Output Committee.

Some measure of the confusion caused by the two strands of thinking can be sensed in a Chamber of Commerce meeting reported in the *Halifax Courier* in late April.[13] The local president of the Chamber of Commerce had received a suggestion from its national organising body, the Associated Chambers of Commerce, to appoint a committee to consider how the area could contribute to munitions production. The chairman of this central body was none other than Sir Algernon Firth, a local Halifax man who appeared to be a supporter of the National Factory scheme.[14] At the meeting the Mayor of Halifax had to point out that they were in danger of having overlapping committees because he 'had been approached by the manager of the Labour exchange, asking him to call a meeting of the engineers of Halifax, the object of considering this very subject'.

Perhaps as a pragmatic gesture, it seems that the personnel from both of these two proposed Halifax committees were initially merged. The problems with inspection proved to be unfounded and so the co-operative schemes, including the one in Halifax, took on a new lease of life. As we shall see later, it would be the engineers who would ultimately emerge as the driving force in Halifax's munitions story.

The two approaches were variously adopted by the country's industrial centres according to local conditions. Leeds, Bradford and Huddersfield, for example, opted for National Shell Factories using purpose-built (or at least purpose-adapted) buildings. Places such as Halifax, Hull, Blackburn, Sheffield, Coventry and Leicester opted for the Co-operative Scheme. In some areas, such as Liverpool, Manchester and Birmingham, National Factories and Co-operative Schemes operated side by side.[15]

As a final footnote, the War Office Armaments Output Committee under George Booth developed into a compartmentalised body. On 28 April 1915 it became authorised to act without further reference to the Secretary of State at the War Office. Its charter gave it the status of a central department for 'controlling the whole of our imperial output' of ammunition. It served as the model for the new department of state, the Ministry of Munitions, which came into existence officially on 9 June 1915, with David Lloyd George as its new minister.

Halifax's response to Lord Kitchener's appeals for voluntary enlistment and the subsequent reaction to conscription is described in Chapter 10.[16] One of the issues was the on-going conflict between the demands for men to enlist in the army and the demands for men to make the materials of war. Indeed, it was said in some quarters that men were fulfilling their patriotic duty by their willingness to work in the production of war material, particularly munitions. This argument is far from convincing as war work was relatively well paid compared with other options. Nevertheless the willingness of Halifax industry and its skilled workforce to adapt to a war economy is beyond dispute, although absolutist conscientious objectors also refused to play any such role in civilian life, anathema as of course it was to their stance.

Anyone examining the changes that took place in Halifax industry during the war should be left in little doubt that such changes were radical. It might be expected that only certain industries transformed themselves to support the production of war materials, but virtually every manufacturing firm in Halifax became part of the drive for total war production. In some cases it was a matter of adapting facilities which already existed. In other cases workshops were turned over to entirely new production. Amongst the earliest to feel these changes were the textile firms. Prior to the war they had been experiencing a trade slump and many were struggling. Initially, it was thought that the disruption of their overseas markets would bring further trade misery. This fear proved short-lived due to the urgent need to equip and clothe Britain's expanding army. Although hard statistics are difficult to come by, it is evident from references in the local newspapers, as early as August 1914, that government orders for khaki yarn were having an immediate impact on the local economy.[17] The 'rush to the colours' experienced in late August and early September fuelled this still further. By mid-September the *Halifax Guardian* commented that 'the unprecedented run upon khaki and woollen at this time places many Halifax mill-hands ... in a particular [sic] happy position ... present orders guarantee full employment for several months to come'.[18]

After a dismal period in the first half of the year, local businessman William Henry Stott was able to note in his diary: 'Woollen trade very brisk. Khaki orders are being done in the neighbourhood. Also army blankets are heavily booked for some time to come.'[19]

John Crossley & Sons Ltd, which occupied a huge complex at Dean Clough Mills, was the largest carpet-making concern in the world. It was badly hit by disruption to the supplies of its raw materials and also because carpets were regarded as a luxury item. Massive orders for khaki yarn proved more than an ample replacement. Webbing – that is, the belts and straps holding in place the military accessories to a soldier's uniform – was also in great demand because there were only two firms who manufactured this before the war.[20] Webbing was traditionally made with fabric and John Crossley was able to undertake government orders, although the installation of new equipment was required. The company was later to claim that it made 'millions of miles' of webbing.[21] Other textile items produced by the firm were spun hemp and linen yarns for tents and for the fabric covering aeroplane frames and wings, along with millions of yards of blanket cloth. The firm was also part of the local Halifax Munitions Cooperative, although it was one of the smaller players.

Another significant local company and beneficiary of the boom in khaki was John Holdsworth & Company Ltd, which occupied Shaw Mills. By 1918 its profits had reached record levels. One curiosity was the commandeering by the Army Ordnance Department of several floors of one of their warehouses to accommodate a boot repair depot. Very little is known about this facility but the prevalence of many shoe manufacturers in the district probably influenced its selection.

Halifax's contribution to the manufacture of munitions must be regarded as a noteworthy achievement. The town already had a large engineering presence, particularly in the manufacture of machine tools, and therefore had many workshops with the necessary expertise to convert to munitions manufacture. One of the requirements of the Armaments Output Committee was that areas must produce whole shells, though this did not include filling them with explosives. As was noted earlier, Halifax responded to the appeals of the Armaments Output Committee by forming a local Munitions Committee which brought local engineering firms together into co-operatives for munitions manufacture. The Halifax Munitions Committee was formed probably in April 1915.[22] Its adoption was in contrast to nearby Huddersfield, which opted for a National Shell Factory scheme. Guidelines had been laid down by the Armaments Output Committee as to the composition of the local munitions committees. They were meant to include all strata of local industry, including labour representation. In the event, labour was somewhat unrepresented in Halifax unless one includes the presence of James Parker MP, who was a member of the Independent Labour Party. In Halifax the founding committee comprised the mayor, captains of industry and representatives of the Chamber of Commerce. However, it was the employers of the engineering firms who became the key players, notably: J.W. Wallis (Drakes Ltd, gas engineers and condenser manufacturers); H. Campbell (Campbell Gas Engine Company, manufacturers of engines driven by oil derivatives); J.W.S. Asquith (W.H. Asquith Ltd, manufacturers of machine tools); H. Butler (J. Butler & Co., manufacturers of machine tools); G. Stirk (John Stirk & Sons Ltd, manufacturers of machine tools); and J. Sagar (J. Sagar & Co. Ltd, manufacturers of woodworking machines). This group made up a delegation party which went to London to present their scheme for approval.[23] Once this had been obtained, the Munitions Committee elected a 'Board of Management', which consisted of the above group.[24] Their function was to deal directly with the contracts of the War Office and ensure that the firms in the co-operative group fulfilled their obligations. Other members of the Munitions Committee ceased to have any real function after this point in time. The firms which made up the co-operative group were the six listed above plus John Crossley & Sons Ltd, Robert Dempster & Sons Ltd, Greenwood Standard Gear Cutting Co., United Brass Founders & Engineers, Wood Brothers, Carter & Wright, and Charles Horner Ltd. Collectively they fulfilled orders for 4.5-inch, 6-inch and 18-pounder complete shells. Their relative contribution can be seen in Table 1.

United Brass Founders & Engineers and Charles Horner Ltd illustrate why the venture had to be co-operative. The former provided the expertise for the manufacture of the brass fuses, while the latter was needed to manufacture the delicate 'cap chambers' for the detonation mechanism. The involvement of Charles Horner Ltd also underlines how war production permeated every corner of Halifax industry. The firm was a world-famous jewellery manufacturer, which, on the face of it, would not have an obvious role in war production, yet here it was, providing a necessary component entirely in line with its workers' specialist skills. These are just two examples of what must have been a collaborative effort of different skills and equipment found amongst the members of the group. It should

Table 1. Summary of Halifax Shell Production

Company	Shells produced	Tonnage produced
Campbell Gas Engine Company Ltd	787,157	12,106
J. Butler & Co.	269,957	1,870
Drakes Ltd	182,380	5,635
W.H. Asquith Ltd	130,880	1,172
J. Sagar & Co. Ltd	63,323	656
J. Crossley & Sons Ltd	52,775	862
Greenwood Standard Gear Cutting Co.	33,301	344
Carter & Wright	32,312	320
Wood Bros	21,809	220
Dempster & Sons	8,160	54

Source: *Halifax Courier*, 15 March 1919.

be emphasised that all of this had occurred before the Ministry of Munitions officially came into existence. Examination of data from the *History of the Ministry of Munitions* reveals some interesting information about productivity. In terms of shell numbers produced per head of population, the record of the Halifax Munitions Committee appears to be outstanding (*see* Table 2), particularly when compared to other industrial areas in Yorkshire. Just why this was so is a matter for speculation.

Table 2. Comparison of shell productivity, 1914–18*

Location	Shells produced** (millions)	Population*** (millions)	Productivity (shells per head of population)
Manchester	9.66	0.74	13.1
Halifax	1.3	0.10	13.0
Leicester	1.02	0.23	4.4
Huddersfield	0.47	0.11	4.2
Birmingham	2.89	0.87	3.3
Leeds	1.5	0.46	3.3
Bradford	0.67	0.29	2.3
Sheffield	0.47	0.46	1.0

   * Blackburn has not been included here as it was a management board covering a vast area that took in numerous towns in Lancashire including Preston, Blackpool, Wigan and Burnley as well as parts of Cumbria.
  ** Data extracted from *Official History of the Ministry of Munitions*, vol. 1, pt III, ch. 1, p. 2.
 *** The Tale of the Tanks, *Halifax Courier*, 23 March 1918.

Halifax's move into shell production did not begin at the commencement of the war. At about the time the Halifax Munitions Committee was putting together its munition plans, there was another important initiative taking place in central government which had significant implications for Halifax. The government was undergoing its own 'learning curve' and it seems that to date nobody had identified that there was a shortage of machines to make the goods of war. A particular deficiency was in the number of lathes necessary for shell production. By April 1915 the Armaments Output Committee was aware of several instances where a lack of machine tools had contributed to failure in supplies of shells.[25] On 27 April 1915 Alfred Herbert was invited to create a Machine Tool Department with authority to issue instructions to firms on the manufacture and distribution of machine tools.[26] It was to be the first of many initiatives emanating from the government which directed priorities to private firms. With hindsight, it seems incredible that machine tool firms were still fulfilling civil contracts and even exporting to neutral countries, some of which were subsequently delivering to Britain's enemies.[27] The immediate consequence for Halifax was an order from the Machine Tool Department that no shell-making should take place to the detriment of its machine tool manufacture. This resulted in twelve of the original twenty-two firms having to drop out from the Halifax Co-operative Scheme in order to concentrate on machine tools. Others, such as W.H. Asquith, also complied with the directive but then adapted unused premises for shell-making. Later in the war Asquith's was to undertake a massive expansion into new buildings where the manufacture of the larger 9.2-inch shells was also undertaken.

There were numbers of themes which emerge from Halifax's Great War story that applied to nearly all of its manufacturing firms. First and foremost, they all underwent a period of unprecedented prosperity, necessitating an expansion in their workforce. Multiple shifts, including at night, became commonplace and in many cases firms expanded their premises. With varying degrees of acceptance, employees began to fill the gaps in their workforce with female employees. A significant obstacle to this was removed by the union acceptance of 'dilution' – the practice of allowing 'unskilled' labour to fill positions normally occupied by 'skilled' labour. Traditionally 'dilution', along with 'demarcation' (that is, who was allowed to do what), had been contentious issues in the engineering industry. Initially, the concession was achieved through an informal 'Treasury Agreement' of March 1915, negotiated by Lloyd George, but was fully implemented later when it became embodied in the Munitions of War Act of July 1915. The concession was part of a wider package which also included the abolition of strike action in companies engaged on war work, an automatic referral to arbitration in the event of disputes and, significantly, a capping of company profits derived from war work. All agreements were for the duration of the war only.

The government also had the powers to make any company a 'controlled establishment'. In a 'controlled establishment' every employee came under tight employment controls. Perhaps the most significant of these controls was that employees could not leave the company without a 'leaving certificate', which in practice was quite difficult to obtain. The purpose of this was to prevent a free market movement of employees between companies, thus allowing companies to retain a stable workforce. A system of 'munitions tribunals' was also set up to arbitrate on employee abuses and in disputes between employers and individual employees. Agreement with the official unions was a considerable achievement which should not be underestimated. The Ministry of Munitions had become a very significant state department with wide-ranging powers over many aspects of industrial Britain, including employment.

The widespread employment of women was one of the most significant social developments of the Great War, which many, though not all, believe had a profound influence on the status of women in Britain thereafter. It seems that the Board of Trade proactively encouraged the employment of women even before the Munitions of War Act became law in July 1915. The *Halifax Courier* reported a meeting held on 30 April 1915 in Halifax Town Hall, attended mainly by females, and called by the Lady Mayoress at the request of the Board of Trade. They were addressed by a Miss Julia Thornton, who was 'senior organising officer for women's work'.[28] It is interesting how tentative the early proposals were. Miss Thornton advocated that the potential female employees would be drawn from those who were 'women of leisure' or who had been made unemployed. She did not advocate that there was any need to use women with families or those in domestic service. The *Halifax Courier* reported:

> Among probable posts for women she mentioned shop assistants, bank and insurance clerks, tram conducting (she would leave driving to men), many openings on the railway such as ticket collecting ... carriage cleaning, chauffeurs for motor vans and the textile trades ... they would not be required in the heavy engineering but they could fill fuses, sort and store them ... There was also a need for nurses.

In the event, women came from all walks of life, including those who had families. Additionally, their employment was far more wide-ranging than Miss Thornton's conservative list, which seemed to imply that women were only capable of light housework. As to being 'not required in the heavy engineering', Asquith's employed women to move the massive 9.2-inch shells, albeit using pulleys and in pairs.[29]

The various women's suffrage movements had prepared the ground before the war for developments that would lead to greater female emancipation, but it was the recognition of the women's importance to the war effort at home that accelerated the process. In 1917 the House of Commons voted to extend the franchise to women over the age of 30 who were householders, the wives of householders, occupiers of property with an annual rent of £5 or graduates of British universities. This became law in 1918 with the passing of the Representation of the People Act. Full voting parity with men had to wait until 1928 but clearly the 1918 Act was a decisive step forward.

The manufacture of explosives required the construction of a considerable number of new 'National Factories'. By the end of 1917 there were two such factories in the Halifax area producing picric acid, one of the explosives commonly used in shells. However, as was noted earlier, the actual filling of the shells – adding the explosives to the shell case – took place elsewhere, outside the

Halifax area. The first of these picric acid factories was HMEF (His Majesty's Explosives Factory) Greetland, near Halifax, which was almost entirely a new build. It was not managed directly by the government but by a local firm, Sharp & Mallett, which already had a chemical works nearby at Copley. Using the powers of the Defence of the Realm Act, the government took possession of a site owned by the Halifax Corporation and the Lancashire & Yorkshire Railway, situated next to the River Calder and Greetland railway station. Work began in January 1917 and was completed by August of that year. The other factory was at Brookes Ltd in Lightcliffe, also just outside Halifax, which was run as a subsidiary factory called Brookes Chemicals. This appears to have been a case of using an adapted building rather than a purpose-built one. There seems little doubt that it was much smaller than the Greetland factory. Picric acid is very unstable and both factories experienced a minor explosion which nevertheless resulted in a handful of fatalities, including a young child living nearby. The two explosions occurred on the same day, 21 December 1917, although this appears to have been nothing more than a coincidence. Neither explosion was as significant as those at the picric acid factories at the Low Moor Munitions Company in Bradford in August 1916, nor at Henry Ellison Ltd in Heckmondwike in December 1914. After the war the Greetland factory was dismantled and all but disappeared from local folklore. The Brookes factory ceased production at the end of the war and had to battle a number of claims made against it by local residents who cited damage caused to local vegetation, water supplies and animals.

Munitions, khaki yarn, machine tools and explosives were the bread and butter of Halifax's war contribution, but there were also several important niche technologies. The Campbell Gas Engine Company was heavily involved in the production of engines for small nautical craft and continued this work throughout the war. Some of the engines were mounted in a handful of the landing craft used at Suvla Bay, Gallipoli, in August 1915. The company also developed the 'paravane' – a kind of small underwater 'glider' that was towed by a naval vessel, with tow-cabling designed to cut through the chain of an anchored mine bringing it to the surface for safe destruction. Related to this were the so-called 'blue otters' or 'blue pigs', which used a similar principle to wrap around U-boats before releasing a detonation which would destroy them.

G.H. Gledhill's peacetime work had been in the manufacture of cash register tills and time-recording machines. The precise mechanical nature of these devices led the company into the production of bomb-release mechanisms, which were fitted to many of the later generation bombers developed by the Air Board, including the Handley Page V/1500, three of which were readied to bomb Berlin in late 1918, each carrying a payload of 7,500lb of high explosive. It reminds us how rapidly war can drive development when you consider that the aircraft which entered the war in 1914 were small rudimentary machines used mainly for reconnaissance, and yet they went on to spawn many derivatives, including the massive Handley Page V/1500 with its intricate bomb-release technology.

One of the most intriguing stories to come out of Halifax is the possibility that it was the home of the iconic 'tin hat'.[30] It was quite unlike the helmets adopted by other countries but it should be remembered that it was developed in response to a very specific need. Shrapnel from overhead exploding shells was a major cause of casualties even in the apparent protection of the trenches, and the 'tin hat' was designed to shield the head from this threat. Alfred Bates, of Willis & Bates in Halifax, claimed to have come up with the basic design for a simple, inexpensively produced anti-shrapnel helmet using a process of metal stamping sheets of steel. By his own testimony[31] he received a French 'Adrian' helmet from the War Office to assess how a British equivalent could be made.[32] His firm made decorative metal lanterns and he was familiar with the stamping of metal sheets to produce lantern shapes. Indeed, one of his lanterns has a component which bears a remarkable likeness to the basic 'tin hat' shape. Bates coupled the simplicity of its manufacture with the use of specially strengthened steel manufactured nearby in Sheffield. No authoritative documentation can be found to back up Alfred Bates' claim outside of the newspaper reports, but the story that he was the 'inventor' of the 'tin hat' was current in many newspapers at the time of his death, including several from around the world. Today, John Leopold Brodie is credited with the invention 'mainly because of patents he took out on the helmet and the improvements he added to it'.[33] Examination of these patents, however, reveals considerable emphasis on the design of the helmet lining. Scant attention is paid to the use of metal stamping in the manufacturing process, although at a later stage Brodie was probably responsible for replacing the original steel type with a stronger alloy of manganese steel.

Halifax may also have contributed some expertise to the manufacture of some early types of flamethrower. The Germans had already employed these in 1915 and inevitably the allies were keen to retaliate. The *Halifax Courier* of 24 January 1919 reported on the wartime activities of local firm Hartley & Sugden, recording that:

> The Ministry of Munitions ... suggested the manufacture of flame-projectors on the model of the German flammenwerfers. Two types were eventually produced – the portable and the stationary ... those manufactured by Hartley and Sugdens are spoken of as the finest type of portable flammenwerfer yet manufactured ... the stationary type were first used on the Somme and have been improved by Messrs Hartley and Sugden on their own designs ... the portable type ... in the Zeebrugge raid were employed by the landing party.[34]

The specific geographical references do corroborate with what is known of the British use of flamethrowers. The *History of the Ministry of Munitions* makes reference to the use of some experimental flamethrowers on the Somme and also on HMS *Vindictive* in the attack on Zeebrugge in 1918.[35] They were, however, very experimental and may be the ones that were designed by Captain Vincent, who is mentioned in the *History of the Ministry of Munitions*. Here, there is a tantalising reference: 'Captain Vincent of the Trench Warfare Department evolved a four cylinder apparatus, or quad battery, in collaboration with a firm which had already had experience in the manufacture of compressed air machinery.'[36] Frustratingly the firm is not named, but Hartley & Sugden certainly had the necessary expertise with compressed air boilers.

There is, however, no clear connection between these and the ones designed by Captain W.H. Livens,[37] which have received more historical attention and were used in a limited capacity and with some degree of success.[38] The military did not ultimately invest much more time and resources in the further development of these flamethrowers. Instead, they favoured simpler and more cost-effective cylindrical mortars designed to hurl barrels of flammable substances, which were then ignited by bursting charges and dispersed over enemy trenches. Here the evidence for Hartley & Sugden's involvement is more clear-cut. The *Halifax Courier* was able to be specific about the company:

> ... Other weapons of modern frightfulness ... were contributed by the Atlas works in the form of gas drums, oil drums and ammonal drums. These drums were a species of shell fired from trench mortars and held more gas, inflammable liquid or explosive than could be fired out of any gun ... [over a] range of 1,500 yards ... at the start, the firm made the trench mortars for the shell, but later concentrated on the drums which they manufactured in their tens of thousands.[39]

The Ministry of Munitions had an Inventions Department and was receptive to ideas from all sources, including the public. For all sorts of reasons, most of them were rejected or failed to get past the prototype stages. A small percentage ultimately formed the basis of a useful idea. The pages of the *Halifax Courier* occasionally featured an idea by a local inventor, as was the case with the Anti-Zeppelin Dart, which was proposed by the Reverend D.R. Lewis of West Vale, near Halifax. The basic idea was that a large metal dart, or a series of them, could penetrate the skin of a Zeppelin when dropped over them from above and then explode inside, igniting the Zeppelin's volatile gases.[40] The development of these inventions often took a complicated path involving many people who all made some contribution, big or small, to the eventual end product. Under these circumstances, attribution then becomes extremely difficult. In the case of the Reverend D.R. Lewis, there is very little evidence to go on. What is officially documented is that an Anti-Zeppelin dart was designed by Commander Francis Ranken of the Royal Navy in 1915 and went into service in February 1916. It bears a remarkable resemblance to the one described in the *Halifax Courier*. All we can do is speculate. The *Halifax Courier* article claimed there was 'much correspondence with the Government', so, like Alfred Bates, did the Reverend D.R. Lewis supply the basic concept and others develop the idea further? More likely, it was a case of great minds thinking alike. The idea of piercing a Zeppelin filled with highly flammable hydrogen gas and igniting it with an explosive device was such an obvious one that it must have occurred to several people at the same time.

The protective shield or 'bullet deflector' for riflemen, developed by G.H.T. Greenwood, has many features in common with the 'Zeppelin dart' story.[41] The army experimented with several ideas for armour protection, particularly in 1915, but the only two concepts to receive any sustained attention were the steel helmet and the tank. Various items of body armour or 'bullet deflectors' were trialled but could never quite get round the problem that anything capable of stopping a bullet was prohibitively heavy for an individual soldier. Nevertheless they served some useful functions in static positions, such as with snipers and machine gunners. G.H.T. Greenwood's submission was probably lost in amongst the hundreds of similar ideas.

Industrial mobilisation, particularly when driven by the Ministry of Munitions, proved to be an all-embracing experience for many communities around Britain. Some companies turned to completely new products, whilst others adapted what they were already producing. The manufacture by Charles Horner jewellers of 'cap chambers' used in the detonation system of shells is a case in point, as is the example of Archer & Tempest. Before the war Archer & Tempest manufactured decidedly unwarlike fancy furniture such as palm stands and artistic tables for theatres. With the collapse of its peacetime trade, the works was turned over from these artistic products to making locker cabinets for hospitals, field service bed-steads and recreational tables for the huts and billets used by soldiers. Someone had to make them! Furthermore, boxes were needed to store shells and these were produced in hundreds of thousands.

The company of Fleming Birkby & Goodall manufactured leather goods and already had experience with government orders. Nevertheless, the impact of war turned the business inside out. The *Halifax Courier* reported in 1919 that 'never in its history has such reconstruction of its business been necessary to meet the needs of the times as during the past four years'.[42]

The production of webbing for soldiers' uniforms was an early priority, as the two traditional suppliers were wholly inadequate to meet the demands being put on them at the beginning of the war. As was noted earlier, webbing is a textile material and the government had to turn to companies such as Fleming, Birkby & Goodall to provide a leather equivalent. The company's involvement with war work took it into many new avenues of leather production: 25,000 sets of reins for driving mules; 40,000 blacksmith's aprons; 100,000 leather gloves for the protection of men from liquid gas; 25,000 nosebags for horses; over 1,000,000 square feet of upper leather for army boots; and up to 20,000 pairs of leather gloves per week for shell-filling factories. And so it went on.

The Great War radicalised British society in ways that could not have been anticipated. Even the most perceptive of people could not have envisaged the full extent of the changes necessary to wage a modern war of national survival. The nation's industry was in a sense the 'second estate' which worked in parallel with the armed forces. The story of how the British Army was transformed into a continental-sized army was remarkable enough, but it also required the industrial base created by the Armaments Output Committee and later the Ministry of Munitions to bring Germany to the peace table where the conditions were dictated rather than negotiated. Halifax had played its part.

Notes

1. See, for example, Simkins, P., *Kitchener's Army: The Raising of the New Armies 1914–1916* (Barnsley: Pen & Sword, 1988).
2. These included Vickers, the Woolwich Arsenal and Armstrong's.
3. For example, Joseph Henry Simpson of Launceston Street, Halifax, was a machine fitter (assembling prefabricated metal parts to build heavy industrial machinery) and worked for J. Sagar

in Halifax (woodworking machinery). The evidence suggests that he relocated with his entire family to Brightside, Sheffield, where he was accommodated in a vast complex called the Tyler Street Huts. The Vickers armaments firm was nearby. Information provided by Jean Simpson, who was Joseph Henry's granddaughter.

4. *The Official History of the Ministry of Munitions*. Vol. 1: *Industrial Mobilisation 1914–15* (The Naval & Military Press Ltd and the Imperial War Museum, 2009), pt III, ch. 5, p. 94.
5. Ibid., vol. 1, pt III, ch. 1, p. 2.
6. Ibid.
7. Ibid., pp. 11–14.
8. George Macaulay Booth (1877–1971) was a partner in the firm of Alfred Booth & Co. (ship owners and merchants) of Liverpool and a director of the Booth Steamship Company.
9. *Official History of the Ministry of Munitions*, vol. 1, pt III, ch. 3, p. 37.
10. Ibid.
11. Ibid., pt III, ch. 4, app. XI, p. 118.
12. Ibid., p. 70.
13. *Halifax Courier*, 29 April 1915.
14. Speech given by Sir Algernon Firth at a British Industries Fair dinner, Hotel Cecil, London. *Halifax Guardian*, 22 May 1915, p. 9.
15. *Official History of the Ministry of Munitions*. Vol. 2: *General Organisation for Munitions Supply* (The Naval & Military Press Ltd and the Imperial War Museum, 2008), pt II, app. V, pp. 166–72.
16. *See* Chapter 10, *How Committed was Halifax to the Great War?*
17. Commercial News, *Halifax Courier*, 29 August 1914, p. 5.
18. Mills at High Pressure, *Halifax Guardian*, 19 September 1914, p. 7.
19. William Henry Stott Diaries, 18 September 1914 (Stephen Gee, private collection).
20. Mills Equipment Company and M. Wright & Sons.
21. War Industries, *Halifax Courier*, 8 February 1919, p. 5.
22. *Official History of the Ministry of Munitions*, vol. 1, pt III, ch. 4, p. 73.
23. Halifax shell-making scheme approved, *Halifax Courier*, 6 June 1915, p. 7.
24. Shells for Halifax, *Halifax Courier*, 19 June 1915, p. 5.
25. *Official History of the Ministry of Munitions*, vol. 1, pt III, ch. 5, p. 82.
26. Sir Alfred Herbert (1866–1957), owner and managing director of Albert Herbert Ltd, a manufacturer of machine tools.
27. *Official History of the Ministry of Munitions*, vol. 2, pt II, ch. 14, app. 5, p. 168.
28. *Halifax Courier*, 1 May 1915, p. 7.
29. *Halifax Courier*, 28 December 1918, p. 7.
30. David Glover of the Halifax Antiquarians made the initial discovery of this claim from the obituary of Alfred Bates in the *Halifax Courier* of 22 October 1929.
31. *Halifax Courier*, 11 January 1919, p. 10.
32. So did about forty other people.
33. John Leopold Brodie (b. 1873). His ancestry is somewhat obscure but he claimed to have been a Russian born in Germany.
34. *Halifax Courier*, 24 January 1919, p. 5.
35. *The Official History of the Ministry of Munitions*. Vol. XI: *The Supply of Munitions* (The Naval and Military Press Ltd and the Imperial War Museum, 2008), pt I, ch. 5, p. 97.
36. Ibid., p. 96.
37. In 2011 Channel 4 broadcast an extraordinary story by the Time Team crew about the Livens Large Gallery Flame Projector. Named after the Royal Engineers officer who designed them, Captain William Livens, these flame projectors were monstrous contraptions which were installed in underground tunnels and squirted a huge jet of liquid fire over a considerable distance.
38. Major-General C.H. Foulkes, *Gas! The Story of the Special Brigade* (1934; repr. Naval & Military Press, 2009), pp. 162–4.
39. *Halifax Courier*, 24 January 1919, p. 5.
40. *Halifax Courier*, 20 November 1915, p. 3.
41. *Halifax Guardian*, 5 May 1915.
42. *Halifax Courier*, 15 February 1919, p. 6.

Suggested Further Reading

Millichope, D., *Halifax in the Great War* (Barnsley: Pen & Sword, 2015)

Wilson, T., *Myriad Faces of War: Britain and the Great War 1914–18* (Cambridge: Polity Press, 1986), ch. 20: 'Men and Munitions' and ch. 21: 'The Largest Buying and Selling Concern in the World'

The Official History of the Ministry of Munitions. Vol. I: *Industrial Mobilisation 1914–15* (The Naval & Military Press Ltd and the Imperial War Museum, 2009)

The Official History of the Ministry of Munitions. Vol. II: *General Organisation for Munitions Supply* (The Naval & Military Press Ltd and the Imperial War Museum, 2008)

The Official History of the Ministry of Munitions. Vol. XI: *The Supply of Munitions* (The Naval & Military Press Ltd and the Imperial War Museum, 2008)

Chapter 12

The Great War in 1916:
A Challenge to Faith?

By Adrian Gregory

There is a deep irony in writing of the challenge to faith in 1916. In December of that year the greatest Christian theologian of the twentieth century denied the very possibility of a history of faith. The Swiss pastor Karl Barth, in his commentary on St Paul's Epistle to the Romans which he began to write at the height of the battles of the Somme and Verdun and published as they came to their frozen ends, stated that faith was only faith in so far as it did *not* lay claim to historical reality. Faith existed outside history. But by contrast the history of the Church and 'religion' was something that existed *entirely* within the world.

Barth wrote in 1916 as a radical challenge to what he saw as the blasphemous failure of the German liberal Christianity which had previously formed his views. In particular he had been horrified at the prominent role played by his mentor, Adolf von Harnack, as a propagandist for the German cause in 1914. Harnack had penned the speech of Kaiser Wilhelm at the outbreak of the war and was a central mover of the infamous declaration of ninety-three German intellectuals. For Barth these actions represented a prostitution of Christianity and an embrace of 'Wodenism', the worship of a war god bound to a particular state. If we were to summarise the long-term significance of Barth's position we might wish to speak not of the challenge the war posed to faith but of the challenge that faith posed to war.[1]

No historian, particularly one from an essentially humanist stance, will ever be able fully to embrace Barth's position, but he remains an important qualifier on what we might or might not be able to say with confidence. We are on much more certain ground in considering the history of religious institutions and writings, including Barth's, which, as the preceding paragraph shows, can in a further irony be best explained by their historical context rather than in trying to probe the mysteries of interior religious experience.

There can be little doubt that Barth's unease about the Church's response to the war was a position that was gaining ground by 1916. Whilst it is not true that all churchmen had welcomed war in 1914 or had unconditionally endorsed the national cause, there was a widespread feeling that patriotism had polluted piety. This could be found coming from the unlikeliest of sources: the Bishop of London, Arthur Winnington Ingram, a man who is often caricatured as the most extreme of patriots, preached a sermon in Chiswick on 23 January 1916 in which he stated that: 'From end to end in England we find people, who at the bottom of their hearts have grown to believe – although they are afraid to admit it – that the war was the absolute breakdown of Christianity.'

The Bishop's quotation came from an essay by Israel Zangwill published in 1916 entitled 'The War and the Churches', which is worth considering as the work of an informed and sympathetic outsider. Zangwill pointed to the 'passive contradiction between "Rule Britannia" and the "Sermon of the Mount"'; he was particularly disturbed by the idea that the churches had gone beyond traditional and conventional loyalty to the state to a position where they were active recruiting sergeants, with some clergy even going as far as to complain that the Military Service Act had exempted those in Holy Orders. The Bishop of Worcester was alleged to have declined to ordain any man who had not attested for military service. Zangwill also claimed that whilst the established churches had been quick to condemn their enemy's abuses they had not been at the forefront in pleading for restraint on their own side. However, while making these fairly conventional criticisms, which have tended to dominate discussions of wartime religion ever since, Zangwill also pointed to signs of vitality. In particular, he praised the collection of essays by the Council of Church Union which attempted to wrestle with the meaning of the war.

But overall, Zangwill felt that the war had overly entangled not only the Established Church but most of the nonconformist denominations with the objectives of the state. This was not purely due to the war:

> The difficulties of the Christian Church are not confined to wartime. They are perpetual and inherent. They arise from it being a Church of a majority and from trying to be everywhere a national Church. But Christianity is a spirit, not an institution and that spirit the spirit of a minority. That the Sermon of the Mount is impossible as the basis of a State has been admitted by the highest ecclesiastical authority. But it was never meant to be nationalized. It was meant to be the inspiration of a few – the salt of the earth, the yeast to leaven the lump. Its hyperbolism, its spiritual extremism is necessary to offset the grossness of the body politic. ... Christianity cannot 'pay'. It is a religion for losers ... This attempt to fit the tragic universe of ours into a comfortable Church establishment is hopeless.[2]

Although Zangwill as a Jew interprets the situation in a more secular manner than Barth, there is the same sense that Christianity is something that cannot be reconciled with powers and principalities. The logic of this would be seen practically in Britain in 1916 by the stance of religious conscientious objectors. The price of liberal and nonconformist support for the introduction of conscription had been the acknowledgement of the legitimacy and possibility of 'conscientious objection' to military service. In the event, a significant number of those who objected did so on broad humanitarian and socialist grounds and they have tended to dominate the historiography. But it is probably the case that a majority of those who objected to military service did so precisely because they were true believers in Zangwill's and perhaps Barth's vision of what Christianity was supposed to be.

A website (www.forthesakeofthekingdom.co.uk) provides intriguing details of the experiences of members of the International Bible Students Association, a group which would subsequently become better known as the Jehovah's Witnesses. Not generally recognised as an historic 'Peace Church' like the Society of Friends, their members often had a hard time trying to persuade Military Service Tribunals of the validity of their objections. In March 1916 a widower in Rugby was reported as having stated to the tribunal that five years previously he had vowed his loyalty to the Almighty. The local press reported on the subsequent exchanges:

> President of the Tribunal: Don't you think it is compatible with the Christian Life to defend your Country?
>
> Applicant: I have no country, sir, I gave up my citizenship. Whilst I have always realized the privilege of being born in this country, yet my oath of allegiance is to the King of Kings.
>
> The Reverend Challoner asked whether he would be willing 'like the Master' to undertake noncombatant work in order to 'relieve suffering'.
>
> The applicant replied: In this I must consider what the Master would do. It may seem very good to alleviate the suffering of the poor soldiers at the front but I hear them say on coming back 'It is ten hells in one'. Take a man from the jaws of death and nurse him back to life. For what purpose? To send him back to those ten hells in one. No, I'm of the opinion it would be better to let him die and await the Lord's coming.

The Tribunal nevertheless was only prepared to grant a 'conditional' exemption based on Noncombatant Service, which the applicant rejected. It is an interesting case in that it shows that some applicants held conscientious views which modern sensibilities might find uncomfortable – that it was better for a wounded soldier to die and face the Lord's judgement than be saved to return to the front. However, the very toughness of this view might be taken as evidence of its sincerity. At least a hundred 'Bible Students' made such 'absolute' claims.[3]

The spring and summer of 1916 saw these performances occurring the length and breadth of the nation. The resonances were powerful. The appearance before the 'magistrates' was resonant of the traditions of Christian martyrdom, both in the days of the early Church and during the Marian persecutions recorded in Foxe's Book of Martyrs. It is likely that both sides of the Tribunal bench were all too aware of it. The nineteenth-century experiences of tithe disputes and then education acts had kept alive the confrontational spirit of 'old dissent' and one cannot help feeling that many religious objectors actively relished the opportunity to testify and suffer for Christ.

Although most nonconformist clergy supported the war, they also were active in supporting conscientious objectors. For example, the leading Baptist Frederick Meyer headed a fact-finding mission in June 1916 in order to examine the situation of those who had been pressed into the army and sent to France.

The energy that conscription and conscientious objection gave to nonconformity in 1916 was not so obviously available to the Church of England. But the Anglicans were about to undertake their own massive exercise in renewal.

At the start of the war William Temple, the son of a former Archbishop of Canterbury and the rising star of the Anglican clergy, had presented the view that the war ought to be an opportunity for the Church to renew itself. In 1915 he was the leading light on a committee appointed by the Archbishop of Canterbury to consider the idea of church renewal. Temple was the principal proponent of the idea of a 'National Mission of Repentance and Hope'. Archbishop Randall Davidson called together the clergy of his own diocese in January 1916 and in the spring of that year Anglican clergy were prepared for a major effort to renew the faith of the nation. Almost all of the parish clergy of Oxford Diocese attended one or other of the retreats that were organised. In Manchester 1,000 out of 1,025 priests attended a related day conference later in the year.[4]

To supplement the efforts of the clergy and to provide material for sermons and homilies, the Church sponsored a major pamphleteering effort. Although the pamphlets would represent most positions in the Church, there was a heavy emphasis on positions that William Temple found most congenial, works which stressed the ideas of sacramental Fellowship and Christian Socialism. Perhaps most remarkable is the fact that the second pamphlet was written by George Lansbury, the leading socialist and active Anglican layman.

Lansbury, with his newspaper, the *Daily Herald*, was by 1916 one of the strongest voices of dissent on the war and on government policy, an opponent of conscription and an advocate of a negotiated peace. It must have seemed immensely strange to many outside the Church of England, and not a few inside, that he was being invited to contribute to the official propaganda of the Church at this time. Lansbury's pamphlet presented the war as a moral opportunity to challenge capitalism:

> Since August 1914 we have lived through terrible days that have brought home to us the futility of the mad scrabble for material riches . . . But if the futility of material things is being proved, there is something else we are all able to recognize. No one hates and detests war more than I do, yet out of it come great and noble deeds which fill us with admiration and love. . . . The trenches call out this spirit of comradeship and brotherhood just because each is striving to do his best for all.[5]

This view that the redemptive values of war and the values of socialism were the same could also be found, at least implicitly, in Temple's pamphlets for the mission. It is worth remembering that the war was the climax of a great wave of Christian Socialist idealism developing since the 1880s and exemplified above all by the inner city missions that had drawn so many young upper middle class men to its centres such as Toynbee Hall. The idea that this was how the Church would reconnect with the masses was already well established.

The National Mission mobilised tremendous enthusiasm for a short while but there is little evidence that it made much of an impact on the laity in 1916. The 'Repentance' part of the Mission drew the fierce criticism of the crooked dema-gogue publisher Horatio Bottomley, who was then at the height of his power and influence. Always hostile to the moralising of the religious, he attacked the Mission for daring to suggest that those fighting a righteous war had anything of which to repent. He also accused the Mission of being obsessed with working class behaviour, particularly in relation to drink and sex. Whilst these accusations did not in fact reflect the spirit of the Mission as a whole, there was just enough truth in them to make many uneasy.[6]

The acerbic Dean of Durham, Herbert Henson, had never had much faith in the National Mission and wrote of it in early 1917:

> The National Mission seemed to me to be a grave practical blunder, for the time was inopportune and there were none of the conditions for success. Its only permanent consequence for the Church was the raising into sudden and unmerited importance a number of foolish persons, ardent, bigoted and ill informed, who would not otherwise have gained a hearing or been given any authority. The problem demanding solution at the hands of the Archbishops is how to end the mission without loss of dignity. In order to save face they are lending themselves to a whole series of continuation movements, crude and ill conceived.[7]

The analysis is rather reminiscent of the traditional view of the Battle of the Somme: badly conceived and continued from stubbornness to no avail. But rather as the Somme can be seen to have carried important low-level lessons for the future of the BEF, so it could be argued that the National Mission did provoke some useful thinking amongst the lower levels of the Church. Henson's hostility to the Mission had been shaped by his conservatism; it shouldn't be seen as the whole story.

For an Anglican layman's view of the situation of English religion in 1916 and its difficulties, it is worth looking at one of the great confessional tracts of the war. Donald Hankey was a Christian Socialist who had volunteered for the army as part of a lifelong quest to break down class barriers. He was killed in action on the Somme in October 1916 but not before he had delivered a manuscript of what would be his lasting legacy, the autobiographical series of essays, some previously published in the *Spectator*, entitled *A Student in Arms*.[8] In it he reflected on the 'inarticulate religion' of the ordinary soldier. He begins by pointing to a commonplace of the first two years of the war:

> There has been a great deal of talk since the war began of the Church's opportunity ... I have seen letters from Chaplains complaining bitterly of the phrase. What did it mean? ... They admitted that they had hoped the war would make men more serious [but] the men still appeared to be the same indifferent careless heathen they had always been.[9]

It is worth noting that Hankey, like most Anglican observers, showed no sense of a crisis in the faith of ordinary soldiers, rather he assumed that their religious involvement was relatively limited in the first place. He goes on to describe a group of soldiers discussing a singularly poor sermon delivered by a Chaplain: 'One man began to scoff at the Old Testament ... Another capped him by laughing at the feeding of the 5,000. A third said that anyone who pretended to be a Christian in the army must be a humbug.'[10] Hankey's reflection on this became

a profound meditation not on the faith of the ordinary soldier but on the articulation of religion in Edwardian England:

> This is surely nothing short of a tragedy. Here were men who believed
> absolutely in the Christian virtues of unselfishness, generosity, charity and
> humility, without connecting them in their minds with Christ; and at the same
> time what they did associate with Christianity was just on a par with the
> formalism and smug self-righteousness which Christ spent his whole life in
> trying to destroy.[11]

Nevertheless the intense anti-biblical and anti-clerical sentiments he recorded to
some extent overshadowed the situation where, '[a]s a matter of fact, I believe in a
vague way that lots of men do regard Christ as on their side'. He concluded that
the bigger problem was that men like himself had been side-tracked into trivia
and failed to focus on the fundamental message:

> It is certainly arguable that we educated Christians are in our way almost as
> inarticulate as the uneducated whom we always want to instruct. If we apply
> this test of actions and objects of admiration to our own beliefs we shall often
> find that our professed creeds have very little bearing on them. In the hour of
> danger and wounds and death, many a man has realised with a shock that the
> articles of his creed about which he was most contentious have mattered very
> little and he had somewhat overlooked the articles that proved to be vital. If the
> working man's religion is wholly inarticulate, the real religion of the educated
> man is often quite wrongly articulated.[12]

In later essays Hankey returned to what this would mean to the Church and saw
some hope in a future where the educated Christian layman and a new clergy
could effect a reformation within the Churches around the idea of a loving god
and a suffering Christ. Hankey was not the only Christian Socialist who would
think on these lines. Richard Tawney survived the Somme despite having been
badly wounded on the first day; his faith would also survive but not without a
traumatic moment. In returning fire against the German soldiers whilst he was
lying in no-man's-land, Tawney would remember a brief moment of pleasure in
killing, followed by profound guilt at the idea that he had become a 'mischievous
ape' destroying the image of God.

In practical terms, an example of what Hankey had in mind had begun to
develop at Poperinghe in the Ypres Salient. In December 1915 a military chaplain, Philip 'Tubby' Clayton, established a soldiers' club called Talbot House in
memory of Lieutenant Gilbert Talbot, who had been killed in 1915. According to
Gilbert's chaplain brother, the original idea had been to name the club 'Church
House', but the military hierarchy objected to the name because they 'smelt
tracts'. 'Toc H', as it soon became known, was both a site and a movement. With
the slogan 'abandon rank he who enters here', the facility was a tea room, a
lending library and a concert/lecture hall. But the small upstairs chapel was able
to attract a congregation at all times. A similar spirit could be found for troops on
leave at St Martin's in the Fields in London, just off Trafalgar Square. Here the

ex-chaplain, Dick Shepherd, was a reforming vicar who saw himself as having a particular mission to the ordinary soldier.

It was also in 1916 that the most famous of the chaplains of the BEF rose to prominence. In recent years the career of George Studdert Kennedy, known as 'Woodbine Willie', has begun to be properly appreciated. Far from being the bluff caricature of a patriotic cheerleader for the war, he was a man deeply engaged with the 'inarticulate' identified by Hankey.[13] In 1916 he wrote to a fellow chaplain:

> Live with the men, go where they go, make up your mind that you will share their risks and more if you can do any good. You can take it that the best place for a padre is where there is most danger of death. Our first job is to go beyond the men in self-sacrifice and reckless devotion. Don't be bamboozled into believing that your proper place is behind the lines – it isn't.[14]

All of which might be seen as the conventional response of a good pastor, but during the course of the year, in his actions, his prose and his poetry, 'Woodbine Willie' would also develop the core of his own theodicy, and would practise an intense devotion to a 'suffering God' who could, through suffering, understand and comfort a suffering humanity. After the war he would take his experiences into the joint causes of the industrial mission and pacifism, and would die exhausted by his efforts in 1929.

The British case, considered above in some detail, was probably not exceptional amongst European nations by 1916. Everywhere the escalation of death and suffering had led to questions. The Russian Slavophil and mystical Christian poet Zinaida Gippius had been ambivalent from the start of the war but by the end of 1915 she had dropped any patriotism:

> In the last hour, in darkness fire
> Don't let the heart forget
> There never has been a true just war
> And never will be yet
>
> And if this is the hand of God outstretched
> This terrible path of blood
> My soul will fight even Him
> My soul will rebel against God.[15]

But at the same time that some wrestled with extreme doubts, others retained a profound faith under challenge. The articulate members of the German middle class were in many respects not dissimilar to their British counterparts. The former theology student Johannes Haas wrote to his parents from Verdun on 13 May 1916:

> Here we have war, war in its most appalling form and in our distress we realize the nearness of God. Things are becoming very serious, but I am inwardly unalarmed and happy, 'Let me go, I long to see Jesus so'. It must be splendid to see God in all His glory and his Peace ... I do not fear Judgement, I am indeed a poor sinful creature but how great is God's mercy and the Saviour's love ...

I thank you dear Parents for having led me to the Saviour, that was the best thing you did.

Haas was mortally wounded a fortnight later but lived long enough to write a final letter stating how glad he was to have time to prepare for his 'heavenly homecoming'.[16] Killed on the same day, the philosophy student Heinz Pohlmann had written that he felt safe in the hands of God, trusting in the resurrection, and that 'Many Roads lead from men to God but from God to men only one'.[17]

The battle of Verdun dominated the psychological landscape of France in 1916 and inevitably it came to dominate the spiritual landscape as well. In April of the same year Maurice Barrès first used the term *La Voie Sacrée* – the sacred route – to refer to the one road from Bar Le Duc which allowed reinforcements to be moved into the battle zone. It was a conscious echo of the *Via Sacra* in Rome but also resonant with the idea of Christ progressing through the Stations of the Cross. Whilst the title was not officially adopted until 1922, there is a sense that the battle had taken on a certain feel of 'Calvary' for the French soldiers who passed through the maelstrom. At Verdun the officer priest Gaston Millon kept a journal through Holy Week in 1916. His final entry was made under bombardment at Mort Homme on Easter Saturday:

> Jesus lies dead in his tomb. I in my death shelter may die at any moment … My lamp has been blown out and a soldier killed. O My God receive my soul. Death is on our midst; it is always near, always possible. My soul is ready to meet it. It will be my deliverance if I survive this war with what fervour shall I seek to save souls. But now I am still a priest, I must set an example of courage.[18]

Millon was killed shortly afterwards when he left cover from the bombardment to minister to casualties. His self-sacrifice was celebrated by Maurice Barrès in his 1917 propaganda work which pushed the idea of Union Sacré. Barrès claimed that the officer in command of the unit concerned, a free-thinker, arranged a Requiem Mass for his comrade and spoke afterwards of how France would require the united efforts of all her children.[19] It might be easy to dismiss this as a propaganda construct and indeed the relationship between the 'spiritual families' of France was not always so smooth. Nevertheless front-line service could often push people together in unusual ways. Georges Duhamel recounted the efforts made by a Muslim orderly to secure a decent burial for a co-religionist. The usual burial detail was two Roman Catholic priests, Monet and Renaud, who were serving as stretcher bearers. After a brief discussion they agreed to act for the dead Algerian whilst 'Rashid represented the dead man's kindred with much dignity. He held something in his hand which he planted in the ground before going away. It was that crescent of plain deal at the end of a stick which is still to be seen in the midst of the worm-eaten crosses.'[20]

Duhamel, an army surgeon, was not religious in a conventional sense but he entitled his powerful memoir of the year of Verdun, *La vie des Martyrs*. The book consciously views the suffering of the wounded in a way that parallels the corporeal sufferings of the early Christians. Duhamel was also clearly aware that the original Greek meaning of the word 'martyr' was 'witness'. These were men who both physically bore faithful witness to the human capacity of suffering and were witnesses to it.

But what of the French civilians who had to deal with separation and bereavement? In the case of Maurice Galle, killed on the Somme at the age of 22 in 1916, his mother composed a poetic prayer at the end of the war thanking God for her son's life:

For the twenty years of happiness given to me
For my dear little son
I thank you Lord
For his sweet infancy
For his loveable adolescence
For his beautiful and sweet youth
I thank you Lord …
For the joy of the reunion on leave in our dear house
Christmas 1915 and to 1 January 1916
I thank you Lord …
Because on 25 September 1916
He volunteered for a most dangerous mission
Because he was a magnificent French officer
And a pure Christian knight
I thank you Lord …
Because you let us know the details
Of his last moments
And we know that he didn't suffer
We thank you Lord[21]

Whilst this might appear to be the complacent and traditional sentiment of a civilian well removed from the front line, the sense that a mother could still use such traditional forms and find comfort in them speaks to a real and not to be underestimated significance of faith amongst many. This is too easily overlooked in standard accounts.

It was towards the end of the year that the classic story of French civilian piety really began. The teenage Claire Ferchaud had been troubled by religious visions since childhood but it was in the autumn of 1916 that her visions of the Virgin became most intense. In December 1916 she was brought before a commission established by the Bishop of Poitiers where she recounted her experiences. It was during her interrogation that Ferchaud revealed her mission: to persuade the anticlerical President of the Third Republic to add the image of the Sacred Heart of Jesus to the Tricolour. In March 1917 when the commission reported, it was somewhat ambivalent. Whilst broadly endorsing Ferchaud's visions as genuine, there was a distinct lack of enthusiasm for pursuing the mission. With good reason: Bishop Humbrecht was well aware that the move would be seen as a partisan assault on the secular French state. In the end, Ferchaud would receive an audience with the President and it would end badly. The Vatican was no more supportive.[22]

Roman Catholic reactions to the brutal *Materielschlacht* of 1916 could be mixed and ambivalent. In his study of Bavarian soldiers during the war, Benjamin Ziemann argues that 1916 saw a widespread decline in piety. In July 1916 only six soldiers from the entire 14 Reserve Regiment had even bothered attending confessional when it was available. In September the chaplain of the 6 Reserve Division described the men suffering 'agonizing doubts about their faith' and large numbers losing it entirely. In one Bavarian battalion only five soldiers went to confession in the whole final quarter of 1916 and in a hospital of more than 5,000 men only 80 attended a Mass.[23] Even the chaplains could be assailed by doubt. Karl Lang, a chaplain at Verdun, felt that the 'tempter' was showing him the thousands of dead in order to make him doubt God's existence.[24]

But the same kinds of caution that Hankey expressed about the British Army might be in order. There may have been a turning against some of the outward and formal signs of piety and an upsurge internally and other more complex reactions as well. Ziemann suggests that front-line infantry still showed a greater tendency towards attending Mass than supporting troops and that severe fighting could still lead to pious manifestations. Private prayer might have grown in significance. Soldiers wrote to their families and in apparent earnestness solicited prayers for their safety. Many of the same practices that Becker noted for France could also be found amongst the Bavarians: Marian Rosary prayers were popular both at the front and at home. *Schutzbriefe*, collections of printed prayers for protection, became popular. Overall, Ziemann suggests that for a pious minority faith remained a significant source of psychic support but that nearly all soldiers developed an intense dislike of those priests whom they saw as too propagandistic in support of the war effort.

One might observe similar difficulties for Irish troops in the course of 1916. The Irish nationalist MP Tom Kettle was killed in the fighting near Ginchy on the Somme in September. In his poem 'To my daughter Betty – Gift of God', he expressed his frustration about how his legacy would be seen in the aftermath of the Republican Easter Rising:

You'll ask why I abandoned you, my own
And the dear heart that was your baby throne ...
Know that we fools, now with the foolish dead
Died not for a flag, nor King, nor Emperor
But for a dream born in a herdsman shed
And for the secret Scripture of the poor.[25]

Kettle was more than aware that the imagery of Christian sacrifice had been central to the uprising against English rule of his now estranged comrades, who had consciously planned the Dublin Rising to coincide with Holy Week. Patrick Pearse and several others of the leaders were deeply devout Roman Catholics and the suspicion has always been that there was an element of a passion play in the voluntary blood sacrifice of the Rising. It should also be said that other leaders were far more secular-minded. Most intriguing perhaps is James Connolly, who helped plan the Rising. He was a militant Marxist but embraced Catholicism before his execution. In a manner oddly reminiscent of Edith Cavell, when he was asked by his confessor to say a prayer for his firing squad, he stated that he would say a prayer 'for men who did their duty according to their lights'.

Initially the Irish Catholic hierarchy was reluctant to embrace the rebellion and a number of bishops went as far as condemning it. But ultimately, the largely subconscious appeal to Catholic piety can be deemed successful and it is notable that the Protestant Roger Casement, captured by the British as he tried to run guns for the rebellion, would also convert to Catholicism before his execution.

Before concluding the discussion of Catholicism, it is worth noting that the end of 1916 saw the accession of the only reigning monarch of the twentieth century seriously considered for sainthood. The death of Franz Josef of the Dual Monarchy saw him succeeded by the Emperor Karl, who would be beatified in 2004. The new Emperor and his wife Zita were known for their intense personal piety. In the course of 1916 this would dovetail with the interests of the Dual Monarchy in their attempt to encourage by means of Zita's relations a negotiated peace, an effort which was strongly supported by Pope Benedict XV.

It might be appropriate to end with some reflection on the greatest non-Christian theologian of the twentieth century who had a powerful influence on Christian theology nonetheless. In April 1916 Martin Buber began the publication of his periodical *Der Jude*. In his editorial he wrote sympathetically of the German cause, hoping that Germany in victory might serve as a broker to bring together the peoples of East and West in a new understanding. This provoked a fierce response from his friend, the anarchist Gustav Landauer, who on 12 May 1916 accused him of simply parroting war propaganda and attacked the idea that *Gemeinschaft* – community – could ever genuinely arise from war and murder. Buber's immediate response was to complain that Landauer had misread him and was being unfair. However, Landauer's prediction that Buber would come to regret his stance does seem to have been borne out. As early as September 1916 Buber wrote critically to his contributor Hermann Cohen, a figure in German Reform Judaism. Cohen in many respects held a standing similar to Alfred von Harnack's prestige in liberal Protestantism and he was similarly patriotic. Buber stated explicitly that 'humanity is greater than the state'. Buber's theology would develop in a way that would in some respects be a polar opposite of Barth's. Whereas Barth would stress the utter separateness of God and man, Buber would push towards mystical unity, the position of his master work *I and Thou* published in 1923.[26]

In fact, in February 1923 Buber tried to arrange a meeting with Barth to discuss the eschatological challenge of their time. The meeting never took place but Buber would later reflect that Barth's utter remoteness of God, and his own idea of complete intimacy with the divine, could be seen paradoxically as opposite sides of the same coin. Both men knew that the God of the nineteenth century, and of the confident progress of Church and State in harmony, had died in the war.

Notes

1. An accessible discussion of Barth's significance can be found in P. Jenkins, *The Great and Holy War* (New York: HarperCollins, 2014), pp. 217–24.
2. I. Zangwill, *The War of the World* (Toronto: 1916), p. 214.

3. www.forthesakeofthekingdom.co.uk/tribunals.html. Accessed Wednesday, 13 January 2016.
4. A. Wilkinson, *The Church of England and the First World War* (London: SPCK, 1978), pp. 73–4.
5. Cited in A. Gregory, *The Last Great War* (Cambridge: Cambridge University Press, 2008).
6. Ibid., pp. 168–72.
7. Cited in Wilkinson, *The Church of England*, p. 78.
8. R. Davies, *A Student in Arms: Donald Hankey and Edwardian Society at War* (London: Ashgate, 2013).
9. D. Hankey, *A Student in Arms* (London: 1917), pp. 98–9.
10. Ibid., p. 107.
11. Ibid., p. 108.
12. Ibid., p. 110.
13. M. Grundy, *A Fiery Glow in the Darkness* (Worcester: 1997).
14. Ibid., p. 44.
15. Cited in 'J. Howlett, 'We will End in Hell my Passionate Sisters', in D. Goldmann (ed.), *Women and World War 1: The written response* (London: Macmillan, 1993), p. 86. Translation by Jana Howlett.
16. P. Witkop (ed.), *German Students War Letters*, trans A.F. Wedd (1929; reissued University of Pennsylvania, 2002), p. 207.
17. Ibid., p. 195.
18. Cited in M. Barrès, *The Faith of France*, trans. E. Marbury (Boston: 1918).
19. Ibid., p. 259.
20. G. Duhamel, *The New Book of Martyrs*, trans. F. Simmonds (New York: 1918), pp. 71–3.
21. A. Becker, *La Guerre et La Foi* (Paris: Armand Colin, 1994), pp. 139–40. Author's translation. *La Guerre et La Foi* has this poem written by the soldier's grandmother.
22. R. Jonas, *The Tragedy of Claire Ferchaud* (UC Berkeley, 2005), pp. 57–61.
23. B. Ziemann, *War Experiences in Rural Germany*, trans A. Skinner (Oxford and Providence: Berg, 2007), pp. 128–9.
24. Ibid., p. 135.
25. T. Kettle, *Bartleby.com*, accessed Thursday, 14 January 2016.
26. M. Lowy, 'Romantic Prophets of Utopia: Gustav Landauer and Martin Buber', in P. Mendes Floher and A. Mali (eds), *Gustav Landauer; Anarchist and Jew* (Oldenbourg, 2015), pp. 76–8.

Suggested Further Reading

Davies, R., *A Student in Arms: Donald Hankey and Edwardian Society at War* (London: Ashgate, 2013)
Gregory, A., *The Last Great War* (Cambridge: Cambridge University Press, 2008)
Jenkins, P., *The Great and Holy War* (New York: HarperCollins, 2014)
Snape, Michael, *God and the British Soldier: religion and the British Army in the First and Second World Wars* (London: Routledge, 2005)
Wilkinson, A., *The Church of England and the First World War* (London: SPCK, 1978)

Chapter 13

Facial Surgery, Rehabilitation and the Impact of Medical Specialisation

By Andrew Bamji

The First World War engendered dramatic advances in facial surgery.[1] The most significant developments took place in Britain, where a single-site unit was developed in Sidcup, in south London, which brought together very considerable numbers of patients under the care of a large international multidisciplinary team. Treatment and outcomes for patients with facial injuries were enhanced by major developments in surgical technique and anaesthesia. Patients were often admitted for lengthy or multiple periods on account of the complexity of the surgery, and these prolonged stays created an environment in which they helped one other. Sympathetic rehabilitation evolved in parallel with a growing under-standing of the potential needs of disfigured men. Together, these developments brought about a profound change in the nature of the doctor-patient relation-ship. The hospital also had a significant teaching function, which was facilitated by standardised record-keeping. By contrast, in France and Germany innovation in facial surgery was limited by a failure to concentrate resources and the main-tenance of surgical autocracy. The development of the French self-group *Les Gueules Cassées* was a direct consequence of the lack of support from physicians and surgeons for patients with facial injuries, compounded by the relative isola-tion of these patients because they were treated in a number of different units.

The medical history of the First World War is of course a flourishing area of research. Much scholarship has concentrated on services on and behind the front line.[2] The diversity of those who were involved in caring for the injured has been an important focus of recent work.[3] Patients have been at the forefront of many other studies, including Emily Mayhew's semi-fictionalised work, *Wounded*, which portrays two patients with facial injuries, although it does not discuss their surgery or post-war experience.[4] This chapter sheds new light on the role of patients within the medical sphere, drawing attention to their agency in terms of their own surgical treatment, and their contributions to the recovery of other injured men. Most of all, however, this chapter focuses on the impact of a single surgeon's determination to concentrate, in one place, medical specialists and patients with facial injuries. The results were momentous in three major areas: positive outcomes for individual patients, medical recognition of the educational and scientific benefits of specialisation, and the development of a new surgical specialty – plastic surgery.

Injuries and Casualty Management

The process by which British casualties were treated developed rapidly in the first year of the war. In 1914 the British Expeditionary Force had a medical service numerically over-stretched for the casualties it would suffer and then one which would need expansion on a huge scale to furnish an army transformed in size to meet the requirements of the war. As the numbers of troops and casualties escalated in early 1915, a triage system which had been devised before the war was brought into play. Patients moved through a series of stages of increasing sophistication, from the basic regimental aid post at the front line, to the large and well equipped casualty clearing stations and base hospitals set in the rear areas. This system was effective, but not effective enough, partly because the transport of injured men was held up while their condition was stabilised. By mid-1915 it was realised that these delays led to a significant increase in the proportion of wounds which became infected, then further worsened by early wound closure so that infection was sealed in. As a result, casualty clearing stations were moved closer to the front, wound cleansing was undertaken at an earlier point, and surgical shock was treated more promptly and effectively.

Surgical practices differed vastly from those of Britain's late nineteenth-century military conflicts because of recent developments which addressed the three main enemies of surgeons: the inability to keep patients still on the operating table, infection, and blood loss. From the mid-nineteenth century surgeons used ether and chloroform to provide anaesthesia during operations which enabled them to perform lengthy operations for the first time. Furthermore, an improved understanding of infection led to the development of antiseptic and aseptic techniques. Surgeons, for example, no longer wore the same blood-stiffened aprons for all their operations. By the early twentieth century, moreover, physiologists were investigating the impact of significant blood loss during surgery and were developing an understanding of how to deal with the resultant surgical shock.

The combination of more effective casualty management and surgical innovation meant that survival rates increased. In turn, surgeons were exposed to complex cases more frequently, and the number of experienced surgeons working nearer the front grew. At the same time the changing nature of warfare had an impact on the kinds of injuries which reached these surgeons. By 1915 warfare in the open had been replaced by war conducted in trenches. Rifles, machine guns and heavy artillery firing high explosive and shrapnel shells replaced carbines and cannon. The infantry were issued with steel helmets from late 1915 owing to the number of fatalities from head wounds. The move away from soft caps reduced the incidence of skull wounds, but men were still receiving significant, even if non-fatal, injuries to their unprotected faces.

The Origins of a Dedicated Facial Injury Service

Plastic surgery was not an established surgical speciality at the outset of the First World War. Although there was a longstanding tradition of facial surgery in India, dating back to the sixth century BC, few European surgeons carried out facial surgery prior to the twentieth century, one notable exception being the sixteenth-century Bolognese surgeon Gaspare Tagliacozzi (1545–1599), who established a technique for nasal reconstruction.[5] Some surgeons had taken an interest in facial surgery in the decades prior to the war. The American Gurdon Buck (1807–1877) operated on men injured during the American Civil War, but his results were poor.[6] Two French surgeons, Charles Nélaton (1851–1911) and Louis Ombrédanne (1871–1956), published two books in 1904 and 1907 which drew on their collection of material about rhinoplasties and other facial procedures.[7]

Over the course of the war more than 15,000 French soldiers were treated for a facial wound, and the French *Service de Santé* recognised the need early in the conflict for facial reconstruction. The *Service de Santé* identified a small number of surgeons whose pre-war work had involved some oral surgery and distributed these surgeons across France. British surgeons who had been transferred from civilian practice to war service soon took an interest in their work. Among them was the ear, nose and throat (ENT) surgeon Harold Gillies (1882–1960). Aged 33 in 1915, he was a man good at everything. His surgery was meticulous and excellent. He was a competent violinist and pianist and a sportsman of note. He had played cricket at school in New Zealand, and rowed at no. 7 in the winning Light Blue boat in the 1904 Oxford/Cambridge Boat Race while studying at Gonville and Caius College, Cambridge. Gillies sometimes neglected his surgical duties when the call of golf was too strong, notably missing a consultation with Dame Nellie Melba. He won the Grand Challenge Cup at Sandwich in 1912 and played for England in an amateur match against Scotland.

Gillies visited the French surgeon Hippolyte Morestin at the *Val-de-Grâce* Hospital in Paris in 1915, and was subsequently posted to Boulogne, where a French-American dentist, Charles Auguste Valadier, had offered his services to the British Army – the French had turned him down – and was trying to develop a facial reconstruction service.[8] Valadier and Gillies 'hit it off', and the army appreciated Gillies' involvement as a trained surgeon since Valadier had no medical qualifications. Gillies recognised that the increasing number of facial casualties would generate a surgical need and returned to Paris to find out more about Morestin's treatment of facial injuries. But this time Morestin refused to allow Gillies into his operating theatre. Morestin was a surgical autocrat who wanted neither to share his experience, nor to collaborate with his dental colleagues, whom he treated as servants.

Finding no way forward, Gillies returned to England. He approached the head of army surgery, William Arbuthnot Lane, and set out his vision of developing a dedicated facial injury service. Feeling that Morestin's self-imposed isolation was reactionary and counter-productive, he outlined a plan for a service which would exploit the specialised expertise of ENT and oral surgeons, dentists, radiologists and anaesthetists. Lane agreed that he should proceed, and allocated him a ward at the Cambridge Military Hospital in Aldershot, Hampshire. Gillies had concentrated a group of surgeons and other practitioners with key expertise in one place, and now needed to ensure that patients reached them. He devised a special casualty tag to be attached to facial injury cases in transit so that they would be directed to his unit. When he took his design to the War Office he was told that it was impractical to distribute special labels, but he took the prototype to a stationer in The Strand and spent £10 on a large batch, which he took back to the War Office and left with a clerk with instructions that they be sent to France and spread round the casualty clearing stations. Within weeks, patients started to appear with his labels attached. As Ana Carden-Coyne has shown, many standard medical cards were lost in transit so people further down the line did not know what treatment had already been administered.[9] By contrast, it appears that Gillies' special labels were rarely lost.

Gillies and his new colleagues set to work. Immediately, they discovered a major snag. Existing reference works which dealt with facial techniques either did not cover the new pattern of injuries or the procedures described were ineffective. Nélaton and Ombrédanne described numerous different operations in their books, which were fully illustrated with diagrams, but when Gillies tried the procedures, they failed. The absence of photographic images from these publications suggests that Nélaton and Ombrédanne had studied accounts of the procedures but had not repeated them in practice. As a result, Gillies and his team went back to basic surgical principles and began to devise entirely new techniques. Gillies was the polar opposite of Morestin and sought to exploit the skills of anyone who might contribute to useful outcomes for patients, whatever their parent discipline. Dental technicians became an integral part of the team because of their capacities in the fixation of jaw fractures. These technicians utilised textbooks published before the war, mainly in Germany, and devised new splints in consultation with the surgeons.

By late 1915 Gillies decided that written operation notes needed to be supported by portraits of the patients. He realised that drawing an occasional diagram to illustrate a procedure was insufficient as an aide-memoire for the surgeons, did not capture change over time, and did not allow case notes to serve as a basis for training other surgeons to undertake procedures successfully. Gillies arranged for a photographer to be attached to the unit, and developed a systematic approach to visual record-keeping, obtaining black and white photographs of full face, profile and oblique (right and left) for each patient. Some surgical details could only be depicted in a colour image, so Gillies was pleased when Henry Tonks (1862–1937) turned up at Aldershot to help the war effort. Tonks had trained as a surgeon but subsequently had given up medicine to pursue a career in painting, teaching at London's Slade School of Art from 1893. Gillies rapidly recruited Tonks, who was working as the Adjutant's assistant and was delighted to be able to use his artistic skills. Tonks produced a series of pastel portraits, including a number of 'before' and 'after' studies of Gillies' patients. He also made lightning sketches of Gillies' techniques while observing operations.[10]

There things might have rested. Gillies and his team were coping at Aldershot and had devised a system of patient rotation, because the surgeons began to appreciate that most patients needed more than one operation. When patients arrived with an infected wound, it had to be cleaned first. Most wounds of mouth and nose were infected by the organisms that normally inhabit these structures, and many patients had poor dental hygiene which aggravated the risk. Furthermore, once surgery had been performed, it was usually followed up with further surgery once it was considered safe to proceed with the next step. To prevent men from blocking beds for days or sometimes weeks, the new system transferred patients to convalescent beds outside the hospital when they did not need to be on the ward.

An Expanded International Service

The system held until the first day of the battle of the Somme on 1 July 1916 when, as Gillies commented, with some exaggeration, 200 patients were expected but 2,000 arrived. Gillies and his team were overwhelmed and he went straight to Arbuthnot Lane to discuss what should be done. Inspired by Queen Mary's Hospital for amputees at Roehampton, Gillies and Lane decided that a special hospital, dedicated to facial injury management, should be established. Although many amputations were carried out at a casualty clearing station or base hospital, there was a parallel in that both adjustment to artificial limbs and the cycles of facial injury surgery were time-consuming processes. In both cases, moreover, it was recognised that severely disabled men should be offered sensible rehabilitation. After all, a man who had been a chimney sweep before the war could hardly be expected to return to his former occupation if he had lost an arm, or if his appearance and speech might frighten ladies and their maids.

Gillies and Lane sought out a site, aided by Charles Kenderdine, the Secretary of Queen Mary's, Roehampton. Kenderdine was aware that the Frognal estate in Sidcup was on the market. The house and grounds were purchased, and Gillies set to work with a firm of architects to design a hospital in the grounds. Fundraising began in early 1917, jump-started by some large donations from wealthy businessmen and aided by a concerted campaign in the press. The hospital's Cuttings Book reveals that articles extolling the proposed new hospital appeared in newspapers across the country.[11] These articles made an emotional appeal to readers by emphasising how difficult life would be for these severely disfigured men and explaining how extensive rehabilitation facilities would be provided as part of the hospital's service. Fundraising efforts were enhanced by HRH Queen Mary's agreement to sponsor Sidcup and it was agreed that the new unit would be known as the Queen's Hospital.

The fundraising campaign said little about the surgical reconstruction to be undertaken by the hospital's surgeons, but surgery was always a central dimension of plans for the new hospital and Lane found Gillies an ideal new colleague, the oral surgeon William Kelsey Fry (1889–1963), whose regimental aid post with the Royal Welch Fusiliers had been obliterated on the Somme, with Fry the only survivor. Gillies also drove forward a further change in strategy. He proposed that the hospital should not be just a British enterprise. All of the Dominions had established separate hospitals in England, where surgeons were carrying out some facial surgery. Gillies argued that it would be much better if they all moved to Sidcup. The hospital opened its doors in August 1917 with a British staff contingent, soon supplemented by staff from Canada, Australia and New Zealand. In the latter case, a certain amount of coercion was required, because Henry Pickerill, the head of the jaw unit at the New Zealand Hospital at Walton-on-Thames, was reluctant to move. Pickerill did not care for Gillies and feared that his autonomy would be constrained with someone else in charge. It was only when Queen Mary herself had a quiet word that Pickerill came on board, although he insisted that his unit should maintain its own separate operating theatre.

The hospital was subsequently expanded from an original semicircle of asbestos sheet wards by a further build in concrete. Gillies replicated his convalescent arrangements at Aldershot by requisitioning a series of private houses and Parkwood Hospital, a large mental health institution in Swanley, providing a total of over a thousand beds. Convalescent beds were a holding point while a patient healed from a previous operation, rather than, as Ana Carden-Coyne has suggested, a halfway-house before discharge home.[12] Gillies' address to the Medical Society of London in 1917 set out his core aims for the hospital: to return men to the front if possible, to do the best for each patient, and to contribute to science and the knowledge of surgery.[13]

More than 5,000 patients passed through the Queen's Hospital. Surgery was highly organised, and the maintenance of standardised records with profuse illustrations facilitated the teaching of new staff who continued to join the unit even after the end of the war. Gillies later used these records when he wrote his seminal 1920 textbook, *Plastic Surgery of the Face*.[14] Following the Armistice, new cases continued to be referred from elsewhere until the early 1920s. Surgery on existing patients also continued for some years after the end of the war until 1925 when the remaining eight patients were transferred to Roehampton and the hospital was closed.

Anaesthetic and Surgical Advances

Effective anaesthesia was a necessary precondition for successful surgery. Both ether and chloroform were available to the surgeons; ether was a stronger anaesthetic agent but loathed by patients because it induced nausea and vomiting. Traditionally, the anaesthetic was administered to the patient via a gauze pad in a face mask. However, this practice obscured the operative field and was impractical in facial work. Moreover, if a patient with a significant jaw wound was laid flat, there was a risk that the tongue – missing its normal attachments – would flop back into the throat and obstruct his breathing. Kelsey Fry had observed this precise issue while serving in France. Initially, patients were operated on in a sitting position, which obviated the problem but meant that the anaesthesia was often too light. Surgeons and anaesthetists experimented with delivering the anaesthetic directly into the trachea via a tube. The drawback of this approach was that the gas, often accompanied by spatters of blood, was expired into the surgeon's face, and the surgeon would start to become drowsy. Anaesthetists resolved the problem by adding an extra tube which redirected the expired air well away from the surgeon. Eventually, the anaesthetist Ivan Magill (1888–1986), who arrived in Sidcup in 1919, improved things further by using a single wide-bore tube for both inspiration and expiration.

Gillies and his team devised and refined numerous new surgical techniques, and carried out reconstructions of all parts of the face, including noses, cheeks, lips and jaws. At the outset, Gillies dealt with soft tissue and Fry with hard tissue, although later their roles were more blurred. Grafts of different kinds were used to reconstruct parts of the face which had been damaged or destroyed, and the surgeons experimented with different techniques, paying close attention to aesthetic as well as medical considerations.

Nasal reconstruction required bone or cartilage support, which was provided using rib grafts. The new cartilage was often embedded first under the skin of the forehead, and a complete flap with support was turned down later. The inside of the nose is lined with specialised epithelial tissue called mucosa, and the surgeons recognised that a graft would fail if this were not recreated. When forehead flaps were raised, the surgeons took care not to run into the hairline so that the nose did not end up with a hairy tip. By contrast, when an upper lip was reconstructed they would deliberately take a flap from within the hairline so that the patient could grow a moustache on his new lip and conceal the repair. Gillies noted the propensity of cut flaps to roll up and experimented with holding it rolled, by stitching it into a tube. He found that this technique reduced the risk of the open underside becoming infected and enhanced the blood supply down the tube which improved the survival of the graft. The use of this 'tube pedicle' allowed skin to be moved successfully to the face from distant parts of the body, even very large grafts. Later, Gillies deliberately included larger blood vessels in flaps to achieve the same end.

Reconstruction sometimes had to be begun by undoing the effects of previous surgery. Wound repair was straightforward at the onset of the war: the raw edges of a wound were simply stitched together. However, shell wounds usually involved major tissue loss and did not lend themselves to being repaired in this way, because the skin was stretched so far that it became distorted, a problem worsened by scar contracture. When Gillies encountered a patient who had received a primary repair elsewhere, he divided the scars and allowed the tissues to return to their original position, later moving new tissue to fill the gaps. The surgeons at Sidcup planned repairs carefully. Once a defect had been delineated properly, a paper pattern was made, often from a plaster cast to ensure three-dimensional accuracy. As with noses and lips, the surgeons always tried to replace like with like. Large full-thickness grafts did not always survive if they were simply moved as free grafts from another part of the body. Gillies found that somersaulting tubes were more reliable. A graft taken from the leg could be moved to trunk or arm. Each time, the next step would only be taken once a new blood supply had been established.

Techniques were also developed in response to how the nature of warfare created particular types of injury. Shell wounds could cause the bone underneath soft tissue to fragment. X-rays were used extensively to delineate loss and to identify the presence of bone or metal fragments. Early attempts to reconstruct jaws using grafts of bone and cartilage were unsuccessful: grafts failed to fuse or were resorbed. The British surgeon Gilbert Chubb (1876–1966) realised that early fixation was key to graft survival, and working closely with the dental technicians developed immobilisation splints. The splints, together with surgical fixation using shaped grafts and firm screws, largely solved the problem.

Some soldiers arrived at Sidcup having suffered burns. The problem of major soft tissue damage was particularly difficult to manage in burns patients, where a large area of skin usually developed a contracture. If the skin around the eyes were involved, the patient would not be able to blink; tears would spill over onto the face and cause chronic irritation. Gillies developed a technique of eyelid reconstruction which obviated this problem.

Despite Gillies' wish to produce results that would allow patients to return to the front, he learned rapidly that it was dangerous to rush treatment. His maxim 'Never do today what can honourably be put off until tomorrow' was exemplified by a severely burned air force officer with severe depression who insisted aggressively that Gillies should raise a large chest flap at once. Gillies agreed against his better judgement with disastrous results: the flap became infected and the patient died. Gillies wrote that he should have taken 'a very firm attitude, and could he have persuaded the patient to wait a year, the operation, as planned, would have had more chance of success'.[15]

Gillies once commented that it was more difficult to get a good case than to hide a bad one. For the most part, the surgeons and other specialists collaborated fully and discussed their cases extensively. Gillies, Fry and Tonks often stayed up late into the night to talk over difficult cases, and sometimes more than one operation was run in the Plastic Theatre at the same time. Surgeons were thereby able to give instant feedback and advice when something was not going right. The extent of collaboration should not be overstated, however. Some surgeons clashed and J.L. Aymard, who had moved with Gillies to Sidcup from Aldershot, returned to his native South Africa under a cloud. Aymard later claimed to have been the first to have performed a tube pedicle operation and made a formal complaint to the General Medical Council that Gillies had stolen his idea, although the dates in the respective case notes confirm that Gillies performed the operation first.

Peer Group Support and Rehabilitation

These techniques and strategies facilitated the capacity of the surgeons at the Queen's Hospital to offer their patients good quality surgical repairs. Treatment was further enhanced by an imaginative approach to recovery which valued each patient's input and which encompassed a comprehensive and sensitive rehabilitation programme. Patients at Sidcup were treated as equals. Elsewhere, surgeons made decisions for them and without them. At Sidcup, by contrast, Gillies included patients as part of the multidisciplinary team. Repeated admissions cemented relationships between patient and surgeon in a way unparalleled in any other surgical discipline. Surgeons worked from pre-injury photographs when reconstructing faces, and also allowed patients to choose their own nose shape from a photograph album of different profiles.

Photographs played other important roles. Each patient had his own photographic record to remind him of his progress and improvement. This record was also a permanent reminder that even if his new appearance were not entirely satisfactory, it was far better at the end than at the start, and certainly better than if nothing had been done at all. Photographic series were also shown to new patients, often as traumatised by their expectations of continuing disfigurement as by the injury itself, to give them hope of eventual improvement. Each patient was also encouraged to contact the hospital if things were not going well, and reassured that his case would be reviewed.

This approach was psychological support before it was even recognised as such. Patients also developed their own self-help structure. The long stays allowed them to get to know each other, and they supported each other as new patients arrived and they moved to and from hospital, convalescent unit and home. Family photograph collections of both staff and patients underline this camaraderie and corporate self-help. Group photographs, produced as Christmas postcards, acted as long-term reminders of hospital friendships which endured for many years after their time at Sidcup. Nurses and ancillary staff also developed deep attachments to their charges, and there were numbers of marriages between staff and patients.

Rehabilitation was planned sensitively. The hospital offered numerous classes, some of which were designed to enable men to stay out of the spotlight if they wished. Four men were trained in cinema projection, and others became dental technicians and photographers. Toys produced at Sidcup were renowned for their quality. Lady Gough, the widow of General John Edmond Gough VC, ran an essay class which aimed to improve patients' literacy; the essays which patients produced attest to their positive attitude and adjustment to their circumstances.[16] As at Queen Mary's, Roehampton, the hospital for amputees, and at St Dunstan's, which cared for the blind, men who returned from the war with a disability and had been treated at Sidcup were set up for productive future lives. Men's minds were kept from introspection by entertainment as well as occupational training. The hospital had football and cricket teams and an annual athletics day.

Many scholars have argued that the incidence of depression was significant amongst patients who had experienced facial disfigurement.[17] Indeed, as Ana Carden-Coyne has highlighted, Gillies himself commented on the incidence of depression in a *Lancet* article of 3 November 1917. However, the outlook of men who had incurred severe facial injuries improved substantially soon thereafter, as techniques were refined and patients were able to observe the excellent surgical outcomes for their predecessors. This argument is supported by evidence of pantomimes written by patients, which were performed at Christmas each year. These performances were pervaded by black humour and reflected the patients' ability to laugh at themselves, as well as illustrating their sense of self-worth. Some surgeons, Gillies included, joked with their patients.

A negative response to facial disfigurement was more widespread amongst the general public than amongst those directly affected. As Sander Gilman wrote, 'no more horrible result of war could be represented in the public sphere than the mutilation of the face. Even the rebuilt faces were understood as so grotesque as to mirror the anxieties about the impact of the war on everyone's humanity.'[18] The emotional impact on patients was exaggerated by contemporary sources such as newspaper articles, because they were designed to solicit financial contributions. Some patients were even encouraged to go up to London, essentially to parade their disfigurements and to reinforce the message of the press that funds were still needed to support the running of the hospital. Patient testimonies of course reveal varied personalities and a range of responses to their disfigurement, but only a minority of the injured sought to shut themselves away. Others even took a mischievous delight in causing a fright. One man, who had been issued with a temporary mask, used to take it off on the bus, causing ladies to scream and faint. He would return to Sidcup holding up as many fingers as people he had terrified. Another patient returned pretending that he had dropped his temporary nose and a dog had run off with it.[19]

The close relationships between staff and patients at Sidcup were wholly exceptional, and it took decades for the medical profession to embrace the concept of a patient being a part of his own management team, with input into his treatment. 'In the line', the passage of severely injured men through the casualty clearing stations was too fast for any prolonged doctor-patient relationship to develop, while in the base hospitals, and home hospitals in the United Kingdom, surgical input was largely a one-off affair, with longer-term support delegated to nurses, physiotherapists and other staff.

French, German and American Approaches

A specialised, centralised service for facial wounds was not developed in either France or Germany, leading to poor outcomes for soldiers with such injuries.[20] In France the *Service de Santé* set up several hospitals, each of which was controlled by an individual surgeon.[21] These hospitals were widely spread in geographical terms, including institutions in Amiens, Bordeaux, Marseilles and Lyon. Wards, moreover, were allocated by site of injury, with one for jaws, one for eyes, and so on. Surgeons did not communicate with each other and reacted rather than developed. No one surgeon saw enough cases to develop new surgical principles, and surgery focused on repair rather than reconstruction. There were few prolonged and repeated admissions and no rehabilitation. Many patients ended up with contracted scars which created substantial disfigurement. By British standards, the surgical work was incomplete and French patients often relied on carefully made masks to hide their injuries.[22] Following the war, only a few unillustrated doctoral theses reviewed the management of facial injuries, and no textbooks on the subject were published. There was certainly much handwringing about the terrible wrong done to these men, and a cohort of *mutilés* was paraded at the signing of the Treaty of Versailles. All the same, Frenchmen with facial injuries were essentially left to fend for themselves. Widely dispersed, as mentioned above, they set up their own self-help organisation, *Les Gueules Cassées*, as a response. A similar organisation did not emerge in Britain because the ethos and environment of Sidcup rendered it unnecessary.

In Germany, similarly, facial work was distributed to a small number of dispersed surgeons and dentists. Repair rather than reconstruction was also the norm here. The priority of German surgeons was to return soldiers to the front line as soon as possible where this was feasible; otherwise, patients were abandoned to their fate. Some scholars have argued that the Prussian culture of parading duelling scars led to a different attitude to disfigurement, in which scars were treated as a badge of which soldiers should be proud, but it is implausible that the ordinary private soldier took this view. The images of 'completed' patients in Ernst Friedrich's 1929 anti-war polemic *Nie Wieder Krieg* attest to the failure of reconstruction and rehabilitation.[23] All the same, it may be noted that state support for German war veterans was reasonably generous at first. War pensions only became unaffordable following the financial crisis of 1929.[24]

The American experience was mixed. Some surgeons had rallied to the French cause, set off for France early in the war and set themselves up either in French hospitals or in American-run hospitals catering for the French. These surgeons included Frederick Allbee, Robert Ivy and Varastad Kazanjian; like the French they worked in relative isolation. In 1918 Gillies suggested that, with the incipient arrival of American troops, it would be sensible if a detachment of American surgeons were 'attached for training' to the Queen's Hospital. The records show that these surgeons did more than just observe and Gillies later paid tribute to their innovations.

After the War

There has been considerable debate about whether the trauma of wartime injury and disfigurement led to significant psychological disturbance amongst those affected. Family accounts of the post-war histories of more than eighty men who were treated at Sidcup lead the author of this chapter to conclude that – remarkably – the majority of men who acquired significant facial injuries lived largely contented lives after their treatment.[25] Undoubtedly disfigurement led to some harrowing experiences: men were jilted by their fiancées or jeered at in the street; some were self-conscious and disliked having their photograph taken, or were embarrassed by a speech impediment. However, most men returned to their pre-war occupations, sometimes they bettered themselves as a result of their occupational rehabilitation, and many raised large and happy families.[26] Certainly, their surgery had wrought wonders in some cases, such as for Pte Thomas of the Cheshire Regiment, who was treated between 1918 and 1924. Men who appeared damaged by the war were traumatised, in the main, by their war experience rather than by their injury, or had pre-existing psychological disturbance.[27]

As the flow of wartime casualties dwindled to a trickle, a large surgical establishment was no longer necessary at Sidcup. By 1925 most of the surgeons who had worked at the Queen's Hospital reverted to their original specialties. Henry Pickerill returned to New Zealand. Gillies remained in Sidcup, supported in his work by Thomas Pomfret Kilner (1890–1964), who had joined the unit in 1919. Archibald McIndoe (1900–1960) and Rainsford Mowlem (1902–1986) joined Gillies' practice in 1930. Civilian surgery brought new challenges because cosmetic surgery was not viewed positively in Britain at this time, in contrast to attitudes in the United States.

The threat of war in 1938 prompted a government review and Gillies and Kilner were asked to plan services in advance, using the principles for surgery and support which had been established in the First World War. Sidcup was considered too risky a site, given the likely flight path of bombers *en route* to London. Provision for the treatment of facial injuries was organised along service lines.

Gillies took army casualties at Rooksdown Hospital near Basingstoke, McIndoe set up his renowned unit for RAF casualties at East Grinstead, and Mowlem and Kilner took casualties to St Albans and Stoke Mandeville respectively. Additional smaller units were established in Birmingham, Bristol, Chepstow and elsewhere. All these units admitted significant numbers of civilians who had received blast and shell fragment injuries in bombing raids.

Conclusion

Harold Gillies, a bright but difficult polymath, predicted that the new kind of warfare would create new surgical challenges, and succeeded in establishing a specialised unit to tackle these challenges. He brought together a multitude of professionals from different backgrounds to work on a mass of patients, whose arrival at the hospital was engineered by his own ingenuity. The sheer number of casualties stimulated important developments in surgery and anaesthesia and established plastic surgery as a speciality in its own right. As Gillies himself wrote in 1957, 'we had witnessed the organisation of a new surgery. The justification for such a bold assertion lies in the fact that plastic surgery had passed from the empirical to a stage based on sound principles.'[28] The careful recording of techniques, in detailed and standardised patient notes, meticulous photographs and vivid pastels, enabled surgeons to learn from each other and to share new insights effectively. Gillies' system was so effective that it was replicated in the war that began little more than twenty years after the Great War had ended. The developments in plastic surgery which were stimulated by the First World War had a close parallel in the field of orthopaedics. Here too, the concentration of orthopaedic resources, coupled with large numbers of casualties, led to a much more rapid exchange of experience than would otherwise have been the case.[29] One outcome was a sea-change in survival rates for fractures of the thigh.

By their nature and length, wars between great industrial powers result in huge numbers of casualties, but when they are over and the casualties have been dealt with, surgical and rehabilitation facilities which have been developed are inevitably in excess of need. However, every major war has led to surgical and other management advances. For instance, the small number of burns cases at Sidcup set the scene for burns surgery on RAF aircrew in the Second World War; the Troubles in Ulster in the 1980s resulted in advances in major trauma management; and in Afghanistan immediate surgical intervention and rapid evacuation extended the original lessons learned in the First World War.

The treatment of facial injuries in the First World War set a pattern for modern patient management in the United Kingdom in other important ways. Long patient stays, and the need for repeated operations, created trust between surgeons and patients and a breakdown of traditional surgical behaviour with the autocratic pre-war attitude of surgeons replaced by a more consensual and supportive approach. Such a change in attitude underpins all subsequent advances in facial surgery, where the fully informed consent of the patient is paramount – not just so that they understand what will happen to them, but also so they appreciate what might go wrong.

Notes

1. Many thanks to Alex Bamji for her substantial input into this chapter.
2. See Mark Harrison, *The Medical War: British Military Medicine in the First World War* (Oxford: Oxford University Press, 2010).
3. For example, Alison S. Fell and Christine E. Hallett, *First World War Nursing: New Perspectives* (Abingdon: Routledge, 2013).
4. Emily Mayhew, *Wounded: From Battlefield to Blighty 1914–1918* (London: Bodley Head, 2013).
5. Gaspare Tagliacozzi, *De curtorum chirurgia per insitionem* (Venice, 1597).
6. See B.O. Rogers and M.D. Rhode, 'The First Civil War Photographs of Soldiers with Facial Wounds', *Aesthetic Plastic Surgery*, 19 (1995): 269–83.
7. Charles Nélaton and Louis Ombrédanne, *La Rhinoplastie* (Paris: Steinheil, 1904), and Charles Nélaton and Louis Ombrédanne, *Les Autoplasties. Lèvres, joues, oreilles, tronc, membres* (Paris: Steinheil, 1907).
8. For a contemporary surgeon's account of Valadier, see R. Ivy, 'The Mysterious A.C. Valadier', *Plastic and Reconstructive Surgery*, 47 (1971): 365–70.
9. Ana Carden-Coyne, *The Politics of Wounds. Military Patients and Medical Power in the First World War* (Oxford: Oxford University Press, 2014), p. 72.
10. The pastels drawn by Tonks are all catalogued, with notes about the patients, in S.J.M.M. Alberti (ed.), *War, Art and Surgery: The Work of Henry Tonks and Julia Midgley* (London: Royal College of Surgeons, 2014).
11. The Cuttings Book is held by the London Metropolitan Archives, H02/QM/Y/01/005.
12. Carden-Coyne, *The Politics of Wounds*, p. 203.
13. Sandy Callister, *The Face of War. New Zealand's Great War Photography* (Auckland University Press, 2008), p. 89.
14. H.D. Gillies, *Plastic Surgery of the Face* (London: Henry Frowde & Co., 1920).
15. Ibid., p. 364.
16. 'Essays entitled "My personal experiences of the Great War"' (1922), Liddle/WW1/GA/WOU/34, Liddle Collection, Brotherton Library, University of Leeds; see also Suzannah Biernoff, 'The Rhetoric of Disfigurement in First World War Britain', *Social History of Medicine*, 24 (2011), p. 670.
17. Biernoff, 'The Rhetoric of Disfigurement, pp. 673–4; John D. Holmes, 'Development of Plastic Surgery', in Thomas Scotland and Steven Heys (eds), *War Surgery 1914–1918* (Solihull: Helion, 2012), p. 276.
18. Sander Gilman, *Making the Body Beautiful: A Cultural History of Aesthestic Surgery* (Princeton: Princeton University Press, 1999), p. 159.
19. I am grateful to Stephen Groves, grandson of Pte George Brooks (AIF MGC), wounded 12 October 1917, for this information.
20. The lack of scholarship on First World War facial surgery in France and Germany reflects the dispersed and fragmentary nature of the surgical response in these contexts.
21. See Sophie Delaporte, *Les Gueules Cassées. Les blessés de la face de la Grande Guerre* (Paris: Noêsis 1996), which focuses on the post-war experience of men with facial injuries.
22. Anna Coleman Ladd, an American sculptress working in Paris, was the best known maker of masks. See C. Alexander, 'Faces of War', *Smithsonian Magazine* (February 2007). (http://www.smithsonianmag.com/history/faces-of-war-145799854/?no-ist)
23. Ernst Friedrich, *Nie Wieder Krieg! No more War! Plus jamais de Guerre! Nunca jamas Guerra! Nooit meer Oorlog! Aldrig mere Krig!* (Amsterdam: International Federation of Trade Unions, 1929). This anti-war polemic was published with captions in six languages, as reflected in its title.
24. For an account of the differences in post-war veterans' support see Deborah Cohen, *The War Come Home. Disabled Veterans in Britain and Germany, 1914–1939* (Berkeley: University of California Press, 2001).
25. These accounts have led me to revise the view I expressed in Andrew Bamji, 'Facial surgery: The patients' experience', in Hugh Cecil and Peter H. Liddle (eds), *Facing Armageddon: The First World War Experienced* (London: Pen & Sword Books, 1996), p. 499.

26. Sgt Bowen of the South African Infantry is a notable example. A railway clerk in pre-war civilian life, he was blinded by a shell fragment and was treated at St Dunstan's Hospital, from where he went to Cambridge to study law. There he met, and married, Gillies' sister Eleanor, and subsequently had surgery at Sidcup. On his return to South Africa he became a noted advocate and Member of the Cape and then the South African parliament, and founded a school for the blind in Capetown. I am grateful to Hilary Marlow for this information.

27. Pte H.C. of the Gloucester Regiment treated his family with great brutality, something they attributed to his injury. However, an essay written by him at the hospital in 1921 revealed that he had been forced to leave home at the age of 14 because he had assaulted his brother. 'Essays entitled "My personal experiences of the Great War"'.

28. See H.D. Gillies and D.R. Millard, *The Principles and Art of Plastic Surgery* (New York: Little, Brown & Co., 1957).

29. Roger Cooter, by contrast, has argued that the development of orthopaedic surgery at the time of the Great War owed more to broader changes in surgical thinking than to the war itself. See R. Cooter, *Surgery and Society in Peace and War: Orthopaedics and the Organization of Modern Medicine, 1880–1948* (London: MacMillan, 1993).

Suggested Further Reading

Bamji, Andrew, 'Facial surgery: The patients' experience', in Hugh Cecil and Peter H. Liddle (eds), *Facing Armageddon: The First World War Experienced* (London: Pen & Sword Books, 1996)

Bamji, Andrew, 'Harold Gillies: Surgical Pioneer', *Trauma*, 8 (2006): pp. 143–56

Biernoff, Suzannah, 'The Rhetoric of Disfigurement in First World War Britain', *Social History of Medicine*, 24 (2011): pp. 666–85

Callister, Sandy, *The Face of War. New Zealand's Great War Photography* (Auckland University Press, 2008)

Carden-Coyne, Ana, *The Politics of Wounds. Military Patients and Medical Power in the First World War* (Oxford: Oxford University Press, 2014)

Delaporte, Sophie, *Les Gueules Cassées. Les blessés de la face de la Grande Guerre* (Paris: Noêsis, 1996)

Gillies, H.D. and Millard, D.R., *The Principles and Art of Plastic Surgery* (New York: Little, Brown & Co., 1957)

Harrison, Mark, *The Medical War: British Military Medicine in the First World War* (Oxford: Oxford University Press, 2010)

Holmes, John D., 'Development of Plastic Surgery', in Thomas Scotland and Steven Heys (eds), *War Surgery 1914–1918* (Solihull: Helion, 2012), pp. 257–80

Pound, Reginald, *Gillies: Surgeon Extraordinary* (London: Michael Joseph, 1964)

Chapter 14

British Telecommunications History in the First World War

By Kapil Subramanian *and* Graeme Gooday

In this chapter the intention is to provide an overview of how various kinds of telecommunications were developed and used by the British military during the First World War. We argue that wired communications, especially telephony, were more significant than wireless telegraphy (radio) in the conduct of the war. More broadly we argue that the army's use of these technologies on a massive organised scale for the first time during this conflict increased telecommunications capacities and fostered an appreciation of the vast potential of wired communications and their limitations, but also made for significantly enhanced technological developments in telecommunications more generally.

Previous histories of telecommunications in the First World War have typically focused on the initial development and use of army wireless. Such accounts focus on the development of pioneering wireless sets for army use during the war, arguing that this wartime innovation was highly significant for later developments. References to usage of wireless by the Royal Navy mostly concern intelligence gathering (intercepting enemy communications) and direction-finding equipment (intercepting enemy movements). We emphasise instead that the navy pioneered its own fundamental developments in wireless technology independently of the army, both before and during the war. Finally, while wartime development of airborne wireless communication by the new air forces is well acknowledged, we argue that further research is needed on this topic.

Of course, we argue that the war did indeed see the rising importance of radio as a small-scale, short-range and convenient mobile communication device in contrast to the gigantic, long-distance wireless communication systems developed before 1914. We emphasise that towards the end of the war this shift to small-scale radio was increasingly underpinned by the development of continuous wave technology in which the navy played a leading role. We argue that the development of continuous wave wireless – as an alternative to damped wave transmission technology that tended to produce much electromagnetic interference – owed more to the solution of production problems than any innovation in the devices themselves. It was in fact the improved production of radio valves, spurred by the war, which played a more important role than innovation and research in this transformation.

We begin with an overview of army telecommunications during the war, drawing from two classic accounts from Royal Signals engineers who participated in combat: Raymond E. Priestley and Reginald F.H. Nalder. While wired communication overwhelmingly remained the mainstay of army communications during the war, efforts were made to induct wireless technology into army practice. Accordingly we move on to describe pioneering army wireless sets and the question of alternative means of communication, ending with an overview of the wartime use of radio. After a brief account of novel uses of wireless systems in direction-finding and intelligence gathering, we shall focus on fundamental changes in wireless technology in which the navy played a leading role. We shall conclude with an account of efforts to miniaturise wireless sets for use in military aviation.

Military Communications before the First World War

Effective communications have always been central to the practice of warfare. Arguably the most important means of communication used by the British Army in the period immediately preceding the war was 'signals despatch' which involved a runner or a man on a horse physically carrying messages. The use of riders continued to be a central feature of communications through the war with significant improvement in the form of using motorcycles instead of horses for signal despatch. Visual signalling was the primary means of communication at a distance and the methods in vogue included the use of lamps, heliographs, flags and flares; these methods were, however, unsuitable for trench warfare as they gave positions away to the enemy.

In the civilian domain, the half century before the First World War saw the development of a global infrastructure of overland and undersea lines to facilitate *telegraphy*, the transmission of messages as electrical signals over wires, coded in 'dots and dashes' (Morse code). While the international telegraph network was indeed an important factor in British military dominance, little use of wired communications had been made by the army for field operations before the war. While telegraphy offered a secure, reliable – as long as the lines remained intact – and more convenient means of communication, the need to lay the lines was a significant drawback, particularly during mobile warfare when communications devices needed to move with the battlefront. This drawback was also shared by *telephony*, the transmission of voice over electric wires, which had seen significant civilian development since its invention by Alexander Graham Bell and others in the mid-1870s.[1]

In contrast to the army, the Royal Navy had built up a substantial infrastructure for electrical communication before the war; indeed it was the world's foremost user of *wireless telegraphy*, the transmission of Morse signals using electromagnetic waves (thus obviating the need for wires), which had been most effectively demonstrated by Marconi around 1900. By 1914 most of the Royal Navy's warships had been fitted with wireless sets and, together with the Marconi Company, had developed a massive network of shore stations to communicate with ships in the North Atlantic and across the Empire. While the elimination of cables meant that wireless technology provided a means of communication effective for ship to shore use, the massive bulk and heavy power consumption of early wireless sets made them perhaps inappropriate for military use outside the navy.

Three scholars have studied the global development of telecommunications during the nineteenth and twentieth centuries. Headrick devoted two chapters to the period, one of which is on wireless intelligence in the main. His general overview of the period focuses to a considerable extent on long-distance communication by wireless and cable, neglecting military use entirely.[2] Burns' schematic volume has a chapter on the Great War which focuses on the development and early use of wireless in the army; although reference is made to the Fullerphone, the story of wired communication is largely told as one of failure which propelled interest in wireless, though he admits that actual use was scant.[3] Hughill's book on the geopolitics of communication technology focuses on communication, command and control during the period and gives an overview of developments in the air as well.[4]

While the latter books argue that both the development of wireless equipment and of valve-production capacity had an impact on later advances in radio technology, they do not explore this point in detail. Together with the almost complete lack of scholarly work on wireless development and use in the immediate post-war period, this has meant that the impact of the war on later developments has not been fully understood. The wartime role of the navy, so central to the historiography of wireless from its inception in 1896, has been neglected entirely in these works – except for the limited cases of intelligence gathering and direction-finding. While the army's usage, as opposed to development, of wireless technology has not received much attention in these books, works by B.N. Hall have made reference in this regard in the European and global theatres.[5]

Histories of telephony in the British Army, like civilian histories of telephony, generally focus on earlier periods; a recent paper by Hall which seeks to challenge the view that British officers were hostile to the telephone covers the period 1877–1914.[6] The neglect of navy wireless and army telephone development during the Great War exemplifies a general trend in the history of technology of exclusively focusing on initial developments and early usage. This has led to a rather limited understanding of later developments and usages at the time – during the war – when these particular technologies became especially significant.

Telecommunications in the Army

Our account of army telecommunications draws substantially from R.F.H. Nalder's history of the Royal Signals written in the 1950s, and from R.E. Priestley's 1921 account of the signals service during the First World War. Known for his pre-war Antarctic expeditions, the geologist Raymond Priestley served in the Signals Branch of the Royal Engineers in France during the war and was seconded to the War Office to write an account of the wartime work of the Signals Branch which was published in 1921. Major-General Reginald Francis Heaton Nalder began service during the First World War and played a leading role in army telecommunications during the Second World War. His historical account of British Army signalling covering the period until the mid-1950s was published in 1958.

The whole conception in fact had to be changed. Wireless could no longer be regarded as a temporary stand-by when the lines were out of service; it must be a genuine alternative for use at all levels over considerable periods.[7]

In referring to the First World War, standard works on telecommunications history focus mostly on developments and use of wireless in the army, indicating that developments were slow but of great significance to the later military use of wireless. But these words by Major-General R.F.H. Nalder referred not to the First World War but to the opening phase of the Second World War. When it came to electrical technology, wired systems were the mainstay of army communications during the First World War, which saw the use of wires on a scale hitherto unseen making not just for an exploration of the full potential and limits of wired systems but also for crucial technological developments.

A telegraph battalion had been constituted within the Royal Engineers in 1884. The Second Boer War (1899–1902) saw the first significant development of a landline network in the field, though telegraphy was seldom used for tactical purposes forward of divisional headquarters. It also saw the taking over of the civilian telephone network in Ladysmith, as well as the laying of new lines for military telephone subscribers. The period before the Great War saw significant reorganisation and a broader reconceptualisation; in 1910 the technology-specific term 'telegraph' was replaced by 'signal' and thus a Signals Service of the Royal Engineers was constituted. The addition of motorcyclists in 1912 meant that the signal units were in charge of all basic communications (telegraph, telephone and despatch). The principal electrical equipment of the new service was the same as that which had been used and developed in the Boer War: 'sounders' from base to divisional headquarters; 'Wheatstone' from base to army headquarters; 'vibrators' forward of divisional headquarters; cable wagons; magneto telephones with switchboards in the rear areas; and buzzer telephones without switchboards in the forward zones, in addition to cable wagons. Despite financial pressures, according to Nalder, the organisation as extant at the outbreak of the war was far more comprehensive than before and 'technical efficiency' was high except in the case of telephones and wireless.[8] But the creation of a hugely expanded national army meant more than a multiplication of signals units; it made for complicated administration and diluted standards of training, making necessary more elaborate signals communication.[9]

Nalder's retrospect on the First World War emphasises that the primary change which took place in the Signals Service during the war was its evolution from an organisation which in the main provided a telegraph service to one which aimed to provide a comprehensive system of telegraph, telephone and signal despatch services. As electrical communication went, the telephone was the principal device newly inducted into the army which saw substantial use; indeed Nalder makes reference to 'lavish' use.[10] In 1914 civilian telephones were taken over for military purposes, but their use was very measured not just because of security considerations but also because the highly trained corps of officers did not feel the need for constant communications; explicit orders were framed and carried out.[11] As casualties mounted and inexperienced 'for the duration' officers became more numerous, the numbers of orders communicated by telephone increased and were less carefully worded. By the end of 1914 casualties and dilution of training standards made telegraphs less efficient, with unintelligible wording and long transmission times even as the volume of traffic was rising.[12]

To meet the ever-increasing demands of their staff, a certain 'kleptomania' took hold in regard to the systematic appropriation of telephones, exchanges and accessories from civilians; thus an informal military telephone system was soon in full swing.[13] By the first half of 1915 the telephone was becoming indispensable and by early 1916 its use was universal. Beyond the initial kleptomanic phase, the role of the General Post Office – which had held a monopoly over UK wired civilian telephone systems since 1911 – became more important. It was required to establish a supply system for newly manufactured telephones and was asked by the army to supply it with magneto telephones. In the meanwhile the Post Office produced the D3 telephone and experimented with various new designs, eventually perfecting the Telephone 100, which was subsequently approved as army standard.[14]

While army signals staff provided the infrastructure and personnel necessary for telephony, they were apprehensive about this demand-driven growth and this made for conflict with the General Staff, which saw no difficulties with telephone usage. According to Priestley, it was impossible to prevent their telephonic 'hobby' becoming widespread[15] and signals officers like him were very concerned about the inclination that had set in by mid-1915 to use the very convenient telephone to the exclusion of all other means of communication. He saw great danger in this near-complete reliance on what was fast becoming an inefficient service.[16] Initially, telephones worked on a system of direct lines, but as telephone usage became more intensive, the need for exchange systems to handle the extra communications traffic became pressing.

A multiplicity of direct (non-exchange) lines placed a great burden on signallers, but the policy of discouraging such lines was resented by the army staff; virulent complaints quickly arose about the shortcomings of exchange operators even though many had been highly proficient when previously employed in a similar civilian capacity by the General Post Office. Indeed on more than one occasion impatient officers invaded the signals office and placed under arrest telephone operators who would not do their bidding. Improved relations between the signals and the General Staff was achieved by army staff visiting signals offices to witness operators' difficulties first-hand, and consequentially instruction cards were issued to all telephone subscribers. A new training system was soon set up, and, together with the enlistment of more GPO men, the army trade of 'switchboard operator' was created.[17]

Army staff had little prior experience with the telephone in combat situations, so the development of artillery in the Great War made for widespread communications demand. This in turn gave rise to such an 'out of control' expansion of forward line systems that they 'became useless in times of emergency'.[18] This was because the 'new craze for telephony' made for a burgeoning but haphazard system of lines, and impatience with repair of frequent destruction by shell-fire made for bitter relations between staff and signal companies and the latter sought to discipline the laying of lines. In the summer of 1915 signal companies were given authority over all lines and a system was implemented for the recovery of disused cables, proper construction and maintenance, labelling, and forbidding new construction without authorisation.[19]

The strategic need for a properly planned telephone network was urgently felt during the Somme offensive. Early in July 1915 it had been realised that fanning out telephone lines from a single nodal point made the system vulnerable to complete collapse if it were directly hit by ordnance. It was thus desirable instead to build a network-like system of arteries, and various configurations of these were tried.[20] Exclusive allotment of separate private telephone and telegraph circuits was often the norm; in many cases these amounted to no fewer than seven classes of users and the need was felt for evolving a more judicious mix of common user and private wire circuits.[21] By 1916 it became clear that only a grid pattern of circuits would be acceptable.

As was hitherto the case, each divisional front had a forward artery with four main communication centres, while lateral arteries were constructed between these communication centres. Concreted test points were built at 400yd intervals and cross-connecting frames were installed at centres and test points and elaborate circuit records were maintained. Subscribers were linked to communication centres or intermediate test points. Route planning for communications thus had to be meticulous.[22]

The war also saw significant developments in the practice of laying telephone cable. To lessen damage to open air lines exposed to shelling, experiments began with buried cables in early 1915. This was a labour-intensive activity, but the advantages were soon realised. After the destruction of lines in the battles of Neuve Chapelle, Second Ypres and Festubert, infantry labour was made available for laying buried systems.[23] By late 1915 buried cables became the norm; to protect them from direct hits by the German 5.9-inch howitzer, they had to be buried 6ft deep, rather than the initial standard of 3ft deep. At Ypres the problem was temporarily solved by using sewers to lay cables, although the sewers were themselves prone to destruction by shelling from guns of still greater calibre. For the Somme offensive construction of 6ft 'buries' began in April 1916 and a system of arteries and spur lines took shape. Although the mammoth target of a full network was not fully attained before the offensive commenced,[24] an impressive 7,000 wire miles of cables were laid before and during the Somme operation[25] and 13,000 miles before Cambrai in November 1917. By contrast, behind the combat zones, in the rear areas, the use of overhead lines continued, and the total wire miles laid early on around the Somme (July to mid-November 1916) was of the order of 20,000 miles.[26]

Further problems, however, were created by the use of buried cables. Their juxtaposition often set up mutual electromagnetic induction between lines and thus interference in communications. Besides the cross-talk experienced on the British lines, there was growing evidence that the Germans were listening in. Experiments in 1915 confirmed that physical contact was not necessary for the reception of signals; orders were issued that earths be run back at least 100yds from the front trenches, and that certain listed subjects were never to be referred to in telephone conversations. However, orders for such discretion were frequently disregarded, even by the most senior of officers.[27] It took quite a while for the effect of such orders to set in, and not infrequent threats of court martial and other means of disciplining were found necessary to eliminate the dangerous practice of open telephone conversations in combat areas.[28] By 1917 it became the practice to entrust all urgent traffic to telegraph and only personal communication to telephones, the use of which was increasingly discouraged by the Signals Service.[29] As discretion set in, according to Priestley, staff lost the telephone habit and the system finally began to atrophy.

Together with disciplining officers to due encryption of telephone communications, infrastructural improvements also took place in other newer telecommunication technologies. Valve-based wireless listening sets (known as IT sets) came into use in early 1916. Their effectiveness in listening in on enemy lines resulted in orders to extend the 'danger zone', where earth returns were forbidden, to 3,000yds. The replacement of earth return circuits by twisted cables was a mammoth task, not least because supplies from home were not available until the end of 1916; for weeks homemade wire-twisting machines devised by the signal companies worked day and night to twist thousands of miles of wire. As some amount of listening in by the enemy was considered inevitable despite these technical precautions, code names were issued for formations and units in order to minimise the information given away to enemy listeners.

A major technology born out of the quest for signals security was the Fullerphone. Despite doing away with earth returns, leaky insulation meant that signals could still be overheard. Private off-duty experimentation in 1915/16 by Captain Algernon Clement Fuller of the Signals Service Training Centre led to the development of the Fullerphone. This primarily telegraphic device used a signal chopping method to render signals unintelligible to those without a paired receiving Fullerphone; it also used a very small current for signalling, making the range over which it could be overheard practically negligible. Prototype Fullerphones were used in France in late 1915 and in large numbers in 1916. Initially, models were apt to go out of adjustment even with experienced operators until the problem was resolved by the Mark III model in 1917. Originally used to communicate between brigade headquarters and company headquarters, Fullerphone use was extended to the rear to divisional headquarters and after the war to corps headquarters.[30]

Technology Choice for the Army: Wires, Wireless and Alternatives

Unlike the Royal Navy, the British Army had hardly taken to using the novel technology of wireless telegraphy before the First World War. The technological history of army telecommunications during the war has usually been told as the story of the development and adoption of wireless sets. It is thus useful to reiterate the key aspects of the history of wireless development for army use.

Wireless saw experimental use during the Boer War, and further experimentation by the Royal Engineers in the first decade of the twentieth century, together with inputs from the Marconi Company and *Telefunken*, which had led to the development of sets carried on wagons and packs. A committee constituted in 1912 under the chairmanship of Henry Norman MP to consider the question of wireless in the army argued, however, that the army's use of wireless thus far had been 'inefficient ... unreliable ... and practically useless'; indeed it concluded that rather than operate with the existing equipment, it was better to abandon wireless technology altogether as 'an inefficient wireless service in war would be a constant source of doubt and danger'.[31] At the outbreak of the Great War the equipment available for use in the field by the British Army consisted of one wagon-mounted and six lorry-mounted 1.5kw Marconi spark sets and an unknown number of pack sets, each of which required four horses. The lorry sets, an improvement on the wagon sets, were carried in a lorry, had a range of about 100 miles and required 70ft masts. They were, however, manifestly unsuitable for the conditions of both mobile and trench warfare.[32]

The army's experimental wireless section, set up at Aldershot in 1905, had been absorbed into the British Expeditionary Force and thus initial wartime experiments were carried out in France, often with the aid of knowledgeable prisoners of war.[33] In mid-1916 experiments were carried out using four Sterling spark sets in conjunction with short-wave receivers borrowed from the Royal Flying Corps with a view to developing a system suitable for trench warfare. This work led to the manufacture of 100 portable wireless sets called British Field (BF) trench sets, which came into service in early 1916. With a power rating of 50 watts, each BF set could theoretically be carried by three men, but it required a further six to transport its spare accumulators. In addition, it had a 12ft aerial which both rendered it awkward to move and attracted unwanted enemy attention; in any case the BF sets had a range of only 4,000yds. Other drawbacks of these sets included an inability to hold their tuning in battlefield conditions, and it was widely rumoured that German direction-finding equipment could locate them with deadly accuracy and thus swiftly destroy them.[34]

These problems were partly addressed in the 20W loop wireless set which entered service in early 1917, with a range of 2,000 to 3,000yds. It had an aerial which could be supported on a bayonet fixed in the ground.[35] In addition, the Wilson 130W spark transmitter, together with a Mark III short-wave receiver, was inducted beginning in 1915 for use at corps headquarters with a 30ft aerial and an ability to communicate with the BF trench sets at a distance of 4 to 10 miles.[36]

In understanding the introduction of wireless technology, it is important to note that there were great vulnerabilities in the system of buried cables that had hitherto formed the mainstay of army communication. In addition to their frequent destruction by shelling, it required only a short advance or withdrawal of troops for this fixed system to be left behind and thus unable to perform any useful service. It was questionable whether the enormous expenditure of labour in building the cable systems really paid a dividend; according to Nalder, there was no alternative and the crux of the matter lay in the failure to find a reliable alternative.[37]

The primary alternative to wired communication used extensively during the war was signal despatch, and a means far from novel but now vastly expanded was the use of carrier pigeons. In September 1914 the service received fifteen pigeons from French sources.[38] The unreliability of the lines and the availability of privately owned pigeons around St Omer led to an organised pigeon service in May 1915 following the Second Battles of Ypres and it grew rapidly to around 20,000 birds and 380 'pigeoneers' in 1918. In addition, a large number of men in regimental units were also trained in handling carrier pigeons. The limitations of the service were confinement of operations to the day, and the need to retrain the birds when lofts were moved. While Nalder acknowledged that the service proved vital on many occasions where there were no means except runners, and thus the service helped reduce runner casualties, he argued that the number of messages sent by pigeons was no measure of the value of the service as messages which could have been sent by line were often sent by pigeons merely to keep the birds in training by releasing them at the appointed time of day.[39]

According to Nalder, wireless and earth induction telegraphy were the most promising alternatives to the wired communications. But 'three imponderable factors' had to be reckoned with. First, commanders had little faith in wireless, perhaps due to their lack of reliability and difficulty in use; this feeling was sometimes shared by the more senior signals officers as a result of which it was decoupled from the normal signals chain of command until mid-1917. Second, the ubiquity of wireless signals made for security concerns born out of the ability of the enemy to listen in without much difficulty. Finally, the War Office organisation that was habituated to the telephone was not adapted to wireless development. Nalder for one was doubtful whether, even had that not been the case, resources could have been stepped up to any marked extent.[40]

The wireless failures were blamed by Nalder on the staff. Trench sets were first used at Loos in September 1915 and the results were promising, with important messages being passed by wireless when all other means had failed, but the trial never received encouragement due to fear of German direction-finders and the sheer amount of work involved in ciphering wireless messages. But even Nalder admitted that the service was not reliable.[41] In the forward areas, where it was most needed, not only was the equipment unsuitable but its use was also constrained by the fact that wireless was a very specialised branch until 1917 when control was decentralised from GHQ. There was thus a great lack of confidence in wireless sets resulting from clumsy equipment, a shortage of skilled operators and challenging security implications.[42]

In contrast to the telephone, where a reading of Nalder's work – and more particularly Priestley's – suggests that great disciplining by signals staff was required to curb the demand for telephone use by the General Staff, much had to be done by the signals to promote any use of wireless by them at all. Officers such as Priestley were clear enthusiasts. While this was in large part due to keenness for new technology, it was also due to a general inclination to promote all methods, including old ones such as pigeons and visual signalling, that were alternatives to wires due to the great demands that building and maintaining wired communications placed on signals staff. However, wireless was looked upon with suspicion not just by the General Staff but by many in the Signals Service due to the implications of its ubiquity for security and the need to encrypt.[43] According to Priestley, this was due to initial improper use of wireless which saw it fall into disrepute for several months early in the war. The problems faced by wireless could only be surmounted by a campaign of education and propaganda, which was soon introduced both within the Signal Service and within the General Staff. Individual cases from 1916 and 1917, when wireless proved to be of particular strategic benefit – notably when intercommunications were otherwise shattered, – were advertised to convert officers from hostility to partisanship. Every wireless officer thus had to be a 'teacher, preacher and prophet'.[44]

However, education to induce demand for wireless services was not felt to be enough; more drastic measures were also undertaken to wean the staff off wired communication. Certain days were set apart each week or month as 'silent days' when only the most urgent messages were permitted to be passed by telegraph and telephone and the rest had to be passed by wireless or visual signalling. The object was to prepare for the time when line signalling became intermittent or impossible by familiarising users with the slower 'but under certain conditions surer' means at their disposal. In one case, exclusive reliance on wireless was made to last for three whole days. The staff retaliated by saving up messages until after such silent days, thus deluging the signals staff when lines became available again. Priestley argued that these measures helped prove to officers that the telephone and telegraph, while convenient and speedy, were not essential. Nevertheless, given the analysis above, it is unclear whether the full potential of wireless was actually realised as a result of First World War experience.

The Use of Radio for Ground Communication and Intelligence

On the whole, telecommunications historians have engaged almost exclusively with the Western Front. However, according to Nalder, when it came to the use of radio it was in the so-called subsidiary theatres of war that wireless proved to be of greater value.[45] According to him, wireless use was encouraged if not demanded by commanders in difficult combat situations where there was no possibility of providing line communication. Wireless thus became firmly established even before the security-related discipline issues arose which inhibited its use in the European theatres. The wide open spaces of the subsidiary theatres proved less of a deterrent to the bulky transmission equipment, and unlike in the closely concentrated formations of European trenches, the lack of wavelength selectivity of early sets was not really a problem. But perhaps the most important reason why wireless took off more in the subsidiary theatres was the 'definite relationship between the degree of effectiveness and the extent of use'. Where wireless was in daily use, it became reliable and efficient. On the Western Front it was held in reserve until emergencies when it was apt to break down.[46]

The army learnt much from the navy during the Gallipoli campaign while participating in a system of amphibious communication, including coding methods and frequency assignment.[47] In Mesopotamia too, the army relied substantially on developments by another institution, the Indian Government Telegraph Department, which had erected a 30kw wireless synchronous rotary spark set in Basra for use by ships and as a back-up to the submarine cable to India. This station was taken over by the Signals Service's No. 1 Wireless Squadron to communicate with forces in Persia, and another 30kw set was installed at Bushire. Wireless was also much used to intercept Turkish messages. The use of wireless in that theatre was encouraged by the appointments of Lieutenant-Colonel H.I. Allen as Director of Army Signals from mid-1917 and of Major A.C. Sykes as Assistant Director (Wireless), making for better use of wireless resources and more effective security measures.[48]

It was in the Mesopotamian theatre that the use of wireless was most notable in wartime signals practice. This was ascribed by Nalder to four causes: first and second, distances and transport difficulties made wireless the only practical means of telegraphy. Third, wireless systems worked well from the start as a result of good training, the simplicity of the sets and the lack of security issues making for acceptance by both the staff and the signals personnel. Fourth, wireless was always in use and not kept as a reserve. Nalder admitted that the reliable working of wireless in Mesopotamia owed something to fortuitous factors as well: there was no mutual interference between transmissions due to the wide distances between signalling units and the absence of enemy wireless for the first two years. Moreover, atmospheric interference was never serious, and a good maintenance organisation had been put in place.[49]

Wireless usage was also seen as notably effective in the East African theatre. There it was initially used exclusively on line of command, but as more sets arrived it was also used for tactical purposes between columns and parts of the same column. While the British lorry, wagon and pack sets were unable to work to their full range in the bush, the South Africans, equipped with *Telefunken* continuous wave sets, did better. The campaign saw great ingenuity in the field with improvised repairs, dismantling of wagon sets where wheeled transport was impossible, a two-wheeled wireless cart built from a broken-down Ford used to transport engines and generators, and leaving the sets *in situ* as long as possible and relaying messages from them to the columns by other means.[50]

Radio for Intelligence and Direction-finding

That radio signals had directional properties had been known for a few years and the patent for a method of direction-finding developed by E. Bellini and A. Tosi had been acquired by the Marconi Company in 1912; Bellini joined the company's technical staff.[51] Henry C. Round, who had been involved in experimentation with valves at the Marconi Company before the war, was seconded as a lieutenant to Military Intelligence[52] and in October 1914 he went to France with C.S. Franklin (also of the Marconi Company) to set up direction-finding stations,[53] the first two of which were established towards the end of the year at Blendecques, near St Omer, and Abbeville. In due course a network of such stations was set up along the Western Front. Using the bearings of German wireless establishments, determined by each of the stations, their locations could be pinpointed. Thenceforward, weekly maps of these positions were forwarded to the headquarters of British intelligence. Besides improving upon accuracy by using bearings from groups of three stations, Round's work was significant as the direction-finders were early users of radio valves.[54]

More significant developments in direction-finding took place at the initiative of the Royal Navy. With long-range wireless communication becoming less important to the Germans with the onset of trench warfare, Round was recalled to aid the Admiralty to help determine the locations of German warships, U-boats and aircraft. A network of receivers known as the 'B' Stations was developed. Six were immediately erected along the east coast of England with another on the coast of Flanders to sweep the North Sea. As U-boat attacks spread, five more 'B' stations were erected in southern Ireland to cover the south-west approaches; three more were built in the south-east for the use of military intelligence and a further six for use in the eastern Mediterranean. These stations telegraphed the bearings of signals from enemy ships to Room 40, which plotted the lines required for determining location. By May 1915 it was possible to track U-boats in the North Sea to a margin of 20 miles.[55]

The British Army had resisted the introduction of wireless into operational use before the war; it was thus perhaps inevitable that existing wireless infrastructure was initially used for intelligence gathered from the enemy's use of the technology. Only one lorry set was initially shipped out with the British Expeditionary Force in 1914 and it was installed at Le Cateau for intercepting enemy messages.[56] Again, larger developments took place in the Admiralty, which operated one station at the beginning of the war to intercept ciphered wireless communication. While civilian radio use ceased at the beginning of the war, three amateurs who had picked up German signals on their sets were installed at the coastguard station at Hunstanton: Leslie Lambert (better known subsequently as the broadcaster A.J. Allen), Colonel B. Hippisley and Russell Clarke, a member of the pre-war wireless telegraphy committee. Round took over the interception station and built four more of the so-called 'Y' stations in the south-east. Reception at the 'B' and 'Y' stations was improved with the use of powerful rectifying and amplifying valves in 1917.

Besides encryption, German forces employed various countermeasures to interception, such as varying wavelengths and intensity and keeping messages as short as possible or transmitting messages through mechanical means so rapidly that they could not be read by ear; this was the so-called 'war of the wavelengths'. Clarke, well versed in German, was responsible for dealing with these countermeasures. Between 1916 and 1918 three continuous wave direction-finding stations operated round the clock with automatic searching devices for changing German wave-lengths. While Clarke's services remained secret during his lifetime, Round was awarded the Military Cross for his work in 1917.[57]

Naval Developments in Communications

Before the outbreak of war, the Royal Navy had built up an impressive wireless infrastructure of ship-based installations and shore stations based on spark transmitters and crystal receivers. While these had been adequate for operations in home and European waters, oceanic operations demanded longer ranges.[58] The spark transmission system which had been the mainstay of Marconi technology at the outbreak of the war had its disadvantages: it took up a large slice of the frequency spectrum, the reception was harder to distinguish from static, and the speed of transmission was slow; moreover it could not be used for voice communication – only for Morse signals. These problems were not encountered by the carrying of signals on continuous waves at a precise frequency. Three methods existed for the production of continuous waves at the beginning of the war, all substantially developed outside Britain. The first, developed by the American Reginald Fessenden, used alternators spinning at the unheard-of speed of 50,000 turns per second, with alternators supplied by the General Electric Company. The second, developed by the Dane Valdemar Poulsen, used an electric arc to produce continuous waves.[59] The third was the use of radio valves. While the operational transition to continuous wave technology began during the war, new spark sets continued to be installed up to the end of the war.[60]

The primary naval wireless establishment was HMS *Vernon*, a training site substantially run by the Marconi Company for the Royal Navy. At the outbreak of war it had two scientific workers under H.A. Madge, a Marconi engineer who had joined the Admiralty in 1908. The first was the Greenwich physicist C.L. Fortescue, who began to supervise experimental work on a part-time basis, and then, at the initiative of J.J. Thomson, Gilbert Stead, a scientific assistant, who was later deputed to work full time at the better facilities at the Cavendish laboratory.[61] The group associated with HMS *Vernon* worked on developing Poulsen arc transmitters of various sizes for shore stations, submarines, large ships and destroyers, while simultaneously working on radio valves.[62] Their work assumed a sense of urgency in April 1915 when Churchill, informed that German ships could communicate with each other at 300 miles, insisted that British ships be capable of the same. Thus, as a stop gap for radio valve-based systems, the Grand Fleet began to be equipped with Poulsen transmitters which, by 1916, were more reliable than the spark sets with which the navy had so much experience.[63]

Problems in the design and production of the valves lay at the heart of the transition to continuous wave technology. Early work on continuous wave wireless was centred on 'soft' vacuum tubes which had been developed by Round for the Marconi Company in 1913. These were hard to manufacture, as Round himself admitted:

> These necessitated, however, trained men in their manufacture, and trained operators for their efficient use ... Again and again we lost the knack of making good tubes, owing to some slight change in the materials used in their manufacture. A thorough investigation was impossible, as all hands were out on the stations. On several occasions we were down to our last dozen tubes.[64]

Soft valves were equally hard to use. As time passed, the gas pressure in the valve fell and it had to be heated – often with a match – for optimal operation.[65] Wartime British efforts to develop new soft valves, as well as the better 'hard' valves with a high vacuum, took place at the Royal Naval College, at King's College, London, and at Royal Holloway, London. These efforts were described by Fortescue as a good example of 'pure research running in parallel with its immediate application', noting how often the 'limits of knowledge' were reached.[66]

The eventual solution of the wartime hard valve problem, however, was the result less of British wartime efforts than of developments elsewhere.

In 1914 Paul Pichon, a French-born employee of the German *Telefunken* company, passed on samples of the latest *Audion* valves, obtained from the Western Electric Company in the United States, to Colonel Gustav Ferie of the French Military Telegraph service. With some modification in design, these valves soon began to be produced in France. The Admiralty received samples of this 'TM valve' in early 1916 and production of the same as the British 'R-valve' soon commenced at various electrical firms including Metropolitan-Vickers, Edison-Swan and GEC Osram. Valve manufacture nevertheless continued to require skilled craftsmanship and the high demand from the navy and the air forces led to a production crisis by 1918. An inter-services committee was set up to assign priorities for valve distribution.[67] The R-valve became the basis for many post-war British valve designs and the production capacity created during the war became the basis of the post-war broadcast boom.

The Miniaturisation of Communications for Aviation

The introduction of aeroplane combat fostered significant developments in wireless technology, pertaining particularly to enhanced portability and ease of use. In 1912 the Royal Naval Air Service had demonstrated the use of the 30W spark transmitter and a crystal receiver mounted on a Short S41 hydroplane over a range of 6.2 miles. By the following year twenty-six seaplanes had been fitted with French *Rouzet* transmitters selected for their light weight[68] (which amounted in fact to no less than 100lb), while its range was about 40 miles. The sole wireless-equipped machine which was initially sent out to support the BEF was fitted with the *Rouzet*. These sets were so susceptible to breaking down that squadrons on the Western Front preferred to use signalling lamps early on for communication.[69] Of course the main reason for the low usage of radio sets in aircraft was that early equipment was so heavy and bulky: not only could two-seater planes no longer carry an observer, but the equipment even overflowed into the pilot's compartment. This was in part due to the initial view that military aircraft would require a long-range capability; it was soon realised, however, that cooperation with artillery did not require long ranges and compact equipment was preferable, even at the cost of range. This led to the introduction in 1915 of the Sterling set, developed by the Royal Naval Air Service, which weighed less than 20lb.[70] Versions of this spark transmitter dominated British military aircraft through the war. Having an enclosed spark gap, unlike the *Rouzet* sets, it was also felt that they were safer in petrol-engined aircraft.[71]

Work on aircraft radio development took place at an experimental establishment that had been set up by the Marconi Company at Brooklands, not far from the Royal Aircraft Factory at Farnborough. The establishment had been taken over by the Royal Flying Corps during the war and amongst the Marconi staff seconded to the RFC was C.E. Prince, who had been assistant to H.J. Round before the war. Recognizing that speech would be easier to use than Morse,[72] Prince began to experiment with wireless telephony in 1915, demonstrating the transmission of speech from ground to air to Lord Kitchener at St Omer in 1916.

A valve-based air to ground speech transmitter was developed by early 1917,[73] but only two squadrons on the Western Front appear to have been equipped with this before July 1918.[74] While there is no evidence of substantial use, this development no doubt hastened the broadcast era in the post-war period.

Besides the futuristic prospect of wireless telephony, developments in continuous wave airborne wireless telegraphy continued through the war, though any substantial conversion to valve technology only began late in the war with the development of hard valves.[75] Nevertheless, the significance of continuous wave wireless development during the war may be judged by the fact that by June 1918 German soldiers had specific orders to salvage the wireless equipment from crashed allied planes.[76]

Conclusion

The Great War saw a significant evolution in the landscape of telecommunications in the British military and this transformation had to do with both the large-scale use of existing systems and embryonic developments in technologies which would acquire significance in a later period. Thus, nearly four decades after its invention and long after significant civilian use began, the First World War saw the first large-scale use of telephony in the army. If there were indeed any hostility or ambiguity towards the telephone amongst officers, it was shattered during the early months of the war; this was in large part due to the induction of hastily trained officers who felt a greater need for constant communication. The army's demand for telephony was viewed with great concern by the Signals Service, which was responsible for supplying it, and this made for some conflict between the technical and the general staff in the army. In contrast to telephony, wireless saw little use in trench warfare despite the enthusiasm of the Signals Service for it. It did see some significant use in non-European theatres, where the more convenient alternative of telephones was not available. Despite the later advent of wireless, the use of telephones, pioneered on a large scale during the First World War, lasted well into the Second World War, when versions of the Fullerphone continued to be used.

The Navy, which had inducted wireless in the decade prior to the war, gained significant experience in its use during the war. The war also saw novel applications of wireless in the navy for direction-finding and intelligence. The latter stage of the war marked the beginning of conversion of the naval communication system to continuous wave and valve technology. While research on radio valves took place within the navy, in private industry and in academia, it was the fortuitous availability of American designs through the French that spurred valve manufacture in Britain. This manufacturing capacity would become central to the post-war broadcast industry. Along with valves, miniaturisation of wireless technology was another wartime development which would assume significance in the post-war period and this work was pioneered to serve military aviation.

Future historical research on telecommunications during the period needs to be guided by a clearer recognition of the significance of both novel and old technologies. Amongst old systems, wired communication – particularly telephony –

more than proved its utility during the Great War and we need a clear account of how the recognition of its utility shaped army telecommunications doctrine and technical development in the inter-war period. In making the move to miniaturisation, wireless development for aircraft use was perhaps the most significant novelty in telecommunications technology during the war, and yet little is known about the same beyond what is summarised in this chapter. The same can be said of radio valve development. Much historical research is needed to establish what was achieved in these spheres in experiment and praxis. To appreciate the impact of the Great War on the history of telecommunications, closer attention also needs to be paid to wireless development in the immediate post-war period to understand how wartime military work influenced commercial developments, including, but not limited to, broadcasting, in the 1920s and beyond.

Notes

1. Stathis Arapostathis and Graeme Gooday, *Patently Contestable: Electrical Technologies and Inventor Identities on Trial in Britain* (London/Cambridge MA: 2013), ch. 4.
2. Daniel R. Headrick, *The Invisible Weapon: Telecommunications and International Politics, 1851–1945* (New York: 1991), pp. 138–72.
3. Russel W. Burns, *Communications: an international history of the formative years* (London: 2004).
4. Peter Hughill, *Global Communications Since 1844: Geopolitics and Technology* (Baltimore, Md: 1999).
5. Brian N. Hall, 'The British Army and Wireless Communication, 1896–1918', *War in History*, 19 (2012), pp. 290–321, and idem, 'Technological Adaptation in a Global Conflict: The British Army and Communications beyond the Western Front, 1914–1918', *Journal of Military History* (2014).
6. Brian N. Hall, 'The "Life-Blood" of Command? The British Army, Communications and the Telephone, 1877–1914', *War & Society*, 27 (2008), pp. 43–65.
7. R.F.H. Nalder, *The Royal Corps of Signals: A History of its Antecedents and Development* (London: 1958), p. 289.
8. Ibid., pp. 48–53.
9. Ibid., p. 73.
10. Ibid., p. 216.
11. R.E. Priestley, *Work of R. E. in the European War, 1914–1918: The Signal Service (France)* (London: 1921), p. 26.
12. Nalder, *Royal Corps*, p. 99.
13. Priestley, *Work of R. E.*, p. 42.
14. Ibid., p. 123.
15. Ibid., p. 126.
16. Ibid., p. 148.
17. Ibid., p. 148.
18. Nalder, *Royal Corps*, p. 98.
19. Ibid., p. 101.
20. Ibid., p. 114.
21. Ibid., p. 120.
22. Ibid., pp. 125–6.
23. Ibid., p. 102.
24. Ibid., p. 112.
25. Ibid., p. 116.
26. Ibid., p. 113.
27. Ibid., pp. 106–7.
28. Priestley, *Work of R. E.*, p. 185.
29. Ibid., p. 186.

30. Graeme Gooday, 'Combative Patenting: military entrepreneurship in First World War telecommunications', *Studies in History and Philosophy of Science – A*, 44(2) (June 2013), pp. 247–58.
31. Mike Bullock and Laurence Lyons, *Missed Signals on the Western Front: How the Slow Adoption of Wireless Restricted British Strategy and Operations in World War I* (Jefferson, NC: 2010), p. 21.
32. Guy Hartcup, *The War of Invention: Scientific Developments, 1914–1918* (London/Oxford: 1988).
33. Ibid., p. 76.
34. Priestley, *Work of R. E.*, p. 225.
35. Brian N. Hall, 'The British Army and Wireless Communication, 1896–1918', *War in History*, 19 (2012), pp. 298–9.
36. Ibid.
37. Nalder, *Royal Corps*, p. 217.
38. Ibid., p. 98.
39. Ibid., p. 104.
40. Ibid., p. 217.
41. Ibid., p. 106.
42. Ibid., p. 122.
43. Priestley, *Work of R. E.*, p. 29.
44. Ibid.
45. An exception is Brian Hall's recent work, see Hall, 'Technological Adaptation in a Global Conflict: The British Army and Communications Beyond the Western Front, 1914–1918'.
46. Nalder, *Royal Corps*, pp. 218–19.
47. Ibid., pp. 158–64.
48. Ibid., pp. 197–8.
49. Ibid., p. 201.
50. Ibid., pp. 208–9.
51. Burns, *Communications*, p. 419.
52. Hartcup, *War of Invention*, p. 123.
53. Headrick, *Invisible Weapon*, p. 165.
54. Hartcup, *War of Invention*, p. 123.
55. Ibid.
56. Burns, *Communications*, p. 406.
57. Hartcup, *War of Invention*.
58. Arthur Hezlet, *The Electron and Sea Power* (London: 1975), p. 107.
59. Headrick, *Invisible Weapon*, p. 125. The aforementioned 1912 committee on the use of wireless in the army had recommended the purchase of two Poulsen sets but it is unknown if this recommendation was carried out.
60. Hezlet, *Electron and Sea Power*, p. 135.
61. Hartcup, *War of Invention*, p. 128.
62. Hezlet, *Electron and Sea Power*, p. 107.
63. Hartcup, *War of Invention*, p. 128.
64. As quoted in Keith R. Thrower, *History of the British Radio Valve to 1940* (Ropley, Hampshire: 1992), p. 33.
65. Ibid., p. 31.
66. Hartcup, *War of Invention*, p. 128.
67. Ibid., p. 155.
68. Burns, *Communications*, pp. 406–7.
69. Hartcup, *War of Invention*, p. 152.
70. Jones, H.A., *The Official History of the War in the Air*, vol. 2 (The Clarendon press, 1928), p. 82.
71. Burns, *Communications*, pp. 406–7.
72. Hughill, *Global Communications*, p. 117.
73. Hartcup, *War of Invention*, p. 154.
74. Hughill, *Global Communications*, p. 151.
75. Hartcup, *War of Invention*, pp. 153–4.
76. Ibid., p. 156.

Suggested Further Reading

Bullock, Mike and Lyons, Laurence, *Missed Signals on the Western Front: How the Slow Adoption of Wireless Restricted British Strategy and Operations in World War I* (Jefferson, NC: McFarland, 2010)

Burns, Russel, *Communications: an international history of the formative years* (London: Institution of Electrical Engineers, 2004)

Hall, Brian, 'The "Life-Blood" of Command? The British Army, Communications and the Telephone, 1877–1914', *War & Society*, 27 (2008), pp. 43–65

Hall, Brian, 'The British Army and Wireless Communication, 1896–1918', *War in History*, 19 (2012), pp. 290–321

Hall, Brian, 'Technological Adaptation in a Global Conflict: The British Army and Communications beyond the Western Front, 1914–1918', *Journal of Military History* (2014)

Hartcup, Guy, *The War of Invention: Scientific Developments, 1914–1918* (London/Oxford: Brassey's Defence Publishers, 1988)

Headrick, Daniel, *The Invisible Weapon: Telecommunications and International Politics, 1851–1945* (New York: Oxford University Press, 1991)

Hezlet, Arthur, *The Electron and Sea Power* (London: Peter Davies, 1975)

Hughill, Peter, *Global Communications Since 1844: Geopolitics and Technology* (Baltimore, Md: Johns Hopkins University Press, 1999)

Chapter 15

'Any little article I would be pleased to have': The experience of British Widows of the First World War

By Andrea Hetherington

Joseph Lamb was a miner living in the village of Trimdon Colliery in County Durham in August 1914. Thirty-two years old, Lamb lived with his wife Mary Ann and their four children. On 2 November 1914, just a few days before his youngest son's first birthday, he answered Kitchener's call and signed up to join the army. His exact reasons for enlisting are unknown.

Anti-German propaganda had found its way to the pit villages of County Durham in the early months of the war. The local newspapers repeated stories of 'brutal outrages' by the Germans on an almost daily basis. In October 1914 the Deaf Hill Church Institute – just across the railway tracks from Trimdon Colliery – hosted a lantern slide lecture entitled 'How the Germans Make War – Fire and Sword in Belgium', during which tales of atrocities were played out to a no doubt receptive audience. Recruiting stations were established at the local collieries and received an enthusiastic response. At the end of August 1914 a motor car tour of the Durham colliery villages involving twenty vehicles lent by 'patriotic owners'[1] from West Hartlepool drummed up hundreds of volunteers.

If patriotism were not the reason for Joseph Lamb's enlistment, sheer pragmatism may have pushed him into uniform. Miners had the opportunity to earn far more underground than could a private in the army. Following the 1912 miners' strike, a minimum wage had been fixed at 6 shillings and 6 pence a day. An infantry private's basic pay at the time was 1 shilling and 1 pence a day. However, the outbreak of war had a detrimental effect on the mining industry in County Durham. Despite the fact that coal was going to be required at home in vast quantities to keep the country at war, the loss of Britain's coal export market was almost immediate. Germany alone had bought around 10 million tons of British coal in 1913, and the pits of the north-east of England were particularly reliant on exports. By July 1915 Britain's coal export figures were down by 30 million tons on the previous year.[2] A number of collieries closed down or placed their workers on short time hours, making it more difficult to maintain a decent standard of living, especially for those with young children to support. Trimdon Colliery itself, after which the village was named, was temporarily closed in 1914 and remained 'stood down' throughout the war years. When Joseph Lamb joined up, the separation allowance given to Mary Ann Lamb by the army was 21 shillings and 6 pence a week, with an extra 3 shillings and 6 pence allotted from Joseph's pay. Considering that there was now one less mouth for Mary Ann to feed, this was not an amount to be rejected given the harsh economic realities of the time. The idea that this would be a short war still held some currency among the general populace and it may be that Joseph Lamb thought he would sit out a few months at the army's expense until the pit re-opened.

Some mine owners magnanimously announced that the wives of employees who enlisted would be allowed to stay in their tied cottages for the foreseeable future. This was not as generous an offer as it first seems. With no one working the pit, the houses were not now required to accommodate miners in the same numbers. However, owners also announced that the free coal to which the miners were accustomed would also continue, and some employers additionally gave families a small monetary allowance while their miner husbands were soldiering. Miners were also actively exhorted to join up by their own organisations. The president of the Durham Miners' Association, Alderman William House, said that his members should be encouraged 'to buckle on their armour and enlist in the great fight'.[3] By August 1915 it is estimated that there were 250,000 miners in the armed forces.[4]

Joseph Lamb initially trained as a gunner with the Royal Garrison Artillery. He was then transferred to the East Surrey Regiment and made his first and, as it turned out, only journey abroad in October 1915, joining the British Expeditionary Force in France. As the war underground became an increasingly important feature of the conflict, burrowing towards and below the enemy trenches to plant explosive charges, Lamb's skills were felt to be more useful as a miner than as a soldier and he was transferred to the 180th Tunnelling Company, Royal Engineers. Life as a tunneller was arguably even more dangerous than that of an infantry soldier and Lamb lasted less than a month in his new unit. On 10 February 1916 he was part of a three-man party attempting to extend a tunnel in the Givenchy sector of the line in France. A German tunnelling party working in the opposite direction heard the British tunnellers and set off a camouflet charge, collapsing the British tunnel. Lamb and his two companions were buried alive, their bodies never recovered.[5]

Lamb's wife Mary Ann now found herself facing experiences which were all too familiar to an estimated 200,000 British women during and after the First World War. Married soldiers comprised around 28 per cent of the immediate casualties of the war.[6] The treatment of their widows by the authorities provides a fascinating insight into attitudes towards women and to welfare in early twentieth-century Britain.

Mary Ann Lamb's first struggle was for information. She will have, no doubt, received the dreaded letter telling her that her husband was dead. It is clear from the correspondence which survives that she was not told of the circumstances of his death. This was a common occurrence for the rank and file of the British Army. Sometimes a commanding officer would write to the family with details of the soldier's demise, but it was often left to surviving comrades to tell them what had happened if they had a contact address or were lucky enough to be allowed home leave. Pacts were formed amongst soldiers that they would each carry out this grim duty should their companions not return home. If a soldier were simply reported missing, the agony of waiting for news can scarcely be imagined. An indication of the usual timescales for such investigations can be gleaned from the fact that in the case of a disappearance, the separation allowance was paid for a full month longer than in the case of a known death.

Widows sometimes managed to find each other and attempted to pool information about the deaths of their loved ones. Official sources did not publicise widows' details but women found other routes to connect. Ernest Blackburn's widow Sarah received a letter from the wife of another member of his company in the 9th Battalion, King's Royal Rifle Corps. Blackburn had been reported missing on 2 October 1916 on the Somme. Sarah finally received notification of his death on 6 March 1917. It seems that reports then appeared in the Leeds newspapers, copies of which found their way to Scarborough, where Lily Davies anxiously awaited news of her own husband's fate. Lily had heard nothing from the War Office about her husband Harold, and sought any further information which Sarah Blackburn could provide. 'The suspense is almost more than I can bear,' wrote Lily. 'It seems too cruel for words that we women should give our men and never get the satisfaction of knowing what becomes of them.'[7]

Neither husband's body was ever recovered. Ernest Blackburn and Harold Davies are commemorated together on the Thiepval Memorial, the date of their deaths being recorded as 15 September 1916.

Death was a familiar companion in working class communities, particularly in mining villages like Trimdon Colliery. Accidents in the collieries were common, ranging from large-scale losses such as the Trimdon Grange disaster of 1882 in which seventy-four miners were killed in an underground explosion, to small mishaps resulting in a single death. Mourning rituals were important to these communities and women were always at the heart of them. Bodies were often received at home and women would play a central role in the laying-out of the corpse. 'Funeral Clubs' had been a feature of working class communities for almost a century. In 1911 Trimdon Colliery housed three insurance agents in a community of only 350 households. It was seen as shameful not to have a 'good send-off' where your family, friends and colleagues could eat and drink in your honour, and the Funeral Club money was for just such an occasion. A death in the fields of northern France rather than in the pits of County Durham deprived the widow of the comfort which may have been afforded by such familiar rituals. There was no corpse and there would be no funeral.

Mary Ann sought to fill the gap by attempting to retrieve anything of her husband's. She wrote to the War Office several times over the next few years to enquire as to the whereabouts of Joseph's personal effects. 'Any little article I would be pleased to have,'[8] she pleaded. Nothing could be forwarded to her as it seemed that Joseph's belongings were buried with him in the destroyed tunnel. The only 'little thing' which has survived with Joseph Lamb's descendants is a studio photograph taken on the south coast somewhere, showing him standing proudly in his uniform. Mary Ann was now left to bring up four young children on her own.

The unprecedented need for manpower at the outbreak of war presented the British government with a large number of logistical and practical issues which the wars of the Victorian era had never raised. Not least was the support that would be given to the dependents of soldiers, both during their service and after their death. The Victorian army was composed of career soldiers in the main and the rank and file did not generate respect in wider society unless they were actually fighting a war. Only a certain number of wives were permitted to be 'on the strength' as it was termed, meaning that they had been married with the permission of the army and were entitled to financial support when their husbands were abroad.

The Liberal government in power in 1914 had been making moves towards welfare reform. Whilst a genuine desire for social reform undoubtedly motivated some in government, the parliamentary progress made by the Labour Party meant that more pressure was applied for working class concerns to be addressed. The poor state of Britain's recruits to fight in the South African War of 1899–1902 had also given impetus to any measure that would improve the health of the working classes. Free school meals had been introduced in 1906, and in 1908 non-contributory old age pensions were on the statute book for the first time. Lloyd George's 1911 National Insurance scheme further eroded the concept that assistance from the state was a form of charity, as it was a contributory scheme, though smaller in scope than originally intended. One of the main reasons for the slow pace of reform was opposition from the 'Friendly Societies', which saw the prospects of their future business disappearing should the state make insurance arrangements for its citizens. Well organised and vociferous, the Friendly Societies forced the abandonment of plans to make payments to widows and orphans under the 1911 National Insurance scheme.

During the South African War pension payments were finally introduced but only to widows who were considered to be 'on the strength'. Charitable voluntary organisations had filled the gap, and the Soldiers and Sailors Families' Association, (SSFA) played the major role in distributing funds. Other charities supplemented these amounts. For example, the *Daily Telegraph* had its own widows and orphans appeal, and some regiments had specific funds raised to support dead soldiers' families. However, this kind of *ad hoc* approach was clearly inappropriate for a citizen army among which deaths were likely to be in far greater numbers than hitherto.

From August 1914 the majority of soldiers were ordinary citizens who had enlisted 'for the duration', not as a career, so the question of how their families were to be supported was of vital importance. The distinction of women being 'on' or 'off' the strength had no relevance to the new situation. Men needed reassurance that their dependents would be looked after or this worry would surely put a brake on the desperately needed recruitment drive. On 4 August 1914 the British Army issued an order outlining the terms of service for civilian recruits to the forces, specifying that separation allowances would be paid to soldiers' families to maintain households once the breadwinner was fighting for his country. Married men had to agree that one-third of their army pay could also be allotted to their families. Widows and orphans would also be entitled to payments from the state. A sliding scale of pensions would be payable for widows, depending on the rank of the soldier. The pensions were not 'means tested' and, like separation allowances, would be paid directly to the woman herself.

War widows were the only widows to receive a designated pension from the state until 1925. Initial payments were fairly modest, with the minimum level of payment being as little as 7 shillings and 6 pence a week. Additional allowances were made for each child of the soldier, with the first child receiving the most and subsequent children less. The hastily introduced arrangements were debated again in November 1914 and new rates put in place. They were raised periodically to reflect a rise in the cost of living, and in 1917 stood at 13 shillings and 9 pence a week for a private's widow. The first child was paid at 5 shillings a week, down to 2 shillings and 6 pence for every child after the third. Speaking in 1916, the Prince of Wales pronounced:

> It is the will of Parliament, expressing the will of the People, that pensions and allowances alike for widows and dependents and for the disabled, should be given upon a higher scale than in any previous war or in any of the European countries taking part in this war.[9]

Though this grand statement was technically correct, the pension payments were not generous. In fact, they were the lowest amongst the English-speaking nations involved in the First World War. A Canadian war widow received more than twice as much every week as a widow in England.

The granting of such allowances has to be viewed in the light of the attitude towards state assistance at the time. Modern Britons have largely grown up with the concept that one of your rights as a citizen is that the state will contribute to your care in time of need. This was not the mind-set of the early twentieth century, where state assistance implied the shadow of the Victorian workhouse and the despised Poor Law. The availability of non-'means tested' benefits to be paid to women by the state was a significant development in welfare history, and arguably the beginning of the end of 'voluntaryism' on which aid to the less fortunate was previously based.

Despite the fact that widows' pensions were now being paid by the government, not by charity, the SSFA was directly involved in their administration. With 800 branches nationwide and 50,000 volunteer 'social workers' listed on their books, the SSFA had the infrastructure to be able to administer payments throughout the country. The involvement of the SSFA caused its own problems as its volunteers struggled with the concept that separation allowances and widows' pensions were not granted on the charitable basis to which they were accustomed. The SSFA itself had proclaimed that its 'cardinal principle' was self-help,[10] and the notion of 'the deserving poor' was clearly still alive. Following a report by a Select Committee on pensions, the Naval and War Military Pensions Act 1915 was passed, doubling the minimum war widow's pension and removing all power from the SSFA. A central body called the Statutory Committee would now deal with pensions, with local War Pensions Committees beneath it. The SSFA's national committee was unhappy, believing it had been snubbed by the new measures and bemoaning the additional bureaucracy which the committee felt would now be necessary to run the system. The Statutory Committee took full control in June 1916. According to its own records, during the first two years of the war the SSFA had assisted over 700,000 widows and had distributed £2.6 million.[11] Though these figures include all war widows assisted by the SSFA, not just those bereaved in the first two years of the war, they are still astonishingly high. However, this was not the end of the SSFA's involvement in the administration of widows' pensions as the local War Pensions Committees often drew their membership from the same body of volunteers.

Mary Ann Lamb now applied for a widow's pension. On the death of a soldier, the separation allowance being paid to his dependents would continue for twenty-six weeks, which was supposedly enough time to allow the pension claim to be processed. However, this was often not the case and widows struggled to fill the gap between the end of separation allowance and the start of the pension. Some organisations offered assistance in the meantime, but this was almost always in the form of a loan which had to be repaid once the pension was received. In order to claim a pension, Mary Ann had to fill in a form listing her particulars and those of the children. She had to have the form signed by a magistrate and a senior police officer, underlining the concept of patriarchal control over this process. The police officer's declaration on the form specifically stated of the widow, 'we recommend her as in every respect *deserving* of the grant of Pension'.

This wording made it clear that a war widow's pension was not seen as an absolute entitlement and although it was not 'means tested', widows had to pass more subjective tests in order to qualify. The terms of the Royal Warrant of 1917 stated:

> Pensions to widows shall not be claimed as a right, but shall be given as a reward of service, and no pension shall be granted or continued to a widow who, in the opinion of Our Minister of Pensions, is unworthy of Our Royal favour.[12]

The 'service' referred to was, of course, the service of the widow's husband, not that of the widow herself. Throughout the Royal Warrant the wording, carried through verbatim from previous versions, left a wide range of discretion in granting payments. Words such as 'may' or 'could' were used in relation to payments, rather than 'shall' or 'will'. The exercise of this discretion by the Statutory Committee and its successors caused a great deal of financial difficulty to thousands of widows. The Army Council would involve the police further in the administration of allowances by issuing a directive to the civilian force that any misbehaviour by soldiers' wives or widows should be reported to them.

Having completed the pension form and had it duly signed, Mary Ann also had to provide proof of her marriage and of the existence of Joseph Lamb's offspring by sending her marriage certificate and birth certificates for all the children. This was a time-consuming and potentially expensive process, as birth certificates were not routinely kept and copies often had to be obtained. If the details provided matched those given by the soldier on enlistment, then a pension could be granted. Unmarried women were – perhaps surprisingly – also catered for under the terms of the Royal Warrant. If a soldier were to have nominated a woman on his enlistment papers as someone he supported financially, she could also be granted a pension despite the lack of a marriage certificate. However, pensions for the unmarried were not as generous as for wives – 10 shillings a week for the duration of the war and for twelve months thereafter.

Mary Ann Lamb's pension claim appears to have proceeded without difficulty and she was awarded 22 shillings and 6 pence a week for herself and the four children. This put her in a worse financial position than she had been in during her husband's war service, the amount being less in total than she was receiving under the separation allowance and portion of Joseph's wage she had been paid since November 1914. This was not an accident. The reasoning behind it was that, with the husband gone for good, a widow could make economies and potentially downsize. Whilst he was potentially coming home, she had to keep things to a certain standard to await his return. How a widow with four children was, in practice, able to downsize is difficult to imagine.

Mary Ann was, however, one of the lucky ones in that she was granted a pension. Many were not, both during the war and thereafter. A series of cruel twists in the legislation and the attitude of those administering the pensions meant that thousands of women were left completely without financial support. For example, one of the first hurdles to be jumped was that the soldier's death had to be 'due entirely to war service'. In Joseph Lamb's case this was straightforward, but for many it was not, and the outcome of applications could not be predicted. Take, for example, the cases of Lieutenant Ernest Roscoe and Lieutenant James Holmes. Both died in very similar circumstances but the end result of their dependents' pension application was completely different.

Ernest Roscoe was managing director of a theatrical sign-making company in Leeds called Gawthorpe's. A prominent figure in local politics, he was an enthusiastic supporter of the city's recruitment drive. As a man of small stature but also with considerable influence, he was instrumental in the establishment of the 17th Battalion, West Yorkshire Regiment – the 'Leeds Bantams' – and joined the battalion himself. During training in Skipton, Roscoe and a number of his fellow officers were granted a night off and proceeded to hire a car and drive to the town of Ilkley. Later that evening the party made its way back to Skipton. The car was overloaded, with passengers standing on the running boards, and in the darkness the driver misjudged the road, crashing the vehicle. Ernest Roscoe was flung from the car, fracturing his skull. He died at Skipton Hospital shortly thereafter. An inquest heard that neither the driver nor the passengers were drunk and the incident was seen as a tragic accident. Application for a pension was made on behalf of Lieutenant Roscoe's grieving widow Edith and the couple's young son. The application was refused on the grounds that his death was not attributable to war service as he had not been on duty at the time of the accident. A one-off gratuity of a year's officer's salary was eventually granted to Mrs Roscoe, hardly a fitting recompense for the loss of a husband and a lifetime's earnings.[13]

In the case of Lieutenant James Holmes, he and his fellow officers had been stationed in Egypt and were granted an afternoon off by their commanding officer. They hitched a lift to Port Said in an army truck and arranged for the same driver to take them back to base later that night. On the return journey one of Holmes' fellow officers decided to take the wheel from the original driver. He crashed the vehicle, causing the instant death of Lieutenant Holmes. In this case, despite Holmes having been off duty at the time, the death was ruled to be attributable to war service and a pension was subsequently granted to his dependents. It is difficult to see any substantive difference in these two cases which would warrant such a disparity of outcome.[14]

The death of the soldier had to take place within seven years of the injury or illness which was attributable to war service in order for his dependents to qualify for a pension. Though this was later changed when the realities of the effects of trench warfare were better understood, it left many women suffering the double blow of the death of a loved one who had managed to come home and the loss of his income. Diseases like tuberculosis, which was rife at the time, were particularly tricky to assess in these situations and must have left thousands bereft of financial support. The seven-year rule was given a further twist by the fact that, in order to qualify for a pension, a widow had to have been married to the soldier at the time he received the relevant injury. In the case of Private William Mellor of the Manchester Regiment, he was discharged from the army in January 1918 suffering from 'phthisis' – known today as pulmonary tuberculosis. Granted a disablement pension of 100 per cent, Mellor married in November 1919. He subsequently died of tuberculosis in 1923. His widow's application for a pension was refused outright with 'married after discharge' stamped on the papers.[15] There are many similar cases contained within the random sample of pension records which survive at the National Archives. Marrying a wounded returning hero may have been much encouraged by the Press and the Church, but if that hero subsequently were to die, the unfortunate woman did not fit the definition of 'widow' as outlined in the Royal Warrant so was not entitled to claim financial support.

Appeals against the refusal of pensions had to be made to the Statutory Committee, later replaced by a body called the Special Grants Committee. This committee had wide-ranging powers to award one-off payments, pay monies in trust rather than direct to the widow, and make education and living arrangements for the children, with or without the consent of the widow. The committee had the option of granting 'alternative pensions' for those who may not have qualified for the usual allowances, or for the widows of the higher paid who could prove their husbands' pre-war earnings. Pursuing an appeal to the committee was difficult for those with little education or lacking literacy skills. The Special Grants Committee's word was law and there was no higher authority to hear an appeal against the judgement the committee laid down.

War widows did have something of an exalted status in the community. Their husbands were seen as patriots who had paid the ultimate sacrifice. The respect due to those soldiers was passed on to the widows, but that respect was a fragile thing which could easily be lost, along with the widow's pension. The war widow was also the subject of a degree of jealousy within the community, seen as receiving money for nothing, and her existence, beyond the boundaries of direct male control, could be perceived as threatening. The terms of the Royal Warrant left the war widow's pension open to attack from vindictive neighbours and associates who wished to have the woman declared 'unworthy of Our Royal favour'. Anonymous letters signed 'A Ratepayer' or 'A Concerned Citizen' came into the offices of the Ministry of Pensions to report the inappropriate behaviour of a war widow or the poor state of her house and children. Investigations were almost always carried out, involving the SSFA volunteers and the local police force, and could result in the ultimate sanction of complete loss of the pension.

Once a widow was under the committee's scrutiny, she could well remain there for years. Elizabeth Percival had lost her husband Ernest on the Somme in March 1918, leaving her with two young daughters. Local reports of 'unfavourable conduct' led to her pension being paid in trust for more than six years despite an apparent lack of hard evidence to substantiate the claims. Constant visits by the Ministry of Pensions spies were understandably resented by Mrs Percival and the visitors' reports back to their masters reflect this. After one visitor complained of Mrs Percival's rudeness, the widow was sent a letter warning her that the committee would 'take a very serious view' of her case if such behaviour persisted.[16] Once a widow had erred, years of good conduct would be required before she was considered to have 'regained her character', as it was described in the Ministry's communications.

The most frequent reason for the anonymous informants to report to the Ministry of Pensions was that the widow had taken up with another man. This was an issue because the pension was only payable by the state in lieu of the soldier being alive to take care of his wife. On remarriage, the widow's pension would cease to be payable, though she could be granted a gratuity of twelve months' minimum pension. If the widow were 'carrying on' with another man, she was no longer the financial responsibility of the dead husband. Electoral registers were used as proof of a person's address, meaning that widows and their partners would consciously lose their vote in lieu of keeping their pension. Public opinion was very much against such women. The *Yorkshire Evening Post* was not alone in describing them as 'widows who dishonour their dead'.[17] The men with whom the widows were living were equally derided as parasites taking advantage of both the women and the state.

In the sad case of Isabella Simpson, the person with whom she was now in a relationship was her dead husband's brother. Her husband, Private John Simpson, was killed in France in the last month of the war. Isabella, having been granted a pension for herself and one child, had taken refuge in the home of her mother-in-law, where John's brother William Simpson was also living. Isabella and William formed a relationship which appears to have brought them to the attention of the Ministry of Pensions.[18]

Although by 1907 a man could marry his sister-in-law, it remained illegal until 1921 for a woman to marry her brother-in-law. Nancy Astor, the first female Member of Parliament to take a seat in the House of Commons, was one of the voices arguing strongly for a change in this legislation. One of the arguments put forward in favour of amendment was that brothers-in-law would then be able to marry war widows, providing them with support and, of course, removing them from the state's pension bill. Despite the change in the law, clergy were still allowed to refuse to officiate at such weddings, depending on their own personal views. Isabella and William Simpson found themselves in a very difficult situation. It seems that the couple had not tried to hide their relationship at all, were regarded as married in the locality, and, indeed, had actually tried to marry only to be thwarted by the vicar who declined to carry out the ceremony. The Ministry pestered Isabella for information about her relationship and its ultimate decision was that her pension should be forfeited. The local War Pensions Committee asked the Special Grants Committee to reconsider their decision in 1939 on the basis that William Simpson too was now dead and Isabella was 'destitute'. Enquiries revealed that William had actually died in 1923. It seems that Isabella, embarrassed by the status of her relationship with William and scarred by her previous contact with the authorities, had failed to make a further application to the Ministry of Pensions in the intervening sixteen years. The final decision of the Special Grants Committee was that she had forfeited her pension and it could not be reinstated.

The birth of a child was often the red flag which brought a widow to the attention of the pension administrators as proof that she was in a relationship with another man. An investigation would ensue and the pension would often be lost, certainly if the new relationship was ongoing. Widows sometimes found themselves abandoned by the new partner on the birth of a child and even if the Special Grants Committee allowed the pension to continue, the widow could expect to find herself under a great degree of scrutiny thereafter. There were cases reported in the press of widows abandoning illegitimate babies in desperate attempts to retain the pension payments which may have been their only source of income.

The reasons described here for the loss of a widow's pension appear to be fairly typical examples of the cases of which records survive. The Ministry of Pensions figures show that between March 1918 and March 1919 almost a thousand such forfeitures were made, undoubtedly leaving some families in a serious financial position.[19]

Even for widows who were granted pensions without any subsequent interference by the Special Grants Committee, times were tough, financially. In 1920 the National Council of Social Service produced a report on the effects of the widows' pension on families.[20] Over 400 families were studied with the assistance of voluntary organisations and information gathered about their income pre- and post-war. It was discovered that the average pre-war family income in the sample was 47 shillings a week, with many families earning much more than that. In one mining family with two breadwinners, the household was earning 110 shillings a week from the husband and his teenage son before the husband enlisted. After the husband's death, this amount dropped to 50 shillings a week, with an additional 15 shillings of poor relief from the local authorities. This amount had to feed the widow and seven children. All but one of the families studied, which were reliant solely on state relief, were worse off than they had been before the war. Only where the widow was able to work did the family income approach its pre-war levels.

Assistance was sometimes given to widows by their husband's former employers or professional body. Gunner William Cove was a bank clerk before his conscription in June 1916. When he was killed in March 1917, he left his widow

Ethel with two daughters aged 3 and 6. Ethel approached the Bank Clerks' Orphanage for help. The Orphanage was not a residential home but a fund founded by the banking industry in 1883 in order to provide for the education of the children of banking staff. It found itself overrun after the casualties of the First World War. Money from the fund enabled Ethel Cove to send her daughters to Bray Court, a private preparatory school near Maidenhead.[21] Other industries operated similar schemes, but many were geared specifically towards the children of former employees, not their widows.

Some widows would have been able to benefit from life insurance policies, but a standard policy would generally require the payment of an expensive extra premium were it to cover a man for going to war. The 'Friendly Societies' who had so begrudged the setting up of the 1911 National Insurance scheme were not slow to develop specific products targeting the soldier. By September 1914 advertisements were appearing in the Press offering life insurance for soldiers without the prohibitive extra premium which would generally need to be paid. The Eagle and British Dominions Insurance Company (which still exists today as Eagle Star) was one of the companies which advertised their products in the local and national Press. With Sir John French, former head of the British Expeditionary Force, and Admiral Lord Charles Beresford as trustees, the company offered life insurance for soldiers for £1 a year. The death benefits ranged from £100 for a death on the Western Front or other theatre of war, to only £50 for a death in the Balkans, which was felt to be a greater insurance risk presumably because of the ravages of malaria. This was hardly enough to maintain a family for life, amounting to the equivalent of about two years' worth of the average war widow's pension of around £1 a week.

In terms of moral support for widows, a number of organisations set up networks of visitors to provide advice and assistance to the bereaved. The Salvation Army was one such organisation, with 500 'widow's counsellors' nationwide by July 1916. A number of veterans' associations were formed in 1917, their main objective being to better the lot of the discharged or disabled soldier, though they also campaigned for better provision for widows and orphans. There were three to choose from, depending on the shade of your politics. Comrades of the Great War was a Conservative organisation with Lord Derby at the helm, whilst the Liberal equivalent was the National Federation of Discharged and Demobilised Sailors and Soldiers. The similarly named National Association of Discharged Sailors and Soldiers had links with the Labour Party, and there is evidence that this association attempted to set up a separate widows' section.

Representatives from these organisations would assist widows to some degree, either by donations and loans of various kinds, or by helping to deal with the Ministry of Pensions. There was sometimes a conflict of interest involved here, as the local war pensions committees often contained representatives from these same organisations. There were also instances of members of the veterans' organisations who held posts on the war pensions committees taking payments from widows to put in a good word for them with the Ministry.[22] The three veterans' organisations joined forces, along with the Officers' Association, in 1921 and thereafter became known as the British Legion. Interestingly, although one of the avowed policies of the Legion was 'to guard jealously the right to Pension' for widows as well as ex-servicemen, women were not allowed to become ordinary members of the new organisation at its inception.[23] In terms of widows having their own body to represent them, nothing appears to have come to fruition until 1971, when the British War Widows' Organisation was formed, ostensibly to have the burden of income tax removed from the war widow's pension.

Charities proliferated during the First World War, some directly associated with the military, like the Grand Fleet Fund, established in 1916 to assist the dependents of sailors. The Royal Patriotic Fund had been established during the Crimean War to assist widows and orphans and was constantly appealing for funds during the First World War. In August 1914 the Prince of Wales announced that there would be a National Relief Fund to assist with the distress caused by the war, including the particular distress caused to widows and orphans. The appeal raised £1 million in a short space of time and the SSFA was at the heart of the distribution of funds. Those who did not qualify for a widow's pension were invited to apply to the National Relief Fund and associated bodies, but with no guarantee of financial assistance. Each charity had its own rules about the issuing of funds to individuals, including the hated 'means testing', and there was concern amongst some widows about making applications for 'handouts' and all that that entailed. In some quarters, the continued assistance available from such organisations was felt to justify the fairly meagre amounts payable under the terms of the widow's pension. The concept that the state should assume total responsibility was not yet fully entrenched in British thinking on social policy.

Application to the authorities for Poor Law relief really was the last resort for the destitute widow. The National Council of Social Services report noted that such application resulted in a loss of self-respect. Their workers reported that such relief 'is not a right and there is a general feeling that it is given grudgingly, and with the implied suggestion that they ought to be able to manage without it'.[24] Some Poor Law Guardians were not prepared to grant any relief at all to war widows, whilst others did so on condition that widows did not undertake any work outside of the home – an approach sometimes taken by the Special Grants Committee too when dealing with reports of unsatisfactory behaviour by widows. Local War Pensions Committees sometimes expressed a similar view. The Edmonton Committee voted to send a letter to the Ministry of Pensions expressing the view that war widows with children should not work unless they had the permission of their local War Pensions Committee.

Women who had worked during the war were chased back to the home once the male workforce was demobilised. Women who wanted to keep their wartime jobs in industries formerly populated by men were seen as wicked and ungrateful for the sacrifices made by men to keep them safe. The War Pensions Committees took a similar stance in relation to their own employees. The Bradford Committee, for example, decided in September 1919 that all its female workers would be replaced by discharged servicemen. War widows' employment generally was not approved of in some quarters as concern was expressed that it reduced wages for everyone. The reasoning behind this was that war widows had a pension to keep them so would not be asking for as high a wage as others, allowing employers to take advantage. This was hardly a new idea, concerns being raised in the 1840s about the same effect resulting from Poor Law Guardians giving widows 'outdoor relief'. Working widows by 1920 were folk devils whose continued presence in the employment market was allegedly contributing to the vast numbers of unemployed men. This was particularly ironic given that the debates around war widows' pensions in November 1914 had specifically addressed the issue, with the government position being that the pensions were not designed to set widows up for life. The Prime Minister himself said 'We all have to work.'[25] The NCSS report showed that the working widows in its sample were by 1920 mostly earning their money in cleaning or domestic service, not in more lucrative factory jobs which may have been available to them during the war. The average weekly earnings for these particular women amounted to a negligible 7 shillings a week.

It is little wonder that some widows found themselves drifting into debt, sometimes appearing before the courts. Magistrates were often sympathetic to such women who had fallen behind in their rates payments or committed some shoplifting offence due to their reduced circumstances. The effects of grief were also sometimes acknowledged. Nellie Preston appeared before the magistrates in Dewsbury in November 1919 charged with stealing clothing from a market stall. It was reported that 'She lost her husband in France in April 1917 and had not been completely responsible for her actions since.'[26] The magistrates gave her a discharge, effectively not punishing her for the offence. The presiding magistrate or judge sometimes made specific pronouncements that their leniency in such cases was entirely due to respect owed to the widow's dead husband, not to the defendant herself. Such judicial sympathy does not appear to have extended to any woman accused of neglecting the soldier's children, such individuals often finding that they were given sentences of imprisonment. They also sometimes lost their children to adoption and, depending on the exact terms of the sentence, forfeited their pensions on release from custody.

The economic realities mean that it is unsurprising that a significant number of First World War widows – around 40 per cent – remarried. This was a development which had been anticipated to some degree by the Ministry of Pensions, and certainly hoped for, given the financial cost to the nation of pension payments. Visiting Leeds in September 1919, Sir Laming Worthington Evans, Minister of Pensions, proclaimed that 'widows were to be congratulated upon the rate of their remarriage'.[27] Despite the loss of the war widow's pension which always ensued, living once again with a working man improved the family income strikingly. Mary Ann Lamb had found it hard to bring up her young family on her widow's pension. Her children were too young to work, the eldest being only 10 at the time of Joseph's death, whilst the youngest was just 2 years old.

Mary Ann remarried in April 1918, having a registry office wedding to a miner called Harry Britton. Harry was also from Trimdon Colliery and was undoubtedly already known to the family, having lived in the next street to the Lambs in 1911. He was also a former soldier, having been invalided out of the army in 1917 due to sustaining a knee injury. The injury was not particularly serious, but the authorities felt that Harry Britton's services were better directed towards mining than soldiering and transferred him to the Class W reserve of recruits. Mary Ann and Harry Britton went on to have five children together.

The National Council for Social Service summed up the experiences of the widows in their sample as follows:

> It requires no special measure of sympathy to appreciate something of the struggle with poverty and ill health that in too many of these cases is added to the sense of personal loss on the death of the husband. Nor is it easy to over-look the evidence of courage and determination with which the struggle is in many cases faced and overcome.[28]

My great-grandmother, Mary Ann Lamb, was one of those widows who managed to overcome the struggle. Many widows were not as fortunate and their treatment is one of the often overlooked stories of the First World War. Their experiences are a snapshot of a society slowly coming to terms with the concept of state assistance as a right and struggling to realign a woman's role in a post-war world.

Notes

1. *Sunderland Daily Echo & Shipping Gazette*, 31 August 1914.
2. See Sir R.A.S. Redmayne, *The British Coal Mining Industry During the War* (Oxford: 1923).
3. *Northern Daily Mail*, 5 September 1914.
4. For example, see G.D.H. Cole, *Labour in the Coal Mining Industry (1914–1921)* (Oxford: 1923).
5. Details from the war diaries of the 180th Tunnelling Company, Royal Engineers, National Archives, WO/95/488.
6. Ministry of Pensions Second Annual Report PP 1920 XIV, Cmd 19.
7. Ernest Blackburn's file at the Liddle Collection, University of Leeds: Liddle/WW1/GS/0145.
8. Letter contained within Joseph Lamb's British Army Service Records, National Archives, WO 363/L229.
9. James Gildea, *Historical record of the work of the Soldiers' and Sailors' Families Association from 1885 to 1916* (1916).
10. James Gildea, *For King and Country – Being a record of Funds and Philanthropic Work in connection with the South African war 1899–1902* (1902).
11. Gildea, *Historical record of the work of the Soldiers' and Sailors' Families Association*.
12. Ministry of Pensions, 'Royal Warrant for the Pensions of Soldiers Disabled, and of the Families and Dependents of Soldiers Deceased in consequence of the Present War' (HMSO, 1917).
13. Lieutenant Ernest Roscoe, National Archives, WO 339/18421.
14. Lieutenant James Holmes, National Archives, PIN 26/21793.
15. Private William Mellor, National Archives, PIN 82/128.
16. Elizabeth Percival, National Archives, PIN 84/29.
17. *Yorkshire Evening Post*, 18 August 1920.
18. Isabella Simpson, National Archives, PIN 84/39.
19. Figures quoted in Janis Lomas, 'Delicate Duties: issues of class and respectability in government policy towards the wives and widows of British Soldiers in the era of the Great War', *Women's History Review*, 9 (1) (2000).
20. National Council of Social Service, 'Report on some effects of widowhood in wage earning families' (1920).
21. Details from W.A. Cove's file in the Liddle Collection, University of Leeds, Liddle/WW1/GS/0398.
22. See, for example, the case of Harry Chadwick, as reported in the *Yorkshire Post & Leeds Intelligencer* of 27 May 1925.
23. Graham Wootton, *The Official History of the British Legion* (London: 1956). This policy appears to have changed in 1922.

24. National Council of Social Service, 'Report on some effects of widowhood'.
25. Reports of the Parliamentary debate on the issue appeared in a number of newspapers, including the *North Eastern & Daily Gazette* of 19 November 1914.
26. *Yorkshire Evening Post*, 27 November 1919.
27. *Yorkshire Post & Leeds Intelligencer*, 14 September 1919.
28. National Council of Social Service, 'Report on some effects of widowhood'.

Suggested Further Reading

Fraser, Derek, *The Evolution of the British Welfare State*, 4th edition (Palgrave MacMillan, 2009)

Gildea, James, *Historical record of the work of the Soldiers' and Sailors' Families Association from 1885 to 1916* (1916)

Grayzel, Susan R., *Women and the First World War* (Routledge: 2002)

Jalland, Pat, *Death in War and Peace – a history of loss and grief in England 1914–1970* (Oxford University Press, 2010)

Lomas, Janis, 'Delicate Duties: issues of class and respectability in government policy towards the wives and widows of British Soldiers in the era of the Great War', *Women's History Review*, 9 (1) (2000)

Pedersen, Susan, *Family, Dependence and the Origins of the Welfare State* (Cambridge, 1993)

Redmayne, Sir R.A.S., *The British Coal Mining Industry During the War* (Oxford: 1923)

Silbey, David, *The British Working Class and Enthusiasm for War 1914–1916* (London: 2005)

Smith, Angela, *Discourses Surrounding British Widows of the First World War* (Bloomsbury, 2013)

Chapter 16

'Keeping the Home Fires Burning': Women's Support for British Servicemen

By Jessica Meyer

'Keep the home fires burning,
While your hearts are yearning.
Though your lads are far away
They dream of home.
There's a silver lining
Through the dark clouds shining,
Turn the dark cloud inside out
Till the boys come home.'[1]

Ivor Novello and Lena Guilbert Ford's famous First World War composition was published in 1914 and rapidly overtook 'It's a Long Way to Tipperary' as the most popular song of the war, a status it retained throughout the war years.[2] This popularity is unsurprising given the emphasis that the song places on the importance of the home to the success of the war effort. As Emma Hanna has pointed out, songs about home were, throughout the war, the most popular single category of popular music in Britain.[3] In addressing their lyrics to the women of Britain who cared for home and hearth, Novello and his co-author Ford were tapping into a powerful trope of the importance of domestic, and particularly feminine, support for men overseas.

Nor can the importance to the war effort of the home and women's work within it be seen only in popular culture. Numbers of historians have pointed to the ways in which the idea of home, both the ideal and the particular, played an important role in shaping men's experiences of war service.[4] Evidence for this comes from letters such as those written by Private D. Manning to his wife and now preserved in the archives of the Imperial War Museum. On 3 March 1916 Manning, a father of three, wrote of his military experience in terms of his worries that 'the kiddies [sic] boots might get bad just now. I know what it is to have freezing feet and I couldn't bear to think you or they had to put up with it.'[5] Men like Manning maintained strong domestic identities throughout their period of service through their continuing correspondence with home.

If cultural expression and correspondence were to have enabled men to maintain domestic male identities in wartime, domesticity was equally important in defining women and their wartime roles. Much of the historiography of women's experiences of the First World War has focused on the opportunities that the war provided for women to move out of domestic spaces and into a variety of public working spaces. From middle class women who sought adventure and service as VADs and Auxiliaries to working class women who eschewed domestic labour in favour of better paid work in munitions factories, the narrative of British women's experience of the First World War has been predominantly one of expanded horizons and opportunities.[6] Yet historians of women's history are increasingly pointing to the limits of these new horizons and opportunities, not merely in terms of the war's aftermath, which saw political and social efforts made to return women to the home,[7] but during the war years themselves when women's identities as war workers were never fully separated from their roles as home-makers.[8] For women like Manning's wife, defined in his letters entirely through her role as wife and mother, war work was shaped predominantly by domestic concerns, the labour of keeping the family together in anticipation of the men's return home. For these women, the war was experienced less as an historic break in gendered roles, providing fresh opportunities, and more as an extension of the labour they already undertook as wives, mothers and sisters.

Yet, as Novello and Ford's lyrics indicated, this domestic labour was understood at the time as an important part of the war effort, a narrative powerfully reflected by propaganda posters, as well as popular culture.[9] Such work continued well beyond enlistment, helping to maintain servicemen's morale throughout their training and overseas service. It is the specific nature of this form of war work that this chapter will examine, looking at the practical work of maintaining homes and businesses, the voluntary work of provisioning and providing, and the emotional labour of caregiving and communicating which formed the bulk of the work of British women of all classes during the war. Using both popular cultural references and personal correspondence, it will argue that this form of women's wartime work not only sowed 'the seeds ... for a new privileging of the domestic with private life, the imagination and public discourses in the post-war era',[10] but also served as an important source for the maintenance of military morale, and with it the national war effort, during the war itself.

One of the reasons why relatively little is understood about the continuities of women's war work is the paucity of relevant surviving material. While Manning's letters illustrating his domestic concerns and his understanding of his wife as, first and foremost, a mother have been preserved, any letters from Mrs Manning about the children's boots, or lack of them, have not survived. Correspondence *to* the front, as opposed to that sent *from* it, was far harder to preserve than letters sent to the relative safety of home, where they could be carefully collected and treasured.[11] Yet, as Maggie Andrews has demonstrated in relation to the West Midlands, 'A range of letters, diaries, memories, newspapers and posters ... [can] be utilised to draw attention to the significance of the domestic activities women undertook in wartime.'[12] In looking at such sources in relation to how men responded to this work in their own letters, diaries and memories, it will be argued that the influence of women's domestic labour in wartime extended far beyond the home and had a profound impact on the British war effort.

Managing Homes and Businesses

As Andrews notes:

> Domesticity in wartime for women varied, influenced by wealth, class, age and geographical location. Some women kept house not only for their families but also for billeted soldiers or Belgian refugees. Wives and children took on new roles and responsibilities in family farms, smallholdings and businesses when husbands and sons left for war. Some wealthier women were alarmed to discover the supply of domestic servants decreasing, whilst others with large houses converted part of their home into a convalescence hospital for wounded soldiers. As the conflict progressed it increasingly interfered with daily life in the home in ways unimaginable to previous generations.[13]

What women of all classes experienced was a profound change in the management of the home in response to the exigencies of war. Home management was, in Victorian and Edwardian Britain, the responsibility of women, the counterpoint to the rise of the male breadwinner norm as a mark of respectability for both the working and middle classes. While the Victorian middle class wife might view the actual labour of housekeeping as beneath her, the cultural expectation was that she would provide 'a clean and well-ordered house, an inviting fireside, an appetizing table, and soothing attentions in the sick-room'.[14] In working class households, while women might engage in work outside the home to make ends meet, they were also responsible for 'the cultivation of the home' as a defence against accusation of a lack of respectability. This included not only the practice of domestic skills of childrearing, cooking and cleaning, but also the management of family finances, with 'respectable' men turning over their weekly wages to their wives for housekeeping, retaining a portion as pocket money for leisure spending.[15] Management of the domestic economy was not, however, limited to control of finances. It encompassed the fundamentals of food and nutrition, with many women denying themselves food they had prepared in favour of husbands and grown-up sons earning a weekly wage.[16]

The war disrupted these arrangements. Men left for military service, first voluntarily, then compulsorily, depriving the household of their wages or income, but also representing one less mouth to feed. For the middle classes, domestic servants were increasingly unavailable to provide household labour. Food economy became more and more necessary as imports were drastically affected by the German U-boat campaign and the loss to farming of men and horses had not yet been redressed by concerted organised effort on the land – another area where women were to make a positive contribution to the war effort.

By 1917 'food was becoming a public obsession'.[17] Edie Bennett, a housewife in Walthamstow, was certainly obsessed by January 1918 when she wrote a series of letters to her husband about the difficulties of getting food: 'we are slowly being starved out, we have to line up for everything now … tea, sugar, marg and a joint of meat is a thing of the past'. Reflecting women's pre-war status as nurturers of the domestic, she commented in another letter, 'It is the kiddies that worry you. They must live on something.'[18] For women such as Bennett, the imperative of war work was to keep the home going by keeping it fed, even as shortages and queuing added to the difficulty and labour of the task.

For Bennett, as for many women, the preservation of domestic continuity thus involved the struggle to maintain the domestic economy within a landscape of reduced resources. For others, it involved shouldering the burden of their husband's labours while they were away at war in order to maintain the family's economic viability. Annie Marriott was one example, running a milk business in Camp Road, Leeds. The labour of collecting and delivering the milk, which she shared with her husband George, became her sole responsibility when he enlisted in the army in 1915. Her success in maintaining the business as a going concern despite his absence is demonstrated by the fact that she and George continued to run it together after he was seriously wounded and discharged in 1918. His determination to remain involved in the business, pulling himself around the floor on his bottom because of the disablement of his legs, indicates further that the business played a role not only in supporting the family but in enabling his return, however complicated, to civilian life.[19] While separation allowances were intended to substitute for the financial loss that military service entailed for families,[20] the maintenance of a small business had value above and beyond the income it provided. Keeping businesses going was an important way in which men remained linked to their homes and the communities where they lived and worked in peacetime, as well as a vital method for reintegrating ex-servicemen into civilian life after the war was over.[21] Women like Annie Marriott thus played a hugely practical role in maintaining morale by literally keeping the home fires burning and civilian businesses in operation.

Provisioning and Providing
Other forms of homemaking which maintained men's ties to home were as practical if superficially more insular. As Rachel Duffett has shown, the provision of food via parcels was an extremely important way for men to remain in touch with their families. Parcels, whether supplied by Fortnum & Mason, as in the case of officers such as Arthur Gibbs, or filled with homemade items, helped tastily to supplement army rations.[22] Women were central to this form of provisioning, either selecting or concocting the items which parcels contained,[23] a form of regular service to men at the front which came at no little cost, both financial and emotional. The parents of the three Stopher brothers, an impoverished labouring family from rural Suffolk, struggled with the costs of supplying parcels as often as their sons wished. As Duffett notes, despite the assurances of one of the boys, George, that they should 'not be afraid to ask anybody for a little gift' to enable them to send more packages, this would have caused shame to the parents, exposing to their neighbours their inability to provide adequately for their children.[24] The labour of providing was thus not unproblematic.

It remained, however, extremely important, not only in terms of actually feeding the men at the front but also in maintaining 'the point of contact between men and their families as a very tangible reminder of the world that had been left behind'. In this context, the actual method of provisioning was a matter of central importance, with 'parcels marketed by shops … accorded a lower status than those individually packed by loved ones'.[25] Men wrote regular letters requesting homemade cakes or biscuits and cigarettes, and expressing thanks for provisions sent. Kenneth Addy's comment that no cake is 'as good as mother makes' reflected a widespread attitude towards the food women provided in parcels.[26] Women's domestic work within the home as the providers of nourishment through cooking thus contributed to the war effort emotionally as well as practically, with food parcels not only providing calorific nourishment but representing 'a fragment of home, lovingly captured in brown paper and string'.[27]

Such contributions were not limited to the family circle, although this remained the primary focus of most women's domestic labour. Women's wartime voluntarism, as Andrews notes, mobilised domestic labour for the national war effort.[28] Charitable work had long been associated with middle class feminine labour beyond the home.[29] The war, however, dramatically expanded women's opportunities to volunteer, as well as pushing back the definitions of voluntary labour to encompass a wider range of domestic options for community service.[30] While the best known form of female voluntarism was probably in support of the medical caregiving provided by Voluntary Aid Detachment (VAD) units, this form of women's work could encounter the discordance of professional and military nurses understandably laying claim to a more elevated status by reason of their qualifications and experience.[31] Similarly, volunteering with Auxiliary units placed women's work in non-domestic contexts challenging to understandings of appropriate gender roles in wartime.[32] Yet more established forms of voluntary service were also undertaken by many women, from the collection of eggs to supplement soldiers' rations to the ubiquitous knitting of socks and other garments, celebrated by Jessie Pope in her poem 'Socks' (1917) and affectionately mocked in the popular nonsense song 'Sister Susie's Sewing Shirts for Soldiers' (1914). As Andrews points out, women's voluntarism predominantly involved 'women … still doing fundamentally domestic and caring roles to support men'.[33]

Caregiving and Communicating

It is the association between caring and domesticity that underpins the significance of the contribution of women's domestic labour to the national war effort. As we have seen, the provision of domestic services in the form of food and clothing were important to the maintenance of morale by providing links to the family circle for men far from home, links which served to reinforce men's sense of what they were fighting for.[34] Charitable work which mobilised the domestic had a similar effect, evoking home associations even if the tangible reality of home were not present. Female volunteers in YMCA huts, for example, were described as 'toil[ing] incessantly to provide the mother-and-sister sense which calls for satisfaction in the heart of every "boy" when far from home',[35] while nurses' memoirs are full of recollections of dying men who called them 'mother' or 'sister'.[36]

Women also played a significant role in communicating men's experiences of war, as expressed in their letters, to others.[37] As both Bennett and Manning's letters indicate, information about the care of children formed an important point of contact between men at the front and women at home. While childcare as provision was viewed as a feminine duty within the home, the responsibility of educating children had long been viewed as a male responsibility, particularly within middle class homes.[38] Men at war continued to maintain their interest in this facet of childcare, writing letters to children about their experiences. Women, however, had a new and significant role in mediating the lessons contained in correspondence. G.R. Barlow, for instance, expected his aunt to be 'the best judge of what [his sister Nora] should learn', although he expressed the opinion that 'I think that the truth is far preferable to any charming fairytale.'[39] Women thus took on roles as repositories and conduits of knowledge as part of their childcare roles. In doing so, they enabled men to maintain traditional emotional ties with home that the distance of war service, with all its horrors and strangeness, might otherwise have severed.

It was, however, through the emotional labour of writing to men that women were able most directly to influence fighting men's morale. As Michael Roper has argued, specifically in relation to mothers, 'letter-writing was a way of mothering at a distance ... [and] most put great energy into it, almost as if it was their equivalent to military service'.[40] Yet it was not only mothers who undertook this form of labour; wives, aunts and sisters were all points of contact, serving as repositories for news which would be circulated around the wider family, as well as conduits for news from home to the front. Precisely what they wrote about is difficult to assess because of the lack of surviving material, but the importance of this communication is evident from the content of letters which men wrote home and which have been preserved.

One of the most common themes of these letters is the request for more correspondence from home. R. MacGregor, for instance, wrote asking his mother to 'Please write a bit oftener. It seems a weary long time since I last had a letter ... one sentence you can bet on seeing in every letter is "Write soon, soon, soon," and you know I value a letter from you more than from anyone.'[41] C.W. Dawson similarly told his mother, 'your letters are always interesting even when you've got nothing frightfully exciting to say'.[42] The news of the health of family members, meetings with friends, the possibility of home improvements, problems with food shortages, the success (or otherwise) of children at school were all topics which provided men with a touchstone of domestic normality that was of vital importance to their sense of identity in the strange and disturbing world of warfare they had entered. The importance of this touchstone can be seen in men's appeals to their sense of home in moments of extremity. When C.T. Newman found 'conditions ... worse than ever' in 1915, he wrote to his fiancée, 'I need a letter from you to lift my heart.'[43] Home, and communication with it, was a powerful influence on men's sense of purpose and on their morale. The emotional labour that women undertook in ensuring that men maintained their connection with home during wartime was a powerful boost to the war effort, so powerful indeed that voluntary efforts were organised to establish pen-pal relationships between women and men at the front who were otherwise without correspondents.[44]

Conclusion

Karen Hunt has argued that 'Highlighting the housewife within the First World War story underscores the importance of the Home Front to the prosecution of the war.'[45] As this chapter has demonstrated, there is an important story to be told about women's domestic and caring labour within the home, but it is also one that extends far beyond it. This story adds to our understanding of the complex interrelationship between fighting men and the home for which they felt they were fighting. Despite the difficulty in accessing the voices of women undertaking such work, its significance to wartime society, as well as to individuals, is reflected in the mobilisation of domesticity and care in popular culture and voluntary work, as well as the expression of its importance in so many men's letters home.

The presence of domestic labour in men's letters in particular provides evidence of the emotional significance of caring for the home in wartime Britain, a significance which directly underpinned morale through its reinforcement of what men felt they were fighting for, namely the home. As Andrews points out, this emotional continuity reinforced post-war social and cultural narratives of the return to domesticity, particularly in light of the fact that many women undertook such labour in addition to, rather than instead of, work in munitions factories and VAD units.[46] Nonetheless, the direct contribution that the maintenance of family homes and enterprise, the care of children and the provision of home comforts and news made to the war effort provided a valuable counterbalance to the sense of alienation from the home which war experience was capable of inducing in some men,[47] giving women an additional role of no little significance in the prosecution of total war. Read in this context, Novello and Ford's famous lyrics become not merely an offer of nostalgic comfort for men, but a declaration of purpose for women as well.

Acknowledgements

The author would like to thank Dr Emma Hanna, Dr Alice Kelly, Dr Lucinda Matthew-Jones and Dr Catherine Feely for advice on various aspects of this chapter.

Notes

1. Ivor Novello and Lena Guilbert Ford, 'Till the Boys Come Home (Keep the Home Fires Burning)' (London: Asherberg, Hopwood & Crew Ltd, 1914).
2. Michael Williams, *Ivor Novello: Screen Idol* (London: BFI, 2003).
3. Emma Hanna, 'Legacies of War: Popular Music and the First World War', talk given at the University of Leeds, 11 November 2015.
4. Joanna Bourke, *Dismembering the Male: Men's Bodies, Britain and the Great War* (London: Reaktion, 1996), pp. 163–4; Laura King, *Family Men: Fatherhood and Masculinity in Britain, c.1914–1960* (Oxford: Oxford University Press, 2015), p. 34; Timothy James Fisher, 'Fatherhood and the Experience of Working-Class Fathers in Britain, 1900–1930', PhD thesis (University of Edinburgh, 2004), pp. 160–74; Michael Roper, *The Secret Battle: Emotional Survival in the Great War* (Manchester: Manchester University Press, 2009); Jessica Meyer, *Men of War: Masculinity and the First World War in Britain* (Basingstoke: Palgrave MacMillan, 2009); Helen B. McCartney, *Citizen Soldiers: The Liverpool Territorials in the First World War* (Cambridge: Cambridge University Press, 2005), pp. 89–118.

5. IWM, Documents 4685, Papers of D. Manning: D. Manning, letter to his wife, 3 March 1916.
6. Kate Adie, *Fighting on the Home Front: The Legacy of Women in World War One* (London: Hodder & Stoughton, 2013), pp. 1–2; Nicoletta Gullace, *Blood of Our Sons: Men, Women and the Negotiation of British Citizenship during the Great War* (New York: Palgrave MacMillan, 2002); Arthur Marwick, *The Deluge: British Society and the First World War* (London: Bodley Head, 1965); Martin Pugh, *'We Danced All Night': A Social History of Britain Between the Wars* (London: Bodley Head, 2008), p. 152; Angela Woolacott, *On Her Their Lives Depend: Munitions Workers in the Great War* (Berkeley: University of California Press, 1994), pp. 188–216.
7. Gail Braybon, 'Winners or Losers: Women's Symbolic Role in the War Story', in Gail Braybon (ed.), *Evidence, History and the Great War: Historians and the Impact of 1914–18* (New York: Berghahn Books, 2003), pp. 86–112; Susan Kingsley Kent, *Making Peace: The Reconstruction of Gender in Interwar Britain* (Princeton: Princeton University Press, 1993).
8. Susan Grayzel, *Women's Identities at War: Gender, Motherhood and Politics in Britain and France During the First World War* (Chapel Hill: University of North Carolina Press, 1999), pp. 1–3; Deborah Thom, *Nice Girls and Rude Girls: Women Workers in World War I* (London: I.B. Tauris, 1997), pp. 164–86.
9. Maggie Andrews, 'Ideas and Ideals of Domesticity and Home in the First World War', in Maggie Andrews and Janis Lomas (eds), *The Home Front in Britain: Images, Myths and Forgotten Experiences since 1914* (Basingstoke: Palgrave MacMillan, 2014), pp. 6–7.
10. Ibid., p. 6.
11. Remarkably little analytic work has been done on the process of family archive creation during the First World War. For related discussions on the role of the printed form in such archive creation, see Michèle Barrett and Peter Stalybrass, 'Printing, Writing and a Family Archive: Recording the First World War', *History Workshop Journal*, 75:1 (2013), pp. 1–32, and on the process in relation to the Second World War, see Margaretta Jolly, 'Myths of Unity: Remembering the Second World War through Letters and their Editing' in Alex Vernon (ed.), *Arms and the Self: War, the Military and Autobiographical Writing* (Kent: Kent State University Press, 2005), pp. 144–70.
12. Andrews, 'Ideas and Ideals of Domesticity and Home in the First World War', p. 6.
13. Ibid., p. 7.
14. John Tosh, *A Man's Place: Masculinity and the Middle-Class Home in Victorian England* (New Haven, CT: Yale University Press, 1999), p. 56.
15. Keith McClelland, 'Masculinity and the "Representative Artisan" in Britain, 1850–80', in Michael Roper and John Tosh (eds), *Manful Assertion: Masculinities in Britain since 1800* (London: Routledge, 1991), pp. 86–7; Wally Seccombe, 'Patriarchy Stabilized: The Construction of the Male Breadwinner Norm in Nineteenth-Century Britain', *Social History*, 2:1 (1986), pp. 53–76.
16. Rachel Duffett, *The Stomach for Fighting: Food and the Soldiers of the Great War* (Manchester: Manchester University Press, 2012), pp. 46–7. While prioritising the energy of wage earners might seem logical, in fact the physical demands of pregnancy and domestic labour meant that women's nutritional needs were similar to those of their husbands.
17. Adrian Gregory, *The Last Great War: British Society and the First World War* (Cambridge: Cambridge University Press, 2008), p. 214.
18. IWM, Documents 3695, E. Bennett to Gunner Bennett, 8 January 1918, 24 January 1918, quoted in Gregory, *The Last Great War*, p. 215.
19. It continued to be the source of income to support her and two young sons when George died whilst undergoing surgery to amputate his injured leg in 1920. 'Oatland Road, Leeds: Impact of War on Women who Lost Husbands', BBC World War One at Home, first broadcast Radio Leeds, 30 July 2014, http://www.bbc.co.uk/programmes/p023hn5y (accessed 8 December 2015).
20. James McDermott, *British Military Service Tribunals, 1916–1918: 'A very much abused body of men'* (Manchester: Manchester University Press, 2011), p. 136.
21. Bourke, *Dismembering the Male*, pp. 164–70; McCartney, *Citizen Soldiers*, pp. 242–57.
22. Rachel Duffett, 'A War Unimagined: Food and the rank and file soldier in the First World War', in Jessica Meyer (ed.), *British Popular Culture and the First World War* (Leiden: Brill, 2008), pp. 47–70; Duffett, *The Stomach for Fighting*, p. 197.
23. Roper, *The Secret Battle*, p. 98.
24. Duffett, *The Stomach for Fighting*, p. 194.

25. Duffett, 'A War Unimagined', p. 61.
26. G.H. Addy, *A Memoir of his Son Kenneth James Balguy Addy, Second Lieutenant* (London, 1916), letter dated 20 April 1915, quoted in Duffett, *The Stomach for Fighting*, p. 200.
27. Duffett, *The Stomach for Fighting*, p. 199.
28. Andrews, 'Ideas and Ideals of Domesticity and Home in the First World War', p. 11.
29. Frank Prochaska, *The Voluntary Impulse: Philanthropy in Modern Britain* (London: Faber, 1988).
30. Peter Grant, 'Voluntarism and the impact of the First World War', in Matthew Hilton and James McKay (eds), *The Ages of Voluntarism: How we got to the Big Society* (Oxford: Oxford University Press for The British Academy), pp. 27–46.
31. Christine E. Hallett, '"Emotional Nursing": Involvement, Engagement, and Detachment in the Writings of First World War Nurses and VADs', in Christine E. Hallett and Alison S. Fell (eds), *First World War Nursing: New Perspectives* (London: Routledge, 2013), pp. 87–102.
32. Krisztina Robert, '"All That is Best in the Modern Woman"?: Representations of female auxiliaries in British popular culture, 1914–1919', in Meyer (ed.), *British Popular Culture*, pp. 97–122.
33. Andrews, 'Ideas and Ideals of Domesticity and Home in the First World War', p. 13.
34. Meyer, *Men of War*, p. 35.
35. Salvation Army, 'The home touch of the hut', p. 10, quoted in Jeffrey S. Reznick, *Healing the Nation: Soldiers and the Culture of Caregiving in Britain during the Great War* (Manchester: Manchester University Press, 2004), p. 24.
36. Santanu Das, *Touch and Intimacy in First World War Literature* (Cambridge: Cambridge University Press), pp. 24–5.
37. Roper, *The Secret Battle*, p. 59.
38. King, *Family Men*, pp. 30–9; Tosh, *A Man's Place*, pp. 91–2.
39. IWM, Documents 2755, Letters of G.R. Barlow, Letter to Alice, 5 January 1917.
40. Roper, *The Secret Battle*, p. 51.
41. IWM, Documents 13511, Papers of R. MacGregor, Letter to Mother, 16 November 1915.
42. IWM, Documents 10921, Papers of C.W. Dawson, Letter to Mother, 23 June 1918.
43. IWM, Documents 12494, Papers of C.T. Newman, Letter to Winnie, 20 December 1915.
44. The most systematic of these schemes was the French 'marraines de guerre' (godmothers of war) scheme, but local versions proliferated in Britain, often coordinated by local newspapers.
45. Karen Hunt, 'A Heroine at Home: The Housewife on the First World War Home Front', in Andrews and Lomas (eds), *The Home Front in Britain*, p. 87.
46. Andrews, 'Ideas and Ideals of Domesticity and Home in the First World War', p. 6. For a discussion of the multiple roles women undertook during the war, see Grayzel, *Women's Identities at War* and Thom, *Nice Girls and Rude Girls*.
47. Richard Aldington, *Death of a Hero* (London: Chatto & Windus, 1929); Siegfried Sassoon, 'The Glory of Women', *Cambridge Journal*, 8 December 1917.

Suggested Further Reading

Adie, Kate, *Fighting on the Home Front: The Legacy of Women in World War One* (London: Hodder & Stoughton, 2013)

Andrews, Maggie and Lomas, Janis (eds), *The Home Front in Britain: Images, Myths and Forgotten Experiences since 1914* (Basingstoke: Palgrave MacMillan, 2014)

Braybon, Gail (ed.), *Evidence, History and the Great War: Historians and the Impact of 1914–18* (New York: Berghahn Books, 2003)

Duffett, Rachel, *The Stomach for Fighting: Food and the Soldiers of the Great War* (Manchester: Manchester University Press, 2012)

Grayzel, Susan, *Women and the First World War* (Harlow: Longman, 2002)

Gregory, Adrian, *The Last Great War: British Society and the First World War* (Cambridge: Cambridge University Press, 2008)

Gullace, Nicoletta, *Blood of Our Sons: Men, Women and the Negotiation of British Citizenship During the Great War* (New York: Palgrave MacMillan, 2002)

Hallett, Christine E. and Fell, Alison S. (eds), *First World War Nursing: New Perspectives* (London: Routledge, 2013)

Kent, Susan Kingsley, *Making Peace: The Reconstruction of Gender in Interwar Britain* (Princeton: Princeton University Press, 1993)

McCartney, Helen B., *Citizen Soldiers: The Liverpool Territorials in the First World War* (Cambridge: Cambridge University Press, 2005)

Meyer, Jessica (ed.), *British Popular Culture and the First World War* (Leiden: Brill, 2008)

Meyer, Jessica, *Men of War: Masculinity and the First World War in Britain* (Basingstoke: Palgrave MacMillan, 2009)

Roper, Michael, *The Secret Battle: Emotional Survival in the Great War* (Manchester: Manchester University Press, 2009)

Thom, Deborah, *Nice Girls and Rude Girls: Women Workers in World War I* (London: I.B. Tauris, 1997)

Chapter 17

Alfred Pollard VC:
Valour in the Trenches

By N.S. Nash

I have had an almost lifetime interest in Alfred Pollard, a revered hero in my first unit during national service in the army, and then, in my first employment, I was further 'captured' by the claim of my new boss that he was serving with Pollard at the time of his great deed which earned the Victoria Cross. More than thirty years later, and having written extensively on military matters, it seemed right to delve deeper and attempt the hero's biography. There was an absolutely invaluable source, his own account written under the title *Fire-Eater*, which was published in 1932. However, this would need a wider context, together with as much detached verification as was possible, and there was the two-volume regimental history of the unit concerned, the 1st Battalion, the Honourable Artillery Company (HAC). The regimental war diaries were available too and I was privileged to have the practical help of the regimental association's librarian, Miss Justine Taylor.

The supporting documentation was essential but as it was the man himself I was after, soon finding him rather different from what I anticipated and quite extraordinary in his 'fighting philosophy', I came to rely principally on the picture he painted of himself in *Fire-Eater*, his autobiography. Accordingly, for the biography and more particularly for this chapter devoted principally to the First World War period of his life, the quotations shown are from *Fire-Eater*, revealing a man exceptional for more than his remarkable conduct under particularly challenging circumstances.

Alfred Pollard was born into a comfortable middle class household in Wallington, Surrey, in 1893, and attended the Merchant Taylors' School from 1906 to 1908. His brother Frank joined the HAC in 1909, and of himself at the outbreak of war on 4 August 1914, Alfred Pollard wrote:

I was twenty-one years and three months, a clerk in the St James's Street Branch of the 'Alliance Assurance Company' and utterly irresponsible. My chief interests in life were rugger in the winter, tennis in the summer and dancing all the year round. Girls? Of course! They added a spice to life in the same way that one uses salt to season food. With the exception of one, with whom I had believed myself in love with from the age of eighteen, none had any influence over me. I invested the one with every feminine virtue and shut my eyes to the fact that her real self might fall short of the wonderful creature of my imagination. She was two years my senior and thought me rather a silly ass.

Alfred was patently besotted with this lady. She remained unnamed throughout the 271 pages of his autobiography, even though it was published some eighteen years after the event.

Fired by his brother Frank's stories of the HAC, Alfred would settle for nothing less than service in this regiment. On the morning after the declaration of war, he found that the regimental HQ, Armoury House, was completely besieged by men wanting to volunteer. On the gates was a notice bearing the stark advice that 'No more volunteers are needed'. Alfred was but one of the besiegers in City Road that day. It is probable that somewhere in the melee with Pollard were Mr Reginald Haine and Mr Thomas Pryce, both of whom were destined, like Pollard, to win the Victoria Cross.

When the crowd in City Road drifted away, Pollard stayed. He was made of stern stuff and he hung around in the bleak environs of City Road for three hours until, at about 11.30am, the notice was removed and the gates swung open. He was first through the gap and ran the 150yds to burst through the doors of Armoury House. An hour later, medically examined and pronounced fit, he was attested, 'joined the Army' and assumed the appellation Private A.O. Pollard, HAC. He then paid his subscription and, as was the regimental practice, signed the Great Vellum Roll. After cursory basic training, he joined the 1st Battalion.

> Every man was a potential officer. Later, when the country needed officers of the right type, the War Office realized the error of using such material as that which composed the 1st Battalion of the Honourable Artillery Company as ordinary soldiers.

These remarks were made well after the event and Pollard's view on the waste of potential officers is not original thought. It is rather the oft-expressed view of many, but only after hundreds of potential officers in the HAC had been killed in the guise of men in the ranks.

By today's different values there is an unattractive flavour of superiority in many of Pollard's views expressed in his book. He could be termed a 'snob'. However, a hundred years ago social distinctions were much more clearly defined and the blunt fact was that the products of 'public schools' did assume a position of superiority because a man's accent and education were the critical yardsticks by which he was judged – in the main, their superiority was cheerfully acknowledged by those who were less well educated.

With 799 'other ranks', Pollard embarked on the SS *Westmeath* for France. Issued with his rifle, though it was of an old pattern, he acknowledged that handling it for the first time gave him a thrill which remained with him for years.

> I was armed. It was a weapon designed to kill. I wanted to kill – not because I hated the enemy but because the primitive instinct was strong in me to fight. A bayonet was supplied with the rifle. How many times I examined that bayonet in secret, feeling its edge and gloating over it. The desire to get to the front had become an obsession.

Alfred Pollard was clearly very different from most of his fellows and surely exceptional in actively seeking close-order combat, relishing the 'kill or be killed' atmosphere of the trenches. It was an attitude that was to single him out from the crowd.

Before going to the front, Pollard was inveigled by two of his comrades into visiting a brothel in Nantes. For some reason he fled from the brothel. He was not a 'man of the world' and it seems likely that he was a virgin at the time. A young French woman called Mugette made him an offer and was almost certainly the first naked woman he had ever seen or touched. Many would be impressed by his extraordinary restraint in the circumstances; others might judge him to be 'wet', and a few would understand that, in that setting, he just had no idea how to proceed. On several scores, flight was a good option to exercise. Today, it is evident from *Fire-Eater* that Pollard was probably asexual, and this would help to explain his curious relationship with his first wife, a relationship which predictably failed. With his second, there seems to have been a very deep friendship but nothing more.

1st HAC was ordered to join the Lahore Division, a component of the Indian Army, located around the village of La Bassée. When it arrived, the divisional commander was vastly disappointed with what he saw. He had presumed, mistakenly but perhaps understandably, that the Honourable Artillery Company had something to do with 'artillery'. He was neither the first nor the last to make that mistake. Someone had to decide what to do with the HAC. In the meantime, Lieutenant-General Sir Horace Smith-Dorrien inspected the battalion and pronounced it 'a fine body of men'. The 'fine body' was put to work digging trenches. The first day's labour was uninterrupted by the enemy but on the second day:

> Fritz decided to give us a lesson. There was a noise like an express train at an incredible speed. A metallic clap, a cloud of smoke billowed out 100 yards in front of us about 50 feet from the ground. A shell! High explosive shrapnel! A woolly bear, as this type was aptly named. I leaned on my spade and watched, fascinated. I was really under fire. My pulse raced with excitement. A second shell followed the first, then a third. There was a commotion a little way along the line. Men were running. Someone rushed by calling for the doctor. A direct hit, we had suffered our first casualty.

Pollard was incorrect. The very first casualty in 1st HAC had been Lance-Corporal Claude Smart, who had been killed in an accident at Le Mans on 26 October 1914. In fact, the minor artillery 'stonk' of 14 November, so vividly described by Pollard, was an inconsequential incident in the context of a world war. However, it was the occasion when the first member of 1st HAC was killed in action.

The battalion, now part of 7th Brigade, 3rd Division, took its place in the line having been gently weaned into trench life by the very wise commanding officer, Lieutenant-Colonel Edward Treffry. Units which found themselves alongside the HAC were nonplussed to discover that their comrades had actually been 'proposed' and 'seconded' to join their regiment and what is more, they then *paid a subscription* to live in the mud and among the dead and detritus of war. One man (S.B. Wood) recalled that when the HAC was relieving a Royal Fusilier battalion one dirty night in 1914, a voice politely enquired: 'Oo are yer?' The resulting explanation was greeted with the remark, 'Lor mates, come and 'ave a look at these blokes wot's paid to come 'ere.' The same man related that when being relieved by another cockney battalion, one of the incoming soldiers asked what the trenches were like. Before a reply could be given, another cockney voice chimed in, 'Don't worry, Bill; wot's good enough fer the 'onerables is good enough fer us.'

Pollard found the march into the front-line trenches an exciting journey as he stumbled through the dark night. The clinking of the equipment provided a muted military overture for what lay ahead. The men adapted to trench life but not to the infestation of lice. The battalion was deployed to 'F' trenches in front of a village called Kemmel, and Pollard later recalled the approach to their position:

> Stray bullets from the German line hummed through the air. Once, while crossing a ditch, I fell. My out-flung hand came in contact with a slimy something that gave to the touch. It was the face of a Frenchman who had been lying dead for some months. It was my first experience of death. I wondered whether it would ever be my fate to lie like that, uncared for and uncaring.

The trench, when 1st HAC reached it, was half full of mud and water. The men set to work to try to drain it. Their efforts were hampered by the fact that the French who had first occupied it had buried their dead in the bottom and sides. A stroke of the pick could encounter a body. The smell was stomach-churning and the cold was very severe. The men were obliged to stand in water and it was impossible to keep warm. Pollard realised that the war he relished was not quite as much fun as he had hoped. Once in the trenches every third man was put on guard and Alfred, rifle loaded and cocked, was prepared. He commented that it was at this time that the commanding officer won his respect:

> I was determined to sell my life dearly. I think we owe more than we appreciated to Colonel Treffry for the tactful way he handled the Battalion at this time. He insisted on our being broken in by degrees. There is not the slightest doubt that, had he allowed us to be pitchforked straight into the thick of things, we should not have given such a good account of ourselves.

The German trenches opposite 1st HAC were about 200yd distant and were manned by a Bavarian battalion containing a disconcertingly high number of excellent shots. Sniping occupied both sides and the HAC lost a number of men to headshots, although the incessant shelling caused the majority of casualties. Alfred took up sniping; he was a slightly above average shot, although inexperienced. He said that he fired about fifty rounds a day, usually from around a sandbag, eschewing the steel plates with loopholes. He described these as 'a snare and a delusion, as several men were killed by a bullet coming right through the plate'. He was learning his trade and made sure that he did not fire more than a few shots before he moved further down the trench. A trained sniper would not fire unless certain of a hit, but that was a subtlety as yet beyond him. Although he may have been enthusiastic, unskilled snipers did not make old bones on the Western Front and he was fortunate not to attract counter fire.

The cold was intense and relief was welcomed. The 4-mile march out of the line to Locre surprisingly exhausted Pollard, and on arrival at his billet, he collapsed. He woke with a raging fever. The medical officer was called, who diagnosed jaundice and Pollard was evacuated to hospital. Casualties in the battalion had been mounting. One officer and seventy men were killed in this period in and around Kemmel, Elzenwalle, Dickebusch and St Eloi, and in this vicinity a further 250 all ranks were hospitalised for frostbite, exhaustion and exposure. These casualties were incurred without the battalion making a single aggressive move.

Pollard suffered agonies of self-reproach at leaving his comrades. He imagined that he would have been classified as a 'miker' or shirker and he begged the doctor not to repatriate him. At Rouen, Alfred found himself in a holding camp and he met up with the first draft of replacements for his battalion. He was delighted to be among friends and enjoyed being able to play the 'old soldier' on the basis of his few weeks' service at the front. The draft was required to rise at 06.00 each morning but Alfred was disinclined to join them: 'I felt to do the same would be undignified.' On the eighth morning the flap of the tent was cast aside and the camp sergeant-major made a brisk and martial entry into Pollard's life. A regular soldier, his mission in life was to 'sort out' people like Pollard. He asked, in an ominously quiet voice, for an explanation for the soldier's horizontal position so late in the day and for his absence from other forms of productive activity. Pollard relates how he explained that, 'coming from the line', as he had, he had no idea about camp routine. The CSM, who had not yet been 'in the line', was outraged by such calculated insolence. Pollard was ordered to report to the orderly room at noon, but he had not the least intention of so doing – instead he made his way over to the HAC draft and found that it was to parade at 11.00am to march to the station. He duly attended the parade and 'lost himself' among the other 300. He boarded the train and was soon reunited with 'C' Company. He speculated, in 1932, that the CSM was probably still looking for him.

Back with his company, he caught up with his mail and was ecstatic to receive a letter from the girl who had been constantly in his thoughts. She did not write regularly or often but, as he admitted, 'Every time she wrote it gave me hope. Poor fool that I was, I read between the lines things that were never there.'

The attrition in the ranks of 1st HAC had caused a number of officers to be selected from the ranks and one of them, Lieutenant 'Duggie' Davis, asked Pollard to be his servant or batman. Of this invitation Pollard later wrote:

> a change was taking place in me at this time. I crossed to France a mere boy, my outlook restricted. War was changing me into a man. I had not yet emerged from my chrysalis, but experience was making me more self-reliant. I began to realize the strength of my own personality (being a servant), would not make [any] difference to my going into the line. If it had I would have refused. On the other hand it gave me something to do when we were out as an alternative to fatigues. It also promised a trifle more physical comfort. I accepted. I went

further. A cook was required in the Company officers' mess. I volunteered and became the cook. I have never been able to decide why I took this job on. I knew absolutely nothing about cooking.

Pollard shrewdly engaged the support of a French woman and her daughter from the village who, in effect, took over his cooking responsibilities. Nevertheless, he was swift to confess his manifold deficiencies in the servant department:

I have never in my life been much good at getting up early in the morning. To have to get myself out of bed, prepare early morning tea for the mess, rouse Duggie, brush his clothes and clean his boots and then cook breakfast was beyond me. Something had to go. That something was Duggie. I'm afraid that he usually cleaned his own boots and brushed his own clothes. His bath I used to leave ready overnight. From Duggie's point of view I was the worst servant that ever happened. But, thanks to Madame I was a very efficient cook. My job consisted of wielding a tin-opener – and of course the servants had to come first. We took the pick; the officers had what was left.

Other soldiers were promoted to fill gaps in the NCO ranks and Pollard was less than impressed by the promotion process. Somewhat defensively he wrote that in January 1915 he had no aspiration for a commission. He claimed that he 'was happy in the carefree life of a private'.

On 8 March 1915 command of 'C' Company passed to Captain E.P.C. Boyle, who had come straight from England. He instantly won the respect and admiration of the officers' mess cook, who described him as:

A kindly personality who understood men and how to get the best out of them. He was the finest soldier we ever had in the regiment. He never knew fear in any shape or form and always carried himself bolt upright in situations where most men crawled on their hands and knees. I gave him my allegiance from the first day I met him. His example and, I am proud to say, friendship, made me the Fire-Eater I afterwards became.

It is clear that Boyle really was an exceptional soldier and leader. Born in 1860, he had joined the HAC as far back as 1886 and served in the South African War; now, twenty-nine years later, at the advanced age of 55, he had an immediate impact on his new command.

Ernest Boyle ordered all manner of culinary delights to be sent out from England and he announced that the officers' servants were to have a share of these mouth-watering and expensive adjuncts to the issued ration. It was a masterstroke and Pollard wrote that, 'It was all very well to help ourselves when the extras were forbidden but it was a different matter when they were freely and generously offered.'

Pollard was close at hand when he heard Boyle announce that he was going to examine the barbed wire in front of the 'C' Company position. He asked for a volunteer to accompany him. Pollard duly volunteered and thereafter 'went everywhere with him'. Boyle was a father-figure to Pollard and he set the younger man an example which Pollard sought to emulate from their first shared sally.

This was man's work and Pollard lived in hope that they would encounter a German patrol. It seems that Boyle spent time every night making nocturnal patrols. For Pollard, these excursions made life worth living. 'The danger acted like a drug, quickening my pulse. At last I was doing something worthwhile. I was as happy as a sand boy.'

At about this time 1st HAC was well placed to observe an attack by 1st Wilts. The Westcountrymen charged into the fire of German machine guns and were slaughtered. The sight had a strong effect on Pollard and it fed his appetite for close, personal contact with the enemy. To this end he asked to be relieved as the officers' mess cook. On 4 May 1915 he marked his 22nd birthday with a large cake from home. He experienced the pangs of homesickness, but less for his mother than for his 'lady', he cheerfully admitted.

> I persuaded myself that each wish for my health concealed a special meaning: each box of chocolates or packet of cigarettes I regarded as a special token. I hugged her image to my heart. I was fighting for England, but now England was personified by her. She was my ever-gentle lady, for whom, if necessary, I would lay down my life. I wanted leave. Yes I wanted to go home and tell her of my love so that when I returned – and in my egotism, I had no doubt of her response.

These words, recalled vividly years after the event with extraordinary and compelling honesty, evoke an emotionally disturbed young man. The reader of this text, when young, may also have felt to some degree the mental turmoil that young Alfred was going through. For most of us, these adolescent yearnings soon pass and reality takes over. Pollard was to be tortured for some time yet and his 'lady' – still unnamed – occupied his every waking thought.

1st HAC was earmarked for an operation in the Hooge sector. In all likelihood many of the men facing this test, for all their training, would have been frightened, some resigned or fatalistic, and some stoically resolved – or any combination of such pre-operation emotions. Pollard was enthused, expectant and excited. It begs the question, was his attitude abnormal? It was certainly not the norm and so perhaps 'abnormal' is a fair description.

The build-up for the attack was conducted in the sizzling heat of summer. Ammunition, food, medical supplies, water and trench stores were all brought forward on horse-drawn limbers. There was an air of excitement, which was enhanced (or exacerbated) by the heavy traffic. The HAC was to cooperate with the 1st Lincolns and the newly promoted Lance-Corporal Pollard was selected as a runner to act as liaison between the two battalions. He was delighted and recalled that he thought at last: 'I was to take part in a real charge. With luck I might bayonet a Hun.' In the event, as Pollard traversed the battlefield on a scorching hot day, he had no chance to bayonet the foe. The HAC took heavy casualties and could only muster 350 men when the roll was called the following day. Over half the battalion had been lost, with many officers killed; both the colonel and the second-in-command were wounded.

Pollard felt less relieved at surviving the battle than aggrieved at not being in the thick of the action. Fire-eater that he was, he had been on the periphery of the battle and had not even had a chance to engage the Germans – all very frustrating. He was promoted to corporal and started to specialise as a 'bomber'. His height of 6ft 2in, combined with his strength, allowed him to throw a grenade further than most. The Mills 36 grenade was becoming readily available and it was a devastating area weapon. It weighed 1lb 7oz (652g) and most soldiers could hurl it about 20yds, while Pollard could probably throw it a critical 10yds further.

Now one of only 100 survivors of the original 800 soldiers who had sailed on the *Westmeath*, Pollard was given leave and rushed back to 'Blighty' to see his 'lady'. It was all very chaste and heavily chaperoned but despite that his ardour was undiminished:

> I knew now what I wanted: for the first time in my life I began to think of marriage. Of course she was ever so much too good for me. I recognized that from the start. She was the most divine, glorious creature that ever breathed. Try as I would I knew I could never reach her standard but I must do my best.

Pollard's non-relationship with this girl, when considered today, appears to be seriously out of balance, but it was clearly of great importance to him. It had the effect of motivating him to 'better' himself and he speculated that, were he to be commissioned, she would see him in a much more attractive light. 'Suppose I went to her as an officer covered in decorations, then perhaps she would deign to smile on me' was how he later recalled his thinking at the time. The woman had actually raised the matter of a commission and laughed at him for not having already applied. The suggestion, albeit lightly made, was sufficient. The seed had been planted.

Pollard was becoming a seasoned soldier and his increasingly daring forays into no-man's-land were a feature of his life with 1st HAC. It was a life-changing experience when he was sent off for two weeks to attend a course at the 2nd Army Grenade School at Terdeghen, a blessedly quiet spot after the Ypres Salient. He enjoyed the course and learned the characteristics and effectiveness of every grenade, British and German, then in use. He was taught the mechanics of trench clearing and admitted that, 'without the knowledge I gained I doubt very much if I would be alive today'. He was taught the composition of a bombing party but later, and in practice, he rejected it and subsequently arranged his bombing parties differently. The graduate of the bombing course returned to his battalion in late September to find that four officers of 1st HAC had been killed by a shell that landed directly on their dug-out. Among the dead was the officer appointed to command the bombing platoon that had been formed in Pollard's absence. The death of four officers was a regimental disaster but it resulted in Corporal Pollard being presented with a rare opportunity. He was selected to take command of the bombing platoon.

During the war senior NCOs often commanded platoons, but rarely did command devolve to a corporal, other than in extreme circumstances – and these were just such circumstances. Pollard rose to the challenge of commanding thirty-two men and worked hard at their training. He was promoted to sergeant and, after an intense period of activity, was recommended for the Military Medal. This was downgraded and instead he received a commendation from the divisional commander.

It was at this time that he wrote to his 'lady' in the most uninhibited terms and, assuring her of his devotion, asked her to marry him. She replied to Alfred's proposal in the most crushingly negative terms. She wrote to say that she was amazed that Alfred had ever considered the remote possibility that they had any sort of personal relationship. She added that her actions in sending him chocolates and cigarettes were no indication that she had any greater regard for him than any other soldier. He was a friend of the family and merely one of the few men she knew personally serving in France. Her letter closed in the most uncompromising manner when she averred that it was improbable that she would ever marry and that even if she did, he was most certainly the last man whose proposal she would consider. Pollard was shattered and took himself off to the village to get drunk. He failed but got tipsy enough to trip over a guy rope on his way back to his tent.

The next day, 30 September, 1st HAC returned to the Ypres Salient. A mine had been exploded under the German line but the resulting crater had not been secured. The bombing platoon, by now under the command of Lieutenant Hammond, was to counterattack and seize the crater. The officer would take half the platoon and Pollard the other half, supplemented by five men from the 1st Royal Scots. It was a savage encounter and only seven of the twenty-one men with Pollard survived unscathed. His party bombed its way forward down a communication trench until faced by a major obstruction. There was a brisk exchange of grenades but Pollard knew that to achieve success his men had to climb the barrier and take the fight to the Germans. In a brave demonstration of leadership, Pollard went first, but four of the six men immediately behind him were killed and, on gaining the far side, Pollard himself was felled by a grenade and badly wounded by splinters. He got to his feet and his diminished party pressed forward. He turned to one man but as he spoke, the man fell like a sack. A little later he was giving orders to one of the Royal Scots, a small man who stood no more than 5ft 4in tall, when the smaller man was shot dead.

The attackers pressed on to a second barrier and again Pollard went over it first. However, by now 'bombs' were running short and Pollard remembered that, 'I sent back a messenger for further supplies. I hopped back onto our side of the barricade to fetch a sack of bombs, which was lying there. I picked them up and was in the act of handing them to a man that had turned to take them when he suddenly pitched forward on his face. At the same time my right arm fell to my side and the sack dropped to the ground.' The round went through the unfortunate man and he fell like a stone. That initial and fatal impact caused the round to 'tumble' once it had exited the dead man's body but it still had sufficient velocity to do serious damage and it went on to hit Pollard in the shoulder, base first. He staggered and then collapsed. A comrade put a water bottle to his lips. He got unsteadily to his feet but did not remain erect for long because he fell again and lapsed briefly into unconsciousness.

Pollard was evacuated and his wounds were treated at a hospital in Manchester. It was here that he heard that he had been awarded the Distinguished Conduct

Medal. His commanding officer later made it clear that he had recommended Pollard for the Victoria Cross but the downgrading process had, once again, worked against him.

The twenty months between 30 September 1915 and 7 June 1917 were the high point in Pollard's life. During this time he won the Victoria Cross, the Distinguished Conduct Medal and two Military Crosses. He was discharged from hospital in November 1915 and was posted to the 3rd HAC, a holding battalion in England, where his new CO told him that he had been selected for the commission he so badly wanted. He put up his new badges of rank on 16 January 1916 and in May rejoined the 1st HAC, once more under the command of Colonel Treffry.

Pollard blossomed as an officer; he was a natural and assertive leader. He led innumerable patrols into no-man's-land and exposed himself to danger constantly and willingly. His right hand had been damaged in the winning of his DCM and so he taught himself to fire his revolver left-handed. He became a marksman with the weapon and used it frequently to good effect.

The winter of 1916/17 was severe but the weather was just another adversary. Colonel Treffry handed over command and this was a valued link lost but worse was to follow because his replacement, Lieutenant-Colonel E.P.C. Boyle, Pollard's mentor and friend, was soon to be killed. On 7/8 February Pollard's company attacked a German position and became involved in merciless close-quarter fighting. Of this he later wrote that 'my eyes focused on two Huns about 10 yards away who had fired their rifles at me, they both missed. I took careful aim and fired.' Pollard did not miss and both Germans were killed. In the mayhem Pollard's leadership proved to be critical in a protracted engagement. His conduct over several weeks culminating in these events led to the award of the Military Cross. A bar to his MC followed in April when he led a hazardous reconnaissance patrol and gathered important intelligence on the disposition of the Germans facing the 1st HAC. In mid-April 1917 he took command of 'B' Company in the trenches facing Gavrelle.

Pollard was now aged 24 and regularly accepted responsibility greater than would normally be given to an officer of his age and rank. He was an extraordinary man. He cheerfully admitted that he felt 'neither fear nor pity' and in a letter to his mother wrote he was in the 'best of spirits and having a good time. By the way, I have killed another Hun, Hurrah!' He really did see trench warfare as an exciting game.

The fighting at Gavrelle was part of the much bigger Battle of Arras. The 1st HAC performed heroically and won two Victoria Crosses. The first of these went to Lieutenant R.L. ('Bill') Haine. The second was won by Acting Captain A.O. Pollard MC*, DCM. Today the site of the action lies on a featureless plain about 400yds from the insignificant village of Gavrelle, which, in April 1917, had a line of German trenches running north–south in front of it. Haine, commanding 'C' Company, tenaciously and courageously pressed home a series of attacks on a German redoubt that dominated the trench line and, fired by his example, his men took the objective.

Pollard and three men from his 'B' Company, armed with sacks of grenades, worked their way up a trench and on the way despatched any number of the enemy, some of whom fell to Pollard's revolver. The speed of the advance did not give the Germans time to regroup and the aggressive bomb-throwing party took several hundred yards of trench. When the supply of Mills bombs ran out, Pollard used the German grenades he found in the captured trenches. This was a bonus because the German weapon weighed only 1lb and could be thrown further. Eventually, enough was enough even for the Fire-Eater and he halted until the remainder of 'B' Company could come up to join him. It had been an exemplary action. All four men were decorated. The *London Gazette* published the citation for Alfred Pollard's Victoria Cross:

> For most conspicuous gallantry and determination. The troops of various units to the left of this officer's battalion had become disorganised ... Second Lieutenant Pollard at once realised the seriousness of the situation and dashed up to stop the retirement. With only four men he started a counter attack with bombs and pressed it home till he had broken the enemy attack and regained all that had been lost and much ground in addition. The enemy retired in disorder, sustaining many casualties. By force of will, dash and splendid example, coupled with contempt for danger, this officer who has already won the DCM and MC infused courage into every man who saw him.

This was the last action Pollard fought. Having been notified of his VC, he proposed, yet again, to his 'lady'. Surprisingly, and probably unfortunately, she accepted. Soon after, the battalion was withdrawn from the line and given a training role. Pollard went home to marry and to be decorated by the King. When American troops reached France, Pollard was one of those involved in the orientation of American troops to trench warfare.

As the war came to its close in the following year, he was of course one of millions contemplating their future. He wrote later that he was aware that he had been 'part of the biggest greatest and most efficient Army in the world. But I knew in my heart, and I know it now, if ever my King and Country have a further need for my services, I will gladly offer them.' These are the unequivocal words of an unashamed patriot and soldier; a man who had met and overcome with distinction every challenge that had confronted him. However, two decades later, when Britain faced the greatest threat in its history, inexplicably and most uncharacteristically, Alfred Pollard did not offer his services. Catherine Boylan, in an article for the journal of the Society for Army Historical Research, described Pollard as an 'enigma' – it is an accurate judgement.

In 1919 Alfred's inclination was towards a commission in the regular army, but his wife was opposed to the idea. Reluctantly he abandoned it. Perhaps Mary Pollard helped him to make the right decision but for the wrong reasons. He went back to see his old employers, who dealt with the young man very graciously indeed, saying, 'consider we have been paying you a premium to insure ourselves against the results of an enemy invasion, you need not return to us if you do not wish, although we should be very pleased to have you'. Pollard was touched and the more so when, having declined the offer, he was given a year's salary as a gift.

After the war he drifted from one form of employment to another, perhaps the high point being his participation in the Westminster Abbey interment of the 'Unknown Warrior' on 11 November 1922. *The Times* reported, 'the Unknown Warrior will be carried to his last resting place between two lines of men who won the Victoria Cross or otherwise distinguished themselves by special valour' during the war. Here was confirmation of national approbation.

Predictably, however, Pollard's marriage failed. He took a short service commission in the RAF which enabled him successfully to achieve his 'wings' but he was now too old for a career in the RAF. He remarried, and then joined and became a director of an aero-engine company, and took to writing adventure novels kindred to those of Captain W.E. Johns with his 'Biggles' books or the Sexton Blake stories. He was more distinctive writing about his idiosyncratic self in *Fire-Eater*:

> I have chosen a title, which aptly expresses my attitude throughout the campaign. I enjoyed the war, both in and out of the line. Despite the discomfort and hardships of life in the trenches, I found pleasure in wandering about 'no man's land' at night. 'Going over the top' struck some chord in my nature, which vibrated strongly to the thrill of the attack. Men called me mad. Perhaps I was.

Fire-Eater was well received. It was by a wide margin the best thing Pollard wrote. He beat the drum of comradeship and patriotism and he had the medals that gave him the authority so to do. He was held in the very highest regard by the HAC and one would have expected him to enjoy the fellowship of fellow survivors after the war but not on a single occasion did he attend the annual 'Westmeath Dinner', just the sort of forum at which he would have been welcomed, between the inauguration of this regimental old comrades' gathering in 1920 and his death in 1960. Furthermore, there is no record of his ever meeting fellow regimental VC Bill Haine, beyond the 1922 ceremony at Westminster Abbey. He was not a gregarious man, and even his family, who knew him as 'Jumbo', reported that 'he was not the life and soul of the party'.

Pollard was 46 when war was declared in 1939. He could have contributed to the war effort in many ways, short of fighting, but he did not offer his services. In fact he moved from London to Stockbridge in Hampshire to avoid the bombing. During the war he wrote a total of sixteen books. He was not in the Home Guard, was not a firewatcher, and made no contribution to the war effort at all. His exceptional row of medals is notable for the obvious absence of any service medals for the Second World War. His earlier protestations of patriotism hence sound hollow, as do his views on comradeship. His First World War gallantry is indisputable but when he wrote of his service in France as patriotism, it may be nearer the truth to see it as a quite extraordinary thrill in action. Pollard the man, his philosophy and the life he lived, remain enigmatic.

Suggested Further Reading

Boylan, C., 'Fearless Fighter, Tender Romantic: The paradox of Alfred Oliver Pollard' (*Journal of the Society for Army Historical Research* 83, 2004)

Clapham, H.S., *Mud and Khaki: The memoirs of an incomplete soldier* (London: Hutchinson, 1936)

Corrigan, G., *Mud Blood and Poppycock* (London: Cassell, 2003)

Goold Walker, Major G., *The Honourable Artillery Company 1537–1947* (London: Gale & Polden, 1954)

Goold Walker, Major G., *The Honourable Artillery Company in the Great War* (London: Gale & Polden; repr. London: Naval & Military Press, 2004)

Pegler, M., *Out of nowhere – a history of military sniping* (London: Osprey, 2004)

Pollard, A.O., *Fire-Eater: The memoirs of a VC* (London: Hutchinson, 1932)

Chapter 18

A 'Teenage' War: British Youngsters and the Great War

By Nick Bosanquet

The generation born around 1900 looked as if it were going to be a very lucky generation – it was not to be. Instead, it had a future with great trauma, but also with opportunities.

In the late nineteenth century adolescents were seen as dangerous, unguided and unreliable.[1] Free associations included words such as gangs, juvenile delinquents and youth unemployment. This image had already begun to change before 1914 with the remarkable rise of the Scout movement and the expansion of secondary education. The war years brought teenagers to the fore although the term itself was not used until after the Second World War. They came to play a much more central role both in the economy and in the war effort.

By mid-1918 one-third of the work force was made up of young workers and 50 per cent of the British front-line infantry was comprised of teenagers. Yet the rise of the teenager has not been a prominent part of the story of the First World War. The contribution of women has been recognised, but not that of teenagers. In this chapter we trace how this position came about – how and why did the role of teenagers in the war effort develop? By the end, it was a war of the young because so many in their twenties and older had already gone. In the gloom of manpower policies, teenagers stood out as a bright exception for fitness and energy. They were key contributors to the machine of war in the air, at sea and on the ground. Without them it would not have been possible to find the new cadres for enlistment and training. The talk earlier in the war of juvenile delinquency and national decline faded away, and retrospectively, even in the Official History, they are recorded as 'well disciplined'.[2]

The teenage girl story was better documented as part of the women's story. In terms of choice of employment and income, young women saw consistent gains. They had work with shorter hours and which paid two to three times as much as jobs in domestic service or in the cotton and textile industries had done before the war – over a pound a week rather than the 10 to 15 shillings which adult women had earned before the war. They had opportunities for jobs as typists and staff in telephone exchanges, in health services and even, towards the end of the war, in engineering. Alone among the combatant nations Britain had women's uniformed services for the army, the Royal Navy and the Royal Air Force. Women entered new occupations, from the interpretation of aerial photos to the nurse anaesthetists who were trained on the Western Front, As well as the more traditional roles in catering, 160,000 people were recruited into the women's services.

The munitions workers were a key, highly concentrated and visible group but there were many other women in lower profile occupations in transport, the postal service and even as labourers in gas supply.

In financial terms, there were gains but along with this came the distress and loss from casualties, which of course brought more general and more diffused family pressures than hitherto. For so many women, war brought bereavement and grief, and related serious practical problems. Throughout society the resilience required from women facing these issues was challenging in the extreme.

However, to return more specifically to the youngsters, there were more young females than young males in the population, given the higher mortality rates of males as infants and children. This 10–15 per cent imbalance was found across Europe but it was only in Britain that this demographic fact was turned into a powerful resource for the war effort through a mobilisation of younger women which was virtually total and furthermore was voluntary.

The fifteen years before the war had seen rapid change in the economy and in society. By 1900 working class parents were literate. In the first thirty years of Board School education from 1870, the literacy rate had risen from 65 per cent to 95 per cent. There was a particularly striking change for women, who had had a much lower literacy rate for centuries, estimated for 1650, for example, as men at 55 per cent and women at 10 per cent.[3]

In the British economy there was a second industrial revolution from 1880 to 1914, based on steel, electricity and oil rather than on iron and coal.[4] Notable too was the rise of the chemical industry with a range of industrial and domestic products. The new technology, with the coming of the typewriter and the telephone, made possible larger national organisations in place of the more local single town or city enterprises of the nineteenth-century economy. New product areas included cars, trucks, radio equipment, specialised cargo ships (refrigeration and oil tankers), larger liners, gas turbine engines, more powerful locomotives and aircraft. For local life there was the bicycle with pneumatic tyres, bringing local transport within reach of many younger people.

Many of these industrial advances were worldwide and led to heightened concerns about national competitiveness. The 1902 Balfour Act aimed to increase secondary education to make up the gap in technical education with Germany and the United States. It was a success – the numbers entering secondary education in state schools rose from 2 per cent of the age group in 1900 to 8 per cent in 1914. The economic change began to make an impact directly on some in the younger generation with new opportunities unheard of in their parents' life experience. However, there was a divide, with many poorer families unable to keep a child at school.

From 1908 boys were seen in a new uniform on the streets: that of the Boy Scout. This youth movement was but one indicator of changing times. The Scout movement was highly successful from the start, through local initiative rather than through central planning.[5] Indeed the rush of volunteers may have influenced the later recruitment approach of Kitchener, who knew Baden-Powell from army service. Within a few months some 300,000 young boys had joined the

Scouts. They paid for the cost of uniform, boots and equipment. The movement also created a new group – adult volunteers – and they acted as local leaders.

Research on this topic has focused on the problem of poverty, poor health and the stunted physical and mental development of the young in the East End of London and in other large cities.[6] Studies have shown that urban working class teenagers were 5in shorter than Cambridge students. However, there was also a burgeoning middle class and growing prosperity in the expanding suburbs and among artisans in the new industrial centres. For some young people in the 'middle England' of Beeston, Nottinghamshire, the time seemed idyllic. Lottie Wiggins, later recruited at the age of 18 as a crane driver at the Chilwell National Factory making munitions, described her experience before the war in such terms:

> I was now in my teens and along with Flo and other friends I loved to take walks over the fields at Chilwell to Long Eaton and there we would enjoy talking to the local boys who would pair off with us and walk back again – what happy days these were. Horace Atkinson would play his mouth organ and we girls would sing along with such tunes as Moonlight Bay, Beautiful Doll and You Made Me Love You. Jazz was just becoming popular. On Sunday after-noons we would put on our summer dresses and make foursomes on the river, the boys rowing. What happy delightful pastimes these were ...[7]

Wartime Teenagers in Industry

In the four years between leaving school and conscription, youths were free to seek jobs. There was not the systematic recruitment of youths which took place with women but the young workforce expanded partly as a result of early leaving from school. This workforce sought jobs in munitions and in a wide range of industrial occupations. Their earnings were far higher than before the war but with the fathers away and mothers at work, there was a lack of family cohesion which led to complaints of delinquency. With auxiliary police on patrol, young people were more closely supervised on the streets than had been the case before the war. From 1916 onwards there was a programme to develop welfare and sports for teenagers and to cut down on their drinking and smoking. The contribution of teenagers to war industry increased, often for such reasons as unfitness for military service, as exemplified by the subsequently famous Alfred Hitchcock, who worked as an apprentice draughtsman in an electrical engineering factory.

The first active organised group of young people at the start of the war to become supportively involved was the Boy Scouts. In the very first weeks they took up roles as messengers, guides on stations, on coastal patrol duty, and scan-ning for signs of invasion – one such group seems to have arrested a spy. How-ever, for many young people the first months of the war were 'business as usual'.

Birmingham Scouts were at the forefront of war-related voluntary work. In 1915 'over 200 Birmingham scouts spent several weeks in erecting huts for soldiers and stabling for horses in Winchester'.[8] Later in 1915, some 450 Scouts worked in their spare time as bell-boys on the city trams and others worked on whitening the kerbs and lampposts. Birmingham Scouts also helped with air raid precautions and 300 Scouts were deployed out of the area for at least three months as coast watchers.

From May 1915 the munitions industry surged into its essential expansion and over the next two years this created innumerable opportunities. Young women were recruited into the munition plants through local and national recruitment campaigns. The work could be dangerous but the number of accidents anticipated was far greater than the number that actually took place. The size of some of the plants meant that recruitment had to take place over a wide area. At Hayes in Middlesex a new plant was advertised for its designer qualities with separate huts for accommodation and for the thrill of being able to send messages to troops across in France on filled shells. At Gretna Green several thousand women were recruited from Glasgow for the plant which stretched for 10 miles along the border near Carlisle. At Chilwell recruitment was more local, by transfer from the large women's workforce employed in lace-making. In Woolwich the factory employed 70,000 people by the end of the war. There was special transport across London by bus, train and river ferry. Hostels were built in nearby Eltham, together with the first garden city planning in south London on the Well Hall Estate.

The munitions workers were the first people in Britain to work in American-type factories with production lines. There were canteens, welfare centres and in due course a successful effort to improve health despite the notoriety of picric acid staining the hands and faces of workers, who as a consequence were nick-named 'yellow canaries'. By mid-1917, with improved materials handling, they still had the name but not the colour.

Teenage boys were not recruited as part of any national drive for the larger munitions plants. They filtered into more local engineering firms as more men left for the forces and as more people left school. There was some recruitment for the lighter jobs in munitions but in general they were a supportive rather than a core group. By mid-1917 H.A.L. Fisher, as Education Minister, was admitting that there were 600,000 child workers who should have been at school.

Sylvia Pankhurst pointed to the effects in London. 'In the general relaxation of the Factory Acts the protection of children was being swept away. It was made permissible to work children of 14 years a 60 hour week ... There were now 60,000 fewer children in the schools.'[9]

Teenage girls were more regimented in the huge National Factories. The young lads had freedom which many regarded as the path to abuse. There were complaints about lack of parental control, juvenile delinquency and that the boys were being led astray by their unaccustomed affluence. A new habit to attract blame was the coming of the cinema, where young people now had the funds to go every week.

Though there was a teenage hero in the shape of the young sailor Jack Cornwell, who stood at his post despite being mortally wounded, there were also teenage villains in organised gangs in Glasgow and the East End of London – in Glasgow, for example, the 'Anderston Redskins' were one of the many gangs terrorising 'their' area of the city in 1916. In Manchester:

> a gang called the Napoo practised their own version of American Indian folk-lore. They'd creep up behind girls and young women in the street ... then

they'd grab the long plaited hair that hung down the back, that was the style of the day, and with a sharp pair of scissors cut off the plaited hair and run off with it as a souvenir. Operating in the industrial district of Ancoats, the Napoo were readily identifiable by their group uniform of pink neckerchief. They became notorious and everyone was talking about them.[10]

The munitions workers were an elite, although the work was hard with a very high turnover of the workforce in the first weeks. At Chilwell workers were given two good meals a day for a daily payment of a small amount. At Gretna Green and Woolwich there were hostels and team spirit. Hours of work fell as the Ministry learned that longer hours did not increase output, and wages rose through generous pay settlements agreed by the then Minister of Munitions, Winston Churchill. Some of the workers were promoted to more skilled jobs in setting machine tools and gauges. Others moved on to the wide range of war outputs now that the shell shortage had turned towards a greater need for tanks, aircraft and scientific instruments.

Outside the munitions works, young women moved into a much wider range of service employment and also to vacancies in journalism and administration occasioned by male conscription. The postman became the postwoman and the 'man from the Pru' became the 'woman from the Pru'.

Young women workers ordered meals in restaurants, went to the cinema, wore nylon stockings and, to the greatest shock and horror, smoked in the streets. They had often moved from smaller towns to the big cities. The *History of Hove* reports:

> Last but not least let us not forget the hundreds of Hove women and girls who in the February and March of 1917 left for London and other places to work in the great shell-filling factories. At that time the government appealed to the country for 30,000 of these recruits. A local Committee was formed in Hove and a meeting held in the Town Hall at which the methods of the great factory at Willesden were fully described.[11]

In the big cities women now formed the majority. For example, in the 1911 census in Birmingham males over 18 numbered 246,881 and females 283,366. By the spring of 1918, the respective totals were 200,251 and 323,911.

The official Ministry of Munitions account of the work at Woolwich – then the world's largest factory complex with 70,000 employees present – was highly positive:

> If there is any man in London who can pass through the workshops of Woolwich without thinking he has been looking at some thousands of the best-looking young women in the world, it is certainly not the present writer. Their hard work does not seem to be doing much harm to their health, for their eyes are bright, and there is hardly any evidence of fatigue among them ... They work day and night in two shifts of twelve hours each, with a break of an hour for dinner and half an hour for tea. Their pay, which is by the piece, is generally large, the minimum being, I think, a pound a week, and the maximum five to seven pounds.[12]

Against this had to be set their burdensome caring responsibilities. Again it was the large families in the East End of London who suffered most. The campaigner Sylvia Pankhurst presented a very different picture of a woman's life from the happy singers in Woolwich depicted by the Ministry of Munitions:

> The War spread its huge tentacles to all sections of the people, breaking them at the front and bleeding them of energy and the joy of life in the munitions factories. Larger and larger numbers were subjected to the poisonous dust and fumes of high explosives. The 'yellow girls' working in T.N.T. were a common sight. They were kept out of view as far as might be. Restaurant proprietors were under orders from their managers not to serve munitions workers.[13]

However, overall, women were gainers with their contribution recognised by the franchise, even though it was delayed until 1928 for young women. It may seem ironic that the main leaders of the women's war effort were some of the suffragette leaders such as Emily Pankhurst, the younger of the celebrated sisters. It must be said, however, that Sylvia, her older sister, was far from endorsing such a stand!

For young male teenagers there were different ways to become involved in the war effort, the avenues open to them being considerably dependent on their social situation. In the upper classes many 18- or 19-year-olds volunteered at the start of the war as officers, or for officer training. A public school record, which almost certainly would include Cadet Corps experience, was enough for a commission or further training for it. For the working class young, there was the option of volunteering if they could pass as 18. From the middle of 1915, with a hugely expanded industrial war effort of paramount importance, many young people left school to earn far more than they would have done before the war. In munitions they were confined to roles as assistants to the older skilled workers or to lighter work alongside the women. Just as with the contribution of women, their usefulness was demonstrable.

In contrast to the new large factories of the women workers, employers running small and older engineering works were encouraged by the Ministry to support canteens, recreation and sport. Some, as recommended by the Ministry of Munitions, employed special visitors for boy workers. The young workers must, however, have been more influenced by the rise in wages as they were likely to be supporting families as well as themselves.

> The Boy Visitors Work is directed to improving the boy workers moral and material well-being and to reducing the difficulties which sickness, ill-discipline etc. cause the factory staff.

> The present abnormal conditions of work, high wages, lack of healthy recreation, and in many cases the absence of the father, tend to thriftlessness, ill-discipline and other evils ...

> The Boy Visitor will by personal guidance work towards getting contented, well-disciplined boy workers and the information he gathers will always be available.[14]

Birmingham was especially active in developing new welfare and recreational programmes.

The problems which had always been present with the adolescent worker were accelerated by the conditions of labour during the war. Not only were the numbers of young people employed in the factories very considerably increased, but the amount of money they earned became substantially greater.

Birmingham set up a Juvenile Organisations Committee and by November 1918 this had led to the establishment of 304 clubs with a total membership of 13,000, and a football league with seventy-two clubs.[15]

The British Army and Teenagers

In the first year of the war there were numbers of recruits who were told to 'go round the park and come back when they were 18'. There was, however, a comb-out of these young soldiers as the war progressed. This was partly the result of parental pressure but also the perception that they were not strong enough to carry the 70lb weight of arms and equipment required on active service. Physically inadequate, inexperienced soldiers were a danger to themselves and to others in forward areas. They needed not just training but time in the support lines and the engagement of what might be called the 'parental care' of older men in the ranks serving with them. The high casualty rate among under-age soldiers came to be seen as a waste of good military potential.

As implied, early in the war some teenagers joined up by advancing their age. The Midlands MP Sir Arthur Markham campaigned for the return of these under-age soldiers and there were changes in policy. From the beginning of conscription in 1916 there were much stricter controls on the recruitment of under-age soldiers. Birth certificates had to be produced and at the front the remaining boy soldiers were combed out and sent to a special camp at Etaples, where they were well treated. Given the heavy use in British propaganda of pictures of German boy soldiers, there may well have been some sensitivity about their use by the British.

With conscription, training of young soldiers became more organised, with special youth battalions, but in the crisis of late March and April 1918 the length of training was reduced and so these young lads had to be sent to the front after three rather than six months. They were vital because so many of the older men conscripted were in poor health and unlikely to be graded adequate for front-line duty.

The desperate emergency meant that 18-year-olds had to be sent to the front, despite the statutory age limit of 19 years for overseas service. In all likelihood this contributed to the heavy casualties suffered by these units, with many soldiers killed in their first days in the line.[16] The period from March to May 1918 in France was a black one for all soldiers in khaki, but particularly for the young soldiers. One American general said of his own troops that 'sending them to the front without experienced officers is little short of murder'.

From July onwards, young survivors and new drafts were involved in the changed circumstances of a victorious advance during the 100 Days offensive, where allied infantry advanced after massive artillery fire on an enemy under demoralising pressure. The drive and energy of the young soldiers and their young officers played a significant part in these months of the British Army's greatest successes of the war. They had a taste of victory in a confident, well equipped army.

Some conscripts and some of the volunteers for the RAF and other services found new opportunities for training as pilots, tank crew and artillery specialists. The increasing use of aptitude tests worked to the advantage of some recruits from less favoured social backgrounds. There was a new potential for finding round pegs for the increasing number of round holes, and many more technical jobs which could be filled by the expanding numbers who had been through secondary education. Only in the Royal Navy, which had traditionally made the best use of young recruits, was there less need for such finessed recruitment. These young men being slotted into the range of new specialised occupations made a huge contribution in the final months of the war. It is not too much to say that Britain would have been unable fully to service and successfully to deploy these new arms without them. They were vital in creating the better armed and innovative British war effort as it was from the summer of 1918.

From February 1916 teenagers faced conscription. Half of all conscripts in the next three years were from this age group. The weight of numbers increased with each year as the supply of fit older adults drained away. In the first year teenagers would have been in the minority as all those adults who had failed to volunteer were now drawn into the net. By 1918 teenagers were the largest single group alongside the adult workers combed out from munitions and mining. They were now also the largest group of workers graded 'A' as fit for immediate service.

One history of Leeds describes the reality of conscription for reluctant individuals one evening in September 1916:

> Queues were waiting at the doors of the theatres and music halls. Hotels, restaurants and cafes were all busy. Suddenly a strong contingent of police, accompanied by a stronger force of military, drew a cordon and all men who looked younger than 40 years were accosted and asked to produce for examination their registration cards, exemption or registration certificates.[17]

On being called up, all conscripts were subject to a medical examination. In 1920 the Ministry of National Service published a report on the examinations of 2.2 million men called up between 1 November 1917 and 31 October 1918.[18] Most were from working class districts of urban areas. The report is not a picture of the health of all males but it gives a unique picture of the health of males in industrial areas. The health of older adults was poor, especially in the Midlands and the industrial north-west. In Stockport and Salford the average man was, for military purposes, an old man before he reached the age of 40. 'Birmingham was particularly unhealthy with pearl makers rot and lead poisoning. Only in mining and agricultural work were there more than 50 per cent Grade I. The colliers as a class are well developed and muscular and strip much better than the cotton operatives.' In Buckinghamshire younger agricultural workers had 'splendid physique' but this had gone by the age of 40.

Much of the report dealt with the effects of occupation but for younger recruits it also reported on their height (on average 5ft 3in) and weight (110–130lb). These results were attributed to poor diet and living conditions in childhood. The years of employment as younger teenagers had not been enough to offset these factors. However, 50 per cent of the young recruits could be graded 1 as compared to 30 per cent of older men. It is likely that the grading of the young recruits was more consistent across the period. There were changes – such as the downgrading of vision standard to ¼ vision in one eye as minimum standard for grade 1 – which would have affected the older recruits more, so that a much lower standard was accepted by 1918.

The recruits then went for basic training. Until March 1918 the age limit for foreign posting was 19, which meant that the training period could be as long as a year for younger recruits.

When they came to us they were weedy, sallow, skinny, frightened children – the refuse of our industrial system – and they were in very poor condition because of wartime food shortages, but after six months of good food, fresh air and hard physical exercise they changed so much their mothers wouldn't have recognized them.[19]

This was not, however, the only opinion. The conscripts themselves recognised this beneficial effect, with comments such as, 'I am keeping fit so far and that's a big item I suppose', and 'Feeling much better for the changed life and developed voracious appetite'. When one boy went on leave, he found 'everyone surprised at how well I looked'. Another said: 'My girl and the folks at home were surprised how I had filled out, put on weight and looked disgustingly fit and well.'[20]

A former clerk noted: 'This time of training had been on the whole an enjoyable period of fresh air exercise which has benefited us all. I suppose five months in the army has made a difference.' Some grew 4–5 inches during the twelve months of training. They also benefited from the firm leadership of the then CIGS, Sir William Robertson, who wrote in his excellent autobiography:

In the winter of 1916–17 a very desirable change was made in the composition of the infantry training battalions at home which had heretofore recruited irrespective of their age varying between boy of eighteen and men of forty-one years. It was clearly objectionable both from the training and the social point of view to mix up boys with men old enough to be their fathers.

Robertson set up 'Young Soldier' battalions for four months' basic training followed by graduated battalions where they stayed for eight months until they reached 19 and became eligible for service abroad. They lived in 'a kind of public school atmosphere'. He saw this innovation as 'one of the best things in which I had a hand during the war'. And, 'when these lads, many being under nineteen, were sent out to help stem the disaster of the West Front in the spring of 1918, they more than upheld the reputation they had deservedly earned while in England'.[21]

During 1916 and 1917 there were some older teenagers who were sent to the front but they were not a distinctive group. The first generation of conscripts also had some chance of being sent to the support services or, if good at mental skills, to the artillery. On the other hand, the first conscripts at the front came in late 1916 and 1917 and they were to endure a desperately grim experience.

In the spring of 1918 there was a surplus of troops in support roles and an acute need for fighting infantry, so nearly all teenagers were drafted there, many of course during the great German offensives. One young soldier remembered his march to the railway station in Norwich:

> The pavements were full, mostly of women; we were their boys. Some waved and said 'Good Luck', some were crying. We could hear comments: 'poor little buggers' I heard one woman say. 'Fancy sending them out to France to die for us.'[22]

They joined an army which had been driven from its long-established positions and had suffered heavy casualties among NCOs and junior officers. The chances of a well supervised induction were almost nil in a war zone where experienced troops had a considerable survival advantage. The allies were wary of placing American troops prematurely in the front line and British teenagers had to fill the gap.

On 5 April Harold Lawton, an 18-year-old lad from Rhys in Wales, was sent in a draft to a battalion of the East Yorkshire Regiment, which had been reduced to just three officers and thirty-six soldiers. Lawton recalled:

> The Regiment was resting after a very nasty time. We were the new boys and the old soldiers took no notice of us whatsoever: they were utterly exhausted and had to look after themselves, but it meant that they told us absolutely nothing.

The following day the battalion moved forward:

> We were to hold a line of trenches which were little more than a scrape in the ground and we had to get digging straight away. We hadn't been there very long when one chap, a lad who had come out with us, John Peacock, looked over out of the new parapet and was immediately shot through the head and killed.[23]

From 27 March to 5 May there were 133,902 such reinforcements hurried out to France, many of them were boys of 18[½] and wounded men who had recovered. They were now penned more restrictively still after the German push in April. Training space to accustom new troops to the line was further reduced. However, the German Army's offensives in May and June exerted less pressure and were now being strongly resisted. There was more time for rotating new drafts through quiet sectors and for much more structured training programmes. Troops had more rest periods and the excellent British support system for food and recreation came back into normal service.

The role of infantry in the 100 Days changed too. The coordination of all arms – infantry, artillery, tanks and aircraft – allowed for changed infantry tactics, giving better protection to troops now advancing upon a weakened foe. Young soldiers came to be seen as a special resource with their fitness, aggression and better training for their new role.

It might be mentioned in parentheses that the Australian and Canadian Corps, so important too during the 100 Days, did not have many teenage soldiers. Their front-line infantry was made up of older volunteers, while the British effort depended far more on young infantry, as witnessed rather grudgingly in the Official History: 'The very young soldiers with whom the ranks of the British battalions had been filled up after the heavy fighting of March and April did remarkably well in the attack: whether they would have fought equally well in defence was not put to the test.'[24]

The German commander, General Georg von der Marwitz, issued an order to his Second Army on 25 August 1918: 'With regard to the enemy's infantry, stress must again be laid on the fact that in most cases they have only received drafts of 18-year-old men. Therefore there are no reasons for any panic.'[25] He was wrong: as long as they could carry out straightforward orders in daylight, the young soldiers were a formidable force.

It is interesting to note that these young lads in uniform had different health problems from their older comrades.[26] They were much less likely to get cardiac strain or 'soldier's heart' but much more likely to suffer from trench fever, a louse-borne infection. Experiments with older male volunteers carried out at the Royal Free Hospital in London had been inconclusive. Older volunteers were rolled in blankets with scores of lice but none contracted trench fever. Their skins were too thick for the lice to bite through, so no infection could take hold. Later research showed that the lice preferred the skins of young conscripts. The disease was rarely fatal but often proved debilitating, requiring long spells in hospitals. In this new war of movement there was less risk of trench foot but greater danger of dysentery from contaminated water.

Few young soldiers suffered from shellshock, which may not have been a matter of age but a result of the less intense and less frequent bombardments from a now harassed and weakened German artillery. Many young soldiers showed remark-able recovery from serious wounds. This was attributed by the RAMC to the fact that they were not yet hardened smokers. However, by the summer of 1918 the British casualty clearing stations were at peak performance, and wounded young soldiers would have had the best medical treatment then available in Europe.

Teenage soldiers made an enormous contribution, not just in numbers but in specialist areas of the better-equipped army of 1918. The first new 'arm' had been the Machine-Gun Corps, formed in 1915. Volunteers had to be fit, mentally alert and also able to take the initiative in changing fields of fire and location. One of the best accounts of service in this unit is by Yorkshireman Arthur Russell, aged 19, who served in the MGC as early as November that year. He wrote that the training was:

> intensive and strenuous . . . For hours at a stretch we would run for a distance of twenty-five to fifty yards with the forty-eight pound tripod, the thirty-eight pound machine-gun and boxes containing the belts of ammunition each weigh-ing twenty-one pounds, then mount our gun and go through the appropriate

actions of loading and firing. Then in our team groups we would sit round the gun to learn the intricate mechanism and working. As we progressed in our training to become machine gunners and became more proficient in the hand-ling of the gun and knowledge of its mechanical parts, there was great rivalry among our various gun teams. We would all strive our utmost to knock off more and more seconds in the time taken to get our gun into action, and to match our skills team against team and gunner against gunner.[27]

George Coppard described his similar experiences in his book, *With a Machine Gun to Cambrai*. He had enlisted from his home in Croydon at 16 and fought his way through until, aged 19, he was wounded at Cambrai.

I should say a few words about the machine gun section. Two Vickers machine guns were now allotted to the battalion. Reserve teams were required and I was picked out of the blue. This was a welcome surprise and I became a keen and willing learner. The Vickers .303 water cooled gun was a wonderful weapon and its successful use led to the eventual formation of the Machine Gun Corps, a formidable and highly-trained body of nearly 160,000 officers and men. Devotion to the gun became the most important thing in my life for the rest of my army career.[28]

Later, when Coppard had transferred to the Corps, came training:

Our first CO was Captain DK Anderson a Scot and a bit of a Tartar to boot. By this I mean he was dedicated to bringing his new company to a condition of almost brutal efficiency … For sighting, the flick of finger sprang the stem of the rear sight into a vertical position. A rapid selection of ranges was provided by a spring-loaded wheel turned up or down as necessary. Part of the drill when practising on the butts was to knock over steel target plates, and we were expected to do this by accuracy of aim and not by watching the dirt fly as a guide to the target. At Gonnehem we practised for hours, day after day, and gradually improvement came throughout the entire company. Captain Ander-son was never satisfied unless our hands were bleeding. The more bits of skin were knocked off the better he liked it.[29]

During the 100 Days the Lewis gun, with its greater portability and lighter weight, became the key infantry weapon. Young soldiers seemed particularly adept at using it once they had learnt the complex mechanism.

A young officer in the Royal Artillery, Frank Paish, had been 18 when he joined:

The month's course at Larkhill concluded with firing practice with live ammu-nition. Each cadet in turn had to act as forward observation officer, while the others manned the guns, taking different positions in turn.[30]

Paish fought through till 1918 when he was wounded, and won the Military Cross for carrying out a dangerous reconnaissance.

Some conscripted young soldiers joined the newly founded Tank Corps from 1917. A cache of letters recently found in Harrogate documents the service of

19-year-old Lieutenant Walter Ogden in the Corps.[31] He was involved in the great tank-led offensive at Cambrai in November 1917 as the commander of what he called 'His Majesty's land ship Harrogate'. He described the attack in a letter to his family:

> When the Germans saw us crawling across with the infantry behind us they offered very little resistance and came over in hundreds and surrendered ... As we got nearer the Germans the artillery barrage lifted, and we entered their wide belts of barbed wire which were 20ft wide and 8ft high. This wire we cut with our tanks. Leaving large gaps through which the infantry came ...

Four days later the young lieutenant was shot in the abdomen and died soon after in hospital.

The largest contribution to any single new Arm was that of young cadets joining the RFC and then the RAF. At the beginning of 1917 it was decided to expand the current twenty service squadrons and thirty-seven training squadrons to 106 service squadrons and 97 in reserve. After the German daylight bombing raids on London in June 1917, greater expansion still was authorised. There was a necessary drive to find the aerodromes and accommodation for the many new cadet squadrons, but it was also decided that the cadets should have more training than hitherto, at least forty hours rather than the previously decreed seventeen which pilots had been given. Training was greatly assisted by the introduction of the Gosport system of dual control. From the end of 1917 suitable telephones were devised to 'make conversation between the instructor and his pupil natural and easy'. Prior to this, if the instructor wanted to speak, he would stall the aircraft for a 'momentary conversation'. This, the pamphlet on the Gosport method states, 'has given a useful indication of the state of the pupil's nerve, as those who are likely to prove unsuitable for scouts generally cling to the side with an unintelligent expression instead of conversing fluently and with confidence.'[32]

Outside the UK, training bases were set up in Texas, Canada and Egypt. Most of the new cadets were teenagers, who could start the course at the age of 17[1/2]. As from July 1917, the need for expansion was such that opportunities for training as pilots, observers and mechanics ran into many thousands. There was also a new initiative in recruiting women as aircraft fitters.

The Training of Young Officers for the Army

Recruitment was not just 'to the ranks' but also for young officers, many of whom were trained in 1917. The six months' Officer Training Course was not reduced, so those who were selected in 1918 hardly had time to get to the front. However, the young officers trained earlier were vital replacements for the dreadful officer toll in the Passchendaele offensive.

The young men selected were trained at Sandhurst or at Officer Cadet Schools set up by Robertson, the first at Bailleul in France as early as 1915. Initially the schools ran a six-week course but the period was later extended to three months and included experience in the line. Instruction was given in all branches of training required by a platoon commander. Later, twelve cadet battalions were formed, each of about 500 cadets, commanded, Robertson confirmed in his memoirs, by 'some of our best officers'.[33] In all, the cadet battalions trained more than 84,000 officers during the war.

Regional Impacts

In this respect, conscription had the greatest effect on young males in suburban and rural areas, where 70 per cent of recruits would have been highly graded. In the Ministry's examinations, clerks in Kingston-on-Thames stood out as the healthiest group.[34] They were also less likely in such areas to be in reserved occupations such as munitions or engineering. Thus the recruitment, as in the 1914–15 volunteering, tended to take in young people from more affluent backgrounds, men who were fitter. Earlier in the war, workers in engineering had been drawn back out of the army but later, in 1918, although some workers were combed out to serve in khaki, overall, men from the poorer areas of big cities were less likely to have to serve at the front as a result of their poor health.

The main centres for munitions production were in the Midlands, in or near larger towns. In Yorkshire the populations of Leeds and Sheffield grew, while the populations of smaller towns, such as Todmorden and Harrogate, and of rural areas declined, accelerating trends that had begun before the war.[35] Thus the effect of the war was to make urban areas more attractive, with more entertainments and more opportunities in work.

With young people being drawn into the cities and with the nation's heavy toll of casualties, rural areas were faced with the problem for the future of an ageing population. On a national scale the issue of an ageing population dates from before the outbreak of the war. The war also made access to the coastal towns and areas more difficult as so much was out of bounds, although exceptionally, and of course explicably, Folkestone and Southampton, outgoing and incoming ports for France, became boom towns.

Post-War Impact on Youth following from Wartime Policy

There was one development at the end of the war which did benefit children and young people. This was the Fisher Act, which became law on 8 August 1918. This Act, unlike other important acts in education, passed with little controversy. For the first time there was established a 'national system of public education available for all persons capable of profiting thereby'.[36] It raised the school leaving age to 14 and set up a grants system for secondary and technical education.

The franchise was extended to all men over 21 in 1918 but there was little discussion of voting for those over 18. Teenagers, after their brief period of prominence in the war, remained a hidden group with few rights and little distinctive presence. It was only after the Second World War that a distinctive teenage culture became a reality and once again teenagers were seen as a threat, a return to the image of the gangs of New York. The contribution of teenagers in the Great War was ignored and forgotten.

Family Impacts

We know little about the personal experience of teenagers in the war. They appear in crowds, in teams, or at training camps, but there is insufficient evidence readily available at present about the impact on individual personality and family life. The most detailed study of the impact of traumatic events upon young people was that carried out by Glen Elder in America on children of the Great Depression.[37] It does seem reasonable to draw some similar conclusions about youngsters in Britain during the years of the Great War. Elder's study suggested that living through the depression gave children resilience and a persistence which served them well in later life. The author of this chapter considers that the British picture is more mixed. Some individuals mentioned here, like Russell, Coppard and Paish, had good careers and long lives. Many others had physical problems and mental illnesses which impoverished or cut short their lives. In *Some Desperate Glory*, a young officer, Edwin Campion Vaughan, reported with great honesty his inability to cope with the responsibility he had to exercise and at the end he experienced something close to a breakdown:

> So this was the end of D Company. Feeling sick and lonely I returned to my tent to write out in my casualty report: but instead I sat on the floor and drank whisky after whisky as I gazed into a black and empty future.[38]

After the war Vaughan failed to settle in civilian life and died young in 1931. There were many who showed resilience but others who never recovered, whether from gas inhalation, war wounds or deep mental disturbance.

It may well be that the First World War had similar effects on family life to those of the Great Depression – the mother becoming the family anchor, teenagers having to help pay the rent and carry out household chores. For many, however, there was the new reality of broken or weaker family ties.

At the start of the war there was separation from their families for the Kitchener volunteers and hardship for many families as prices rose rapidly for food and coal. Over the course of the war such pressures on families increased and more mothers went out to work. Nearly half of the under-40 adult male population was in uniform and for so many families there was the shock of the telegram or letter announcing the loss of a father and husband, either killed, wounded, missing or taken prisoner. All at home lived with the dread of such a communication.[39]

However, we should not ignore that there were new opportunities as well. From 1915 until the early spring of 1918 young workers could now choose their jobs. After decades, even centuries, in which many young workers were harshly disciplined and mistreated, they were suddenly in demand. Young women workers were simply vital to the war effort, and in 1918 it was Britain's teenage soldiers who supplied the courage, initiative and skill in new arms which played so significant a part in a victory earned surprisingly within the same year as defeat had threatened.

Recently a manager in a British car plant, after recruiting several hundred new young workers, said they 'had brought a charge of energy through the whole plant.' Something similar happened to the war-weary British Army in 1918.

Acknowledgements
With my thanks to Adrian Denney, John Davies and to Paul Stamper, who will know how they helped me.

Notes

1. Hall, G. Stanley, *Adolescence* (1909).
2. Edmonds, J.R., *Military Operations France and Belgium 1918*, vol. XI (London: MacMillan, 1937), p. 13.
3. Porter, G.R., *The Progress of the Nation* (London: Methuen, 1912), p. 147.
4. Ibid.
5. Baden-Powell, Robert, *Scouting for Boys* (1908; repr. Oxford: Oxford University Press, 2004).
6. Pankhurst, E.S., *The Home Front* (repr. Peterborough: Cresset Press, 1987), p. 379.
7. Haslam, M.J., *The Chilwell Story* (RAOC Corps Gazette, 1982), p. 2.
8. Brazier, R.H. and Sandford, E., *Birmingham and the Great War 1914–19* (Birmingham: Cornish Brothers, 1921), p. 307.
9. Pankhurst, short title, p. 379.
10. Savage, J. *Teenage* (London: Pimlico, 2008), p. 162.
11. Walbrook, H.M., *Hove and the Great War* (Hove: Cliftonville Press, 1920), p. 32.
12. Caine, Hall, *Our Girls* (London: Hutchinson, 1917), pp. 24–5.
13. Pankhurst, short title, p. 379.
14. Ministry of Munitions, *Health of the Munitions Worker* (London: 1917), p. 29.
15. Brazier and Sandford, *Birmingham and the Great War*, p. 304.
16. Edmonds, J.R., *Military Operations France and Belgium 1918*, vol. III (London: HMSO, 1939), p. 9.
17. Scott, W.H., *Leeds in the Great War* (Leeds: 1923), p. 48.
18. Ministry of National Service, *Report upon the Physical Examination of Men of Military Age by National Service Medical Boards. Nov 1st 1917–Oct 31st 1918* (London: HMSO, 1920).
19. van Emden, R., *Boy Soldiers of the Great War* (London: Headline, 2005), p. 266.
20. Bet-el, I. *Conscripts: Lost Legions of the Great War* (Stroud: Sutton, 1999), p. 61.
21. Robertson, W., *From Private to Field-Marshal* (London: Constable, 1921), pp. 304–5.
22. van Emden, *Boy Soldiers*, p. 235.
23. Ibid., p. 273.
24. Edmonds, J.R., *Military Operations France and Belgium 1918*, vol. IV (London: HMSO, 1947), p. iv.
25. Montgomery, A., *The Story of the Fourth Army in the Battles of the Hundred Days* (London: Hodder & Stoughton, 1919), p. 69.
26. Bosanquet, N., 'Health Systems in Khaki', in Hugh Cecil and Peter H. Liddle (eds), *Facing Armageddon: The First World War Experienced* (London: Pen & Sword Books, 1996), pp. 451–65.
27. Russell, A., *The Machine Gunner* (Kineton: Roundwood Press, 1977), pp. 10–11.
28. Coppard, G., *With a Machine Gun to Cambrai* (London: Papermac, 1986), p. 13.
29. Ibid., p. 32.
30. Paish, F.W., *War as a Temporary Occupation* (Peacock Press, 1998), p. 15.
31. *Harrogate Advertiser*, 22 May 2015.
32. Jones, H.A., *The War in the Air*, vol. V (1922; repr. London: Naval & Military Press, 2009), p. 433.
33. Robertson, *From Private to Field-Marshal*, p. 267.
34. Ministry of National Insurance, *Report*, p. 36.
35. Lee, J.A., *Todmorden in the Great War* (Waddington: 1922).
36. 'Fisher Act': Education Act 1918, 8 and 9, Geo. V c.3.
37. Elder, Glen H., *Children of the Great Depression* (Westview Press, 1999).
38. Vaughan, E.C., *Some Desperate Glory: the Diary of a Young Officer 1917* (London: MacMillan, 1981), p. 232.
39. Freud, A. and Burlingham, D., *War and Children* (Medical War Books, 1943).

Suggested Further Reading

Baden-Powell, R., *Scouting for Boys* (1908; repr. Oxford: Oxford University Press, 2004)
Bet-el, I.R., *Conscripts; Lost Legions of the Great War* (Stroud: Sutton, 1999)
Coppard, George, *With a Machine Gun to Cambrai* (London: Papermac, 1986)
Elder, Glen H. Jr, *Children of the Great Depression*, 25th anniversary edition (Westview Press, 1999)
Emden, Richard van, *Boy Soldiers of the Great War* (London: Headline, 2005)
Freud, A. and Burlingham, D., *War and Children* (Medical War Books, 1943)

Chapter 19

Conscription, Conscience and Courage: Resisting War from 1916

By Clive Barrett

Conscription

'For an individual to attempt to resist the power of the State would be a tremendous venture.'[1]

You may remember Hosea Biglow's saying:

> 'Ef you take a sword and dror it,
> An' go stick a feller thru',
> Guv'ment ain't to answer for it,
> God'll send the bill to you'

Personally, I believe that the ethics of the question ought to be applied to the individual soldier. I know what will be said – that it is impossible to allow the soldier the right to the exercise of his individual conscience; that whatever the Government decides the soldier is bound to do. If the Government makes war, the soldier is not to ask any question; and if the Government murders, the soldier is to be exonerated. Personally, I hurl that from me. I believe – and, I think, the feeling is growing in this country – that no Government in the world, no tribunal in the world, can answer for the individual conscience, that every man is responsible, to himself if not to some higher power, for the right of the faculties which he possesses ...

This prescient 1901 lecture, drawing on the writing of James Russell Lowell during the US–Mexico War of 1846–8, was delivered in the unlikely surroundings of a military exhibition at Earl's Court, London. The lecturer, Arthur J. Waldron, was a curate in Camberwell, and his sentiments ran counter to the spirit of the age. However, the peace movement of the time was invigorated by the rise of international institutions, congresses and friendly cross-border exchanges. From the Nobel Peace Prize to the International Court of Arbitration, it seemed that structures for the non-violent resolution of international conflict were being established, and, as Jan Bloch and Norman Angell appeared to argue, there could be little military or economic case for war anyway. If nations were not going to fight again, then the question of an individual's position in time of war was immaterial.[2]

Thus, in 1914, when such peace was seen to be an illusion and dreams were shattered, the pre-war British peace movement fell apart as well. In little over six months a new set of organisations emerged, with the Union of Democratic Control being the largest and broadest, embracing not only those who opposed the war but also many who tolerated it without enthusiasm and looked for ways to control and end it as soon as possible. The Women's International League was formed early in 1915 and Christian opponents of the war rallied to the call of the Fellowship of Reconciliation (FOR), founded in the last days of 1914.

Perhaps the most important anti-war organisation to emerge, however, was the No-Conscription Fellowship (NCF), 'presently to become the most abused institution in England'.[3] From the moment war had been declared, it was obvious that large numbers of men would have to be recruited quickly into the military. Would they come voluntarily, or would the state impose compulsory conscription into the armed forces, something which the National Service League had advocated since 1902, and which it had pursued more rigorously in the months before the war?[4] Lilla Brockway feared their arguments would win over even those with Liberal sympathies. It was her idea, put into action by her husband Fenner, editor of the *Labour Leader*, the journal of the Independent Labour Party, to form the No-Conscription Fellowship. The NCF quickly established itself across the country as the natural home for anti-war activists of all persuasions and backgrounds, whether Socialist, Christian or independent-minded. Thinking against war in general, or this war in particular, was rehearsed, refined and reinforced. Whatever their backgrounds, NCF members knew what they stood for, what they were against, and why. There is a temptation to regard opponents of the war as lonely pacifists, but through bodies like the NCF and the FOR there was an established support base. The literature of these organisations would have had a reach beyond the immediate membership, and national expressions of opposition to the war were regularly printed in, for example, George Lansbury's *Herald* newspaper. In many cases there were strong war-resistance movements in local communities too.[5] For men who would themselves become liable for conscription, the NCF provided the means by which they moved from being vulnerable individuals to becoming part of a movement with all the solidarity that provided. That there would be consequences for each man who made a stand was foreseen by the NCF's Statement of Faith:

> The No-Conscription Fellowship is an organization of men likely to be called upon to undertake military service in the event of conscription, who will refuse from conscientious motives to bear arms, because they consider human life to be sacred, and cannot, therefore, assume the responsibility of inflicting death. They deny the right of Governments to say, 'You shall bear arms,' and will oppose every effort to introduce compulsory military service into Great Britain. Should such efforts be successful, they will, whatever the consequences may be, obey their conscientious convictions rather than the commands of Governments.[6]

In Stanton's unpublished manuscript diary, he summed it up: 'One had a growing sense of isolation – that one was surrounded by people who thought in different terms and spoke as it were a different language.'[7]

The NCF's fears of the inevitability of the introduction of conscription were well founded. Initial military recruitment, cheered on by the Press, led to willing volunteers coming forward at the rate of up to 170,000 a week. Kitchener's recruitment drives took place in a climate of strong social pressure and hostility towards 'cowards', 'slackers' and 'shirkers' who did not put themselves forward to serve their country. White feather campaigns were waged by women who felt moved by patriotic feelings – campaigns which were subsequently discredited as stories emerged of wounded soldiers, even a VC in civilian dress, receiving white feathers.[8] However, principled resistance to social pressure led some to regard with a degree of pride their association with this sign. One conscientious objector (CO) even entitled his autobiography, *White Feather*.[9]

As military operations expanded on new fronts, as numbers of the fallen grew, and as numbers of volunteers unsurprisingly declined, the clamour for conscription became unstoppable. The legal preliminary to conscription was the national registration of men and women aged between 15 and 65 on 15 August 1915. Through a process promoted by the Earl of Derby, the results were used by canvassers during the following November and December to persuade men to 'attest' their willingness to join a military reserve, to be called up in groups as required. Still the numbers coming forward were insufficient for military purposes, and the Bill to introduce military conscription was introduced to Parliament in January 1916. The Military Service Act came into force on 2 March 1916, with single men aged 18–41 being regarded as having been 'duly enlisted in His Majesty's regular forces ... for the period of the war', unless they were in reserved occupations. In May 1916 this call-up was extended to married men, and in 1918 to men aged 17–51. This latter amendment also included a politically controversial attempt to extend the military draft to Ireland, an extension that was never put into practice.

In response to these parliamentary moves towards conscription in 1915, the NCF strengthened and extended its statement of purpose:

> The members of the Fellowship refuse to engage in any employment which necessitates taking the military oath. Whilst leaving the decision open to the individual judgment of each member, the Fellowship will support members who conscientiously resist compulsory alternatives to military service involving a change of occupation.[10]

By the time conscription was introduced in 1916, there were probably around 15,000 NCF members who were committed to resist any call to bear arms.

Conscience

> The average 'local tribunal' was one of the most stupid and incompetent institutions known to English history. Composed for the most part of elderly and ardent patriots, it was particularly unfitted to pass judgment on the most intimate problems of the individual human spirit.[11]

One feature of the Military Service Act, reflecting the influence in Parliament of two Quaker MPs, Arnold S. Rowntree and T. Edmund Harvey, the member for

Leeds West, – 'the soldier and military system belong to a stage of society which has to be transcended' – was a clause allowing exemption on 'the ground of a conscientious objection to the undertaking of combatant service' – subject to the approval of a tribunal.[12] Exemption could be absolute, temporary or subject to such conditions as undertaking work of national importance.

From the outset, the tribunals had difficulties with their brief, as Army Council Instructions for administering the Military Service Act somewhat enigmatically implied: 'it is not sufficient [for an objector] to show that opinions are held against war; there must be proof of genuine conscientious conviction'.[13] When does an opinion become a conviction, and that become a *genuine* conscientious conviction?, it might well be asked.

Exemption on conscientious grounds was generally expected to apply only to combatant roles, and, apart from a special status granted to members of the Friends' Ambulance Unit, most COs were still expected to join the army and to undertake non-combatant duties. Those who made trouble from the outset – by refusing a medical, for example – would immediately be posted to combatant units and any arguments from conscience automatically dismissed.

From this point on I draw heavily from the words and experiences of individual conscientious objectors, the stories of many of whom are recorded in the Liddle Collection in the Brotherton Library, University of Leeds.

> Whilst there was certain service which I was very willing to do for my country, I could not agree to do anything which would facilitate the prosecution of the war.[14]

What might have seemed a tidy proposal on paper did not take account of the diversity of human thought, conscience, commitment and resolve. Some COs so opposed the system that they refused to deal with a tribunal at all. Others saw their tribunal as an opportunity for public proclamation of their opposition to war. The testimony of Harry Stanton was succinct:

> I am convinced that all warfare is utterly contrary to the will of God, as revealed in the teaching of Jesus Christ, and therefore cannot undertake any service to assist in the prosecution of this or any war. I claim absolute and complete exemption.[15]

Stanton's 'genuine conviction' was acknowledged, but he was ordered to undertake non-combatant service. Appealing that decision, he was offered work for a public body, but, arguing that any compulsory change in his employment would only be designed to further the war effort, he declined. As a result, his claim for exemption was dismissed and he became liable for military duties. On the date he was ordered to report, he preferred instead to attend a national convention of the NCF in London which went ahead despite a hostile crowd attempting to break up the meeting. The convention gave him strength for the struggle to come.

> It was a thrilling experience to see so many hundreds of men, many of them already awaiting arrest, solemnly pledging themselves to refuse all forms of

military service, and to maintain the claims of a higher authority than the state, where the taking of human life was concerned.[16]

I was determined not to take part in any service which had for its object the more efficient prosecution of the war.[17]

Stanton was a Quaker, his conscientious objection religiously motivated, and he was what came to be known as an 'absolutist' – that is, he refused under any circumstances to cooperate with a system at war. He would not replace a worker in an innocuous or non-war-related employment, for example, because that would simply allow that worker to join the army. Such absolutists were actually in a minority among the 17,000 or so COs who came from a range of backgrounds and responded in diverse ways to non-combatant and other offers made by tribunals. There were members of the historic peace churches, principally Quakers; there were also members of larger denominations, especially Nonconformist Churches with a history of independent thought and action, motivated both by biblical sentiments – 'Thou shalt not kill', 'Love your enemies', – and by the non-violent example of Jesus. Other religious bodies were strongly represented, including the Plymouth Brethren, Christadelphians, Adventists and International Bible Students, now known as Jehovah's Witnesses, some of whom restricted their opposition solely to direct responsibility for killing, while others refused to be told how to act by the state. There were humanists opposed to all war, having a sense of solidarity with all human life; there were anti-capitalists who were opposed to this particular war but who would have been prepared to man the barricades of revolution; other socialists held to a solidarity with workers of other nations and would not fight against their 'brothers'. There were anarchists opposed to cooperating with any concept of conscription, let alone the war.[18] Add to that list Irish nationalists opposed to the British state and its involvement in Ireland and the breadth of opposition to conscription is seen to embrace a huge range of contrasting, even conflicting, attitudes and philosophies.

Adding to the complexity, within each of these groups there was a spectrum of responses to conscription. Some accepted a role within the non-combatant corps – which the supportive *Herald* newspaper described as the 'No-Cowards Corps' – who could be asked to undertake any task short of taking life – even, in some bizarre cases, guarding other COs.[19] Some chose to face the perils of the front line in the Royal Army Medical Corps or, outside direct military control, in the Friends' Ambulance Unit. Even the acceptance of non-combatant or medical service did not bring an end to unforeseen challenges to conscience. Imagine this hypothetical scenario at the front:

Officer: 'Put that wounded man on a stretcher.'
CO: 'Yes, sir.'
Officer: 'And pick up his rifle.'
CO: 'No.'

Disobedience in such a setting would or could lead to court-martial, brutal detention and an extended sentence of hard labour.

Others, unwilling to join the NCC, were prepared to accept work of national importance, ranging from farming to, in some cases, even manufacturing munitions. Tribunals' misdiagnosis of what COs would be prepared to do led to many men being arrested and imprisoned when their preferences might otherwise have been accommodated. Florence Lockwood of Huddersfield described such misunderstandings as 'tribungles'.[20] Over time, the Committee on Work of National Importance – known as the Pelham Committee, after its first chairman – became influential in placing successfully many COs in work appropriate to their objection.

As for the absolutists, how many would crack when facing the ultimate test of their resolve? Or could they be bought off by a Home Office scheme designed to tempt them into doing work of national importance? Notoriously harsh work centres were set up around the country, not least at Knutsford and Wakefield. At Princetown Work Centre, Dartmoor, there were so many COs that the FOR set up its own Dartmoor branch.

The best statistics available immediately after the war estimated the total number of conscientious objectors as 16,100. That figure is now known to be at least 1,000 short, with new names being regularly added to the 'Pearce Directory of COs'. From the post-war figures, over 6,000 men were arrested, nearly 5,000 – most of whom had been settled by the Pelham Committee – were in some kind of employment, 3,300 joined the non-combatant corps, and 1,200 joined the Friends' Ambulance Unit, with an additional 100 in the Royal Army Medical Corps.[21]

Courage

'In cases where the claims of the State were in conflict with those of God, I must obey the higher authority'.[22]

The 'Frenchmen'

The first instinct of the military authorities was to test the resolve of absolutist COs to the limit, if possible beyond the gaze of public scrutiny. One diverse cohort of absolutist COs, drawn from the initial intake of prisoners gathered at Harwich, and soon to be joined by others from Richmond Castle, Kinmel Park and Seaford, was taken by the military to France. The first group to land in France was taken from Landguard Fort, Harwich, in the small hours of 8 May 1916, escorted by military police and additionally with nearly 100 NCC men. To the frustration of the military authorities, members of the group from Harwich managed to get word out about their movement. As they passed through the capital, Alfred Evans persuaded a London station porter to post a letter to the NCF. Although others managed to get letters out later at Basingstoke via a guard, Jack Foister wondered whether the Evans' letter eventually saved them, being the means by which their plight eventually became public and political.[23] When one of the party, Rendell Wyatt, in due course received a telegram from the Friends Service Committee, they all knew that their plight was in the public domain and that allies in Britain would work hard in their support.[24]

Arriving at Southampton, where they boarded a ship carrying troops returning to France, Jack Foister recalled, 'We had a boisterous time singing … We were permitted to group on deck for a few minutes to take a last look at England, but warned to keep our own company, for many of the troops were the worse for drink and might entertain hard thoughts for us.'[25]

The Richmond group, men who left evidence of their convictions graffitied on the cell walls of Richmond Castle, went to France three weeks later. At least superficially, their common resolve overcame their trepidation, leading to a bizarre scene on the platform of Darlington station on the evening of 29 May. During the long wait for a train to take them to London *en route* for France, a group of sixteen COs formed a square of platform seats. 'We indulged in hymn singing, which was joined in by the Non-Combatants with much zest.'[26] Even the station porter wished to shake their hands, saying 'There's some spirit there.'[27] As they left, there was 'only a slight evidence of derision being manifest'. On the night-train to London, a friendly sergeant exchanged anecdotes. Having been bussed from Kings Cross to Waterloo, they started hymn singing again on arrival, '"Simply trusting" being a prime favourite'.[28]

At Southampton docks the group boarded a boat to Le Havre, together with NCC men and '8 C.O. *out & outers* from Seaford … the spirit manifest now was beyond description and we, although being a very mixed gathering Agnostics – Artists – Christians of different sects joined in our hymn singing with great fervour'.[29] For all the fears of what might be to come and the discomfort of dark, overcrowded conditions, there was gratitude in 'realising what a glorious privilege we were allowed – to be pioneers of such a magnificent cause'.[30]

Arriving in France, one of the Richmond cohort, Bert Brocklesby, doctored an official postcard home to convey the message that 'I am being sent to … b … ou … long' and some of the group even managed to buy ice-creams from the window of a French train.[31] The presence of extroverts like Brocklesby kept their spirits high. Their diversity enhanced the sense of solidarity in the days ahead, as they organised their own Adult School evenings in taking turns to introduce such subjects as prejudice, elections and materialism, as well as regular Bible study and hymn singing. Yet soon the diary entries thin, the mood changes and conditions worsen. By mid-June Gaudie was writing that 'We felt this day, that our former respectable habits were conspicuous by their absence.'[32]

By then, the group from Harwich had been in France for over a month. For both the objectors and those in positions of authority this was new territory. Those who were used to being obeyed found the open non-cooperation of the COs infuriating. Stanton's diaries recount incidents in which the COs were dragged onto parade grounds only to cause confusion among ranks of soldiers by their disobedience, and consternation among the officers by their blatant insubordination. In answer to taunts that they would not kill anyone by keeping in step, came the retort that there must be no letting up in their disobedience.

> We could see that by refusing to obey even in the most trivial matters we should keep the issue clear, both in our minds and those 'in authority'. Had we obeyed such orders we should have gradually found ourselves up against

more serious ones, and it would have been impossible to logically draw a line and say 'Thus far and no farther![33]

As the numbers of incidents of disobeying orders increased, so too did the levels of punishment. Detention cells, solitary confinement, a bread and water diet, and inadequate sanitation – treatment not dissimilar to that which some had already experienced in uncomfortable conditions at Harwich Redoubt – gave way to characteristically military punishments. Stanton and others were sentenced to '28 days of Field Punishment No. 1', colloquially known as 'Crucifixion':

> Provision was made for this by means of a wooden framework, consisting of uprights, four or five yards apart, with connecting beams at a height of about five feet. We were placed with our backs to the posts and arms outstretched. Our ankles were then tied together and our arms tied tightly at the wrists to the crossbeams. We were to remain in this position for two hours.[34]

This was tough on the wrists of all those being punished, but especially so for smaller men who had to stand on tiptoe. The following day Stanton and his companion, Harold Brewster, received a variation of this, attached to the inner of a double barbed-wire fence surrounding Harfleur prison.

> We two were on this occasion placed with our faces to the wire of the inner fence, and tied in the usual manner at the wrists and ankles. As the ropes with which we were fastened were tied around barbed-wire instead of the usual thick wooden posts, it was possible to tie them much more tightly, and I found myself drawn so closely in to the fence that when I wished to turn my head I had to do so very slowly and cautiously to avoid my face being torn by the barbs.[35]

At the Field Punishment Barracks in Boulogne a similar punishment was 'exquisite torture', leaving several on the point of fainting under the strain.[36] Further disobedience led to days in irons, which meant being handcuffed with hands most of the time behind one's back. When the irons were removed, surprisingly, in the middle of one night, there was a hopeful sense that external forces were at work which could yet come to the aid of the COs. The intensity of the privations meant that occasional kindnesses received or expressed were specially remembered:

> Presently two of the warders came along and asked me what it was all about. As I began to explain, they became very interested, and, when they found that I was a Quaker, quite sympathetic, saying that the government had no right to treat Quakers in such a manner. I begged them not to think that only Quakers could be genuine conscientious objectors. One of them released me from the hand-cuffs on condition that I would not leave the tent, which I readily promised.[37]

One soldier guarding Stanton's group had heard that they were going to the front where any disobedience would result in their being shot. '"I would sooner shoot the officer who gave me the order," he said fiercely, "than shoot one of you fellows!"'[38]

In amongst long periods of 'sweet silent thought, whose healing effect became increasingly necessary', the COs found solidarity in their common experience of punishment, and in their diversity, holding debates on such subjects as Marxism, Tolstoyan philosophy, Esperanto, vaccination and the existence of a personal devil. At last the COs were permitted to receive 'letters of burning faith and courage which came from those left behind to continue the struggle at home'.[39]

> We were, indeed, becoming closely knit into a fellowship which multiplied the strength of the individuals comprising it. It was an indication of the sincere regard which we bore for one another that during the whole of that long and trying four weeks, which we spent in such close contact, there was no trace of ill-feeling displayed, though radical differences of opinion were continually in evidence.[40]

At the start of June the imprisoned COs in Boulogne were visited by Hubert Peet of the Friends' Service Committee, acting as secretary to an elderly cleric, the Revd F.B. Meyer, who had come to find out in more depth the basis of the men's opposition to the Military Service Act.[41] Would the hopes raised by such a visit prove to be a false dawn? Soon afterwards, the Harwich cohort was joined in Boulogne by the group from Richmond, and confidence was boosted by their tales of extrovert humour and song. The military authorities, however, still had cards to play. Courts-martial were about to begin.

> I was not a soldier and so did not recognise the right of any military officer to command me, nor the right of any court-martial to judge me. Whether the orders in question were lawful or unlawful, I had disobeyed it, and should continue to disobey similar commands in the future.[42]

One by one, between 10 and 13 June, the Boulogne COs were brought before a court-martial, charged with disobeying orders whilst undergoing field punishment. On the following Thursday, 15 June, a large escort collected four of the COs – Howard Marten, Harry Scullard, Jack Foister and John Ring – to have their sentences read out. Over the next ten days thirty-four men would be called in shifts to a parade ground in front of ranks of hundreds of soldiers. With pauses for dramatic effect, the announcement was made for each man, a sentence of death by being shot ... confirmed by General Haig ... commuted to ten years' penal servitude. Seven others received long sentences directly. Only two out of forty-three COs taken to France had succumbed to the intense pressure; the rest had held out even to the point of being sentenced to death. It had been a close thing, but the parliamentary campaign of Edmund Harvey, Philip Snowden and others had just been sufficient to thwart those who wanted to make an example of the COs by carrying out the death sentences.

> Slowly we came to realise that a great, perhaps a decisive, victory had been gained. Once for all, we hoped, the Government had been brought to face the question of its ultimate treatment of C.O.'s and had decided not to shoot them.[43]

Stanton's sentence was read out on 19 June in the bizarre setting of a parade ground next to a cricket pitch:

> Death! Penal servitude! The words seemed to mean little as I stepped back among the others. But as I stood listening to the sentences of the rest of the party, each man standing calmly in the midst of these menacing symbols of military power, a sense of joy and triumph flooded my mind. This was not so much an ordeal as a privilege ...
>
> The ceremony was soon over, and the crowd of soldiers dispersed – the cricketers to their game, the gossipers to their gossip. A small group re-assembled near us and gazed curiously at the men who could accept with equanimity so dismal a prospect.[44]

In the words of Clifford Cartwright, one of the men so sentenced: 'Whilst many suffered bodily torture far more than we did, yet the separation from the outside world, the entire suspense, along with the possibility of what might have happened, demanded the existence of a principle with which to face it.'[45] Their motivations were manifold, but each had stood up for that in which he believed.

Prisons and Work Centres

After a few more days of military discipline, Stanton and most of his party returned to Southampton and were transported to a civilian prison in Winchester.

> The main buildings, with their long rows of tiny windows, at once indicating the restriction and uniformity of the prisoners' living space, impressed the mind with a sense of grimness and rigidity which was new in our experience. In place of the sketchy and improvised penal machinery of the military arm, we were to know the full weight of the law, the unfaltering methods and systematic pressure upon the human spirit, which had been evolved during a century of the penal code.[46]

This was the penal system experienced by the majority of COs who did not comply with the verdict of their tribunal. Although what follows is closely linked to Stanton's story, the places and experiences referred to would have been familiar to many of the thousands of COs who were imprisoned in 1916–19.

From the outset, individuality was not recognised; it was an effort for Stanton even to be acknowledged as a Friend, as the only permitted religions to register were Church of England or Roman Catholic or, *in extremis*, Wesleyan. Foister had no chance of being allowed to put down 'Socialist'. Those with responsibility for trying to get COs to change their opinions were openly hostile, often brutally so. 'Quite the most unpleasant guards' Stanton met were New Zealanders, escorting a party of COs in Winchester: 'they told us several times that their rifles were loaded, and that nothing would give them greater pleasure than to use them on us'.[47]

Other guards, civil or military, were far more open-minded and, on occasion, prepared to listen to an objector's case. A number of ex-soldiers in Maidstone prison were very supportive of the COs.[48] Even the work centres varied: the

Warwick Work Centre was in the charge of a Quaker, Edwin Gilbert, who tried to make the Home Office scheme as tolerable as possible:

It was said that all C.O.'s who were considered genuine were to be allowed to work upon a scheme controlled by the Home Office. We began to picture a Home Office run by C.O.'s, but this vision was too good to last. It appeared that cases were to be reviewed by a central tribunal, in London. This was confirmed by the 'Quaker chaplain' during his next visit, and the question of whether or not to accept this chance of 'alternative service' became the main topic.[49]

Most COs, after the failure of their appeal, either accepted the verdict of their tribunal – usually to join the NCC – or awaited arrest. Many of the latter were sent to the central tribunal at Wormwood Scrubs, where they received prison sentences with hard labour. The regime at Wormwood Scrubs was brutal. Thomas Attlee's experience was not untypical. He started his three-month sentence with a month sleeping on a bare plank in solitary confinement, for the first fortnight of which he was on a bread and water diet. On release, he was sent to barracks, court-martialled once again and taken to Wandsworth gaol for another month of solitary confinement. The pattern was repeated and a third term at Wandsworth followed.[50]

Stanton and another group of Winchester COs were taken only briefly to Wormwood Scrubs, the towers at the entrance to which have inset plaster reliefs of the philanthropist John Howard and the Quaker reformer Elizabeth Fry. 'The wheel of Fortune had completed its circle. Once again Quakers were entering the London prisons – would they too emerge as prison reformers, speaking from bitter experience of the evils of the modern prison system.'[51] Reform was certainly needed: the cells were filthy and reading matter scarce. Attempts to enforce a regime of silence failed, as an entire wing was populated by conscientious objectors. Strains of 'The Red Flag' could be heard.[52] On 14 August Stanton appeared before the central tribunal – 'three men, whom I judged to be rather more competent than my earlier inquisitors'. They tried unsuccessfully to persuade him to accept alternative service under civil control. Some of his peers gave an unconditional refusal, others said it would depend on the terms of the offer. The immediate outcome for Stanton was a return to Winchester. From here, dressed in oversized second-hand civilian clothes, he was to travel with other COs to a Home Office camp at Dyce in Aberdeenshire. They were met at Waterloo by men and women from the Friends' Service Council and the NCF, who had received advance word of the planned journey and had come to express support.

Resistance

Controversy over the treatment, even the concept, of conscientious objectors continued throughout the war. Their parliamentary champion, Philip Snowden MP, received 30,000 letters in 1917 expressing concern for the welfare of COs and asking him to pursue their cases. He was outspoken in calling conscription a 'weapon for enforcing the chains of slavery on democracy' and stating that 'I refuse to ask any young man to sacrifice his life for me. I am not going to eternity haunted by the ghosts of slain young men who lost their lives because of my inducing them to join the army.'[53]

This was one area where Church leaders, few of whom had dared to criticise the war, were prepared to stand up against public opinion. The Congregationalist preacher J. Morgan Gibbon disagreed with the COs' stand but reminded his congregation that they stood 'where the majority of them stood yesterday and where they would all be standing again to-morrow or the day after'.[54] He likened the spirit of the times to that of Judge Jeffreys. Similarly, Edward Hicks, Bishop of Lincoln, alluded to the Inquisition when he argued that conscience is a sacred thing, and that it is perilous to trample on it:

> That there are among us conscientious objectors, all agree. The Friends are such, and are exempted. There are others outside that body, in the Church of England for example – in spite of the Thirty-nine Articles. Need any man be ashamed of interpreting the Gospel as did Tolstoy? Such a man may be useless for war, but he may be a useful citizen. We want prophets and visionaries, and we shall need them still more. The will or capacity to take an enemy's life is not the only element in good citizenship.[55]

In the months ahead a number of other bishops and even the Archbishop of Canterbury would speak out in support of the right to conscientious objection and the importance of humane treatment of those who were COs.[56]

Not that everyone made such humanitarian concerns a priority, as may be seen in some soldiers' letters home. G. Faraday Davies was 'jolly sick' of the clause permitting conscientious objection.[57] Thomas Bayley Gresham, a machine-gunner in Egypt, wrote that 'if the *conscientious objectors* could only hear the language their objections cause out here & the names they are called, they would be ashamed to be seen in the streets'.[58] Harold Victor Jones, writing from the Western Front, rued, 'What would I not have given to have got amongst them with a bayonet. (Just to tickle them, you know.)'[59] E.G. Bates of the Northumberland Fusiliers was not alone in thinking that all COs should be shot.[60] Even if it didn't happen officially, 'wait till a few million soldiers get back to England! Then there'll be a few little changes – & a few little bits of dirty work at the cross-roads with nasty messy results for some of the objects!!! They're all marked men. You've only got to see that in the men's letters. And everyone has realised that LIFE IS PRETTY CHEAP AFTER ALL!'[61]

Another soldier, E.R. Collins, was not impressed by suggestions that the COs were on a par with early Christian martyrs. He wanted 'to rope in the whole lot of them & give them a chance of hearing a shrapnel come whistling through the air, followed by the sharp crack of the exploding shell'.[62] Even fifty years later A.J. Cripps of the 8th Battalion, Rifle Brigade, was adamant that he 'would have shot the lot'.[63]

Time, however, did change the perspective of Charles Raven, who later became an inter-war pacifist theologian of high repute. In 1917 he opposed the 'poor blind sentimentalists' who rejected war, and in casual discussion suggested that 'a drastic slaughter of the Pro-German peace-mongers would do more than the establishment of a war council'.[64]

Such controversy divided, even shamed, some families. For many, however, views were expressed more temperately than as detailed above, particularly in families where there were members on both sides of the issue. Howard Victor Hart regretted that his sister Sybil and her husband Andrew – an imprisoned CO – opposed the war. He recognised that she was in a similar position to many women, separated from their husbands, but argued that from his perspective it was a privilege to have to bear some burden in the war.[65]

Members of the Brocklesby family had also responded differently to the war. Philip Brocklesby, in the forces, headed for France knowing that his brother Bert, one of the Richmond COs, was already there in detention. Passing through Boulogne, Philip sought him out, finding him at Henriville camp on the day the first death sentences were read out. Their meeting in the guard room was not a time for them to change each other's mind, rather to offer mutual support at a critical moment for individuals and wider family alike.[66]

That sympathetic responses from the public stand out is perhaps an indication of their rarity. Crossing London en route from Winchester to Dyce, Norman Gaudie went to a barber's shop, 'where he had satisfied the curiosity of the company and enlisted its sympathy for C.O.s, so that he left the shop to a chorus of good wishes'.[67]

> Most of us had refused to sign the undertaking required by the Home Office; that we were not aware of being compromised so far, and that if we found that our testimony against war was being impaired, we should have to refuse the work offered to us.[68]

The good wishes were required, as Dyce turned out to be a work camp, based in a quarry where heavy labour was needed to move stones. Accommodation for some 200 ill-fed COs was in a set of leaky tents, ill-protected from the elements, with inadequate sanitary provision. The health of a number of COs deteriorated sharply. Walter Roberts, a Stockport architect and member of the Independent Labour Party, died at Dyce; he was one of ten COs to die in captivity, a subset of seventy-one who died as a direct result of the treatment they received.[69]

From the close of 1917, deaths in prison or after release on medical grounds began to be numerous. They were nearly all of one type. A man was emaciated by want of exercise, nourishment, and by mental and physical suffering, so that he was unable to resist influenza, bronchitis, pneumonia or consumption, when they attacked him.[70]

The majority of COs at Dyce rejected Home Office pressure to work ten hours a day, and that of representatives from the Committee for the Employment of Conscientious Objectors, including Labour MP William Brace. When it was suggested that the granite being crushed at Dyce could be used for the construction of a military road, many of the COs protested. Brocklesby announced he would go home and await arrest. The viability of the quarry, especially in winter, meant that its days were numbered and it closed in October 1916 before the issue came to a head.[71] Stanton commented: 'Looking back over those weeks at Dyce, I saw that we had done nothing to further the cause of pacifism.'[72] After being granted a week at home, Stanton was required to attend Wakefield prison, converted into a work centre for COs:

> I had felt a renewal of the doubts as to whether 'work of national importance', at Wakefield or elsewhere, was really the right thing for me. It held the prospect, not of an easy conscience, but of a series of compromises. I was uncomfortably aware that in discussions on 'alternative service', the fact that 'Frenchmen' were working under the Home Office scheme was being used as an argument in favour of compromise ... Surely to 'work the scheme' was to abandon our opposition to conscription.[73]

For other COs, who had arrived at Wakefield from other prisons and who were more used to the enforced obedience of prison regime, there was curiosity at the attitudes of the men from Dyce whose reputation had gone before them. 'One or two told me that if we were not willing to obey the orders of the Home Office, we ought to go back to prison. I replied that if we were ready to obey all orders we should soon be in France again, having betrayed the cause for which we had stood.'[74]

When ten Wakefield men refused to go to Wigan to undertake quarry work of unknown purpose for a private contractor, possibly releasing other men to join the army, the Home Office threatened imprisonment. The resultant short strike at Wakefield led to a division among some 400 COs, with two-thirds voting to resume work. Of the remainder, seven wrote an open letter to resign from the Home Office scheme, acknowledging it was a mistake for them to have obtained release from prison under the present conditions. 'Unless a conscientious objector is free to follow his vocation, he has no sure guarantee that he will not be involved in many evils which he cannot condone.'[75] Receiving a negative response, they laid down their tools, walked out and awaited re-arrest. When it came, they were taken in chains from Armley gaol in Leeds, where Stanton received abuse from a prison warder, to Maidstone convict prison, where Clifford Allen, Chairman of the NCF, and a number of other COs were already gathered.[76] Stanton would stay there for over twelve months, working in the print shop binding ledgers, though refusing to be involved with forms to be used by the military or naval authorities. As a poem from the *CO Clink Chronicle 1916* expressed it:

> Men who hae called Allen head,
> Men whom Russell sometime led,
> Welcome to your three-plank bed,
> With a conscience free![77]

Stanton again: 'We had long recognised that consciences rooted in such diversity could not be brought to a unanimous decision.'[78]

Perhaps it should be restressed that not all COs were pacifist. Political objection to this particular war was strongly held by some. In prisons, work centres and places where COs came together, they were far from sharing a common mind. In some places there was a degree of harmony, in others not. A. Barrett Brown wrote cheerily of the scene in Canterbury prison:

Socialist and Anarchist, Catholic and Quaker,
We're a motley crowd of pilgrims when you come to write the Tale,
But we're vowed to Lady Peace, and we never will forsake her,
So here's to good St Thomas and the Canterbury gaol![79]

On the other hand, one otherwise sympathetic visitor to the Princetown Work Centre on Dartmoor in 1916 was taken aback by meeting the 600 COs held there:

> Was there ever gathered together so strange a collection of individuals? – quiet Quakers, who sat unmoved while men stood up and shouted around them, wild-looking men from the Clyde and Rhondda Valley whose hopes for the regeneration of society lay in a class war, strange melancholy men whose message was the immediate coming of the Messiah and the end of the world, men of all trades and professions, mathematicians, scholars, musicians, actors, miners and farm labourers, with nothing to unite them but a refusal to bear arms in the present war.
>
> I was distressed and dismayed by the clash and conflict of theories and personalities with which I was confronted. Some brandished Bibles, accusing me of not knowing the Word of God as revealed in the Book of Daniel, others with red flags proclaimed me as a traitor for not accepting class war and the dictatorship of the proletariat.
>
> Their feelings and passions, conviction and commitment were strong; they had to be for the men to be prepared voluntarily to undergo the privations and pains imposed by a State trying to break their resolve. Their principles were no more likely to be surrendered to each other than to a military tribunal.[80]

Hopes, False and Real

Those principles were constantly being put to the test, for no sooner had an objector's prison sentence expired than, in a process known as 'cat-and-mouse', he was liable to be re-arrested immediately, court-martialled and imprisoned again. It seemed that there was no end in sight, and it placed a particular strain on the families of COs.

For Kathleen Attlee, the impact on her health was on a par with that of her CO husband, Thomas. She had been active in the Poplar Labour League, working alongside George Lansbury in the local council, as well as being a lecturer for the Oxford University Extension Course. Trying to juggle meetings, motherhood and time-consuming prison visiting, when that was permitted, took its toll, especially when a deterioration in her husband's health coincided with news of other COs dying in prison. A rumour that Thomas might be transferred 200 miles away to Wakefield nearly broke her spirit completely.[81]

Eventually, the Armistice was declared. Would there now be a general release of military prisoners, perhaps even an amnesty for COs? It was not to be.

> The months following the Armistice were perhaps the most difficult of our prison experience. The reasons for detaining us seemed no longer to be valid, but the months crawled by, with no word of release.[82]

When it was announced that those who had served two years would be released, most of the 'local' COs were allowed to go, but the 'penal servitude' COs continued to be detained, fearing they might have to serve their full sentence. Release came in April 1919, and Stanton returned to his Luton home one Sunday morning:

> That evening, as I sat in our Friends' meeting, so quiet, yet full of emotion, I thought of the many who were returning home with broken health, perhaps embittered, and without hope for the future; yet knew that to them would come better days, and the realisation that they had taken their part in this great struggle for human freedom, and not in vain.[83]

Some weeks later Stanton received his discharge papers, citing three years and one day in the army, with fifty-two days' service abroad. It carried with it a warning that those who had been discharged for misconduct must not attempt to re-enlist secretly. There was little chance of that.

Conclusion
The cumulative impact of those who resisted the war reached far beyond the few thousands directly involved. It has, if anything, grown with time. Indeed, the principal aim and motivation of many COs was to make a lasting impact on society. Harry Stanton wrote:

> While many of us were not able to express articulately the faith that was in us, it had so laid hold of us that nothing else counted – that this was to be our particular contribution to the thought and progress of the world, and that to be unfaithful would be to betray our fellow-men, even those who were most bitterly denouncing us.[84]

Clifford Allen described the protest of the COs as:

> a great effort of citizenship, the object of which was service to the community through the defeat of an evil system. In other words, the struggle ranked itself with many of the great rebel movements in history. Technically unconstitutional perhaps, but far less so than those which secured the Magna Charta or frustrated the claims of the Stuarts or drove James II from the throne. Henceforth the outlaw conscientious objector, rejecting every compromise which might have lessened his personal suffering, claimed that his rebellion was an act of citizenship.[85]

Allen maintained that the stand of the COs was a supreme act of patriotism. He added: 'Of our fellow-countrymen who once hated us, I would only beg that they will believe us when we say we acted as we did because we loved our country.'[86]
The author of this chapter believes that 'their stand was for us all'.

Notes
1. Stanton, H.E., *Will You March Too?*, unpublished manuscript diary, Liddle Collection, WW1/CO/092, p. 4. All the Stanton material in this chapter comes from this source.

2. 'The Great Illusion ... gave us some assurance that the attitude which seemed to be dictated by conscience had also a certain economic validity.' Stanton, p. 3.

3. Stanton, p. 4.

4. For an example of the pre-war debate on conscription in Huddersfield, see Pearce, C., *Comrades in Conscience, The Story of an English Community's Opposition to the Great War* (London: Francis Boutle, 2001), pp. 93–7.

5. The Huddersfield story, see Pearce, *Comrades in Conscience*, is the best documented, but it was far from unique.

6. Graham, John W., *Conscription and Conscience* (London: George Allen & Unwin, 1922; repr. New York: Augustus M. Kelly, 1969), p. 174.

7. Stanton, pp. 2–3.

8. For a thorough study of the phenomenon of giving white feathers, and on the complex issues surrounding them, see Gullace, Nicoletta F., 'White Feathers and Wounded Men: Female Patriotism and the Memory of the Great War', *Journal of British Studies*, vol. 36, no. 2, Twentieth-Century British Studies (April 1997), pp. 178–206. Published by Cambridge University Press on behalf of the North American Conference on British Studies: http://www.jstor.org/stable/176011 (accessed 30 July 2015).

9. Marten, Howard C., 'White Feather: The Experiences of a Pacifist in France and Elsewhere, 1916–1918', Liddle Collection, WW1/CO/061.

10. Graham, *Conscription and Conscience*, pp. 174–5.

11. Stanton, p. 8.

12. Graham, *Conscription and Conscience*, p. 55. National Archives, MH 47/142/1_1: 'We doubted whether the proposed Tribunals would prove capable of judging consciences' – Stanton, p. 5. For an overview of the work of the tribunals, see Gregory, Adrian, *The Last Great War* (Cambridge: Cambridge University Press, 2008), pp. 101–8.

13. *Registration and Recruiting*, 21 August 1916, p. 43. National Archives, MH 47/142/1_2.

14. Stanton, p. 120.

15. Ibid., p. 9.

16. Ibid., pp. 11–12.

17. Ibid., p. 26.

18. Members of the International Bible Students Association facing the uncertainties of conscientious objection received encouragement from the words of Charles Taze Russell, the first IBSA president, who asked, 'Would it be any worse to be shot because of loyalty to the Prince of Peace and refusal to disobey his order than to be shot while under the banner of these earthly kings and apparently giving them support and, in appearance at least, compromising the teaching of our heavenly King?' Cited in Perkins, Gary, *For the Sake of the Kingdom*, http://www.forthesakeofthekingdom.co.uk/theology.html (accessed 13 August 2015).

19. *Herald*, 18 March 1916.

20. Lockwood, Florence, diary, July 1916. Liddle Collection, WW1/DF/077.

21. Graham, *Conscription and Conscience*, p. 349.

22. Stanton, p. 128.

23. Foister, Jack, Diary, pp. 9–10, 8 May 1916. Liddle Collection, WW1/CO/032.

24. Stanton, p. 93.

25. Foister, Diary, p. 10, 8 May 1916.

26. Gaudie, Norman, Diary, p. 12. Liddle Collection, WW1/CO/038.

27. Ibid., pp. 12–13.

28. Ibid., p. 13.

29. Ibid., p. 14.

30. Ibid., p. 15.

31. Ellsworth-Jones, Will, *We Will Not Fight* (London: Aurum, 2008), p. 159.

32. Gaudie, Diary, 15 June 1916.

33. Stanton, p. 109.

34. Ibid., p. 87.

35. Ibid., p. 90. This sort of treatment was not restricted to British COs. Perhaps the most brutal experiences were undergone by New Zealand COs who had to face 'crucifixion' and worse in France. See Grant, David, *Field Punishment No. 1* (Wellington, NZ: Steele Roberts, 2008).
36. Stanton, p. 101.
37. Ibid., p. 89.
38. Ibid., p. 93.
39. Ibid., pp. 108, 112.
40. Ibid., p. 112.
41. Shortly afterwards there was another Quaker visit, from J. Rowntree Gillett. Ibid., pp. 132–3.
42. Ibid., p. 127.
43. Ibid., p. 130.
44. Ibid., pp. 134–7.
45. Cartwright, Clifford, 'The Death Sentence'; Daniell, Derek L. (ed.), *For His Name's Sake: Being a Record of the Witness given by Members of Churches of Christ in Great Britain against Militarism during the European War, 1914–1918* (1921), p. 69. Liddle Collection, WW1/CO/102/Box 1/Item 4.
46. Stanton, p. 157.
47. Ibid., p. 179.
48. Ibid., p. 283.
49. Ibid., p. 178.
50. Barrett, Clive, *Subversive Peacemakers, War-Resistance 1914–1918, an Anglican Perspective* (Cambridge: Lutterworth, 2014), pp. 159–60.
51. Stanton, p. 181.
52. Ibid.
53. Philip Snowden MP in the House of Commons debate on the Military Service Bill, 12 January 1916. http://hansard.millbanksystems.com/commons/1916/jan/12/military-service-no-2-bill-1#S5CV0077P0_19160112_HOC_319 (accessed 28 October 2015). The second comment had previously been Snowden's response to an appeal from a local mayor for assistance with recruitment. Schofield, Gerald, 'Lower Darwen, A History', http://archive-org.com/org/c/cottontown.org/2013-11-26_3234156_17/www_cottontown_org_Lower_Darwen_A_History_by_Gerald_Schofield/ (accessed 28 October 2015).
54. Unattributed press cutting, almost certainly from 1916, inserted into Lockwood, Florence, Diary. Liddle Collection, WW1/DF/077.
55. Letter to *The Times*, composed 3 April 1916.
56. Barrett, *Subversive Peacemakers*, pp. 154–5.
57. Davies, G. Faraday, Letter 19, 18 April 1916. Liddle Collection, WW1/GS/0427.
58. Gresham, Thomas Bayley, Letter 30, to his father, 2 May 1916. Liddle Collection, WW1/GS/0662.
59. Jones, Harold Victor, Letter 111, to his mother, 9 June 1918. Liddle Collection, WW1/GS/0868.
60. Bates, Edward Giles, Letter to Miss M.B. Dunn, 28 March 1917. Liddle Collection, WW1/GS/0098.
61. Bates, Edward Giles, Letter to Miss M.B. Dunn, 11 November 1917. Liddle Collection, WW1/GS/0098.
62. Collins, E.R. (ed.), 'War Diaries and Correspondence 1914–1919', p. 150. Liddle Collection, WW1/GS/0342.
63. Cripps, A.J., transcript of interview with Peter Liddle, 1970. Liddle Collection, WW1/GS/0392.
64. Letters from Charles Raven to S.W. Burgess, 22 October 1917 and 19 November 1917, held by Faith Raven.
65. Hart, Howard Victor, Letter, 6 August 1916. Liddle Collection, WW1/GS/0718.
66. Ellsworth-Jones, *We Will Not Fight*, pp. 1–3. For a wider discussion on how attitudes to the war, including but not only conscientious objection, caused family and social division, see Hochschild, Adam, *To End All Wars: How the First World War Divided Britain* (London: MacMillan, 2011).
67. Stanton, p. 189.
68. Stanton, pp. 188–9.
69. Graham, *Conscription and Conscience*, pp. 312–13 and pp. 323–4.
70. Ibid., p. 313.

71. Stanton, p. 209.
72. Ibid., p. 211.
73. Ibid., p. 210.
74. Ibid., p. 212.
75. Ibid., pp. 215–17. The seven were Cornelius Barritt, Norman Gaudie, Arthur Helsby, Rendell Wyatt, Harry Stanton, L. Hughes and Archie Moon, the first five of whom were 'Frenchmen'.
76. Ibid., p. 222.
77. Augli (pen name), 'The CO Battle Song', originally from *The Literary Outlet*, a clandestine prison journal edited by William L. Dixon, a socialist CO from Huddersfield; reprinted in *The CO's Clink Chronicle* (London: National Labour Press, undated *c.*1919), p. 8. Liddle Collection, WW1/CO/102/Box 5/Item 12.
78. Stanton, pp. 203–4. The comment was made when a minority group of around sixty of the Dyce camp men agreed to work ten hours on road construction. The group included 'Frenchmen' Bonner, Brewster and Bromberger; it was mainly IBSA people. About twice that number declined.
79. Brown, A. Barrett, 'The Pilgrim's Way', originally from *The Canterbury Clinker*, edited by A. Barrett Brown; reprinted in *The CO's Clink Chronicle*, p. 11.
80. Walke, Bernard, *Twenty Years at St Hilary* (London: Methuen, 1935), pp. 120–1.
81. Barrett, *Subversive Peacemakers*, p. 161. The full account is in Attlee, Peggy, *With a Quiet Conscience* (London: Dove & Chough, 1995).
82. Stanton, p. 289
83. Ibid., p. 301.
84. Ibid., pp. 131–2.
85. Graham, *Conscription and Conscience*, p. 16.
86. Ibid., p. 23.

Suggested Further Reading

The most important resource in researching conscientious objectors is the Pearce Directory, a database of over 17,000 known conscientious objectors; the Directory is available online at https://search.livesofthefirstworldwar.org/search/world-records/conscientious-objectors-register-1914-1918.

The Liddle Collection in Leeds University also provides a comprehensive resource of personal material relating to conscientious objectors.

Overviews

Barrett, Clive, *Subversive Peacemakers: War Resistance 1914–1918, an Anglican Perspective* (Cambridge: Lutterworth, 2014)

Bibbings, Lois S., *Telling Tales About Men: Conceptions of Conscientious Objectors to Military Service During the First World War* (Manchester: Manchester University Press, 2009)

Pearce, Cyril, *Comrades in Conscience: The Story of an English Community's Opposition to the Great War* (London: Francis Boutle, 2001)

Pearce, Cyril, *Communities of Resistance* (London: Francis Boutle, 2016)

Classics

Bell, Julian (ed.), *We Did Not Fight: 1914–1918 Experiences of War Resisters* (London: Cobden-Sanderson, 1935)

Boulton, David, *Objection Overruled* (London: MacGibbon & Kee, 1967)

Graham, John W., *Conscription and Conscience, A History 1916–1919* (London: Allen & Unwin, 1922)

Rae, John, *Conscription and Politics* (Oxford: Oxford University Press, 1970)

Chapter 20

Drawing on the Front Line

By Juliet Macdonald

On 21 July 1916 an aspiring young artist called Adrian Hill had just arrived at the French port of Le Havre. At the outbreak of war Hill had been an art student with a promising career ahead of him but in November 1914 he signed up, following his brother into the Honourable Artillery Company (HAC). After an extended period of training and a stint of duty at the Tower of London, he finally got to France a year and a half later as a 21-year-old corporal, and reported in a letter to his parents that he was delighted to be 'doing something at last'.[1] Hill was later to join the HAC's 1st Battalion, which had an infantry role, but when he was not busy being trained in bombing and anti-gas warfare or out on fatigues, he was already weighing up the possibilities of artistic activity. Seeing the pleasant wooded landscape around the town of Le Havre on his first day there, he wrote: 'It's quite a picture & for that reason they've pounced down on all the cameras, so I'm wondering whether I shall be shot at dawn if I risk my hand at a sketch.'[2]

In later life, Hill was to become well known for three things. First, he was commissioned by the newly established Imperial War Museum from late 1917 onwards, as their first official war artist, to make a pictorial record of the war as it was in progress. With over 190 artworks in the IWM collection and at least 100 drawings in the Archives of the Honourable Artillery Company, based at Armoury House, Hill has left an astonishing visual legacy of the First World War, including some of the most intense and detailed observations of war-damaged landscapes and towns. Second, after suffering from tuberculosis in 1938, he became a leading proponent of the idea that artistic activity could be an aid to healing for those suffering long-term illness, and is said to have coined the term 'art therapy'.[3] Third, he was an enthusiastic communicator about art, writing a number of popular instructional manuals on drawing and painting for the amateur market. From 1955 to 1962, in the early days of television, he hosted the regular children's programme 'Sketch Club', and he continued to promote the benefits of art making until the end of his life.[4]

During the First World War Hill wrote frequent letters home to his parents, always signed 'Joe' and filled with vivid and humorous descriptions of daily life, and they contain a number of lively ink drawings of billets, camps, funny incidents and characters. They also give an indication of how he carved out a role for himself as an artist during his first year in France. As the months progressed, and particularly during the bleak days of winter 1916/17, drawing for Hill in some senses a 'lifeline'. It was a skill that, once recognised, provided him with a distinctive role, saving him from tasks that were unattractively routine or potentially even more hazardous, and in the midst of danger and devastation it was an activity that made him feel invigorated, even elated.

Risking a Sketch

During the war drawing had military uses. New technologies of reconnaissance were being introduced, aerial photography for example, but on the ground, with of course the use of binoculars and telescopes, pencil and paper was often the primary means of notation for information gathered. Territory was surveyed and maps drawn out, but freehand sketching also had a role in communicating information about the lie of the land. For example, panoramic views were drawn from forward artillery observation posts, marking out the landscape against a grid to calculate the arc of fire for shelling purposes. At an even more local level, reconnaissance sketches were used to plan lines of attack and make tactical decisions. Although elaborate drawings required specialist training, all officers were expected to have the ability to make a rough sketch of the key landmarks to supplement a map.[5]

Soldiers in the ranks, on the other hand, were not allowed to exercise this type of skill. A drawing or photograph of a landscape or village was seen as potentially dangerous or even seditious; if it fell into the wrong hands it could give away vital intelligence as to the location of troops. For this reason, cameras could be confiscated and any outdoor sketching, even of the most innocent variety, was generally forbidden. For example, Private H. Atherton, a stretcher-bearer with the 28th Field Ambulance, 9th Scottish Division, managed to carry a small sketch-book around with him and make a number of detailed pen and ink drawings of his billets and immediate surroundings, but he records in his memoirs, 'I had to do it on the quiet as it was against army rules; if I had been caught I should have been for it.'[6] The artist John Nash, who is famous for such paintings as *Over the Top, 1918*, was a corporal. He recalls that he could only scribble quick notes on letters or envelopes in his pocket. Any overt drawing would have been treated with suspicion, even in the Artists Rifles.[7]

Hill was initially with the 6th Entrenching Battalion on the way up to the front, and was temporarily promoted to the rank of sergeant so perhaps this gave him greater freedom. By 30 July, as his unit moved on towards the line (in the Somme region, as it later became apparent) he asked his parents to post him a 9-inch sketchbook. The French countryside was apparently going to be 'a happy hunting ground for sketching'.[8] A later letter includes a caricature of himself drawing, closely watched by a group of inquisitive locals, and the caption 'Oh I love it!!'[9]

He must have done enough to get himself noticed. His sheer speed and skill in draughtsmanship and his acute powers of observation had potential uses that were soon recognised by his superiors, and he was directed to do specific drawing tasks. On 11 August he wrote:

> Just a line before I start on a two days sketching trip. The weather is again wonderfully fine & the prospects are ideal. The adjutant has sent me on the job & I'm thinking I shall want that other sketch book as soon as you can let me have it. I've packed up my kit and I'm all ready to start. It makes a ripping break

in the routine & I think it's awfully good of him to let me go. I feel frightfully privileged. I'll let you know all the bits on my return. No more time now as I want to get in a long day & it's a fair distance to the field of operations.[10]

At the bottom of the letter is a comment scribbled in pencil by the censor, presumably one of his battalion's officers: 'Your son is invaluable to the Battn,' with the word 'invaluable' triple underlined.

What exactly Hill had to do on that first sketching trip is not recorded but in all likelihood it would have been an attempt at drawing features of the enemy line facing the battalion. He mentions that it was too misty to draw a panorama, and that he had to hitch a ride back with a Red Cross vehicle that was travelling 'hell for leather'.[11] He clearly enjoyed the experience, writing: 'The last two days have been ideal. Sketching all day & for the first time since I joined I forgot I was a soldier.'[12] The colonel was apparently pleased with the results, and Hill asked his parents to send Indian ink and a pen so he could make better copies for higher command.

The Wood

In late August and throughout September Hill was stationed in a camp in a wood somewhere behind the lines. After the excitement of his reconnaissance outing, he returned to fatigues. His letters mention road building, chopping down trees and leading a party of men for a week away from the camp. This took him into areas further out of the line. He remarks on the fact that rural life was still going on and crops were being tended, despite evident damage to villages.

Hill's frequent letters keep up a persistently cheery tone to reassure his parents. With two sons on active service in France they had legitimate cause for concern. Staying positive was also a requirement of the censors. Some sections of Hill's letters are missing, the paper cut off crudely mid-sentence or pages completely gone. Complaining about conditions was strongly discouraged and of course revealing any military information was completely forbidden. Unable to report any major items of news, Hill exercised his creative abilities instead. He tells anecdotes and provides humorous snippets of information, helping his parents to build up a worry-free picture of the everyday pattern of army life. For example, one domestic scene shows Hill reclining on a camp bed amid the clutter of the sergeants' mess reading a copy of *Punch*. In another early letter he states mournfully, 'I'm getting my head shaved today – (tears) as they advised it for the sake of "the busy people"'[13] – rather a nice way of admitting the universality of head-lice. A couple of days later he includes a before-and-after cartoon of himself; on arrival in France he is neat, trim and clean but after just a few days on fatigues he has a shaven head, muscular build, square jaw, pockets bulging with equipment and uniform looking decidedly worn and dishevelled.[14]

His time in 'the Wood', as he called the camp, seems to have had genuine compensations. He loved the trees themselves. There are sketches at the top of some letters showing the tents and huts nestling amid graceful trunks and foliage. Writing paper was a scarce resource and his letters are on thin sheets of whatever came to hand, now yellowing and fragile. The drawings are very small, just occupying a corner of the page but they still evoke a sense of the place. Produced using pen and ink, his quick fluent lines provide just enough detail to capture the scene, such as the smoke curling from the chimney of the hut. The linear technique seems particularly suited to drawing trees, eloquently expressing the distinctive character of branches and the lively movement of leaves.

Lacking painting equipment, Hill compensated in language. Sitting with his back against a large beech tree that had an 'uncanny combination of silver-grey-green',[15] he wrote a letter to his father which seems to express a mixture of excitement, apprehension, home sickness and optimism. The intensity of his experience is conveyed in vivid descriptions of the scene before him. 'The whole forest is one mass of loveliness – after the rain, great-ragged clouds doing a bayonet charge through the drenched trees & sparkling sun making vain efforts to dry the place up a bit.'[16] Even his description of the community of soldiers has a rich sensory quality:

> A party have just come in & are drawing their evening meal. The fires are glowing – throwing up purple snakes of smoke – Comments are chucked about concerning the food & soon the ground in front of me is full of little groups with their steaming rations – balancing too much on one knee & blowing on tea that will not cool. Then the news of the day is discussed & the amount of work is published. Singing follows which makes writing even more difficult than ever.[17]

In mid-September there was heavy rain and a drawing in one letter shows the huts of the camp as arks floating in a tempest. Another illustrates Hill's role in enforcing an extra drill as punishment to one of the men. In mud that he describes as being 'of exceptional depth & quality', he orders the man to keep marching until they both gradually sink into the quagmire.[18]

A Grey Day

There is much less correspondence from October, perhaps indicating a move nearer to the front lines. In one letter Hill writes that he is missing the woods but gives no further clues as to his new location.

At some point during November Hill transferred from the Entrenching Battalion to the 1st Battalion, HAC. He may well have been involved in their front-line actions at Hamel (3–6 November) and Beaucourt (13–14 November), during which heavy losses were incurred.[19] He also learnt that his brother had died in action at Warlencourt, further up the River Ancre. Receiving the news, he wrote in a very brief message to his father, 'It's been – a grey day for me – my worst.'[20] By December, as the battalion moved away from the lines, Hill tried to resume his regular correspondence and up-beat tone, anxious for his mother's health. He reassured his parents: 'The Battalion have done their bit & have suffered for it. I think "the Chiefs" see that it is throwing away prospective officers in sending us up in "the thick of it" again – they are certainly going to give us a long rest.'[21]

Apart from the sketches in his letters, one of the few drawings from this period that exists in the archives holding the letters – the Liddle Collection at the University of Leeds – is *On the Somme 1916*. It is a pencil sketch showing a mound of earth. In the foreground lies the body of a soldier, head tilted away from the viewer, one hand clenched on his chest, the other lying limply above a shape on the ground which could be a gas mask or a skull. Around his head is a cluster of stabbing pencil marks – flies perhaps. A density of lines in some areas indicate earth scooped out by the action of shells. The figure was later reproduced in an ink drawing entitled *Pozières: An Australian Episode*,[22] but the first pencil sketch retains the roughness and immediacy of a drawing made there and then, on the battlefield, in the face of death itself.

The Frost

By late January 1917 Hill was on the move again, marching in deep snow up to the line. Conditions must have been pretty grim, but his letters are still humorous, albeit ironically so. Describing an incident when he slipped head over heels on the ice, he remarked, 'Everybody was very kind & offered numerous suggestions. Meanwhile the column moved on and I was left like a beetle on its back.'[23] However, a letter of 22 January suddenly announces to his parents a new position as 'artist to the snipers'.[24] The change would mean 'all kinds of privileges' and freedoms.[25] It was a few days before he admitted that it also meant demotion to the rank of private. The costs of drawing equipment would be reimbursed by the battalion. He requested a waterproof sketching case that could be slung on his back, just large enough to hold paper of 12 inches by 8 inches, and more pencils, ink and nibs.

The letters of the following days were written in pencil. In contrast to his usual flowing pen lines, the marks are constrained, more like a succession of short vertical strokes. He explains that the pen is frozen, his fingers are frozen, his sponge, cap, boots and putties are frozen, but despite all of that he is extremely happy because of his drawing tasks. It is technically demanding: 'there's map reading & drawing landscapes from the contours of maps – a devil of a job',[26] but he expresses pride in his role in military intelligence. 'I live in a cloud of maps and diagrams.'[27]

The new job was officially with the Snipers Platoon and Hill was expected to combine the role of scout and sniper with that of artist, using his observational skills and taking a sketchbook along with him as well as a rifle. Reconnaissance sketches were made on the spot in pencil and then worked up later in ink. A drawing of this type in the collection of the HAC shows a light railway and a road at Martinsart.[28] Sweeping lines define the main contours in a simplified, almost diagrammatic form so that key features can be picked out and annotated. There are no details apart from those that would serve a military value, and yet there is a sense of elegant design, and the unique shape of each tree is carefully articulated.

By 27 January 1917 the battalion was back in the Somme region again and stayed in the line for five days in the same sector as before, near the River Ancre. Without giving away any details, Hill stressed that his new role was a safer one, writing that he was in a 'luxurious' dugout, manning an observation post.[29] The work was no doubt dangerous and difficult as it involved drawing in awkward positions under shell fire and in extremely cold conditions. The situation was not improved when the dugout accidentally caught fire and he lost all his kit. A letter of 4 February, scribbled on a little piece of grid paper, is uncharacteristically bleak:

> I live in such rushing times I hardly know whether I am living in next week or tomorrow fortnight. Out here one is used as a pawn – you find yourself where you never thought you would ever be & back again where you never thought of returning.[30]

The pencil drawing at the top of the letter shows three bedraggled soldiers walking across a pitted landscape with explosions in the background. Each has a question mark above his head.

The battalion was involved in further action on 7 February and managed to capture the strategic position of Baillescourt Farm, suffering casualties in the process. Hill wrote a couple of hasty letters from an observation post on 6 and 8 February claiming there was absolutely no news. 'We muddle along & enjoy ourselves.'[31] A few days later he revealed in a sealed letter that they had indeed gone up the line and suffered many casualties, some to frostbite. On a personal level, however, there was a significant development. A small drawing he had done 'of a certain important position under fire' had been seen by his commanding officer, who asked Hill to make an enlarged version that could be sent back to the regimental headquarters as a record of the HAC's achievement.[32] This was perhaps the first sign of another direction in which his artistic skills could take him. Eyewitness drawings depicting the military campaign could be valuable additions to the regiment's historical records.

Indeed, there is a small, faint drawing in the HAC's archive, showing in sharp detail a section of ruined building and a few shattered trees in the foreground with a partially wooded landscape receding behind it. It is captioned 'Baillescourt Farm' and then, in softer pencil, Hill has added, 'In no man's land'.[33] The top of the paper has been burned as though it has been held too close to the flame of a candle, perhaps as Hill tried to make his copy. The regiment also has in its collection a larger version. Like the original, it is drawn in pencil but with some shaded areas and darker lines. Flecks of red chalk pick out the damaged brickwork and tiles. In the foreground Hill has added craters and he has adapted the landscape behind so that it seems enveloped in mist, conveying an even greater sense of desolation.

Hill somehow managed to evoke a sense of the extreme cold in this and other artworks from this time. For example, a drawing from 1917 shows the ruined village of Mesnil lying under deep snow. He has used a very small amount of coloured chalk in addition to the pencil and black ink, and although the yellow ochre and rust red are warm hues, they are applied in such a sparing and muted fashion that they serve only to intensify the contrasts in his depiction of the frozen, snow-bound village. The wrecked buildings, as casualties themselves, lie against a yellow-grey sky and the depth of the frost is almost palpable.

The HAC's operations in the Ancre valley were not yet over. The battalion was called back into the line from 21 to 28 February, attacking Beauregarde, Dovecot and Gudgeon Trench. In a letter that appears to be written on 28 February 1917,

Hill seems excited, almost beside himself. He describes drawing in no-man's-land, slithering into a shell hole, becoming covered in mud and recovering himself, as though it were an entertaining escapade. The letter could be read as bitter irony: 'Taking the joy ride on the whole I wouldn't have missed it for the world.'[34] On the other hand, his flippant dismissal of the dangers is accompanied by a suggestion of genuine elation:

> If you could have seen your little Joe in a shell hole in no man's land sketching & loving the birds for singing whilst the shells were whistling over us – you would have felt anxious – I'm sure of it. But I had heavenly luck all the way through.[35]

The battalion must by this date have been severely depleted and the troops exhausted, but they had significant achievements to the unit's credit and this may, in part, explain Hill's hyper reaction. After weeks of hardship punctuated by periods of violent conflict and extreme danger, there was at last some prospect of respite. Not only had he escaped unscathed, but through his daring actions Hill had proved himself an asset to the regiment and in more than one sense had drawn something from the chaos.

Years later, in 1930, Hill wrote an account for *The Graphic* recalling a time when he was asked to make a detailed drawing of a tree that the Germans were using as an observation post. The skylarks were singing then too and the weather was fine as he ventured forward of the front line. 'I advanced in short rushes, mostly on my hands and knees with my sketching kit dangling round my neck.'[36] Once he was near enough, he lay on his stomach resting the sketchbook on the ground to make his sketch: 'At first I was too excited to draw with any certainty of touch, but as I recovered my breath, and no shell came to disturb my labours, I made a deliberate drawing.'[37] Whistling as he drew, he managed to capture every detail of the trees, and then, pulling the sketchbook out of the thick mud, he crept back to the line, diving into craters when shell screams or nearby explosions demanded it. The accuracy of his drawing enabled the artillery to target the disguised observation post precisely. Hill's memory of this incident as something almost pleasurable and satisfying seems to support the idea that as long as he was drawing he had a way of coping with the war.

A Private with Special Privileges
From that point on, Hill's role was established, and when the HAC fought again in April at Gavrelle he was there to document it in the dual capacity of artist/scout. Increasingly he worked up sketches when he could find a table in a billet, producing enlargements for the HAC command. Sometimes he would be asked to make particular reconnaissance drawings, but there were also times when he was at liberty to choose for himself. In an interview with the Imperial War Museum towards the end of his life, Hill recalled this period:

> I think in the end it was 'anything that's opposite to us would be interesting to record'. So I was given a lot of privileges to do the villages, and the general terrain for record purposes. You know, 'This is what it was like.'[38]

Given this position as a 'private with special privileges', he was able to make his own artistic decisions:

> In a way I was not always under orders. Mostly the things that struck me as being so horrific, or so unreal, that I thought I must get this down, because this will never happen again. Trees will never be blasted like this. Holes can't be made in any building like this, or a whole village completely obliterated, just the stark remains, the skylarks singing above.[39]

Artists at the Somme

Hill was not the only artist to have been a witness to the battle of the Somme. The Scottish printmaker Muirhead Bone was commissioned in July 1916 to make drawings for the government's propaganda unit, known as Wellington House. He was the first of a number of war artists to be employed on a similar basis when the Ministry of Information later took over this role. Bone made sketches on site, albeit mostly from behind the lines. The illustrator E.H. Shepard, who later became known for drawing Winnie the Pooh, had a commission in the Royal Artillery and in addition to many humorous sketches, he also produced atmospheric watercolours showing the effect of artillery blasts on the rural landscape. Other examples are given in Paul Gough's survey, *'A Terrible Beauty': British Artists in the First World War*, which pays careful attention to artists who were making reconnaissance sketches and smaller drawings, as well as the more famous artists such as Paul Nash.

These were professional artists, but the work of amateurs also has value as an insight into wartime experience. Private Atherton, mentioned above, found time to do some sketching. His small battered sketchbooks contain drawings of billets – farmhouses, barns, tents – and sometimes the villages and countryside nearby. Some of these appear at first glance as peaceful rustic scenes, with small figures sitting chatting, washing hung out on the line and summer trees, until you notice that every single building is a ruin. The sky of a picturesque rural landscape is punctured by the addition of exploding shells, which are depicted according to a standard cartoon convention: a point surrounded by radiating lines and a few swift curves to indicate the clouds of smoke. Such artworks are scarcely startling or radical examples of war art. The wrecked buildings are attractively quaint. The depiction of shelling is safely contained within a stylised format. However, the worn, fragile, discoloured paper of Atherton's sketchbooks gives them the air and the affective power of an authentic record. Produced with limited means and economically used materials, and employing the artistic conventions that were familiar to him at the time, they show details of daily life in war.

Officers sometimes had greater freedom to draw. For example, Robert Charles Perry, who served with the 10th Gloucester's and gained a Military Cross for action at the Somme, maintained his artistic activity throughout the war. His early drawings from the Gallipoli campaign are in pen and ink, but once he found a set of watercolours on the dead body of another man he began making the most vivid, colourful images of landscapes, towns and billets. He later added labels, which provide further significant information about the circumstances in which they were drawn. For example, the painting *Gunners' Farm: Le Touquet Sector*, of December 1916, was apparently drawn while wearing a gas mask. Another, from August 1916, is entitled *Sarton, Somme: A Good Billet*. It shows an apparently peaceful scene of a man sitting reading a newspaper or looking at a map in the sunny courtyard of a rustic farmhouse, but in stark contrast the label states, 'The man in the sketch was a week later buried with all the other Company batmen by a shell. Three were killed: this man was rescued alive but was seriously injured by a trenching tool while being dug out.'[40]

Drawing for the Record

At the same time that Adrian Hill was slithering around in the Ancre valley, plans were being set in motion on the other side of the English Channel. On 27 February 1917 a memorandum from Sir Alfred Mond to the War Cabinet proposed a National War Museum. Its function would be to collect and preserve military trophies and gather publications, maps and pictures relating to the war. Exhibitions of such items would serve not only to boost public morale as the war dragged on, but to provide a commemorative function in the future. The Cabinet approved the idea on 5 March. Later in 1917, the drawings that Hill sent back to the HAC were seen by those associated with the new museum. Hill himself was slightly wounded in August and was granted his first home leave for thirteen months. He took the opportunity to present his drawings in person to the museum's officials. The director-general, Sir Martin Conway, was impressed with them, and on 1 October he wrote to Field Marshal Sir Douglas Haig: 'We have to-day received eight admirable drawings from the war-area done by Private Adrian Hill, H.A.C. They are among the very best war-drawings I have yet found. I think this artist is excellently suited to do the work we need.'[41] A few days later Hill was issued with a pass stating that he was working for the National War Museum and had permission to paint and sketch in the area controlled by the Third Army. On 27 December 1917 he was granted an honorary commission as a second lieutenant and was officially seconded to the War Trophies Section of the Imperial War Museum, as it was by then named.

In retrospect, the role of the War Trophies Section in 1917–18 seems extraordinary. The war was being documented for posterity even as it was being most fiercely fought. On the one hand, every sort of shell was being supplied to the front from both sides with deadly purpose. On the other hand, samples of the same were being picked up from the battlefields, preserved and catalogued as relics for the planned museum. A specimen of every sort was required – bullet, shell, equipment, badge, uniform – from large guns to de-lousing apparatus. Hill's role was to generate authentic pictorial records from the battle zones. In the early part of his secondment to the War Trophies Section he had considerable freedom and made a number of drawings of the war-torn landscapes of France. Trees shorn of their branches by shelling were a subject that preoccupied him, and given his love of woods and foliage must have saddened him. He also produced careful linear drawings of wrecked towns, showing buildings with sides ripped away so that only a skeletal structure within remained. His artistic approach was to invest the insensate and the inanimate with feeling and life and show that 'everything suffers'.[42]

The museum later issued more specific directions. In June 1918 Hill was requested to draw particular topics, such as soldiers from the colonies working on engineering projects. The museum, through its collecting policy, had by then gathered numerous works of art from other artists, including those whose names were known for their Modernist approach to the topic of war, such as C.R.W. Nevinson and the brothers John and Paul Nash. Hill was not regarded in that category. The museum's secretary, Charles ffoulkes, put it bluntly: 'It is suggested that we have now sufficient records of the devastated landscape type.'[43]

Hill did not have the chance to return to Britain to work on a bigger scale in oils – a requirement for getting oneself noticed as a painter at the time. The museum kept him continually occupied making reportage drawings for the rest of the war and into 1919. Everything had to be portable, and although he made larger copies from his sketches, he was restricted to a size that he could, in practice, work on in a tent or billet. Two sample oil paintings were rejected by the museum in February 1919 and he was told to stick to drawings. In consequence, Hill has been seen in the literature on war art as a journalistic reporter of the war, making documentary records rather than significant artworks.[44] He had a prodigious ability to draw and paint using a range of techniques, but his work did not have the startling novelty of works such as those by Nevinson or the Nash brothers. Hill admired their work, on being interviewed, citing for example, John Nash's painting of Oppy Wood.[45] In that painting, the broken trees, pitted landscape and torn clouds have a stripped-down quality that could only have been drawn from the reduced reserve of memory rather than from the fullness of direct observations.

'A Certain Liveliness'

In the first draft of an unfinished autobiography that Hill began in the early years of the 1920s he reveals how much he missed the war:

> How can I explain that? I hated the war – in spasms, then I grew used to it, as I grew up in it. And then almost imperceptibly pre-war days became dim, unreal & finally remembered only as a kind of first time on earth. And then? Well the war somehow got hold of me, and life became very vital – a militant rival to death. Existence, from day to day, was held most precious.[46]

The practice of drawing brought Hill pleasure during the war, perhaps helping him to stop hating it. Artistic activity – and presumably the creative exercise of writing letters also – provided him with a sense of vitality and purposefulness, and the message that art could promote well-being, even in the most desperate of circumstances, was one that he continued to communicate throughout his life.

Notes

1. Adrian Hill, letter addressed to 'Dearest Ones both', 21 July 1916. Over 260 of Hill's letters to his parents from the period July 1916 to March 1919 are in the Liddle Collection at Special Collections, Leeds University Library.

2. Adrian Hill, letter, 21 July 1916, p. 4, Liddle Collection.
3. Hogan, Susan, *Healing Arts: The History of Art Therapy* (Jessica Kingsley Publishers, 2001), p. 25.
4. Adrian Hill, Interview with Joseph C. Darracott, Imperial War Museum, 1975, catalogue number 561. Speaking at the age of 80, Hill is a fluent and engaging raconteur and still keen to promote the benefits of artistic activity.
5. HMSO, *Manual of Map Reading and Field Sketching* (1912).
6. Atherton, H., *During the War: World War I The Western Front 1914–1918* (typescript recollections), p. 92. Liddle Collection, WW1/GS/0057.
7. J. Nash, Interview with Joseph C. Darracott, Imperial War Museum, 1974, catalogue number 323, Reel 1.
8. Adrian Hill, letter, 30 July 1916, p. 3, Liddle Collection.
9. Adrian Hill, letter, c.18 August 1916, Liddle Collection.
10. Adrian Hill, letter, 11 August 1916, Liddle Collection.
11. Adrian Hill, letter, 13 August 1916, p. 2, Liddle Collection.
12. Ibid.
13. Adrian Hill, letter, 23 July 1916, Liddle Collection.
14. Adrian Hill, letter, 26 July 1916, Liddle Collection.
15. Adrian Hill, letter, 16 August 1916, p. 1, Liddle Collection.
16. Ibid.
17. Ibid., p. 2.
18. Adrian Hill, letter, c.20 September 1916, Liddle Collection.
19. A letter from the HAC to Adrian Hill, dated 16 February 1976, in the Liddle Collection states that Hill joined the 1st Battalion on 26 November 1916. A letter from Hill to his parents dated 27 November 1916 mentions their understandable shock at learning of his move from the Entrenching Battalion. All dates for HAC actions are taken from Goold Walker, G., *Honourable Artillery Company 1537–1987* (Honourable Artillery Company, 1986).
20. Adrian Hill, letter, 5 November 1916. A date of 20 November has been added later. Liddle Collection.
21. Adrian Hill, letter, 8 December 1916, Liddle Collection.
22. The watercolour, *Pozières: An Australian Episode*, is in the Imperial War Museum, Art.IWM ART 322. The pencil sketch *On the Somme 1916*, which is dated 1916, is in the HAC archives at Armoury House, London.
23. Adrian Hill, letter, 18 January 1916, Liddle Collection.
24. Adrian Hill, letter, 22 January 1917, Liddle Collection.
25. Ibid.
26. Adrian Hill, letter, 24 January 1917, Liddle Collection.
27. Ibid.
28. Hill, Adrian, *Reconnaissance Sketch Showing Position of Light Railway & Martinsart Road Looking South*, c.1917, pencil, ink and paper, 290 × 228mm.
29. Adrian Hill, letter, 27 January 1917, Liddle Collection.
30. Adrian Hill, letter, 4 February 1917, Liddle Collection.
31. Adrian Hill, letter, 6 February 1917, Liddle Collection.
32. Adrian Hill, letter, 18 February 1917, Liddle Collection.
33. Hill, Adrian, *Baillescourt Farm*, c.1917, pencil and paper, 203 × 136mm.
34. Adrian Hill, letter, dated 'Wed 28th'. It is not clear which month or year this applies to; later additions suggest December 1916 but the content of the letter and the day of the week are more consistent with the events of February 1917.
35. Ibid.
36. Hill, Adrian, 'An Artist in War and Peace', in *The Graphic*, 15 November 1930, p. 303.
37. Ibid.
38. Adrian Hill, Interview, Imperial War Museum, 1975, catalogue number 561, Reel 1.
39. Ibid.
40. Robert Charles Perry, label on reverse of painting of 21 August 1916, Liddle Collection.
41. Martin Conway, letter to Field Marshal Sir Douglas Haig, 1 October 1917. Imperial War Museum, Adrian Hill war artist archive, ART/WA1/084.

42. Adrian Hill, Interview, Imperial War Museum, 1975, catalogue number 561, Reel 5.
43. Charles ffoulkes, letter to Adrian Hill, 14 June 1918. Imperial War Museum, Correspondence with Adrian Hill, ART/WA1/482.
44. Despite his status as their first official war artist, Adrian Hill is not mentioned in the Imperial War Museum's publication *Art from The First World War* (2008).
45. The painting's full title is *Oppy Wood, 1917. Evening* and it was painted in 1918.
46. Hill, Adrian, *A Certain Liveliness*, manuscript autobiography, pp. 1–2, Liddle Collection.

Suggested Further Reading

Campbell, James, *Shepard's War* (London: LOM Art, 2015)
Gough, Paul, *'A Terrible Beauty': British Artists in the First World War* (Bristol: Sansom & Co., 2009)
Harries, Meirion and Susie, *The war artists: British Official War Art of the Twentieth Century* (Michael Joseph in association with the Imperial War Museum and the Tate Gallery, 1983)
Hill, Adrian, *Art Versus Illness: A Story of Art Therapy* (London: George Allen & Unwin, 1945)
Hill, Adrian, *On Drawing and Painting Trees* (Oxford: Oxford University Press, 1936)
Imperial War Museum, *Art from the First World War* (2008)
Malvern, Sue, *Modern Art, Britain and the Great War: Witnessing, Testimony & Remembrance* (New Haven CT and London, 2004)

Chapter 21

Vestiges of the Home Front: An Archaeological Approach to Recording the Great War Landscape in Britain

By Emily Glass *and* Nicholas J. Saunders

Introduction

This chapter highlights the level to which the British[1] home front was militarised during the years of the Great War. This occurred on an unprecedented scale over a relatively short time, yet its influence persisted in the physical landscape and society throughout the twentieth century to the present day. While there has been significant public interest in the Great War for many years, archaeological research has become increasingly poignant as the last veterans of the conflict have passed away and the war era disappears from living memory. This chapter will discuss the vast breadth of research potential for an archaeological study of the home front. It will also examine what impact the centenary has for generating and collating knowledge for the future, as great numbers of people are re-engaged with the conflict of 100 years ago. These issues will be examined through a recent pilot project which created an archaeological research methodology for use by volunteers to document traces of the Great War in their locality.

Currently, the home front archaeological record is inadequately understood in terms of the extent, survival and condition of the remaining built heritage and material culture. It was this deficiency which led to the initiation of a pilot project, known as *The Home Front (1914–18) and its Legacies*, to demonstrate the depth and diversity of Great War urban and rural landscape change. We shall outline the approach used in the pilot and synthesise some of the results taken from the final report.[2] The methodology employed by volunteers to record Great War buildings, places and spaces – all termed in an archaeological manner as 'sites' – will also be discussed and the benefits of incorporating these results into local and national heritage listings will be highlighted.

An Archaeological Approach

An archaeological approach to studying Great War legacies within the streets and spaces of twenty-first-century Britain does not require actual excavation. The 'digging' is metaphorical, and is undertaken in archives to generate documentary evidence – maps and photographs – to illustrate the wartime use of a particular building, place or space. Once collated, a field trip is undertaken to test the validity of the information, confirm the recorded location, make an assessment of any visible remains and document current land-use. Any new photographs, notes or sketches taken on the field survey can be added to existing records and enable comparisons to be made against previous investigations. The benefits of taking this approach towards the Great War on the home front are immense. This can be demonstrated through the emphasis on encompassing a broad research scope, or at least one that extends beyond the military establishment, and an approach which uses the widest range of documentary sources possible. In addition, the desire accurately to record the location of a place in the landscape is crucial for undertaking spatial analysis. In more specialist terms, this technique uses historical archaeology and modern conflict archaeology, which encompass elements of social archaeology, public archaeology and anthropological archaeology, and is one of the many so-called 'archaeologies of the contemporary past'.[3]

Modern conflict archaeology is an anthropologically informed interdisciplinary approach towards conflicts of the twentieth and twenty-first centuries. It incorporates social, cultural, psychological and technological matters in addition to the military complexities surrounding recent conflict. Conflicts and their powerful and unpredictable legacies are a multi-faceted phenomenon which may leave a variety of physical and social traces in many different places, rather than being solely restricted to the detritus of a battlefield. These vestiges of wartime can possess multiple meanings that may change over time as new experiences and memories are endured by people and their environs.[4] It was through these concepts, combined with an increased level of public interest, that the centennial period was viewed as the opportunity to improve our comprehension of the Great War through the focus of change to the wartime landscape.

Research Potential on the Home Front

The landscape of Britain was transformed on an unprecedented scale to facilitate the needs of an ever-demanding war operating on an indeterminate timescale. It was crucial to respond quickly to these wartime needs on an industrial scale, despite the financial cost. This was compounded by continuous military, technological and mechanical innovation and production. This was the socio-economic setting for four years of home front militarisation that ultimately left an enduring imprint on the physical landscape and on the collective psyche of the British people.

These vestiges of the Great War are embedded in the fabric of urban and rural landscapes, but the extent to which they are recognised and understood is variable. A greater awareness of what occurred on home soil would enable a deeper appreciation of how people and places were affected by the pressures of a war that concerned all sectors of society. Away from the trenches, innumerable catastrophic events occurred on the home front resulting in an indiscriminate loss of military and civilian lives. Shelling of coastal towns by German warships, bombing by aircraft or Zeppelins, explosions at munitions factories, accidents in military training and in transportation of troops or munitions, all took their toll. These incidents were memorialised in the minds of local people and family members as well as physically by way of commemorative tributes. Areas that suffered such an ordeal are indelibly scarred – an enduring legacy of the Great War and its consequences.

Locations with tragic associations by no means dominate the British home front landscape legacy. There remain many, many buildings, places and spaces which were utilised or adapted for a wartime purpose or manufactured a product which differed from the building's or (location's) pre-war function. These relatively short-lived changes may not be commonly perceived or widely documented but they are all crucial components in the story of how town and country engineered a militarised home front. To prepare, supply and cope with the demands of the Great War, innumerable town hall, church, school and domestic buildings were converted into refugee shelters and temporary hospitals. Areas of land were requisitioned or donated for military training or to increase food production, while factories were given war contracts to supply the country with what was necessary to sustain the national war effort. In some instances, these adapted functions were maintained beyond the 1918 Armistice, as demonstrated by medical facilities tending to the needs of wounded, sick and convalescing soldiers until the early 1920s.

Away from the obvious military nature of the home front, there is the potential for an archaeological study of the landscape to be truly inclusive and reflect social, gender, religious, ethnic or underprivileged experiences. The Great War was a uniquely literate war, whereby the experiences of all classes were documented through diaries and letters sent to and from the trenches. The diaries and papers of prominent persons who operated during the conflict were usually deposited in local and national archives and have since been thoroughly examined. Comparable material was produced by many soldiers and civilians on the home front, including the diaries of young children, such as those contained within the Liddle Collection at the University of Leeds. These voices of the conflict made fundamental contributions to the creation and progression of post-war society and their narratives are embedded within their home front experience. It is possible to draw them out through an examination of archaeological and architectural Great War legacies on local, regional and national societal levels to create a broader appreciation of wartime events.

The Great War was an inclusive conflict, meaning the majority of people today have at least one relative who went to war, while the remainder were affected on home soil. A significant amount of community research regarding wartime places, people and events has been undertaken by local groups and societies over the past 100 years. This work has been shared on a regional level through talks, publications and contributions to local newspaper articles. Studies of this type are usually intensely researched by people who have an intimate and life-long knowledge of their physical and social environs. This enables members to assign names to people in otherwise anonymous photographs and utilise the minutiae of their local landscape to comprehend the layers of wartime modification and subsequent changes that have occurred. In some cases, collections include varied source material such as taped interviews recollecting life during the First World War and contemporary magazines which detail local events or stories. These works represent a goldmine of home front information, but their distribution is often limited to the locality in which they were created.

The centenary of the Great War provides an opportunity to remember the sacrifices made by those in the military and civilians who suffered and grieved, as well as those whose lives were physically and mentally damaged in the aftermath of war. In addition, this important milestone of historical significance can provide us with a unique opportunity to consider home front research, re-evaluate previous studies and undertake new investigations. Projects can cover a broad range of subjects and utilise specific themes to generate interest and encourage the community to get involved. Studies that focus on the landscape and material culture of the home front can employ aspects of the military, art, literature, poetry, genealogy, regiments, gender, war-work, refugees, war diaries, hospitals, rationing or industrial and agricultural practices to consider Great War legacies. These vestiges are as diverse as they are profound, meaning that their complex spheres of enquiry will inevitably overlap and intertwine.[5]

The archaeological heritage of this period has already benefited from projects carried out across Britain, capitalising on the upsurge in interest due to the centenary. These have primarily been funded by grants from the Heritage Lottery Fund, which since 2010 has awarded over £70 million to more than 1,300 projects exploring Great War heritage. The majority of these projects involve community level collaborations and encourage findings to be disseminated through public events and exhibitions. These endeavours are accomplished through the capacity and willingness of the participants who donate their time to ensure that project aspirations are achieved. Ultimately, this centenary-driven body of work will make a significant contribution towards new digital resources, exhibitions, educational trails and commemorative legacies that will improve the comprehension of Britain's role in the Great War.

The Home Front (1914–18) and its Legacies Pilot

The Council for British Archaeology led the *Defence of Britain* project (1995–2002), which engaged almost 600 volunteers to record the physical remains of roughly 17,000 Second World War military structures across the UK.[6] The results were provided to local and national heritage agencies to enhance their twentieth-century modern conflict archaeology listings, quantify the existing Second World War resource and consider protection outcomes. It was anticipated that by using a similar archaeological approach towards the vestiges of the First World War, it would be possible to document buildings, places and spaces which reflected civilian as well as military involvement across the home front. This led to the creation of a pilot project, *The Home Front (1914–18) and its Legacies*, which was aimed at establishing the feasibility, public appetite and potential for investigating the heritage of the Great War within local communities.

The pilot study was funded by Historic England[7] as part of its wider agenda to record the Great War footprint left on the fabric, landscape and coastal waters of England. The investigation was conducted by the Universities of Bristol and York with coordinated volunteer researchers during 2012–13. A methodological framework was created which would enable people systematically to research, locate and document sites within the two case study test areas of Staffordshire and the Lea Valley in Greater London. These regions were chosen as they contained a rich diversity of Great War remains and had both hosted recent archaeological research, including excavation, on wartime military installations. Upon completion of the pilot project, eight groups had documented a total of 111 sites in these two areas.

The methodological framework and critical feedback from the pilot experience were supplied in support of a national-level recording project called *Home Front Legacy*. This Great War initiative is scheduled to run throughout the centenary and is being coordinated by the Council for British Archaeology with funding from Historic England, Historic Environment Scotland[8] and Cadw[9]. Using an online documentation system, this project encourages community groups and individuals to identify and map elements of the Great War landscape.[10] An archaeological handbook for this project has recently been published which details the specifics of how to undertake the research and covers the range of places that could be recorded on land and at sea.[11]

Recording Scope

Landscape modifications in response to the Great War did not simply stop after November 1918; indeed, a robust influence was sustained across the twentieth century. This can be revealed through the abundance of war memorials and the erection of memorial halls, schools, gardens, sports facilities and Lloyd George's 'homes fit for heroes'. These types of commemorative structure, along with statues, plaques and free-standing war memorials, are material representations of bereavement. They can hold the details of dates, people, regiments and places which, in the case of those with no known grave, have since become the physical embodiment of the missing. The memorialisation of the Great War dead is an ongoing phenomenon, and one which has intensified as the centenary approached. This has been demonstrated by recent works to repair or conserve existing war memorials and construct new monuments. One of the most recent commemorative structures to be unveiled is located at the National Memorial Arboretum in Staffordshire and is the first dedicated statue to honour the contribution of Sikh soldiers who fought in the Great War.[12] This twenty-first-century war memorial is the physical manifestation of 130,000 men whose sacrifice has been newly symbolised and therefore remembered in the present, a century after the conflict.

Considering this depth of impact, it could be argued that the recording scope for *The Home Front (1914–18) and its Legacies* pilot could have included much of this memorialisation and necessary post-war redevelopment. However, in order to keep the research tightly focused, all home front examinations were bounded within the Great War years of 1914–18. If a degree of flexibility were required for sites that dated to beyond the close of 1918, then they could be considered for inclusion under the 'legacies' aspect. These parameters were also beneficial in avoiding any overlap with other commemorative initiatives, primarily those which had been instigated by the War Memorials Trust and the Imperial War Museum.[13] Within the scope of the pilot project, there remained significant potential for recording formal and informal wartime memorials – as the typology of these extends beyond the obvious – and landscapes and buildings which were produced, recreated or reshaped during the four-and-a-half years of war. Some of these would still be extant in their physical form, whereas others may only be traceable via personal knowledge, archives or local library research.

Since the Great War a century of change, redevelopment and the loss of industrial and manufacturing facilities means that key indicators of that particular home front conflict landscape have been lost. Historic England recently completed an assessment of Great War National Factories in England which has revealed that some physical elements survive at only 46 out of 174 sites. These remains range from standing buildings to earthworks on the ground as evidence of their previous land-use function.[14] This illustrates why it was of paramount importance for the pilot project to document all sites within the landscape, whether visible or not, to comprehend the full degree of home front militarisation. When recorded and mapped, this would reveal the true extent of urban and rural landscape change over the years of war by making visible what was hitherto invisible.

Research Strategy

It was important that the pilot project methods for undertaking research and documentation were accessible and usable, and could enable volunteers of all ages to get involved in recording built heritage and archaeological traces of the Great War. The first task for the volunteer groups was to create a brief inventory containing different types of site within their local environment, from which a representative sample would be selected for investigation in the field. This was achieved by examining the contents of archives or any collections that could be accessed to find buildings, spaces or places that were created or modified as a response to the Great War. Visits to local authority Historic Environment Record (HER) offices and the use of their online resources via the Heritage Gateway website were encouraged as this was where the pilot data would eventually be deposited. However, it was noted that within the Historic Environment Record it was predominantly the better known places, such as the Royal Ordnance Factory at Enfield or the Cannock Chase camps in Staffordshire, that had their 1914–18 wartime phase of use indexed. For many of the sites that were requisitioned or donated for the war effort, particularly eighteenth- or nineteenth-century country houses, there was no information regarding their change of use during the Great War. The pilot project hoped to address this by facilitating the production of quality data to enable Great War phases of use to be indexed.

It was decided only to record sites which had associated documentary evidence to verify their wartime role; anecdotal stories were not sufficient proof to enable inclusion. The volunteers established that photographic images were particularly useful to assist with the inventory of sites, as were contemporary maps. These not only helped to comprehend sites which have since been destroyed, but were also of benefit for places which are still extant, so a comparison of the landscape between then and now could be made. In addition, local newspapers were identified as an invaluable resource for identifying sites and for detailing the minutiae of local life during the war. Finally the internet was mentioned as a useful and rich resource for background knowledge, ideas for possible sites and for finding information on people, institutions and places which no longer exist.[15]

Throughout the twentieth century a significant amount of research regarding wartime places, people and events has been undertaken by local groups and societies. Collectively this has generated a major resource which is usually disseminated through local publications, talks and open days, which means it tends to have a very local distribution. Collections such as these often include varied source material such as taped interviews recollecting details of Great War life and contemporary local magazines which illustrate events and capture the mood. The pilot project group operating in the Enfield region of the Lea Valley used a locally produced book, *Enfield at War 1914–18*, to document sites. This 1982 publication used council minutes and local newspapers to detail wartime events and reveal the region's contribution to the war effort. The aim of the book's author was to 'rescue some stories from oblivion for future generations',[16] which was realised when the publication was updated and re-released for the centenary.[17] Nuanced wartime accounts such as these are invaluable as they reveal the physical and social changes required on the home front and they should be consulted prior to any investigation.

Recording Methodology
A proforma sheet, known as a Site Report Form, was designed to record the details of each Great War site. These forms were completed by the volunteers during their field visits to the places they were recording. Each site required detailed information, including the name, location, description, type of site, construction materials, any associated documentation, names of people associated with the site and names of the volunteers who recorded it. Details of the current nature of site use, present condition and any visible or known threats were given as supporting information. Additional provision was made to collate any myths, folklore or commonly acknowledged hearsay about the site to give weight to local perception. The possibility of linking named people to a particular wartime place, especially when evidenced through photographs, is a particularly poignant and pertinent undertaking. There are innumerable anonymous faces captured in images of the home front that could potentially be identified and future-proofed through this combination of detailed local knowledge and archival research.

The position of each site was recorded as a twelve-figure National Grid Reference number to enable a locational accuracy of within 1m. This was crucial to generate pins in the pilot home front map of sites, which, when clicked, would display some of the information from the Site Report Form. If used on a much wider scale of recording, this spatial data would enable home front activity hotspots to be identified and draw attention to areas which were much less affected. Mapping site data in this way acts as a visual tool to demonstrate the impact of the Great War on the landscape and communities of Britain by highlighting the scale of the physical and social reorganisation that took place.

It was a mandatory requirement that some of the Site Report Form recording adhered to a standardised format which would enable the data to be passed on to heritage bodies. Primarily, this was through the creation and use of a Great War

Site Type thesaurus to facilitate consistency in recording and allow sites to be absorbed into regional Historic Environment Record and national Historic England lists. Two of the most commonly used Site Type thesaurus terms were 'Requisitioned Building' and 'Requisitioned Land', which demonstrated the degree to which the landscape was reconfigured during the conflict. Some sites were subject to multiple uses or changed their function over the war years. This was illustrated by the pilot project's recording of Alexandra Palace, which initially housed Belgian refugees, but from 1915 operated as an internment camp for Austrian and German civilians.

One of the intentions of the pilot project was to explore and test how Great War events or occurrences on the home front could be recorded. This would allow the social dimensions of landscape to be considered and enable incidents that took place over a broad area, rather than in a specific place, to be documented. In this way royal or celebrity visits, parades, fund-raising, military sports days, outings and entertainment for injured soldiers, recruitment drives and demonstrations, riots, and any other happenings of note could all be researched and added to the map. It was in this manner that the pilot project recorded the location of a 'day-too-early' announcement of the outbreak of war at a bandstand in Enfield, a tank-led military recruitment drive in Hackney and the locations of three 1919 peace celebration events.[18] Despite the level of post-war redevelopment in these areas, the volunteers were able to use an intimate knowledge of their local historical landscapes to pinpoint these locations in the present.

Volunteer Engagement
By definition, 'engagement' is a two-way process involving listening and interaction to generate mutual benefit. Projects which include a collaborative element need proactively to manage the expectations and abilities of participants and consider how best to raise skill levels and build confidence rather than alienate potential volunteers. This is best achieved by developing project objectives within a community-building framework to ensure that the aspirations of both sides are structured effectively and consistently throughout the duration of any work. The wider impact of involvement in a scheme such as this pilot project is validated when people feel empowered and inspired to make contributions towards other community projects.[19] This has been demonstrated by some of the pilot volunteers who have subsequently sought involvement with other Great War centenary projects utilising the skills and confidence gained during their pilot experience.[20] Another group has incorporated the work members did for the pilot into a Great War exhibition at Waltham Abbey Town Hall and the group has continued to unearth interesting information about wartime life through the local museum.[21]

There are obvious benefits in collaborating with groups which have an extensive knowledge of their local area, people and associated histories. This potential memory bank of regional information is a crucial advantage for local-level Great War research, particularly when taking a century of change into consideration. Local research projects can capture the essence of communities and demonstrate the importance of forging links between generations and improving communication between diversities. The pilot project engaged a total of twenty-three people undertaking the research and recording Great War sites. Upon completion, each volunteer (or group) was asked to complete a feedback form and provide information on the experience. Through this they were able to assess the archives or resources they used, critique the recording methodology and make suggestions for the future. Some volunteers noted that they had not only discovered and mapped new Great War sites in their local area, but also generated a deeper level of understanding for established places.

Pilot Results

The sites recorded by the pilot project have been divided into five broad themes for discussion: civilian, domestic and agriculture; military, defence and training; hospitals and convalescent care; industrial and manufacturing; and finally, memorials and gravestones. This grouping was facilitated by the use of Historic England's Great War thesaurus of Site Types. Although there are inevitable crossovers, the standardisation enabled by the thesaurus permitted consistency throughout the pilot records to create a uniform and searchable dataset. It is not the intention of this chapter to discuss each recorded site in detail, rather to give a concise overview of the pilot findings within each category and illustrate this with case studies. A complete description of sites recorded by the pilot can be found within the final report, which is available online as a free download via Historic England's website.[22]

Civilian, Domestic and Agriculture

The key to comprehending how the home front was militarised is to move away from considering only those places identified solely with the military. There was an inordinate reconfiguration of everyday spaces within towns, cities and the countryside 'over here' as a response to the war that was going on 'over there'. These changes were initiated soon after war was announced as people gathered in meeting halls to hold public information meetings, form civil committees and organise war effort groups to raise funds for a range of purposes.

Civil defence groups were set up, which, having no pre-war precedent or base, organised recruitment in school halls and nightly patrols from members' houses. Domestic dwellings were offered by women who took part in the war effort by sheltering Belgian refugees or accommodating army personnel. Group activities would also take place in houses, often those belonging to middle-class women who arranged recycling collections, war work and afternoon teas for injured soldiers. The pilot project recorded the house of Miss Edwards in Newcastle-under-Lyme, who registered her house as a war hospital supply depot in 1915. From here, she coordinated work parties of ladies who would meet and stitch garments, create roller and triangular bandages, swabs and dressings, knit and cut patterns for the war effort.

To counteract food shortages, rural areas and green spaces were requisitioned or encouraged to be turned over for growing food, and farms were enlarged to boost production levels. The pilot recorded a school playing field and a golf course that were both converted into allotments and the site of Vernon's pig farm which extended its footprint to house more animals. It was noted that during the war a lady from Vernon's farm was nicknamed 'Boudicca' by the locals as she drove a float around the area collecting food scraps to feed to her pigs.[23] This 'make-do-and-mend' mentality became increasingly important as the war progressed, and food and fuel shortages began to bite before rationing of those commodities was introduced. To counteract these shortages, logging was undertaken by army troops and the Women's Land Army, and public kitchens were set up in cities to discourage people from cooking in the home. An examination of non-military home front sites such as these can inevitably reveal the level to which everyday places and lives were required to adapt and reconform during the Great War.

Military, Defence and Training

The military response to the Great War on the home front was, as might be expected, phenomenal. Existing army barracks and facilities were soon full to capacity due to the unprecedented numbers of soldiers from home and abroad requiring accommodation while training. Additional buildings, places and spaces were utilised for military organisation, training, supply and mobilisation. Vast networks of service provisions needed to be coordinated over great distances and with prolonged necessity. Disused buildings were taken over by military units and used as organisational headquarters and equipment stores; for example, the pilot study recorded that the Bethel Chapel at Waltham Abbey was used as the Essex Yeomanry's 'C' Squadron store. Newly formed military units were created and quartered in reused buildings or temporary tented camps before departing for the front. This usually began from an official muster point before a parade through town, an event often captured by local newspapers.

Large houses and estates were offered by the owners or requisitioned by the government for conversion into military headquarters and billeting accommodation. Soldiers in various forms of training, including musketry and trench-digging, have sometimes left an enduring legacy on the landscape. The pilot project recorded Folly Farm, near Barnet, which had functioned as a pleasure garden with entertainment, rides and a very large tearoom prior to the war, being requisitioned. The infrastructure meant that the land and buildings were beyond those of an ordinary farm, hence its being taken over for military use. In general, the provision of entertainment and other trades was not usually very far away from where soldiers were billeted. Large camps on rural estates, such as Rugeley and Brocton on Cannock Chase, attracted the setting up of tearooms, dance halls, shops and the postal service. Smaller camps would utilise nearby church halls for snacks, reading, board games and letter writing. Soldiers in convalescence could play cards and table games in patriotically decorated homes or converted shops offered as places of rest and shelter. One such location was recorded by the pilot project in High Barnet, where a former greengrocery shop had been converted into a quiet space for soldiers by the business owner, Mr Davies.

The Great War was, of course, the first time that the home front was threatened by bombardment from the skies. In those first days of the advent of air power, existing airfields were further developed and new home defence airfields established, Stow Maries in Essex being a truly remarkable survivor in terms of architecture as well as location and space. Much construction was needed for air-craft production, airfield use, and accommodation for personnel and administra-tion as the Royal Flying Corps and the Royal Naval Air Service expanded. Sometimes nearby buildings could be utilised for accommodation, for example, an officers' mess or a sick bay.

The aerial threat was to be countered not just by home defence aircraft but by combinations of air defence measures: the installation of barrage balloon aprons, listening posts and fixed sound-recording concave concrete constructions – some of which survive – plus anti-aircraft gun emplacements and searchlights at key vantage points. The evolution of anti-aircraft artillery in the Great War took its pace and character from the development of air power among the European nations. Its emergence was swift.[24] It is believed that most Great War anti-aircraft sites in England were previously identified through Dobinson's 1996 study of twentieth-century fortifications, which located 376 Great War gun positions.[25] This depth of coverage was reflected within the pilot study as all four recorded sites were included in Dobinson's Gazetteer of Great War anti-aircraft sites.[26]

The majority of military sites were dismantled in the aftermath of the Great War, leaving little or no evidence on the ground. However, some of the more substantial installations were reused for the Second World War, when the aerial threat was much more intense.

The legacies of the first strategic aerial bombing campaign in history were observed more acutely in the Lea Valley study area than in Staffordshire. Two bomb sites from the same raid on 31 May/1 June 1915 were recorded by the study. The LZ.38 Zeppelin, commanded by Hauptmann Erich Linnarz, first dropped an incendiary bomb through the roof of a terraced house at 16 Alkham Road, then carried on to hit the garden of the Nevill public house. In its entirety, this par-ticular raid killed seven people and injured thirty-five, and caused £18,596 of damage.[27]

German bombing raids across the home front destroyed infrastructure and buildings and killed civilians, having a very serious impact on the morale of the population. Some of these events were marked by contemporary commemoration and were utilised in propaganda for the war effort.

Councils responded to air raids by providing civilian refuges in existing sub-terranean spaces and sheltered places, including cellars in civic buildings, railway viaducts and Underground stations. The threat from the air was maintained throughout the war as reflected by the 1916 construction of Barnet Court House, which was recorded by the pilot project. This building was used as a first aid post and had a basement air raid shelter capable of holding up to 100 people incor-porated into its design. Employers at high-risk locations such as ports, military transport sites, munitions factories, manufacturing plants and the chemical indus-tries provided on-site shelters for workers. This was the case at the Waltham Abbey Royal Gunpowder Mills, where a series of 2-metre surface air raid shelters were constructed to protect factory staff. The danger from the air was recognised beyond that of protecting workers in key industries, as witnessed, for example, by the survival of an air-raid shelter installed for watercress workers at Waltham Abbey gardens. This site was recorded for the study by members of the Waltham

Abbey Historical Society, whose knowledge of their local environment enabled them to map the location of the shelter and identify the female figure in the wartime photograph as Mrs Julia Pryor.

Hospitals and Convalescent Care

Early in the war it was recognised that existing military medical facilities and additional hospital services within army camps would not be sufficient to cope with the predicted level of casualties. This was counteracted by transferring existing civilian hospitals over for military use, increasing bed capacities and, in due course, adding specialist operating and treatment facilities for amputees, mental health and gas poisoning cases. Further hospital support was supplied by auxiliary and private facilities as well as those run by the Order of St John and by the Red Cross. It was not only the military that required amendments to be made to hospital and treatment provision on the home front. The implication of reduced civilian bed space and changes in the population demographic meant that some specialist medical services were obliged to broaden the scope of their admissions. In Hackney the Mothers' Hospital had previously been for the exclusive use of unmarried mothers but this policy was changed during the Great War to admit married mothers whose husbands were away fighting or who had been killed in the conflict.

After less than a year at war it became necessary to provide further places on the home front to accommodate convalescent soldiers. From March 1915 public and private buildings were requisitioned or offered for use as hospitals to deal with the great numbers of war wounded brought back from overseas. In addition to town halls, schools, church halls and workhouses, this included private residences ranging from terraced houses to large stately homes. Country houses were particularly suited for the treatment of wounded and soldiers in convalescence. They were spacious and quiet, and had large gardens and grounds, all circumstances which aided healing. This was the case at Grovelands House and Park in Southgate, which was recorded as becoming an auxiliary military hospital in July 1916. This grand building had an extension for wooden annexes built out from the colonnaded frontage and specialist gas decontamination facilities were installed in the basement.[28] Local entertainment, musical concerts or outings were often provided for soldiers as part of their recovery. At the time of the Great War the Enfield Palace Cedar and Garden was owned by the Enfield Constitutional Club, which held regular concerts in support of convalescing soldiers, and in Waltham Abbey the owners of Joyce House served teas and entertained wounded soldiers from the nearby town hall military hospital.

Industrial and Manufacturing

Being at war meant that traditional import supply lines were disrupted and foreign contracts could not always be fulfilled. This led to the adaption and expansion of home front manufacturing and processing industries to provide the country and the armed forces with the materials needed for the struggle. Government war contracts were issued to factories across the country to produce whole supply chains from nuts and bolts to weapons and clothing for the army.[29] By guaranteeing manufacturing outputs across trade networks, the government hoped to keep pace with wartime requirements and increase output still further where and when needed.

A colossal increase in munitions output became necessary and in one area this involved the expansion of existing cartridge works and the creation of new facilities. The pilot project recorded the Ponders End Shell Works in Enfield being built in 1916 as a direct response to the increased demand for shells on the Western Front. At its production height it employed 6,000 people, including a large female workforce, on day and night shifts to meet quotas. An examination of how factory buildings changed during the Great War can even illustrate the evolution of the need for a particular type of shell: the high explosive. So insistent became the demands for cordite from the Waltham Abbey Royal Gunpowder Mills that earlier buildings were modified and newly designed facilities were created to produce cordite. An architectural examination can also show how prior societal norms were adapted during the conflict as the size and number of factories increased and additional workers were required. Within the footprint of the Royal Gunpowder Mills, this was manifest through the pilot project's recording of Sandhurst Hospital, which since 1894 had operated as the sole on-site welfare facility for the predominantly male workforce. As this situation changed during the war with greater numbers of female workers, it became necessary to construct an adjacent hospital for women only.

Factories which previously produced non-military items were engaged to fulfil national requirements for an extraordinary quantity of military uniforms and equipment. This led to factories which had produced blouses and coats being turned over to make shirts and tunics, with boot and shoe industries supplying military footwear. Equipment and supplies for military camps were also sourced through adapted production as makers of fine tableware created considerable quantities of canteen crockery. The pottery industry also contributed new items for chemical manufacture by making moulds, acid stoneware tanks, nitrate pans and corrosion-resistant containers. Some continued to create designs for the domestic market, albeit designs that reflected the austerity and attitude of the times. The Grimwade factory at Stoke produced pottery marked with propaganda messages about food economy and cartoons by the British author and humorist Bruce Bairnsfather, depicting his 'Fragments from France' drawings.

Many of the industrial or manufacturing complexes used during the Great War have been lost through a century of closure, relocation and landscape redevelopment. It would be of great benefit to map the location and wartime output of all Great War industrial and manufacturing sites, from large mustard gas complexes to small family clothing companies. In this way the magnitude of reconfiguration could be demonstrated and the home front industrial landscape re-envisaged.

Memorials and Gravestones
It is important to note that any investigation which involves gravestones and memorial inscriptions to the wartime dead is immediately situated within a complex, multi-layered and emotional process that involves different stakeholders, sections of society and politics. The pilot project's methodology was designed to

enable the recording of memorials, commemorations or gravestones for both military and civilian casualties. This could include members of the public or workers who died as a result of the country being at war, due to aerial bombardment, nurses who contracted disease or through disasters at munitions factories or other warfare industries. Military accidents also occurred during training across home front landscapes, seascapes and in the air. Within the confines of this pilot study, some of the volunteers found their examination of memorials and gravestones to be the most moving of all site categories. The young age of the dead and the possibility that the families of non-local soldiers were unable to visit regularly were cited as the main reasons why such recording was an exceptionally poignant experience.

The Great War memorialisation response was immense due to the enormous number of military casualties. Soldiers who died overseas were either interred in cemeteries or mass graves; in cases where no identifiable remains were found, there is no known burial site but their names are incised on huge commemorative structures such as at Thiepval on the Somme or at Ypres. Wounded soldiers were transferred back to the home front for specialist care and rehabilitation. Those who failed to recover, and the many servicemen who succumbed to the 1918/19 influenza pandemic, are interred in military and municipal cemeteries throughout Britain. Numerous formal and informal memorials to the dead and missing were created on the home front. These took the form of local and national rolls of honour, plaques for regiments or individuals, and war memorials. Although occasional wartime examples of these do exist, predominantly they were planned and implemented after November 1918.

In local landscapes, the names of soldiers who went off to the fighting fronts were detailed within informally created 'street shrines' – sometimes the names of regiments too. Such shrines included name lists outside churches and within neighbourhoods. They acted as collection points for donations of cigarettes and chocolates for the men and their regiments. During the war these shrines were ever-changing entities as names were added and crosses put against the names of those who had died. Most street shrines were removed after the war, often in advance of an official war memorial being constructed, although there are rare cases of survival into the present day. Closing a street shrine usually involved a public religious ceremony and as such would undoubtedly have been documented by local newspapers. An examination of press archives would be the most effective way to locate and record these emotive yet transient memorials to the dead.[30]

Conclusion

The imprint of the Great War has been demonstrated by the influence it had on society and the landscape during the inter-war years, through the Second World War, into the Cold War and to the present time. The centennial 2014–18 period is an exceptional opportunity for researchers, groups, schools and academics to contribute towards a deeper understanding of the Great War and its inheritance through commemorative archaeological and architectural projects. In addition, this is a timely opportunity to re-examine previous records, make additions, analyse and possibly correct commonly held myths. The sheer number of centenary projects means it is paramount that partnership-working and sharing are encouraged between groups, archives and national heritage bodies. This creates effective investigation routes and inclusive support to ensure that ventures are successful and any data is sustainably future-proofed.

This type of research should make still clearer that, although the Great War was a relatively short-term event, it created a devastating social and physical aftermath. Away from the trenches and the fighting fronts, the impact of the Great War at home was powerful enough to permeate into the routines of daily life and leave a deep physical mark across large swathes of the landscape. This has produced considerable scope for military and civilian research that is rich, varied and socially comprehensive. The 1914–18 voices and experiences attest to the resilience of the human spirit against the backdrop of war and can be comprehended through a multi-perspective examination of the home front. Fully to understand and to analyse physical vestiges of the Great War, an archaeological approach combining archive research with field examination and recording should be the way forward.

Through the creation of a framework to generate quality, standardised data for home front sites, *The Home Front (1914–18) and its Legacies* pilot project demonstrated that it is possible to measure the physical response to Britain being at war through the experiences of urban and rural communities. The investigation work for this pilot project was undertaken by volunteers who tested the research and the recording system in their local environments. The pilot was also an opportunity for local people to create their own engagement with the communal heritage of war by comprehending and recording places in their own locales. The results of the pilot clearly demonstrated the value of information that can be found within local archives, local publications and local newspapers. Working with people and groups from within their regional areas proved to be the key to creating meticulous baseline data and undertaking a successful examination of the home front.

Finally, this pilot project demonstrated that the change of use experienced by home front buildings, places and spaces during the Great War can be researched, recorded and highlighted through volunteer engagement coordinated with local Historic Environment Record Offices. With the sheer volume of research being undertaken by centenary projects and the mapping facilitated by the *Home Front Legacy* project, it is anticipated that by the close of the centenary the home front landscape will be better understood than at any time previously. By enhancing local Heritage Environment Records and national listings, this data can benefit future planning decisions and enable home front heritage to be considered for the designation of protection measures. Most significantly, the combined efforts of all of the above will leave a socially inclusive, lasting legacy for the nation and secure for the future Britain's Great War narrative of the home front.

Acknowledgements
The pilot project was indebted to Wayne Cocroft of Historic England and John Schofield of the University of York who provided invaluable advice, direction and knowledge. In addition, the study could not have been completed without the volunteer participants who gave their valuable time to make this contribution

towards Great War research on their own home fronts: Doug E. Ball, Jean Church, Bryn Elliott, Lawrence Greenall, Janet Grove, Barbara Headland, Peter Huggins, Kirsty Johnstone, Ian Jones, Ian MacFarlane, Rachael McMillan, Odette Nelson, Allie Nickell, Lucy Oldnall, David J. Pracy, Mary Salton, Raymond Sears, Michael Seymour, John Mason Sneddon, Len Stuart, Chris Sumner, Guy Taylor and Les Tucker.

Notes

1. The term 'Britain' is used to encompass the whole of the United Kingdom, as it would have done during the Great War.
2. Saunders, N.J., Schofield, J. and Glass, E., *The Home Front (1914–1918) and its Legacies: A pilot study for a national public archaeology recording project of First World War legacies in Britain: 2014–2018*. Project No. 6113 Historic England typescript report, 2014. Available at: https://historicengland.org.uk/images-books/publications/home-front-1914-1918-and-its-legacies/ (accessed 30 August 2015).
3. Saunders, N.J., *Killing Time: Archaeology and the First World War* (Stroud: History Press, 2007), p. vi.
4. Saunders, N.J., 'Introduction: Engaging the Materialities of Twentieth- and Twenty-first Century Conflict', in Saunders, N.J. (ed.), *Beyond the Dead Horizon: Studies in modern conflict archaeology* (Oxford: Oxbow Books, 2012), pp. x–xiv.
5. Saunders, Schofield and Glass, *The Home Front (1914–1918) and its Legacies*, p. 85.
6. Defence of Britain Project (2006 version updated on the Archaeological Data Service Website), http://archaeologydataservice.ac.uk/archives/view/dob/ (accessed 15 September 2015).
7. Formerly part of English Heritage which split into two organisations on 1 April 2015. Historic England continues the statutory role of giving advice to owners, local authorities and the public.
8. Name changed from Historic Scotland on 1 October 2015.
9. Cadw is the Welsh government's historic environment service. Cadw is a Welsh word that means 'to keep' or 'to protect'.
10. See www.homefrontlegacy.org.uk.
11. Appleby, C., Cocroft, W.D. and Schofield, J., *The Home Front in Britain 1914–18: An archaeological handbook* (York: Council for British Archaeology, 2015).
12. The statue is the first to commemorate Sikh soldiers who fought in the British Indian Army. It was crowd-funded through a Kickstarter campaign by the WWI Sikh Memorial Fund and unveiled at the National Memorial Arboretum in Staffordshire on 1 November 2015.
13. See www.warmemorialsonline.org.uk.
14. Kenyon, D., 'First World War National Factories: An archaeological, architectural and historical review', project no. 76-2015 Historic England typescript report, 2015 p. 106. Available at: http://research.historicengland.org.uk/Report.aspx?i=15388&ru=%2FResults.aspx%3Fp%3D1%26n%3D10%26a%3D4805%26ns%3D1.
15. Saunders, Schofield and Glass, *The Home Front (1914–1918) and its Legacies*, p. 26.
16. Gillam, G., *Enfield at War 1914–1918* (London: Enfield Archaeological Society, 1982), p. 2.
17. Gillam, G. and Jones, I.K., *Enfield at War 1914–1918* (London: Enfield Archaeological Society, 2014).
18. Saunders, Schofield and Glass, *The Home Front (1914–1918) and its Legacies*, p. 79.
19. Ibid., p. 86.
20. Kirsty Johnstone (Barnet Independent Researcher), involvement with the 'Herts at War' and '8th in the East' projects, pers. comm. emails, March 2014 and November 2015.
21. Mary Salton (Waltham Abbey Historical Society), pers. comm. email, November 2015.
22. Saunders, Schofield and Glass, *The Home Front (1914–1918) and its Legacies*.
23. Ibid., p. 48.
24. Dobinson, C., 'Twentieth Century Fortifications in England: Volume 1 Anti-aircraft artillery 1914–1946', 1996 Unpublished Report for Historic England, accessed at Historic England Swindon Archives, October 2012, p. 11.

25. Ibid., p. 3.
26. Ibid., p. 274.
27. Castle, I., *London 1914–17: The Zeppelin Menace* (Oxford: Osprey Publishing, 2008), p. 26.
28. Gillam, *Enfield at War 1914–1918*, p. 14.
29. For detailed listings, see: Great Britain and Northern Ireland. Ministry of Munitions. Department of Engineering, *Directory of Manufacturing in the Engineering and Allied Trades* (London: HMSO, nd). Located at Leeds Royal Armoury Museum Archives, MOD Pattern Room archive.
30. Saunders, Schofield and Glass, *The Home Front (1914–1918) and its Legacies*, p. 67.

Suggested Further Reading

Appleby, C., Cocroft, W.D. and Schofield, J., *The Home Front in Britain 1914–18: An archaeological handbook* (York: Council for British Archaeology, 2015)

Castle, I., *The first Blitz: Bombing London in the First World War* (Oxford: Osprey Publishing, 2015)

Cocroft, W.D., *Dangerous energy: the archaeology of gunpowder and military explosives manufacture* (English Heritage, 2000)

Connelly, M., *The Great War, Memory and Ritual: Commemoration in the City and East London, 1916–1939* (Royal Historical Society Studies in History New Series, 2002)

Faulkner, N. and Durrani, N., *In Search of the Zeppelin War: the archaeology of the First Blitz* (Stroud: Tempus, 2008)

Forbes, N., Page, R. and Perez, G., *Europe's Deadly Century: Perspectives on 20th century conflict heritage* (Swindon: Historic England, 2009)

Gillam, G. and Jones, I.K., *Enfield at War 1914–1918* (London: Enfield Archaeological Society, 2014)

Lewis, J., *From Gunpowder to Guns: The story of two Lea Valley armouries* (Hendon: Middlesex University Press, 2009)

Lewis, J., *Weapons, Wireless and World Wars: The vital role of the Lea Valley* (Hendon: Middlesex University Press, 2010)

Saunders, N.J., *Killing Time: Archaeology and the First World War* (Stroud: History Press, 2007)

Schofield, J., *Modern Military Matters: studying and managing the twentieth-century defence heritage in Britain* (York: Council for British Archaeology, 2004)

Sears, R. and Foster, J., *Waltham Abbey: Reflections of the Past Volume 1* (Waltham Abbey: Raymond Sears Publishing, 1991)

Whitehouse, C.J. and Whitehouse, G.P., *A Town for Four Winters: Great War camps on Cannock Chase*, 2nd edn (Stafford: Staffordshire County Council, 1983)

Notes on Contributors

Andrew Bamji is a retired consultant rheumatologist who worked at Queen Mary's Hospital, Sidcup, between 1983 and 2011. The hospital appointed him as consultant archivist in 1989, and in this role he acquired the extant case files of the British and New Zealand Sections who worked at Sidcup during the First World War. These records are the only surviving clinical records from the Great War and comprise 2,500 files, including surgical notes, diagrams, X-rays and watercolours. The archives also comprised a collection of plastic surgery images and ephemera, and a collection of contemporary and historical works about medicine and surgery in the First World War. The archives were decommissioned in 2011, and the material was divided by subject specialism and relocated. The case notes are now at the Royal College of Surgeons, London, and other material can be found at the British Association of Plastic, Reconstructive and Aesthetic Surgeons (where Bamji is Gillies Archivist), the Army Medical Services Museum and the Brotherton Library, University of Leeds.

Bamji has written extensively about the history of plastic surgery and the work of the Queen's Hospital, Sidcup. A chapter on 'Trauma, violence and medicine' is forthcoming in the *Oxford Handbook of the First World War*. He has lectured to medical and lay audiences in the United Kingdom, the United States, France and New Zealand, as well as contributing to a number of television programmes and exhibitions.

Dr Clive Barrett is Chair of Trustees of the Peace Museum, Bradford, which holds a unique collection of peace movement artefacts and memorabilia. He has a quarter of a century's interest in academic peace movement history, looking mainly at the period up to 1945, from a doctoral thesis on 1930s pacifism to his most recent publication, *Subversive Peacemakers: War-Resistance 1914–1918, an Anglican Perspective*.

Nick Bosanquet, Emeritus Professor of Health Policy at Imperial College London, has a long-standing interest in the Great War, an interest linked to his professional work. He wrote on 'Health Systems in Khaki: The British and American Medical Experience' in Hugh Cecil's and Peter Liddle's *Facing Armageddon* (1996 and 2016) and recently published *Our Land at War: Britain's Key First World War Sites* (2014).

Dr James J. Cooke is Emeritus Professor of History at the University of Mississippi (Oxford, Mississippi) with a specialty in military history, World War I and II. He has published *The Rainbow Division in the Great War, 1917–1919*, *The U.S. Air Service in the Great War, 1917–1919*, *Pershing and His Generals*, *The All-Americans at War*, and *Billy Mitchell*. He continues to research in the area. During the First Gulf War (1990–91), he served as a lieutenant-colonel, was the

US Army's liaison officer to the French division and saw combat in Iraq. His service memoir was published as *100 Miles From Baghdad: With the French in Desert Storm*. For his combat service he was awarded the Bronze Star.

Just as this volume was going to print the Editor learned that James Cooke, his long-term generous friend, had passed away, a loss recorded here with a regret which will be shared by all who knew him.

Emily Glass is a post-graduate researcher at the University of Bristol, undertaking research on communist-era defences in Albania. Her research uses a modern conflict archaeology approach to explore the perception and identity of concrete bunkers from the socialist ideology under which they were created to the capitalist mentality of the present. In addition, she was the lead researcher on the *Home Front (1914–18) and its Legacies* pilot, the project upon which Chapter 21 is based.

Graeme Gooday is Professor of the History of Science and Technology and Head of the School of Philosophy, Religion and History of Science, University of Leeds. He was educated in Natural Sciences at the University of Cambridge, with a PhD in History of Science at the University of Kent. He specialises in the history of electrical technologies in Britain from the 1870s to 1920s, with major book publications, *The Morals of Measurement* (Cambridge: 2004), *Domesticating Electricity* (London: 2008) and *Patently Contestable* (Cambridge MA: 2013) co-authored with Stathis Arapostathis, which won the BSHS Pickstone prize in 2014.

Professor Adrian Gregory of Pembroke College, Oxford, has published on the Great War, is in the final phase of a new short history of the First World War to be published by Oxford University Press and has recently contributed a chapter on 'Religion and Belief' to the new Cambridge Encyclopaedia of the war. He was the Historical Consultant to the Jeremy Paxman BBC 2014 series on the First World War.

Andrea Hetherington is an independent researcher and writer with a particular interest in the social history of the First World War. She completed a Heritage Lottery-funded research project on behalf of the Friends of Lawnswood Cemetery in Leeds, resulting in the book *Lawnswood's Great War Stories*. She has also acted as a consultant to a number of First World War projects in the Yorkshire area. Andrea regularly delivers talks to history societies and has just completed a commission to write the history of one of Leeds' oldest family firms.

Dr Rob Johnson is the Director of the Changing Character of War (CCW) research programme at Oxford University. His primary research interests are in the history of strategy and war, and their contemporary applications. A former British Army officer, he now acts as a specialist academic adviser to NATO armed forces. He is editor of *The British Indian Army: Virtue and Necessity* (Cambridge Scholars Press, 2014), as well as other works on conflicts in the Middle East, and the Indian Army. He is currently working on a monograph on the history of partnering irregular indigenous forces and a strategic history of the First World War in the Middle East.

Dr Spencer Jones is Senior Lecturer in Armed Forces and War Studies at the University of Wolverhampton and currently serves as the Regimental Historian of the Royal Regiment of Artillery. His research focuses on tactics, training and combat leadership in the British Army. He is the author of *From Boer War to World War: Tactical Reform of the British Army 1902–1914* and the editor of *Stemming the Tide: Officers and Leadership in the British Expeditionary Force 1914*, which was runner-up for the 2013 Templer Medal. His latest work is *Courage without Glory: The British Army on the Western Front 1915* (Solihull: Helion & Co., 2015).

Dr Peter Liddle for more than forty years has been concerned with the study of the First World War. His work in rescuing personal experience evidence of the war led to the establishment of the Liddle Collection in the Brotherton Library, University of Leeds, which documents the wartime experience of some 4,500 individuals through original letters, diaries, photographs, art work and recollections.

He has written and edited numerous books on the Great War including volumes on Gallipoli, the Third Battle of Ypres, the Armistice and two volumes of his interviews with men and women who had striking war experience. His most recent book, published in 2016, is a reconsideration of the 1916 Battle of the Somme. He was the Founder/Director of the Second World War Experience Centre in Walton near Wetherby and is Life President of the Centre.

Dr Juliet MacDonald is Research Fellow in Art at the University of Huddersfield. Her research focuses on the practice of drawing, the First World War and human–animal relations. Recent exhibitions include *Drawology* at the Lanchester Gallery, 2014 and *Thought Positions in Sculpture* at Huddersfield Art Gallery, 2015. In 2014–15 she was Leverhulme Artist in Residence with the Legacies of War research project and the Liddle Collection culminating in the solo exhibition *Inhalation* at the Stanley & Audrey Burton Gallery, University of Leeds.

Dr Jessica Meyer is University Academic Fellow in Legacies of War at the University of Leeds. She holds a PhD in Modern History from the University of Cambridge and has published on the history of masculinity, shell shock, the wives of disabled ex-servicemen, popular culture in the First World War and the Friends Ambulance Unit. She is currently completing the manuscript for a book on the work of non-commissioned servicemen of the Royal Army Medical Corps during the First World War and is also working on a European Research Council-funded project on the provision of medical and social care by the state, charities and families to British disabled ex-servicemen after the First World War.

David Millichope was a school teacher and later photographer. He is an MA graduate of the Centre for First World War Studies at the University of Birmingham and chair of the Halifax Great War Heritage Society which explores the impact of the Great War on the local communities of Halifax and the Calder Valley. He is the author of *Halifax in the Great War* (2015) and is currently engaged in research into Lieutenant-General Sir Richard Butler, considered by some to be Douglas Haig's right-hand man.

Brigadier N.S. 'Tank' Nash was a regular soldier for thirty years, serving in the Far East, the United States, throughout the UK and in various posts in the Ministry of Defence. His lifetime interest in the army and in history has resulted in the publication in military magazines of a long-running series of humorous articles on army life, and a range of books on military subjects, including a study of the failure of the experimental 'K' boats, and biographies of Major-General Charles Townshend and the subject of his chapter in this book, 'Bombo' Pollard VC. His work on the Mesopotamian campaign is to be published by Pen & Sword in 2016.

William Philpott is Professor of the History of Warfare in the Department of War Studies, King's College, London. He writes about the history of the two world wars, the British and French Armies in the twentieth century and Anglo-French relations, and has published widely on those subjects. Recent publications include *Bloody Victory: The Sacrifice on the Somme and the Making of the Twentieth Century* (Little, Brown, 2009), which won the Society for Army Historical Research's Templer Prize in 2010, and *Attrition: Fighting the First World War* (Little, Brown, 2014). He is a councillor of the National Army Museum, and a former Secretary General of the British Commission for Military History.

Dr James Pugh is a Teaching Fellow in War Studies at the University of Birmingham. His research interests focus on air power during the two world wars, the relationship between drugs and warfare, and the use of stimulant drugs in both British society and Britain's armed forces. His first monograph, *The Royal Flying Corps, The Western Front and the Control of the Air, 1914–18*, is in preparation and is due for publication with Ashgate's First World War Series. He has also published on military and naval air power doctrine and air power leadership.

Dr Duncan Redford, formerly a Royal Naval officer with hunter killer submarine service, is a naval historian specialising in the relationship between the Royal Navy and national identity since 1870. He has been Head of Research at the National Museum of the Royal Navy, and Honorary Senior Research Fellow in Modern Naval History at the University of Portsmouth. His doctoral research, awarded the Laughton Naval History Scholarship by King's College, London, formed the basis of his first book, *Submarine: A Cultural History from the Great War to Nuclear Combat* (2010). He is currently the general editor of a fourteen-volume series examining the history of the Royal Navy. To this series he contributed *The Royal Navy: A History Since 1900* and *A History of the Royal Navy: World War 2*. His volume in this series dedicated to the Submarine Service is in preparation.

Nicholas J. Saunders is Professor of Material Culture at the University of Bristol, specialising in the archaeology and anthropology of modern conflict, and in particular that of the First World War. He is co-director of the 'Great Arab Revolt Project' in southern Jordan, and of 'The Isonzo Valley, 1915–1918: Conflict Landscapes on the Slovenian–Italian Border' project. His most recent books include: *Killing Time: Archaeology and the First World War* (2010), *Bodies in Conflict* (2014) and *The Poppy: A History of Conflict, Loss, Remembrance and Redemption* (2014).

Gary Sheffield is Professor of War Studies at the University of Wolverhampton. He has previously held Chairs at King's College, London, and at the University of Birmingham. He has taught at the UK's Joint Services Command and Staff College and at the Royal Military Academy, Sandhurst. He has published extensively on the history of the First World War, most notably a biography of Field Marshal Sir Douglas Haig. His most recent book is *A Short History of the First World War*.

Dr Jack Sheldon served a full career in the British Army, retiring in 2003. He is a graduate of the *Bundeswehr* Command and Staff College, Hamburg, and carried out numerous international assignments in Germany and elsewhere. Since retirement he has devoted himself to researching the German Army on the Western Front 1914–1918. Amongst his published works are seven full-length books on the subject and currently he has three more at various stages of preparation.

John Spencer is a writer and historian specialising in the Great War. He has an MA in First World War Studies from the University of Birmingham and is now doing doctoral research into Field Marshal Sir Henry Wilson at the University of Wolverhampton. He has been a journalist for the past thirty-five years, including thirteen years as managing editor of the Press Association, the national news agency for Britain and Ireland.

Dr Kapil Subramanian is a Postdoctoral Fellow in Telecommunications History at the School of Philosophy, Religion and History of Science at the University of Leeds (2015–2016). He completed his PhD on irrigation and the Green Revolution in India at the Department of History at King's College, London, in 2015.

Index